The Story of David

This is the true story of a young man reincarnating back to earth to join his mother for their work on earth. He came back choosing to give his life for others to learn from. The covenant they made had been sealed with their promise in the beginning of Creation.

BY

Ruth Ann Friend

The Story of David

Copyright © 2014

Library of Congress

Ruth Ann Friend

All rights reserved

ISBN: (Soft Cover) 978-0-9898255-2-8

ISBN: (e-book) 978-0-9898255-3-5

Published by Friend Publishing

Ruth Ann Friend

Other published books by author

Under The Rainbow Crossing

1995-2013

(Revised edition)

ISBN: 978-09898255-1-1 (Soft Cover)

ISBN: 978-0-9898255-0-4 (e-book)

My web site

www.UniversalConversations.com

CONTENTS

Why We Both Came Back To Earth One More Time.

Chapter 1   David's Early Years and Our Family (1)

Chapter 2   David's Young Adult Years (12)

Chapter 3   The Difference Between an Old and New Souls (20)

Chapter 4   David's Grandparents and Their Passing (31)

Chapter 5   Learning His Gifts (41)

Chapter 6   David in Heaven's Doorway (57)

Chapter 7   A Long Journey (73)

Chapter 8   Reiki, the Energy Healer (93)

Chapter 9   Building His Rose Garden in Life (105)

Chapter 10   Charley's Spirit Returns at Christmas (119)

Chapter 11   Living in a Broken Body, St. Odilia Heals His Eyes (127)

Chapter 12   David's Suffering and a Praying Mantis (140)

Chapter 13   Mother Mary, the Miracle Healing (156)

Chapter 14   Evil Was Lurking in the Church. A Soldier's Spirit Appears.

Chapter 15   Angels, Miracles and Messages Lighting Our Way. (176)

Chapter 16   David's Incredible Passing into Spirit (185)

Chapter 17   David's Many Visits in Spirit (205)

Chapter 18	How David Would Care for Everything	(237)
Chapter 19	Spirits Messages	(245)
Chapter 20	What Happens When We Leave Earth Questions Answered	(251)
Chapter 21	Escorts for Souls	(258)
Chapter 22	Experiencing Beings of Light, Spirits Caught on Camera	(276)
Chapter 23	Death Experiences	(290)
Chapter 24	Coming Back	(294)
Chapter 25	Suicide	(299)
Chapter 26	Getting Through Time	(302)
Chapter 27	Spiritual Growth	(311)
Chapter 28	A New World	(317)
Chapter 29	Conclusion and Final Thoughts	(334)
Epilogue	The Sunflower that Wouldn't Die	(343)
Appendix	Letters and Messages	(347)

Acknowledgments

I thank my beloved son David, he is the reason this book is to be written and shared with the world. Through his struggles and hardships he was a spiritual teacher loving others.

Thank you my beloved daughters and loved ones for your support and loving me as you do. I have been truly blessed. Thank you to my friend Michelle for your time when I needed it and never questioning my mission.

I give my love to our Creator for your blessings and to the Divine beings in our vast universe. You have held me upon your wings though life after life. Those who choose to live life through the Divine will live with joy and peace.

In Memory of my dear friend Alex

who crossed over in May 2014

"You are never given a wish without being given the power to make it come true,

You may have to work for it, however"

"Here is a test to find whether your mission on Earth is finished: If you're alive, it isn't."

These quotes are from the book Illusions by Richard Bash.

David comes home shortly after his Air Force service

Dedications

I dedicate this book to all parents who have endured the loss of a child or a loved one. I know my son would want to give each one of you a hug if he could with his understanding of the separation one feels, called death. Your loved one will never forget you there is only life after life, we go on and you will all unite one day.

I am hoping with David's story and his words you can believe you will be together again. Love is forever, Love never dies and your loved ones will be waiting for you. Love is the ultimate key to everything there is. We are all a part of everything.

PREFACE

This is a true story of the reincarnation of my son and me coming back! I will be honest with you about our life; it has not been easy living in this world again when you come from a world of love and Light. We chose to return here to help others and to teach what we were given. My son and I had much to accomplish in our lives while we were here. We would do our best in our Covenant to the Creator of All. This was the commitment we made and sealed our Covenant with our given promise and complete love.

The part we loved so much was being back in this world to be with our loved ones. In the plan to return, I was to be the mother first and later the children would come when it was their time to be born. While on the other side I did not realize how much I had promised to do out of my happiness and the love I feel in my heart. We seem to overload our new lives before coming back because we are in a place of complete ecstasy and bliss, filled with love and peace, it is called Heaven. Later on, in our earth years I jokingly said to my son David, "I can't believe how much we said we would do." He agreed, but in our happiness we gratefully choose too. I am certain I heard Heavenly laughter at that instant rolling across the Heavens! The other side knew we were proud to be here again!

For those of you who know what reincarnation is, my story will make complete sense. For those who are not acquainted, please read on to find out more of why we were sent back after our death experiences. The Universal Creator, who is all of everything, knows the plan of everyone on this earth, and this was a large part of mine and my son David's. We were enthralled with choosing to do this and felt totally blessed in this way.

The Story of David

Based On a True Story

Foreword

I had written my first small book years ago titled, *Under the Rainbow Crossing*, and was hesitant to write very much about what was happening. When I wrote my first book I could only reveal certain things. I was actually afraid and fearful to write everything, so I held back most of it. I not only did not want to be labeled as a little crazy, but I felt I needed to protect my family from ridicule. That's what fear can do; it held me back once, but never again! Other than that, I didn't care how anyone thought about me on my unusual journey, nor did my son.

Over the last several years, book stores have become full of other's experiences. People have been opening up more and wanting to know the truth of life after life. David and I would say to one another that those who are interested understand that everyone who has an experience can't be crazy. I admire the doctors, specialists, nurses, scientists, housewives, and the many others who put their careers on the line to tell their story. Some have much to lose as far as their work and reputations. But those of us who are on a certain mission stand up strong and do our work. We drew the line there and wanted to tell it all as we said we would when we were told to.

After my son crossed over I was told when I became well to write his story, and that's what I'm doing. This second book I am now writing exposes to the world our truth and our promise to the Creator as it is. Don't ever be afraid to follow your path when it is of love, sincerity, and from the light. You may not think you are doing anything with your life but you are, and it is perfectly in place. All lives count for something. Your soul is teaching others.

In the beginning of our Creation, a very important promise was made between David, me, and our Heavenly Creator. This covenant and agreement was agreed upon between the three of us and sealed long before

David's birth. David would be returning back to earth in order to finalize his last lifetime here. His journey was to accomplish a final mission not only to himself, but more, and most importantly to the Creator. There were certain others he asked to be reunited with again in his new life and those he asked for would be appointed to him on his journey, and not by accident. He would be led knowing who to go to, and he would be joining me once again in our service on Earth. David was given extraordinary gifts of spiritual medium ship, teaching, healing, prophecy, forgiveness, compassion and a great love for others. This was his life to be...

David's Story will tell of the life plan he chose and his extraordinary life on earth. The Christ and Heavenly Beings have led me to write The Story of David and to "to tell the world." I have vowed to do my best with their guidance.

Now the story will continue from the beginning. This is David's Story.

Chapter 1

David's Early Years
And Our Family

My Children

Only a mother knows the joy of seeing her newborn baby for the first time after birth. My heart was filled with joy as my baby son was put into my arms. This little miracle made my heart spill over with a complete and magical love. He was so tiny and warm as I cuddled him up against me to study his little face. My baby had dark hair and knowing eyes as if he knew he was my son to love, along with his beautiful sisters. I am thankful that at that time I did not know his journey to be and the suffering he would go through in his short life. That would come later. I will always remember when the doctor told me, "Now you have a little King to go with your two little Queens." I was a very happy mother!

My beautiful little daughters, Pamela Deanne, and Robin Lynn were just babies themselves and full of excitement about their new baby brother who would be coming home soon to join them. I named my little son David Michael without having to think about choosing his name. I seemed to know it was perfect for him. He would turn out to be as brave as King David throughout his lifetime.

All of these first early memories are still strong in my mind and forever will be. A little over one year later there would be four children in all, making three daughters and one son. I named this beautiful little baby girl Cynthia. I was feeling very fortunate to be a mother with children who were healthy and amazing little babies. Looking back now I would never have traded the coming years if I could, because through the suffering came an everlasting love and devotion between the children and me. We had a magical connection to one another that we would realize as the years went on. We had one another to lean on and draw strength from; with a bond so deep there are no human words to describe our connection. Only a parent can understand the emotions that are tied to our children becoming even stronger with the anguish and feeling of loss.

David's Illnesses as a Child

The second winter of David's baby life he was hospitalized for some time and had had a close brush with death. He had a new flu which took the lives of many babies and children. I was afraid to leave him, staying beside him day and night, except to steal away in the early hours to see about my new baby girl, who was one month old at the time. In the middle of the night, I would hurry home for clean diapers and make formula, and on my way back to the hospital drop these things off for the baby at my mother's home. I wasted no time rushing back to him at the hospital. He never slept much waking up soon after I left and then he would be crying for me the nurse said. This was a close call for my little son who was barely two years old at the time. In due time he pulled through and was released to come home.

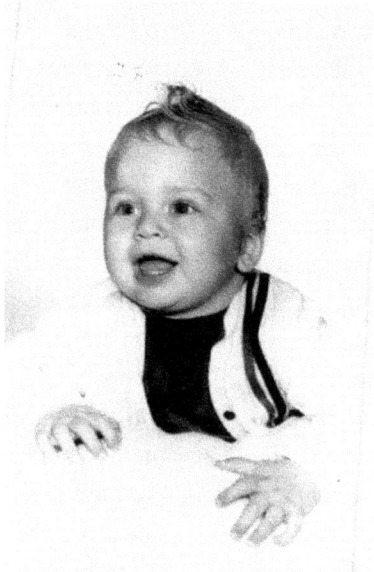

David Michael at 11 months

We both slept on and off for three days catching up on our rest after all the frightening trauma. He had been secured to the hospital bed with bags of fluid running into his small body. I cannot imagine the relief he must have felt being freed from all those tubes! I used to wonder when he became sick as an adult, maybe what happened to him as a baby had returned in some way. I wondered if it was this terrible illness once more reappearing later in life. His childhood doctor had told me after his childhood illness that complications could possibly return years later, even when David became an adult. Years later as an adult when he became sick his doctor then told me that wasn't what had happened to him. This illness he had now was much worse!

Getting to Know Him

Now, I will go back to when he came into this world and was a baby. When he was still small, I had no doubt he knew beyond time and space, and was of something very different. I couldn't begin to know what it was. I could see and feel unknown emotions in him at times, but I did not fully understand in the early years that he really was gifted. And, when he was older and in school, he told me that when he was a baby he used to think me into his room to pick him up out of his crib! Soon, I realized my son had a family ability. After I gave more thought to his statements, I knew I would have to wait to know what he meant. Later his remarks made more sense to me by knowing he had a gift. I would find out his gifts would become extraordinary in his life.

He had come into this world having a difficult time adjusting to life even as a baby. I believe the struggle was that he already remembered and knew why he came here with his given promise to fulfill on earth. It is a beautiful thing for a soul to be in total bliss, in another time and place, surrounded in an amazing warm light, full of love and peace then quickly find your soul in another strange world so completely different and in chaos! His gentle soul deeply felt the strong vibrations of earth, the hurt, cruelty, deceit, hatred, meanness, and worse, a world covered in a layer of darkness. The only light here is the never ending Holy Light penetrating our world with bright spurts here and there struggling to pour through. He was experiencing our human world filled with depression and with people surviving the best they could. His world was pure love and light so his return here was an enormous shock to his soul! But, he would keep his promise and fulfill his covenant with God.

Looking back, I recalled that he couldn't stand to be separated from me as a baby. When he could walk and get out of his toddler bed I would find him asleep hiding under my bed at night, even on cold winter nights. As hard as I tried to keep him in his bed, I quickly learned to check under my bed each night for he never gave up trying to stay close to me.

As a baby and throughout his youth, he was a very good and contented child. He was happy and usually bubbling over with childish giggles. He dearly loved his sisters and they him. As he grew older, he knew things ahead of his time at a very early age which really surprised me. David knew future events and had a strong intuition of people, places, and things.

Pam, Cindy, Robin and David

Much later in life, I would begin to understand more and know it wasn't just a baby stage, this had to do with the connection he and I had and planned for this lifetime. I believe, without a doubt, that he struggled with what he had to do by entering this hard world again knowing the complete plan for his life on Earth. After all, he was back again in a difficult place and couldn't turn back with what he was to finish. David was restless and his life here on earth was going to be hard for him. I knew when he was older why he had trouble adapting to his new life. You will understand more of his life that he shared between other worlds and here, as you read on.

David spoke like he was a much older person while growing up and yet played as any child would. I wondered at times how he knew so many things ahead of time and I always tried to understand his comments. He knew I wasn't ready to understand the promise he made to God because it was too early yet. He was still gentle even when treated badly by others at school and quickly forgave them. In those years I had taught him not to hit back and that it was the right thing to do just as I had been taught. Even if I had never told him this, he would not have ever hurt anyone.

I had nicknamed him Flash as a little boy and he was just that all through his life. If you heard the back door close when he came in he was already upstairs in his room. I could hear boom, boom, boom on the stairs and his door shut in record time! He was the fastest kid and he was so funny! Sometimes we joked and asked, "Did you see a kid just go through here?"

When David was very small I remember placing a message in the newspaper one year on his 12th birthday. The message was giving my thanks to him for coming here as my son and joining his sisters to complete our family. Years later I realized what I had done. Inside of my memory I knew our plan but did not realize it at the time. This became a clue for me.

As a young child he loved Charlie Brown and Snoopy. His room was all in Charlie Brown bedspread, curtains, clock, waste basket, watch, and so on. Growing up and as an adult his favorite movies were *White Christmas*, *The Sound of Music*, *The Three Stooges*, *The Wizard of OZ*, History, and whatever else was uplifting and funny. His favorite song at Christmas was also mine, *Ava Maria*. His favorite prayer was the *Our Father*. The books he read growing up and as an adult were basically the same kind he always loved, spiritual, positive, studies of countries, unusual places in the world and the people in them. He had a strong interest in Mysteries of the Universe, the Stars, Aristotle, Egyptian Times, The Lost Emperors of China and many others. He also studied the planets, weather changes, written predications from Jeanie Dixon to Nostradamus, and many other interesting topics. I know he felt at home with these reminders and was remembering his journey. There were so many subjects he was drawn to, he enjoyed learning something new and meaningful that was educational to him. We both had a great interest in the same time periods of history especially Egyptian, Native American Indians and Ancient History. Watching some of these on a History or National Geographic channel often produced certain past memories to the both of us. At that time I felt what I knew was Déjà vu, recalling the past.

The Seer

While growing up he was interested in things far above his age. He would occasionally talk about these in our conversations. He had knowledge of future events in the world, seeing spirits, knowing his spiritual teachers and guides, the Angel Beings of Light who helped him, plus seeing into the *Beyond*. He had the gifts of a *seer*. He knew past, present, and many future events, with the uncanny blessed gifts that he was born with. Christ knew David would need all of these to use for his spiritual journey on earth. He had been given an invisible SPIRITUAL armor in order to protect him from the negative here on earth. My son understood the meaning of this dark world with clarity, knowing he could not change or do anything about the present and future events he knew would take place. His intuition and abilities made him the Mystic he was and he would only use his skills in a good way.

The word Mystic, according to the *Second College Edition of Webster's New World Dictionary of the American Language* states: "that it is possible to achieve communication with God our Creator, through contemplation and love, without the medium of human reason, and attaining knowledge of spiritual truths by meditation beyond human comprehension, filling one with wonder or awe. One who professes to undergo mystical experiences by which he intuitively comprehends truths beyond any kind of human understanding. God had equipped him with all he needed to complete his short life here.

David was very clairvoyant and a teacher to me since he was tiny. He was armed with his spiritual knowledge that he brought into the world with him when he was born. That's what I was seeing in him as a very small boy, and didn't know just what I was recognizing or understanding at the time. I did not know he would be as a Savior to all of us, his loved ones, friends, and those he touched.

His mind was filled with every emotion with what he felt was going on every day in our world and with certain people he saw. Through this he never became a victim of his life, with his illness, or the coming events he received for the present and future. This must have been very hard to bear when he was a young child.

There were future warnings of airplane crashes, tornados, hurricanes, accidents, and new souls getting ready to cross over into the other side that he would be aware of, combined with all kinds of negative changes in this world. This of course, disturbed him greatly since he felt helpless in situations knowing he could not change anything. Plus, living in different worlds every day was not an easy place to be, especially for him as a very young person.

My family continued to grow up; and David, while growing up, endured some severe illnesses that he was very fortunate to survive through. Years later, I wondered if his childhood disease of Encephalitis was what started his health to decline later on when he was an adult, but it wasn't. I would never change anything if I could, except to take away the pain and illness from my son and take it on myself. I believe everything happens according to each person's life plan no matter how painful it is to us.

To have been given the love of a child, even for a short time, is worth everything, more than to never have this love at all. I feel I have been learning all through my life to use my positive thinking as much as possible, knowing that the human mind controls a very large percentage of how we survive and heal in our hard times. As Edgar Cayce once said, "the mind is the builder." As human beings, we all have an inner strength to call upon at any time to help us through our hurdles. Through mine, I would find out how to survive the obstacles which looked like mountains at times, no matter how long it took, and to be able to help others by using the strength I was given.

As a protective parent, I was not prepared for time to pass so fast. I would sometimes blame myself for my children's problems as they were growing up which seems to be natural for a parent. I wanted their lives to run smoothly as I am sure most parents do, but then comes the time no one can change or soften the blows in their life. We think we know what is best for them but many times it isn't. I guess that is called, wanting it our way.

When sickness, accidents, or the loss of a child happens with their final departure occurring, we as parents usually blame ourselves for whatever happens to them, as if we could have somehow done more to change the circumstances. Many of us try to realize that in another place or time we will be together again, but we continue to torture ourselves with thoughts of, "if I had done this or that, maybe I could have changed the outcome." These thoughts can continually go on in our mind, never ending it seems.

Gifts to Use

David could look at a person and feel their sadness, illness, joy, negativity, goodness, or whatever they were made of inside. He knew their very heart and soul, and he felt the emotions they had chosen to use. Many people change course in their lives by getting off track and by not using their choices in a good way in order to spiritually grow. We all get off track at times which is natural. Earth is the learning ground where one can learn and persevere for those of us to choose from.

His emotions were not something he could turn on and off like a light. David completely accepted his promise to help the negative people he was meant to assist on Earth with a complete and deep responsibility. He came here full of love and suffered for them in his heart and soul and had deep regret for them. Even though this was their own personal journey, he sometimes became wounded watching a soul having traumatic difficulties, and unpleasant changes to make in order to better their selves. He knew they needed to meet themselves, but had never reached this moment in their life simply by not caring. They wanted to stay where they were living in a negative lifestyle of their own. This was something he knew they chose to do for themselves, and the choice was theirs.

Those people are comfortable where they are and do not want change in their lives. He could only show them true kindness and his friendship, and not judge them. He was not here to judge anyone and was happy to see some hard hearted people begin to slowly change, knowing they were not judged by him, and that he showed them respect that they had not ever received before. This had a positive effect on several people changing their lives for the better. By changing, this allowed those people to raise themselves up to a higher level of being a good human, earning respect for themselves, and others with learning what they hopefully needed to achieve in their lives. Through David's spirit, he felt their new positive emotions to a much deeper degree than an ordinary person could ever begin to which made him happy for them.

My son suffered by the way some people were living a life of hatred, evilness, and cruelty, those people did not want to change, and they had adjusted to their broken lives. He felt the emotions of not being able to do more, knowing they knew not what they were doing to their own soul, but also knowing they were here to choose their own path. He would always be available to help them if and when they became ready. He would work with those people to no avail; and they never knew what he was doing to reach their heart, he was so kind to them knowing they were lost. By his caring, many people responded to him by changing to a better way of life.

Those who had turned to his kindness and empowering ways could shed some of their hardened hearts. This was a joy to him knowing they were slowly getting back "on track" in life and making amends. Some of these people even came forward to help others. They had softened their hearts, by seeing how they had hurt others with their crude behavior they had shown.

Love is a very powerful emotion and many of us have been blessed in our lives by having good parents and loved ones guiding us along. Then, there are those who have NEVER experienced love and may grow in other ways and they are as important as anyone to our Creator. We never doubted that with love and positive changes anyone can be lifted to a higher level of self and become closer to the Creator, we just have to work towards it.

Those who recognize they have a gift can graciously accept their gift from our Creator, or one can ask for it to be taken away. I have no idea how many gladly accept theirs. Some are afraid of being gifted. This is a God given gift along with ones free will for your work on earth. We are all born with free will for eternity. The other gifts are such as telepathy, clairvoyance, clairsentience, and so on. Accepting to do this means making a very big change with this new shift in one's life. It is not always welcome for anyone who feels they are not ready, and may never want to be for this type of gift. This is usually out of fear of what this new change may require in their life to go forward. This may mean they need to straighten up their life and do better. There are many reasons one may hold back. Some are afraid of change and are too comfortable where they are.

As a young boy David knew to be aware of those who were negative, and with his abilities he could handle all kinds of problems with tact, strength, and the right words. He knew how to stay above their level of negativity and not give away his energy. Human energy can be used in either a positive or negative way; it is up to each one of us with what we do with it. We are all made of energy everything is energy. We never die, because energy cannot die, it merely changes course into something else. Ours go to spirit.

Now, I can understand why when David was a baby he would get under my bed. He could see energies no one else could, and hear all kind of words being spoken to him from other dimensions. He was probably terrified at times, but too small to explain any of this to me, or understand it himself. In his life plan he would not remember some things immediately in his new world and life. This would begin to enter into his memory, a little at a time. He didn't cry much especially considering all that was going on in his new life change, he just came to me and I held him, and he knew he was safe. I was always his safe place to be. I would protect him and his sisters always.

My son and I were the same in our thoughts and humanness. As he grew, I grew; he slowly opened me up to my own abilities and insight. They had been stored inside of my soul waiting to be unlocked for me to use. I was growing on my own spiritual journey, and getting closer to being elevated. He was patiently working with me a little at a time about past memories, without me actually realizing this for awhile. I didn't realize then, that I was being taught anything. He never pushed me by trying to hurry my recall of certain memories, with his answers to my questions.

We would have a casual talk on various subjects when he was growing up. Some were about spiritual experiences, and non-visual Beings that he could see, which others could not. He quickly helped teach me more about the positive and negative Beings. This was helping me to start on my own awareness with a new way of sight. I will never forget the night I was given multi-dimensional vision! The other side was speaking to me to look across the bedroom. As I did the wall instantly moved to in front of my face! The best I can describe this, is with how a telescope works! This was how my sight was changed. Since then when this happens it is only for that second and then back to normal. I was so dumbfounded, now I was in more of David's world. These were his worlds; this is who he was on Earth, and again in Universal Heavenly Places, and the paranormal world. I would continue to have other new experiences happen to me time and again. One day I realized that we both had always had these gifts and mine was waiting for the right timing!

Growing Up

Through David's grade school years, he was a good student with average grades and his teachers spoke highly of him. He never needed to be coached to do his homework. David would be teased some of the times because he would not cause trouble or get into fights like other young boys. He was good, always asking permission before doing something and staying close to home.

Before school every day, David would make sure that his room was all straighten and clean, and he would make his bed without being asked to do so. He was always so considerate of me and also everyone else, but he did have the typical childhood arguments with his sisters. They would all make up quickly though and life went on.

In high school, David's grades improved and he was a model student as some teachers would say. He played trumpet in the band, but didn't participate in other sporting activities at school. He loved art and photography and thought that he would like to work in the medical field someday. The kids would always come home after school and we would go out and play baseball as a family all the time, at least until the cold weather started. I didn't need to worry about him being all over the countryside doing who knows what. He would either be at home or down at his grandparents house spending time with them.

Spiritual Well Being

One of David's favorite things to do was to go to church two or three times a week, usually with one or two of his best friends. He loved church at a young age and it carried on into his adulthood. When he was old enough and going to high school he got himself a part-time job at the local sporting goods store.

Sometimes he found a religious figure to buy for his room if he had enough extra money left over from his allowance. He had a large collection of figurines of Jesus, Angels, Mother Mary, Saints, Crosses, small church buildings, religious pictures, and just about anything along those lines you can imagine. Needless to say his room was very peaceful to be in. With his allowance money he didn't buy anything for himself, he would enjoy bringing me home a gift from a yard sale. He didn't go around preaching to others in life. He empowered others by uplifting and understanding them. He knew how to reach their hearts without judging them. He lived his life and enjoyed his life, and his heart was always ready to serve. He loved church and helping others.

Chapter 2

David's Young Adult Years

Grown and Married

After high school, David married and soon joined the Air Force. He and his wife traveled to each of the bases that David was assigned to during their time together while he was in the Air Force. They were very active in the different base church programs often working with youth groups and helping wherever needed.

After a couple of years they were expecting twin sons and David was on top of the world with happiness. Then the unexpected happened, the twins were miscarried before birth. David's heart and soul were shattered along with his dream of being a father. He changed for a while fighting his deepest sadness along with the end of his marriage. Throughout his life, David has grieved for the boys he never got to hold, but he knew that they were happy and at peace and would be waiting for him when they would be united.

Startling Discovery

After joining the Air Force my son studied medicine at Walter Reed Hospital in Washington. My telephone rang one day and it was David and he was very excited to tell me something that happened in his class.

In one of his medical classes they were studying critical injury cases that day. They were being shown a file of pictures that day and one was showing a young female who had been DOA (dead on arrival) from a car wreck. Her face was destroyed and crushed and the first pictures were pretty bad David said. Little by little as she healed bandages were removed from the patient, and pictures were taken of her on each visit, to show her improvement. The pictures also revealed how the healing process had taken place over time.

After the final bandages were removed David couldn't believe what he saw! It was me, his mother! I was the DOA case! I had been told when this happened to me the pictures were for student learning, and I would be in medical journals. I never thought anymore about this. At that time I was injured so badly I had a long way to being healed. Never did I dream my own son would find me in this way!

I had never told my children about the wreck. It had happened so long ago and before they were born, but what a shock to see his mom, David said! He called out, "That's my mother!" in class, and he was overwhelmed with what had happened to me! My son told me that he hurried as soon as he could to the telephone, calling me to tell me what had happened. He was still in shock and wanted to know all about it! I did explain it had been so long ago I never thought to even mention this to him and his sisters. And later I thought what a way for my son to find out I had died and been sent back, to finish out things I promised to do. And how extraordinary to find out like he did! What are the chances of that happening? Our connection and work was putting more pieces of the puzzle together I would later realize.

David in the Air Force

A Pilot's Tragedy

David became a Medical Technician in the Air Force and was stationed at a pilot training base. A tragic experience which involved my son happened at his base one afternoon as he was getting off work at the clinic. He had become friends with a female Major instructor pilot, who would come to the clinic occasionally. Early one day, his Major friend came to the clinic and received a required shot that David administered. Then they kidded around and briefly chatted before she was scheduled to fly with a student pilot

Later in the afternoon the siren went off indicating a plane crash had occurred on the base. David was also working on the ambulance that day, and responded with the other hospital personnel. When the ambulance arrived at the scene of the accident, he jumped out to do what he could. In the tangled wreckage of the plane my son found his friend, the female flight instructor pilot. He began resuscitation, though knowing it was too late! Her body was quite mangled with the lower part of her leg found close by, still in her flight boot. He was crushed by what happened to his friend even though he knew it had to be her when the siren went off that day.

David called me in the evening to tell me of his friend's accidental death. He explained how he had just given her the regular shots that were due about noon that day. They kidded around and laughed at small jokes while she was there, and he thought the world of her. A few hours later he was trying to save her life, but it was too late. I could feel his broken heart over the telephone that evening, and I still have the base newspaper with his dear friend's picture on the front of it. She was a beautiful young woman who gave her life for her student. The student had not followed her command with only time for one to bail! She gave her life for him in those moments and went down with the plane. What a brave soul she was.

Even with David knowing where her spirit was now, he was still crushed by the young woman's death and that he couldn't help her. He knew she was now in her transition and that she was trying to figure out her own death. He had his human side we were created with, his human emotions, and he suffered over her loss, yet knowing she had crossed over into our real home. David found out later after the investigation it did confirm his friend the female instructor pilot had saved her student pilot by having him eject first, knowing there would not be enough time for her to save herself. The student had not followed her direct command and this is why the crash took place.

The Attack

While my son was on active duty in the Air Force, he was walking to the base one morning because his car had broken down. As he walked along his regular route a higher-ranking officer picked him up to give him a ride. For some reason suddenly the man pulled over stopping his car and began attacking my son severely beating him, and in the process broke his arm for no reason at all! David later told his sister, Robin, that the man had stopped to give him a lift to the base was his neighbor who he knew! No one ever knew the reasoning he just went berserk! David suffered through what happened alone. He never told me about this when it happened, and when he came home to visit with his arm in a cast he told me he hurt his arm by accident.

His sister knowing what really had happened from her brother later on told me the story of how his arm was broken several years later. My daughter said, "He did not want to worry you at the time that he would wait and tell you about it later on." This was how he was in his life it was never about himself. I know my son suffered with the emotional brutality and beating. The officer being of higher rank probably thought David would never report him. David told his sister he reported what the Officer did since he had to go to the clinic to get his arm x-rayed and put into a cast. He told her the officer was punished for what happened. I never knew this man's name but it took a toll on my son as it would anyone. I thought so many times about this wondering why some people are so cruel. I would not have known what happened if his sister hadn't told me about these years later. He gave wholeheartedly and with an understanding of human emotions but not with violence. We all have certain lessons we need to work on, and the journey is about how we handle the hurdles not the end result.

David's Church

In David's years of Air Force service he helped the Chaplin on each base where he was stationed, and his heart was always ready to serve. I feel sure he received comfort in his church on base at that time, and in his sadness. He loved helping and going to church. I remember as a little boy, he always wanted to go to church more than to play. He grew up that way and remained so all his life. I know most young children go to Sunday school but many need to be coached to attend.

One day at home I had a surprise call from his Chaplain where he was stationed. He told me how much David helped people and gave his extra time to the church you sure did raise your son right, you can tell by how he is and with his kindness to everyone. I was so proud and happy to get this call, knowing David would never leave his path. I thanked the Chaplin for such a nice call and I felt so proud of him and I was uplifted all day long!

He knew his church was within his heart and soul. It was not about a label of what kind of religion a person chose that counted. He loved the presentation of church, the order of learning what each human being needs to know to live life as well as possible. He loved churches of all kinds. We knew the labels (religions) did not matter in order to learn compassion and love for one another. The label is not what counts and this comes from the spiritual world. Go where you feel good and keep an open mind and as long as the words you hear are full of love, uplifting, and good that is what matters.

All of the faiths and names in this world (Protestant, Catholic, Jewish, Methodist, and hundreds more) will not make one bit of difference one day in the end. It's how we live our life here and what we learn in our churches about loving one another. Love is the key and the most important way to live. My son and I were told long ago by the Beings of the Christ Light that one day there will not be all of these different religions. There will be only one spiritual way for all people united together, without fighting over which is right. Wars will be non-existent and a new world will begin without prejudice.

People will care about one another over the world. This will be the new beginning, a new world on earth with people in it who were meant to survive. All of this is possible if man will only change to a higher way of life with love. If our Earth does change with any kind of a fatal disaster, there will be good people taken to a place of safety and needed in the future. Those will be taken to an amazing place and returned here afterward to help organize a new world of peace.

Some years back in the night I was given an important message. I was simply told by the Heavenly voice in this way "THE CATHOLIC CHURCH WILL CRUMBLE!" Up to that time I knew nothing of what was to come. Under a year later the horrible truth surfaced about certain Priests and higher up church officials molesting children for years! The world was shocked with these secrets which had been hidden for so long! David and I both received this same message when it came. He was at his home and I at mine, and we were given the same information. The premonition was soon brought forth as we were told. The rest is history now. This is to affirm our information, and that it comes from the highest source! It's not easy to know certain things, but we know there is a reason involved. Since then the Catholic Church had been very exposed in the cover up.

David's encounter with a Creole Woman

I have a strange story to tell you about my son, that he told me while he was still in the service. He rented an old farm house and included with it were several animals. He was to feed them and take care of them for part of the rent. This was great since he loved animals, dogs, cats, horses, and whatever. He had just returned from a TDY (temporary duty) assignment and while there, he went into New Orleans to check it out and see the sights.

An older Creole woman took a real interest in him one day in a shop. He was looking at all kinds of objects that visitors do. The shops are full of tee shirts and trinkets. The old woman was also a reader, a clairvoyant, and could see into him knowing he was on a spiritual journey. He omitted his bright light around him (aura) which she could see and soon she began talking with him. David knew she was able to do both things, good and bad if she needed. He was somewhat uncomfortable but was polite. She told David that she did more good than bad, unless it was for bad people. But he knew that doesn't make anything right. They exchanged telephone numbers because she asked to stay in touch with him. She had seen the light in his soul which was why she wanted to know him more.

After he returned home to the farm he called me one day to tell me what happened during the night at his home. It had snowed heavily through the night hours. The Creole woman had called my son early asking him if he knew she had visited him in the night. "No." He said. She continued by telling him to look outside his window, look out your bedroom window and you will see my foot prints in the snow, when I came to visit you. He did, and in the fresh undisturbed snow were footprints up to his window! Nothing else, anywhere around! He didn't really want any further communication but also did not want to make her upset. So they had a short conversation and both hung up. I don't think he ever heard from her again by telephone, but she did send him a set of homemade dolls with little bags around their necks meaning protection for him. I knew she could feel his gentleness and goodness with his bright aura light around him. She was not used to experiencing this, and I feel she was intrigued and did put her protection around him.

My Meeting a Priestess

A few years ago I made a trip to New Orleans where I met a Voo Doo Priestess. She had been a surgical assistant in a Chicago hospital for years. She always had the abilities to help others and she did. I was surprised at her back ground for 21 years working in the operating room in the hospital. She also worked with the poor and helped many others. She only practiced goodness and was a compassionate lady.

Then she had to move to New Orleans due to personal reasons and opened her shop as a Priestess. That's when I learned that Voo Doo is really the name for their religion. Those who use it in malevolent ways called this Doo Doo, meaning bad! So after we met her and listened to her talk to a group of us, she took us a short distance to show us her church. It was a Catholic church that she attended regularly.

The quaint and beautiful church was small, and I felt good vibrations all around me. I thought, how nice to share this part of her life with us. She is a very good person who helps unfortunate people in many ways. She shared the day with us making me feel uplifted. Before we left she took my hands, looked deep into my eyes and gave me a blessed message. I told her about my son's experience in New Orleans years ago and she wished she could have met him. She also listened to me about his story meeting the other Priestess and her sending him the dolls.

People naturally think the worst when the subject Voo Doo is mentioned. There again, don't jump to conclusions when you don't know, because of the word. There are good and negative vibes everywhere around us. The Priestess gave me a big hug when we left and I could see her heart is in the right place, she had so much compassion for others. Sometimes Voo Doo scares people with just the name and then their imagination runs wild because it sounds scary, and movies don't help. She is a very spiritual lady who loves Christ with all her heart and keeps busy helping others with the gift she was given. David would have liked meeting her I know. I feel I have learned much from her, the culture, and about her life.

AIDS and a Child

When my son was station in Texas, David worked in the clinic at the base hospital. He loved his work there and the people he met. One day there was a small boy who was admitted to the hospital diagnosed with AIDS. This was a disease that not much was known about yet. David said, "The little boy was isolated and some of the staff was afraid of him and did not want to go near him. Even the parents didn't seem to come around that he knew of." My son told the staff that he would take care of this small boy on his shift because he felt so badly for the child. He would kid and talk with him of childhood things and attended to him. He came sometimes bringing him a toy and to check on him. The evenings he was off duty he would spend with the little boy, the two of them would just talk and laugh together. My son kept him company doing his best to keep him cheered up.

This little boy had taken to my son early on and knew he cared about him very much. I remembered when he would call and tell me about this child. His heart was broken for him. It was hard for me to realize then that this disease could scare people so badly. Here was a little boy who was probably so afraid and did not understand what was going on. He must have been so glad to see my son, feeling so alone in his isolated world.

I thank God my son was meant to be there at that time in this child's life, in his greatest time of needing human compassion and a friend. David took this part of the small boy's empty life very hard and was sad wanting to help him all he could. The child's outcome was plain to see living with AIDS.

David carried on in life assisting AIDS patients and some years later he was a speaker for AIDS. At that time we both were working with AIDS patients and educating others. We soon received our minister's recognition for our energy healing work, which we both considered to be an honor. We cared very much about each sick person without judgment. Yes, we were so blessed to work with these people and we both felt honored.

Someday those who have judged these sick people will have to look back at their lives and how they reacted to them. This goes for some church ministers and people who preached in judgment of those people! In case they have forgotten, Jesus mingled and cared for the prostitutes, robbers, Lepers, and many others who needed him, all the while, never pointing His finger at them. Our Supreme Intelligence God, who created us, will reward those with compassion and love and who doesn't judge those who are different. He doesn't make mistakes when we were all created. I have thought on this for many years knowing Christ would never turn His back on anyone. The ministers who judge have no right to do this and should know better.

Chapter 3

The Difference Between an Old And New Soul.

Old Souls, New Souls, and Premonitions

Several people have told me they could see an old soul in my son's eyes and I knew they did. They saw wisdom, knowledge, compassion, and love. David had been here in many life times and we both have been shown several of our past lives as healers and teachers. He chose to come back continuing to return again and again, to be with loved ones and do his work here. He was learning new lessons that he wanted and to see how this world had changed. Do you know what the difference between an old and new soul is?

A new soul is the expression of a soul without having achieved its experience of earthly lessons. There is an expression called a *turn around*. This means going back and forth from this side never staying long enough on either side to learn what the soul needs to learn. It also is when a soul returns early to do a certain work. There are souls who have returned as the new baby to the same family. They have returned out of love and with their free will to be held and loved by those they love. Free will belongs to all of us for eternity to use as we choose. We all have the opportunity to learn on both sides, which is very important in order to further our spiritual growth. When one has learned their lessons on earth through the different life times, you need not repeat your lessons again once completed, unless by choice.

Some life times are very short, but those souls have completed what they came here to do and are very important. We all have a date of birth and a date to cross over when our work is finished here. A young soul was created at the same time as all souls, as we are all sparks of the Creator. A new soul is still learning their experiences and lessons needed which may take many times to evolve on Earth or on the other side. We are here in Earth school to learn what each of us came here for. It may be to make up for something from the past or another life time. This may be for many reasons such as: to learn about jealousy, envy, murder, faithlessness, and stealing; to having compassion, learning how to love, forgive and other reasons. It may be because one loved it here and wants to experience life here once more. Each person has a different agenda to work on and hopefully to correct over time. There are still many people who have no idea of this learning on Earth and that we are in school here for many reasons. And not the school where you learn your ABC's at.

The goal is to live the best that one can. When the time is right they will realize this and hopefully make the changes they need to so they can move forward. Earth school is the hardest of all in the Universe and this information comes from the Christ Light Beings. This is why many passed over souls told the both of us they never wanted to return here again. Once was enough!

To define an advanced old soul (The Encyclopedic Psychic Dictionary) they have a greater amount of knowledge, experience, and wisdom that they have achieved through the ages than a young soul. The old soul has incarnated innumerable times; acts more mature than a majority of people of his or her time; and excels in creativity that is not always understood by others. They are free from unnecessary worry both inside and out. People are drawn to this soul's magnetic personality rather than to what the person stands for. They lead a good and righteous life and feel material things are insignificant to the point that most others do not understand them, even their close friends and family. These old souls have a great amount of gained knowledge and have a much higher learning from the experience of these many life times. We all go through our learning until we reach the ultimate place we are reaching for.

David, being an ancient and old soul, was a protector to us even when he was bed ridden, sick and could not stand. He vowed to reprimand whoever had hurt one of us. It did not matter that he was so sick that a strong wind could have blown him down at the time; he persevered with an amazing inner strength. When he made that statement, he didn't mean by hurting a person, he would never fight in a physical way. But with his words, he was a superb speaker reaching out to most hearts. He had such an uncanny way of dealing with negative people without shouting or making a fool of himself. His words flowed out to them in a stern but loving way. It was that the words were his and yet blended together with his spiritual teacher from the other side.

In those times he would be shaken and was sad to see the world seemingly getting such an "I don't care attitude." The cruelties, deceit, and the attitude of what they can get, and not caring who gets hurt in the process is what grieved him so much all his life. His thoughts were on how we lived and that we have lost what really counts in life. He kept his life as smooth as possible with his heartfelt laughter; he enjoyed life, no matter his illness. He held life in deep reverence and we all (his family) prayed we could follow his path to the best we could.

David's Thoughts of the World

His thoughts focused on the beauty of nature and how terrible man has treated mother earth. We both have such a deep love for all that has been created and this Earth has been created for mankind to take care of. Man has already destroyed so very much of this Earth, including many species of animals killed to the point of near extinction and not to mention the rain forests being destroyed that this planet needs so desperately. He wanted to save the world, but of course knew he couldn't. He knew the consequences coming ahead for the human race. This would likely be the only way to begin a new world. In order to unite all people together in love and peace unless a great change suddenly came soon.

To this day, with the future space endeavors happening and space trips made into our Universe, he wondered if man will find a way to finally respect other new places? He knew this is a strong statement but we must learn to respect life first and our creation here on earth. He admired those who have committed to travel into an unknown space; they are heroes. But man in general, seems to destroy what we need to have to survive. It all has to change soon.

He knew there is only so much the Universe can do for us here. Maybe we have to do our own selves in to let change come. We have to learn like little children do growing up. The bad part is that man should have learned long ago how to treat one another and our beautiful planet. My son and I thought of how respect and caring has left so many, now not caring anymore. I hope his life experiences will help others to view life in a new way.

As the years rolled by, we continued working in our spiritual ministry. I felt I was gaining through David's wisdom and knowledge as he continued to teach me along with learning from the other side. My teachers and guides had been working tirelessly with me and my memories were expanding rapidly. David was my spiritual teacher on Earth, and one day I would understand so much more about whom he really was and knowing why he was so different from the time he entered this world. I would learn why I was different inside myself from the time I was a small child, my feelings, and strong compassion. I felt like I was such an odd ball growing up. It hurt my ears to hear curse words and ugly remarks. I had trouble with the hardness of my small world as David did. I was blessed to have had such good parents who were gentle and caring people, who would never intentionally hurt anyone. There are others who have no parents at all in this hard world, so I knew how blessed I have been to have had them.

David grew up learning more through his life once more on this Earth which was showing more of his spiritual life. He was so easy going and accepting of whatever came his way retaining his big enormous smile for everyone he met. He had an enormous inner strength and empowerment with a reverence for life no matter what happened. Even as a young child, he often became the victim of older kids, but no matter how tough the hurdle he had the ability to be brave. He never could understand the cruelty in this world it was very hard for him. He never got over this and where he was now, but he also embraced the goodness and beauty, much more than the cruelness. He saw the beauty that God created all his life, which were David's treasures he held in his heart.

Knowing what he faced of the daily *dark ones* sometimes weighed on him and me, but we were spiritually protected, and we always persevered ahead. I know he was deeply hurt many times feeling a deep disappointment in life here. He didn't understand the intentions of some people and how they treated one another, children, the elderly, and animals. This alone crushed his gentle heart. How could there be people in this world who felt nothing? This is a question that I am sure many of you have also thought about. Most people can't imagine being without compassion and love for others. There will be a time and a place for those who live their life so recklessly and mean without feelings for anyone or anything.

My daughters and my son all have very tender hearts. They never made fun of others who were different. In fact, it was the opposite, they were defenders of those who suffered and were mistreated. They only thought of how to find a way to help others if possible. I was very proud they didn't see race, culture, rich or poor, gay or straight, as any different, knowing God makes no mistakes. We are all special beings from the one Creator, our Divine Source. David had a wise understanding of human faults and actions and was dedicated to the promise he made without regrets.

I have seen him actually give most of his clothes away to help someone who needed them. He surprised others with meals, clothing, heaters, and above all respect, anything to better a person's life if he could. His heart was so big, compassionate, and soft, and when he shed tears of sadness or happiness he didn't try to be a macho type person. He was secure in his own skin. He didn't have to impress anyone, he was himself.

Machismo vs. Good Hearts

The *macho* type behavior shows how insecure the person is. It is a cover they wear to look tough. This type of person usually likes to throw their weight around so people are afraid of them. Others like this probably have all kinds of reasons when they act out in a macho fashion. I don't know all of the reasons I can only speak from certain experiences. I'm not trying to judge and this doesn't make them all bad. Some want to feel superior and stand behind their hardened image. That wasn't David; but, he wasn't a wimp either. He could speak his mind very well if he had to and hold his own ground. This was without going to a person's lower level of lost control. He had a way to talk with others to make his point, to resolve things in a good way without being loud and disrespectful. He knew people could have such better lives by learning to use kindness to others.

We knew each ones soul is different, and each one is on a different level of learning. He felt as if everyone had a tender heart he knew it would be a different world all together. He prayed for this to come and be here forever in the future. His thoughts centered on our world and he kept this in his prayers. The real person doesn't have to feel superior by hurting others. The hardened people do not have the important kind of strength one needs. This is a strong inner strength with a compassionate and loving heart.

Those who are cruel are not confident in whom they are. But God loves them just the same as you or me, they are His children too. They have much to learn and if not on this side hopefully on the other. This may be with consequences to pay accordingly for each soul. Hopefully they will find the never ending love that waits for all of us.

Growing up my son did all kinds of things to make people happy. His sisters and I marveled watching his happiness blossom. He loved his sisters with all his heart even though they sometimes gave him a hard way since he was the only boy and they had the normal sibling love. When they were all grown they laughed about those early years and fun times as kids when they fussed, and he was still teasing them just the same, they loved it! We would get together and laugh until our ribs hurt going over so many fun times and precious memories. We couldn't go anywhere together without laughing all day. We laughed during the bad times as well as the good times all the while keeping a good attitude. I am sure we all wanted to live our best for him because that's what he did for us. It was like one for all and all for one! What would one do without the precious memories of our loved ones?

David stood for being a highly evolved teacher to those who were around him and a mediator for what he stood for and we recognized this fact all of his life. Others who knew him did not know this, even though he changed some lives with his kindness and caring alone. He had an important magical way of living as a good example with faith. He wasn't trying to be anything other than what he was. I very much doubt he ever thought of himself in this way of being a teacher, but perhaps he did on his mission of love to others. He was a humble person and didn't want to be known as anything but a regular human being. He was never into himself. It was always the other person he wanted to help if he could and he never asked for anything in return. He kept still about his missions.

He kept and used his gifts, despite his grave illness, over all the years he lived by still kidding and helping others all he could. I know in all his sickness he would never let on that he was so ill. This made us feel hope that he was getting better. Through those many years he helped us with so many issues and problems. He always knew how to make us feel better with a big bear hug and above all, the biggest I LOVE YOU! He was our cement holding us all together.

Premonitions

One of David's main gifts was being able to foretell future events and this was, at times, a very difficult ability knowing what was to come, but being powerless to do anything about it. He was unable to stop the visions, which made it hard, yet he knew there was a reason. One day I found him extremely sad and upset and he told me he felt so helpless! I could see the tears in his eyes. "Why?" I said. He responded that the other side had told him there was a little girl seven years old who was locked in a closet. She had been kept there since she was small. She was starved and weighed very little and was living in filth and she lived in New York. Except, the good news was that she would be discovered soon and be safe.

It wasn't but a few days later when the child was found through a tip from someone! Apparently, she was mainly kept in the closet! When this came out in the news I kept the clipping. We were so relieved for this poor little girl who had suffered so much, but now she was free! Hopefully, she would be able to recover in time to have some kind of a normal life. Everything either one of us received was for a reason, whether we understood it or not.

When we received information of the past, present, or the future, we don't always get every detail and the timing. Rarely, we may get quite a lot of information at once; it just depended on what was given to each of us. We had no control over the situation. Most of the time David would get part and I would get another portion of the same information, then we put it together. The main thing in the above case was we knew this small child would be found very soon and it turned out to be a good outcome. David knew how horrible this child's life had been and we prayed for her health, mind, and body to be completely restored with love.

Going Where?

David knew of future places and premonitions coming and what he needed to finish and accomplish yet. Soon he knew what he needed to do. He was given his mission from the other side with information of where he would be going next. It wouldn't be long and he said, "He would go to Canada to help a young man die that he had not met yet!" Before I knew it, that door opened for him and he was led to meet Jerry, a young man who had AIDS.

The man needed council and a friend on how to tell his parents he had AIDS and was dying. Jerry's parents lived in another city away from him. He needed a compassionate person to help him die without fear, which ended up being my son. Through the unusual connection of how they met, David flew to Canada bringing Jerry back here for a while. He did energy healing on him to rid the pain he was having. The healing energy also stabilized his mental, emotional, and spiritual states.

During the time Jerry was here, my son counseled him giving him added support without judgment. Jerry was a good man and my son let him know having AIDS did not make him or anyone a bad person, and not to be ashamed about whom he was as a human being. Those souls are loved as much as any human, but many are treated terribly because they are different. I noticed Jerry seemed to perk up, laugh more, and was even eating more normal. He was very thin with the illness he had and was picking himself up even gaining strength. He repaired his mind, body, and soul for what was ahead. Then it was time for the young man from Canada to return home.

Jerry eventually flew back to his small apartment of loneliness. He once again called to confess he just couldn't tell his parents yet. David immediately returned once more to Canada to give him more support. He went with Jerry and helped him tell his parents of his illness and coming departure. In the beginning, before I knew my son's mission to Canada, the other side told me to understand David would be gone with his work and that during the trips that he would be making he would be fine; he was doing his spiritual work. I was so proud of my son to help this young man who was suffering. I knew whatever needed to be done for this stranger was an honorable mission David asked for. Jerry became my friend at first sight too when I had met him. He was kind, polite, compassionate, and fearful of so much. He needed to know he was as important and loved as anyone else on this earth. We gave thanks for Jerry coming into our lives. Jerry was a warrior to take on what he did to teach others!

I remember I was so concerned when David first flew to Canada. He was to change planes in New York and would call me when he landed. It was now past the time for his call and I was watching the late news that evening. The weather report came on and suddenly BEHIND the weather man the small figure of a plane passed behind him! It was white and in blue letters it said Canadian Airlines! I was shocked yet knew this sign for me meant David was fine and on his way into Canada! These things never seem to be anything short of a shock, but a great comfort in my life.

The Plane Crash

Months later in another one of David's premonitions, he told me a plane would crash in Africa! It would be carrying 267 passengers and would crash in Kinshasa, Africa and all would perish! The plane would hit a crowded market. As he told me this, I also began to get information; I was getting something about Russian, Russian pilots, or a Russian plane. "Yes, it would be a Russian Cargo plane," he said. It was maybe two to three days later that it happened and all 267 people perished! We both knew it would happen soon, but were not given an exact date. The date was January 8th, 1996, which happened to be David's birthday! We both knew these people had a mass crossing over together.

Katrina

I will always remember when David experienced a vision of Katrina! He told me early that day what he saw in his vision. He knew a horrific catastrophe was coming, but did not say what it was going to be called since he did not know. This horrible event was going to happen in the United States which had not had such a large scale event of this type before, and it would happen very soon. We don't always get every single bit of some information and every detail in a vision, but he said, "It would be devastating when it came and there was nothing anyone could do." What we do know is that there is a reason we each get future information. Many times without an exact date, or exactly when or where it will be, or the result. We get what we are given to prepare us in different ways; we don't always understand where our part is in things, but there is a reason in the big picture.

9/11

This is similar to when we both saw parts of a vision of 9/11, but neither one of us knew what it all meant or where this would happen. I saw the destruction of a building with debris flying in a whirlwind of rage. David called me a few minutes after I had this vision, he also had a vision in which there was blood, and concrete blasted into pieces, fire, and so on. Whatever it would be was now ready to happen or had just happened!

My daughter called me a maybe two hours after our information to us on that early morning to tell me of the first plane that hit the first tower in New York! We were devastated as everyone was! Then everything we had gotten fell into place with the horrible destruction of the second tower being hit and the plane crash! There was nothing we could have done, but what a sick feeling realizing what the visions were warning us of. This was such a horrible ending for so many innocent lives and families, I could never have thought it possible that something like this would happen in our United States!

Yes, a seer's life is hard but it also has some small amount of joy and bliss in it. We had dedicated ourselves to helping others and to accept the gift God has provided us. This is an honor, yet it sometimes is very sad for our human hearts. We know the reasoning and answers will come later with the full understanding of it all. It all will fit together like a puzzle after we cross over, that's what we have to remember to keep our head straight in this world.

Not getting all of the details on information makes it hard to do anything. But it does not matter since we cannot do anything about these events, our hands are tied, and we are not supposed to intervene. We realize we cannot change anyone's destiny or how they will crossover, only God knows this. We couldn't have done anything to stop this and we felt sad in that respect. Yet, we knew in the bigger picture, they were all together and fine where their souls were now in the best of hands. That is part of the reason we are not told the whole story. One thing we do know for sure is that it has to do with our learning in some way. This type of passing with a large group of people is called a *mass crossing over*. Mass crossings' have occurred often throughout history from events such as war, the sinking of the Titanic, tornados, hurricanes, disease, shootings, and so on. There are any numbers of people who cross over at the same time together. They experience their own passing with one another.

More Examples of Premonitions

Another premonition that occurred to David was while I was driving him to the hospital one early morning when we passed through a very small town. He suddenly said to me, "They are going to build a new high school here, mom, and call it Christ Our Rock!" I answered, "Really, in this small town?" "Yes," he said. In a few more years this small town built a new high school and named it Christ Our Rock! The town had never had a high school before; the kids were always bussed to the next town.

One day while crossing the railroad tracks going home, I passed by a large empty building which had been a candy factory at one time. My son told me he knew what this place would be in the future, the other side had just told him. "What?" I asked. He said, "In time it would be sold and become a cake mix factory." "What kind of cake mix will they make there?" I asked him. "All kinds" he replied.

"Do you know what the new factory will be called?" I asked. "Gilster Mary Lee," he said. I had never heard of it. This happened exactly as he predicted several years later, after the empty building was finally sold. It had been empty since a major fire when it had been a candy factory, now years later after sitting empty it is a cake mix factory, just like he said. I never doubted our information when either one of us was told something. And on top of that our town really needed a new business, so this was a very good thing. Even today, the Gilster Mary Lee factory is busy making cake mixes.

Another day when I was kidding around I asked David how much I might get back on my income tax. He gathered his information from the other side in his head saying $667.56. I filed and I knew I would get this amount.

When the tax man told me the same amount I really had a big smile. We each have our own expertise on certain things with information we are given. We would get information every day on many things.

During the night when it was quieter I could see and hear my messages much sharper when I received them. Then the next morning when David came down from his room, we would compare our information. In later years when David was in the Air Force or was living away, we would call each other to see what each of us had received. We did this most every day. It was truly amazing how we would each receive information or experience something about the same thing, not necessarily the same information or experience, but something related to the same event or occurrence. We were always working together.

There were many wonderful future events we were told of ahead of time and as you can see, they weren't all sad information. I strongly feel much of what we went through was building up my future strength. I would need it in order to carry on our spiritual work without my son after he passed over. We didn't discuss this, we didn't have to, and we knew this inside ourselves. Later, after his passing, we would continue working together from separate places his side and mine. I would miss him more than I can ever find words to say.

Chapter 4

David's Grandparents And Their Passing

My Parents, David's Grandparents Attending Their Own Services

I have recalled many times through my life a small amount of the other side that my mother taught me. As a child growing up, my mother spoke to me and my Dad about seeing and hearing spirits. I always wished I had asked her the many questions I thought about later on. I doubt she really knew why she was able to perceive other beings and the passed over souls that she did. She would not have shared her gift with any others in that day and age. She knew it would be taking a terrible chance just knowing what most people would think. They would never understand her life, just as we both felt now. My mother was sweet, gentle, soft spoken and kind to everyone she met and had great compassion for others.

I can recall when homeless men called hobos rode the trains and came to our home asking for food. They knew a regular route to our house. Even when food was scarce my Mom would always find something to give them with a cool drink. I remember them sitting under the big shade tree in our back yard grateful to have the food they ate. Mom would always say, "Help others; you never know when you may be in their shoes." She also turned the other cheek when someone was rude to her, which was what I admired so much in her, she was strong with knowledge. She was always such a gracious southern lady and a great mother to me and grandmother to my children.

David and his grandfather were very close. Dad being a railroader, taught him how to tell time when he was a small boy on his railroad watch. He would tell my son that when he died he wanted him to have his watch. Even when dad's memory had gotten bad and he wasn't in this world most of the time, if he heard the back door open he always called out, "Is that you Davy?" This was when my dad knew nothing else with his mind failing. Somehow he always seemed to know David and his sisters.

Growing up, the children loved being with grandma and grandpa staying overnight and watching movies together at least once a week. Mom and Dad loved them like their very own. I remember when my mother taught all of my children how to make art creations out of her holly hocks; these are tall stemmed beautiful flowers in different colors that she grew in her yard. She would make dolls and other creations for them. It was as if my son and daughters had two sets of parents with my family living only a few blocks from us. They grew up loving my parents with all their hearts, as mom and dad did them.

Through the next few years my Dad's health problems began and did not get better. He became very sick after a lengthily illness of several years with cancer and Alzheimer's which was hard to accept. He was a loving, kind, and hardworking man who helped others in his life, by being his gentle self. He was a railroader taking pleasure in his work and those who worked for him. He cared about them and had many friends there. He was a fair and gentle man respecting others.

Becoming Sick Together

Our world changed when my parents both became very sick at the same time. I was extremely worried as I watched both my mother and father become helpless together. My mother couldn't walk or talk, she became completely helpless in her illness with Cerebellum Spinal Degeneration. Dad was eventually the same, except he could walk and talk, but with Alzheimer's he had no memory. It was hard to see both of my parents together like they were. We needed help around the clock in no time. We were in and out each day and I vowed to keep them home as long as possible. This worked for over eight years, and then the doctor said they needed more medical help than we could provide.

This was a very sad time in our lives. My mom knew what was going to happen even though it wasn't discussed. She could not talk because her voice was long gone. My dad only existed. I had one parent with a terminal disease and a sharp mind and the other who was gone in mind and did not know it. The doctor asked me to let him make all of the arrangements because he could see how devastated I was. He also told us that he did not know how we had kept both of them home for so many years. They needed more care than we could ever give them now it would be soon and they would both be leaving their home where they had lived for many years. Everything was changing so quickly and would never be the same. This was so sad for me, I felt completely numb. This was a very sad time in all of our lives.

David wished that he could be here to help, but with being in the Air Force and living away from here at that time, made it impossible for him except when he could take leave. He did come as often as possible though.

Beautiful Ball of Light

Before too long my son's tour was finally over in the Air Force and he was now working and living in Dallas, Texas. As my dad progressed into his final illness, one evening my son was in his living room talking to his friend, Jim. Suddenly, he noticed a large ball of bright light that kept moving around the ceiling. Jim could also see this strange ball of light and both commented on it with David knowing this was a phenomenon and a visit! He knew why this was happening; he suddenly knew his grandfather had passed over. He was seeing his grandfather's spirit in this beautiful light. When he called to tell me, I told him grandfather had just passed away a short time earlier in the hospital.

My son being so close to him knew his grandpa was making his rounds and had come to say his goodbye. David checked on his grandparents all the time and had called me the night before to ask how grandpa was. He had seen him in his bedroom in spirit standing at the foot of his bed. The appearance of him in spirit let him know his grandpa was getting ready to leave this world; his spirit was already out of his body.

David was on his list that night to say good-by to for now, but not for long. My dad was kind of quiet, yet funny and a very wonderful hard working man. The men who worked for my dad were treated like family. At his funeral years later, many railroaders came to it. I heard over and over from them how good a man my dad was and how good he treated them! That he was the best boss they had ever had, and he was the best dad I could have ever had!

A Grandmother's Illness

That same evening my Dad passed, after I made his arrangements at the hospital, I went home exhausted and lay down on my bed. My entire body was depleted of energy. I was so sad for my dad's suffering and the years he lived in pain. I thought of my mother who had watched everything change in both of their lives still residing in the nursing home. My poor mother was a prisoner in her body and completely helpless. I stayed with her all I could and for many nights to come after Dad passed over.

Her intelligence was good, but she could not speak, walk, swallow food or water, and was being fed intravenously. She could not move any part of her body. And now, her love was gone from her. How alone she must have felt. I thought of how she couldn't even express her sorrow because she was frozen in her own body unable to release her tears and feelings, or to be able to grieve. The one thing I did know was that my mother was able to see my dad after he passed with her clairvoyance. This would be a blessing for her the rest of her life. Even though on different sides, mom and dad were still together, just in a new way. They would be together in this way until she could join him. How did it all end this way, I asked myself? I remembered them as young and healthy. Where did their lives go so fast?

Dad's Celebration

I lay there in my bed thinking of how I never thought my parents could get old and sick, and how they had suffered together for years. As I lay there, running all of these things through my head, I gazed around the darkened bedroom to suddenly see what looked like flashes of light! They were beginning to form very fast, filling the room! This display looked like fireworks on a 4th of July evening! There were bright colors hurling across the room and erupting across the ceiling! For a second I couldn't grasp what was happening, and then I knew my Dad was here! I suddenly knew Dad was with me and I understood his visit with the words he was saying to me!

The main word he would say was celebration! This was his celebration; he was free of his pain riddled body! He was in his spirit body ready to cross over into his heaven! He was giving me this loving message making his rounds for me to tell the others that he was just fine! It was some time before the bright colors quit flashing and the firework display slowly disappeared. I knew Dad had needed to let me know how happy he was and so totally free now! For him his death was a grand celebration! I could actually feel his happiness very strongly and I called out to him, "I love you dad! I love you!" After it ended I was much more at peace by feeling his joy. I slowly found myself content, asleep and dreaming.

Dad apparently had gone on quickly to my daughters and other loved ones that night. He enjoyed his granddaughters and loved them so much and did appear with a visit to them. Dad had come to all of us to say his goodbye for now as he had for David. He would be back many times to leave his messages for us for years to come. He even showed up in spirit in a camera picture one Christmas watching my granddaughter open her gift! No matter what you are taught or told we go on, we live, and keep living, we don't die, the soul can never die! This was a wonderful experience and I gave my thanks to him for coming with my devoted love every time he appeared. Now I felt assured by always knowing how happy he is. On the night my dad crossed over I knew he would be watching over all of us returning often with his visits.

I was called by my daughter, Robin, early the next day to tell me of her grandpa being present with her on that last night too. When she woke up, her bedroom window, which had been painted shut for years, was up and open! A wonderful breeze was gently blowing in her room. An alarm clock grandpa had given her that sat on a shelf across the room had been placed on her pillow beside her head when she woke up! Robin had been the one to release my dad into the other side.

I can still see dad's celebration that night in my memory, and the happiness he was relaying to me so I would be at peace for him and to tell others of his visit. I had such a feeling of his deep love for me now, I could be at peace for him. My dad was really counting on me to tell the family that he would be back. Being human, I still knew I would miss him greatly but we would continue our visits in this way. My son, daughters, and I would have many visits, and he would be helping David and me in our work from the other side now. He would be watching over all of us as our protector and guardian.

Dad would be with my mother knowing she could see and hear him in a way that only she understood. My mother had been sick for nineteen years and everything in her body was being destroyed slowly day by day, a little at a time. Her mind would always stay good. On our visits to her, David and I could talk to her with telepathy, mind to mind, using only our thoughts. She understood this clearly as she was blessed in that way too. I thank God my mother could see dad after he crossed over and appeared to her in her room.

It made my mother happy to know David and I could see dad too. This was a great comfort to her. Just knowing we could also experience him made her happy and she tried to smile at us with her eyes sparkling. By now, even her eyes were not able to shut and focus anymore. I knew she was hoping to go soon and join him to be released from her imprisoned illness.

I recall after my Dad passed over and I was staying with my mother at the nursing home I began to hear her thoughts to me on a particular day. She wanted a pen or pencil and a paper. She couldn't speak, so I repeated to her that I knew what she needed and got the items. I took her fingers and slowly bent them around the pencil; she had not been able to use her hands at all for a very long time. Each of her hands was tightly in a ball in a frozen state, but somehow she held the pencil when I wrapped her fingers around it. I was totally surprised by this but I knew then something wonderful was going to happen! She managed to write, daddy is here! I was so excited!

She managed her message in her own writing, it was so unbelievable! This was a miracle in her condition since she could not move. I had noticed a ball of light near the ceiling for some time that day and I knew dad was here. I told mom, I can see dad too! She tried to manage a slight smile which was impossible for her to do.

No doubt this made her happy to know that I could see him like she did and that I believed in her and what she could see. This took a great amount of energy for her to write her message and it meant so much to her. We always knew when he was present. I know she had my dad's help to be able to hold the pencil. There was no way her fingers could have bent to hold it. I knew he would always stay near to her.

Mom's Celebration

Years later, when my mother crossed over I was with her at the hospital. The other side said to me that she would pass over that evening. She seemed to be in a coma but I knew that she knew that I was there and that she could hear me. Her spirit had been moving in and out of her body getting ready to leave the last few days. I told her how much I loved her; she was the best mother in the world, and many other things I continued to express to her. I had said these things many times before and wanted to again. I knew I wouldn't have this chance much longer, her time was short. My children were already grieving for their grandmother knowing time was short.

As her time grew shorter I saw her soul was moving out of her body. Our life force energy exits out of the crown which looks like a transparent mist to me. I knew she was so tired and wanted to go and would leave soon. I stored her every way I could in my memory as best as I could. My heart was wounded, but also peaceful for my mom's time here to be over after suffering 19 years. She never once complained even when she could have. I sat there thinking of how she always used her Indian courage with the strength of a warrior. She was such a great and silent teacher to me and my children through her illness. These were the times we were taught so much through the courage she had with her perseverance in life and she had not been able to speak for the years that she was ill. Yes, she had suffered long enough.

My beautiful mother waited for me to say the words she needed to release her. Finally, I made myself do this. David was living away out of state then, but would be here later on. He was very upset; he loved his grandma so much! For certain reasons I didn't know exactly why then, but the other side repeated to me that I was to go home and I would be called soon. I talked to Mom awhile longer and although she never opened her eyes I know she heard me. I kissed her goodbye and went home which was devastating! A couple of hours later the telephone rang with news of my mother, she was gone!

She was not alone when she passed, no one ever is. It had been hard for me to not be there, but I obeyed the other side knowing I did the right thing. I wasn't supposed to be there the other side said, "That's the way my mother wanted it to be." I think she knew how hard this would be for me. There is always one who is to be there for a certain reason. The one for her was my dad who came to get her as he said he would at the end.

No one ever dies alone; a person most always is surrounded by their current loved ones, or their loved ones from the past, along with Heavenly Beings in this final transition. Mom had stayed these many years for a certain reason. There was one person in the family she waited for, to know they would be alright without her. One thing I had needed to do and did was to tell my mother that last evening we would all be ok. I said, "I know you want to go and be with Dad and it is okay," that's what she was waiting for to release her.

My dad had been coming to me in the last weeks of my mother's life more often now, preparing me by saying, "I will come for your mother soon. I will take her by the hand and we will be together again." I still wasn't prepared; no one ever is for the final moment. Knowing now my dad and my mother would finally be together again I was relieved and I knew how happy they were now. Now they were together and she was in a perfect state, smiling and looking as young as my dad after he crossed over. They were young in spirit and in perfection and once more together.

At mom's funeral when the minister was speaking, I looked up to see both my mother and dad standing close by her casket! They were smiling and looking directly at me while holding hands with a red heart symbol between them! They looked like young sweethearts in love and they were once again! It was wonderful! I experienced this gift of their love and visit that they presented to me! I must have smiled back at them in my happiness, because later the minister asked me what I saw. He told me he knew something happened that I was witness to. He continued by saying he had seen me looking directly at something he couldn't see and I had a contented smile on my face. He took me by surprise asking me this. I had no idea he saw or noticed my happiness. I had met another person who truly believed and seemed to understand! His eyes could see through the windows of his soul to know this. After the funeral, I spoke to him more about my visit. This wonderful minister understood my experience, adding that he could see the connection through my eyes to something amazing!

I was feeling very happy and content inside myself after seeing my parents as sweethearts once more! They both were united again without a hint of sickness and looked as young as I usually see spirits come. I felt a great peace, but would miss both of them very much in physical form. This happening was by the grace of God, that nothing is impossible. I would see my parents many times over the years and they would be helping all of us.

One summer day a long time later, David was sitting on the steps to their home which he planned to move into one day when he was well enough. The house was empty for now and it was my dad and mother's anniversary. All of a sudden he heard a song she used to sing, It Had to Be You! She loved that song and dad used to record her singing it when we were kids. He stood up, checked the locked door and walked around the house to check. He knew it was his grandmother and granddad doing this for him there was no one anywhere else! He felt this was to comfort him letting him know they were with him that lonely day which had made him sad thinking of them. This lifted his soul and gave him comfort.

Funerals

The way of funerals had changed greatly for David and myself. Not only with seeing my parents, but also others who have passed on. Most of the time the passed over soul will stand close to their loved ones at their funeral. Even though this happens, David and I could not tell people who were grieving as most are already in shock and this information could send them over the line. We always wished we could tell them to hopefully ease their hearts.

After a period of time we were sometimes able to tell people of what was happening and provide them with information that helped them. I do not know how all of this works yet except that we both are clairvoyant, and to see my parents appear together in front of me on mom's celebration day was amazing! David and I wished that all people could know that their loved ones who cross over to the other side are aware of things going on and are usually at their own funeral. They seem to stay close by their loved ones for about three weeks then go back and forth as they choose.

These souls are sometimes surprised at the full attendance for them and with who comes to their final departure on earth. Some of the passed on souls have chuckled and pointed out a certain person saying, I didn't think that person ever liked me. And the souls are sometimes amazed at how loved they are by so many others. They can feel how sorry some people are about how they got along in life with the deceased one. The soul seems to understand those things once in spirit. So much of our understanding of things is made clear to our soul.

After the Loss of Someone

Life has many unknown changes waiting for each of us and the one dreaded the most is death. At some point we all seem to go through a certain part of our life with this trauma and learning of how to let go of a loved one crossing over. When they do, it's the hardest time in our life. This is a long and sad process for those who are left behind. When you begin to venture out again after a tragic loss in your life it is a huge step. It is a different step for each person who is going through the painful loss of a child or any of your loved ones.

One appreciates kind people who want to help you and who are concerned, yet in my case I found it extremely difficult to engage in a conversation during this time in my life. I knew I would break down. I found comfort in hiding away most days for a long time after David's passing. I certainly appreciated people who called and contacted me. This helped me to know others cared and wanted to help in some way. We are all different and I needed to be alone except for my daughters and other loved ones. I was too sick in my spiritual body, mind, and soul to respond to others, my world was upside down! I was working on keeping my sanity and from feeling as if I was in a bad dream.

Your world has forever changed now. It is a different time starting a new life without your loved one. There is really no getting over it! We are humans who have suffered the worse separation in our life. We will, in time, go on as our loved ones want us to do because we have no choice. Our life journey is important to the soul who has crossed over. Each one of us needs to keep going; this is important to them and to us. Most people who experience a loss can't just get over it, like you sometimes hear from others. What a terrible remark to say. I suppose they have no idea realizing the damage their words can do. Something as harsh as the wrong words at this time can be devastating!

Chapter 5

Learning His Gifts

Starting to Develop

David soon began to find his true calling in life as he began to settle down into a new life after the Air Force. Since he was unable to find the types of jobs in his hometown that could provide him with real satisfaction and some room for advancement, he moved to Dallas and began his life as an adult. Unfortunately, it was not soon afterwards that the illnesses that would plague him throughout the remaining years of his life began.

This is also where David and I began to learn and work together, just not in your normal ways. During his time in the Air Force we communicated often, but after leaving the Air Force we began talking every day and sometimes more than once in a day. This is where we became more involved in our learning process with David being the teacher along with our spiritual teachers. We would share our own experiences of the previous day or night and compare these experiences to find out the meanings that were being relayed to us. It was a great joy working with him on a daily basis and so much fun when he would have a chance to come home.

Lessons We Learned Regarding Intervention

David and I had many conversations over the years with the heavenly Beings of Light, sharing and explaining their heavenly answers to our many questions. This was for us to learn for preparing us for our work together through the future. We had one mind between us. In reality, we were one soul divided; we did only have one mind between us from when we were created in the beginning of existence! We had been told of this before, which is why we were just alike in mind and soul.

Our learning was wonderful and another lesson we received to remind us, was more information about intervention. That no one should intervene and try to change other's lives, or their destiny. No one has the right to interfere with another's life. It is wrong to take life lessons away from others. They are learning what they came to earth school to learn, let them learn. It is the hardest thing to not want to give out advice and so easy to say, I wouldn't do this or that. We humans seem to want to orchestrate other's lives so much of the time. We had been reinforced on this once more; we would not forget this lesson to pass on.

We knew it was fine to try and guide, suggest, or offer positive information which is a different thing to do, but others need to make their own decisions. We all come here to learn and need to go through what we need to, no matter how painful we all have a mission. There will always be those who want things their own way and will try to change others. It is the hardest to stand back with the intention of wanting to help a person, especially our children or a loved one.

With prayer, which is the strongest power, there are miracles which can and do happen someplace every day. This can give one the opportunity to change their life and begin learning by getting back on track with a better and positive attitude. No one is perfect that's for sure, we all have Divine help reaching out to us, understanding that we need this help which comes from prayer to our Creator, our God force. Sometimes, something wonderful turns the tables and intervenes at the last minute with Divine intervention. One hopefully learns to never give up hope, continuing to persevere in the hardest of times. There is a time and place with one's own destiny what we each can do with our own free will.

Our lives are set in motion from our beginning, with all the things we need to experience that no one on earth can change and we can't turn back. No one can heal the world in human form and we are not meant to, even though we may want to desperately make things turn out in our way or what we may think is a better way to do something. If you think about it, all of us get up every day and design our own lives without thinking about it in this way. And when we get mad at ourselves, knowing we shouldn't have done something that we did anyway, we feel regret and hopefully learned our lesson. This is part of being human.

One can easily neglect the *small voice* inside of us trying to tell us not to do something. This can also be a helpful secret to listen and learn by. We have the option of bypassing our thoughts with free will and can feel miserable, or feel good with the right actions; this is the way a lesson can come. This is a human emotion and our intuition talking to us this way. To our advantage we can learn from our mistakes for the next time. It is up to each one of us in our learning to listen to our intuition. Everyone has the gift to do well by learning to listen to it. When you don't feel right doing something then don't do it and save yourself the regret.

The other positive way to look at this is, perhaps we needed to go through this lesson again to relearn it. You've had another chance to make something right. Maybe we have another shot at it! One way or another, or time after time, whatever we took on to do and fix, there are no short cuts. No matter how long the learning takes. This explains our many lives over and over being able to evolve to higher levels by learning through our mistakes.

The things we need to accomplish must be done before one's soul can move to those higher levels thus growing closer to our Creator in our Heaven. But in all of this, don't be so hard on yourself about making mistakes. Mistakes are extremely important to help us wake up, learn and do better the next time.

David and I studied our lessons intently wanting to live our lives the best we could, making many mistakes along our way and hopefully learning more. Life is an extraordinary school of learning, but it is also a mystical place of beauty to enjoy what has been created for us. The world is a place of our Creators handiwork.

Lessons Learned Regarding Pleasing Others

Another tough part of life we had to let go of and learn is that you can't please everyone no matter how hard one tries, and really we shouldn't be trying to do this anyway. There must have been hundreds of those occasions when we went overboard and hurt ourselves. Everyone isn't going to like you either, even when you do nothing to them. Learning how not to go the entire length from those who expect you to be a door mat is important. One can still try to find a way to show them a loving and good friendship that may be possible! Even being a door mat is not going to please people who are that way, just be you. That is how David was; he would try his best with these individuals and would just move on.

You are a beautiful, precious being on this earth with your own journey before you. There will always be those for whom one cannot be good enough. The negative can always find fault with something, or someone every day. Do not blame yourself when you know in your heart you have given your friendship to a person, and that person turns on you without reason. Some people are never happy no matter what; they seem to thrive on anger, jealousy, complaining, or another emotion. I think that is their job here on earth in a way. We are learning in this respect that this kind of behavior is not a good way to be. The Universe is made of negative and positive, creating a balance. By experiencing this, try to realize we will always meet those types of individuals, which makes a balance in our universe. It is easy for a negative person to tear down others without reason and expel negative energy that is staggering to others.

The other side reminds me that each person has the right to spend their time with who they want or need to in life. I hope you choose the positive person who will lift you up instead of tear you down. This was a tough lesson for the both of us and still is in some ways of thinking that all people have a generous heart, they don't! We wanted to hang onto this conception to believing in all people though knowing better. It was about searching for the goodness somewhere in them.

It is easy to stay clear of those who live in anger, just look at their face and their eyes; this shows who they are in their soul. Always remember too, that people can and does change sometimes due to circumstances, there is always hope though. Usually a person is different when they have aged further and have matured. Hopefully with further knowledge they have changed for the better. Others, who are sweet, kind and happy, no matter what comes their way, are wise with wisdom and knowledge of having compassion and love.

David and I were set to live our lives in the best way we could, we were a team together and made our mistakes along the way, but hopefully gained in knowledge. We knew all humans make mistakes over and over, just as we hopefully would continue to learn from our own, and one another.

I didn't realize for a long time we both kept the dream of hope alive wanting to heal the world if we could have. This was ingrained in ourselves. If we could accomplish this it would entail taking away lessons from others and that would not be right to do and eventually this soaked into me. I know that is why we both asked to work in a spiritual healing energy world working with those who are ill in body, spirit, mind, heart, and soul. We followed our hearts and our spiritual work was brought to us by the other side in the life plan we had chosen and we both loved our work.

Telling the World

We had learned to live in different worlds without sharing our gifts for years, until we were told to tell the world. The time would be coming in the future to write of our experiences, and to continue our work. A wonderful enlightening thing has happened in the last several years with questions answered and unanswered by others in their search. There are no answers exactly right for everyone; each soul has a different outlook coming from their own experience.

Also, many more books have been written for people who are curious and loaded with questions. People want to know about other's true experiences and have more information about the paranormal world. People's experiences are more out in the open now for which I am excited about. We are not all crazy in this world having different and strange experiences. To those of you that are interested I suggest, staying open to new positive experiences and keep open minds to happenings everywhere in the world. Continue to learn from those who share their stories with accurate reports and good positive books. I think life would be completely empty believing there was nothing after death! Life is forever! This is just a prelude to what we come here for in our earth school. After life comes something so indescribable and beautiful it is like a dream.

Telepathy

David and I didn't always use words to talk which was handy when he was having very sick days. My son and I knew what the other one was thinking (telepathy) and some of our conversations were no words at all or perhaps just a couple of words to each other. Other times when he felt more energy we chatted away, laughing and kidding. We could read one another clearly, but this did not happen all of the time. On many occasions we were saying the exact same thing at the same time. This always gave his Dad a startled look; he would just shake his head asking "How in the world do you two know what you're talking about?" But this was common for us and wasn't anything we deliberately did, it was telepathy (thoughts), which my mother also did at times in her life. We could read each other's minds without trying.

I suppose this was unnerving at times to his dad, but we just giggled and went on with our strange conversation. I noticed later on my daughters began doing this at times and I felt there would be the four of us one day talking with our minds to one another. David would help me so much through his illness in our everyday life with his beautiful positive messages and his humorous and loving ways to me and to his sisters, through his use of telepathy.

The terms *telepathy* and *clairvoyance* explains communication used by some people who are psychic and gifted people. Everyone is psychic in some way but all people do not have to use these methods or even know this. It's a choice, like riding a bicycle or driving a car and some people can do it better with practice. No one has to practice what others do. Everything is a choice and needs to be your choice. There is no right or wrong if one uses the ability or not.

Clairvoyance

David would love to investigate topics related to our Other World and he would dive into finding out as much as he could. One thing my son and I explored and researched information on was mental hospitals. We wondered how many patients have been put into those over the years because a patient had the gifts of clairvoyance. More than likely, those people who were put into hospitals never knew they were gifted and in a sense, were losing their mind. David and I supposed some doctors thought if the patient said, they were hearing voices, seeing spirits and so on, they must be crazy! What a shame it was for the people who were locked away for this because they were different. Perhaps some people did go crazy not knowing why they were different in this way, especially a long time ago when nothing much was known about this subject.

David was interested in everything and easily realized because one is different that they can be cast aside, labeled and treated cruelly. We went to great lengths in talking to a nurse who worked in a Mental hospital in our research to find out what her experience was. She agreed with us in our interest of gifted others who had been hospitalized over the years, and were more than likely normal and thought to have lost their mind. They had been left in hospitals for the remainder of their lives because of so little knowledge on this subject. Doctors then may have rejected any reasons of clairvoyance as to why the patient was like they were. With this gift one can see and hear what others cannot. I shudder to think of those who were labeled as insane for life. I am sure this has happened with many people over the years. They never had a chance.

Different Types of Communication

Another gift that we found very interesting about David was that he could speak in foreign languages at will without learning them! He had never been to school to learn any language other than English. Sometimes he would start talking in another language out of the blue! I was quite amazed at hearing some Italian, Spanish, French, Hebrew, Greek, and so on. It was so natural to him! I could never get over how he could speak in these languages when he did. I usually picked up enough dialect of the language to know what it was even though I had no idea of what he said. The languages he spoke were very fluent when this happened. He would begin talking to me or his sisters and our attention was glued on him! I never saw anything like this!

He, himself, did not know how he did it. He would smile and go on. Was this from his past times before or something else? He also spoke in what is known to him and me as Universal language that the other side taught to both of us. They tried patiently to teach me the Universal language, what a challenge I must have been for them. I know this was a struggle but they were so patient with me and I did learn much of it. I was good with the symbols they taught us, this was easier for me and I enjoyed putting them into my memory. We used our symbols much of the time in our learning from the Universal school.

Quite often, he would talk in what is known as tongues. This is when I found out that talking in tongues is for real! The Universal Beings let me know what it really is, I feel much better knowing that it is a true language. I had wondered if it was an expression of group hysteria by many people getting hysterical at the same time. I am sorry about that, but not knowing until the other side informed me, I didn't have a clue.

The other side wants every person to know that going through our worst times is when we grow the most. That's why our mistakes are so important to learn by. We must have them to learn by or we would learn nothing.

More Energy Lessons

David had more than the typical six senses, he was multisensory and I knew there was much more behind his thoughts and his spiritual work that he was doing. He gave messages for better lives, a new understanding of trust, belief, and goodness. I also knew much more would be revealed to me in my own schooling. Most days and nights our information was coming in faster and faster. We were told by the Christ Light Beings that this information was inserted into my brain stem, as was my son's. I knew at times we both experienced this being done. It was like watching a movie at terrific speed without pain. This is the best I can explain it for now as to how this happens.

To define multisensory, here is a version as provided by in the book *The Seat of the Soul, by Gary Zukav.*

The multisensory human is able to perceive, and to appreciate the role that our psychical reality plays in a larger picture of evolution, and the dynamics by which our physical reality is created and sustained. This realm is invisible to the five-sensory human.

It is in this invisible realm that the origins of our deepest values are found. From the perspective of this invisible realm, the motivations of those who consciously sacrifice their lives for higher purposes make sense, the power of Gandhi is explicable, and the compassionate acts of the Christ are comprehensible in a fullness that is not accessible to the five-sensory human.

All of our great teachers have been, or are, multisensory humans. They have spoken to us and acted in accordance with perceptions and values that reflect the larger perspective of the multisensory being, and, therefore, their words and actions awaken within us the recognition of truths.

From the perception of the five- sensory human, we are alone in a universe that is physical. From the perception of the multisensory human, we are never alone, and the Universe is alive, conscious, intelligent and compassionate.

From the perception of the five-sensory human, the physical world is an unaccountable given in which we unaccountably find ourselves, and we strive to dominate it so we can survive. From the perception of the multisensory human, the physical world is a learning environment that is created jointly by the souls that share it, and everything that occurs within it serves their learning. From the perception of the five- sensory human intentions have no effects, the effects of actions are physical, and not all actions affect us or others. From the perception of the multisensory person, the intention behind an action affects both us and others, and the effects of intentions extend far beyond the physical world.

Your personality, like your body, is the vehicle of your evolution.

I wondered in those years what and who we really were underneath of the cover we wore over our human body and soul? How did we come to choose this work on earth? I had many questions in my head all the time. The other side told me, "The answers would come later on this." I was so hungry to learn more of the other worlds and was not afraid. I knew my answers came from the highest source there is, Our Heavenly Creator.

We both were taking a part of an unknown road this time around with all the energy we had, and were blessed to have one another to share the experiences and teaching with. If our lives had been arranged differently in how the plan was made, it would have been extremely hard for us to fulfill and neither one of us could of alone.

This was a challenge at times and I thanked God we made the promise that when we returned here to work together that we would complete what we had promised to do. Now things were on track, I received confirmations from the other side of more steps coming. I was told "I had graduated from my baby steps to the next phase in my journey." I felt at that point I would be finished before I knew it, I was totally wrong! I had a long way to go with many people and much to do along with my son. We were going to get even busier in our work. More than I could have ever thought!

Crystal Children

Many people may have heard of a veil of matter being over a baby's head when it was born to indicate it had been given the gift of knowing. Some of us have the sign of crosses in our palms that we were born with, such as my son and me, meaning the same thing. And now many children over the last few years who have been entering our world, have amazing intelligence, and will have new ideas for the future of the world. There are names for those advanced groups, the Indigo, Crystal, and Omega children. They will be able to help rebuild a new world, and have brilliant minds, knowledge and wisdom not seen before by man. They sometimes have little patience for their parents and others, they are so intelligent. They each have their own mind of high intelligence; they are highly sensitive and have psychic abilities. This new advanced arrival of them will be superior to us and we will need them. Over the last couple of decades and even before, several of these souls have been returning here to help us. They are here to change things and have important purposes here for their lifetime.

Astral Travel

Our *secret* lives went on each day as what is termed as a normal human being but certainly wasn't for us. Just like when David was in remission and when he was critically ill. The Christ Light Beings were always with us helping my son to heal. They continually gave us strength and courage, to lift us up in this fight. We were blessed beyond what I could ever have imagined, so our work could continue together.

Many times in the hospital my son was out in astral travel when it looked as if he was sleeping. This is one of the ways people can heal, although others are thinking they are asleep. Funny thing is the sick person rarely ever knows they were out and about, while their body rests. But he did know and where he went in this resting period for his body.

Astral travel is defined as: usually happens when one is asleep and the spiritual body leaves the physical body traveling to other places. The spirit body is moving to where it needs or wants to go, while the physical body looks motionless and perfectly asleep. Many people do not believe in astral travel, but only feel that it is a dream that they have had. Very sick patients in hospitals, nursing homes, and other places, do this without this knowledge escaping from their pain and broken bodies. They only assume they were sleeping and dreaming. The same occurs in comas. It is a blessing when one can get out of a paralyzed, old, ill, or diseased body when they sleep by going into astral travel. This is also how an Alzheimer patient can escape for a while to a better place. Healthy and sick people both astral travel without ever knowing it, some to escape awhile and/or to let healing take effect. All of us do this especially at night while sleeping and in meditation or in sickness.

Our Traveling Through the Underworld

The best example I can give you myself, is looking at earth as the round shape it is. Then imagine a dark band around the earth which David and I know as the Underworld. After passing through this terrible structure we are free to travel into the beautiful wonder of the other side. The spirit world is all around us in all reality, in the big picture.

The Universal worlds' and dimensions are full of *worm holes* which makes traveling any distance at an unheard of speed, in a very short time. Let me explain the best I can. Take a piece of paper fold it in two and put a hole through it in the middle. This is a simple explanation of time travel that I can give. If one leaves the paper in the larger form it takes longer to get to the other side of the paper, see what I mean? This is the best way I know to explain it. You would have to remove your regular thinking to this to understand the amazing speed of light travel! This was the most incredible experience to ever be able to dream of! I explain this kind of travel in my first book when the other side worked with both of us for months on end.

Here on Earth this seems impossible to most people, but we are entrenched by time. In the other dimensions there are many other worlds. Man will have trouble gaining much more information until he realizes in space, time means nothing and there is no time there. We here live by minutes, hours, days, weeks, months and years to have a measure to go by. Space does not.

We, who are on earth, have a much slower vibration. Those of us who have raised their vibrations higher (faster) are able to travel and use the other gifts they may have. When one raises their vibrations they excel to a higher spiritual learning. We are very limited in our world, and some are unable to understand all of this. We are bound to our measure of time and what we could do without it. And the worm holes makes distance so quick, it seems like nothing! This has been a great part of our teaching with the experience.

Our Spiritual Lives

I was excited at my new life living between new worlds and, even balancing them very well now with everyday life. The girls and their brother were long grown. They had had a regular up bringing like any other family. We played baseball, basketball, ice skated and other games through those early years. Although, I had kept this life hidden and thought I would never tell of it for many years, or perhaps forever I gave thoughts of hope that perhaps the real meaning of our spiritual lives could be told one day. This information could hopefully help others to wipe away some of the fears we each carry and how our truth had led us.

I also wondered if by time the children were all grown I would be told the time was right to share the information somehow, but the heavenly beings still made clear it was not near time yet. I was so relieved to know this. David and I also knew what a risk this would be trying to explain our chosen work and our missions. We could not risk being labeled psychotic and put into a mental hospital so we knew we could not yet expose our true accounts at that time. Who could understand this? In our world, with people living in other places, there had to be others such as us. Those who have come here with this type of work may now know why they did by reading these true accounts.

I knew the children had experienced many changes growing up and had been very aware of our sometimes *invisible* friends that we co-existed with. Luckily, the Christ Light Beings who came to teach us were not the ones they could see or knew about, for a long time. It would be too hard for them to comprehend. Our home was full of goodness and I knew this, no matter how it may seem to some others, it was full of light! The house was protected with the Christ Light all around it. We had witnessed this on occasions and in several pictures. I kept this part of our lives about the house private for many years. It was home and I wanted it to stay that way.

The Council

There was always so much to be thankful for when the heavenly Council came in the night. This was the Ultimate for us and we were excited! They were shining brightly as they were speaking their blessed messages. These occasions were usually when David was critically ill. Their presence gave me strength to keep us both going. I knew after they spoke to me he would heal, "for he shall be well" was the blessed words conveyed to me to always remember and we never doubted! During the times he was hospitalized or bed ridden at home we both would hear their words of healing. They sent their light on numerous occasions lighting up my room, and his, and even the hospital rooms he was in over the years and we knew they were there! They were beside us all the way.

Now our life was becoming extremely different and I had so much information swimming around in my brain that no one could understand if I had tried to tell them, and I didn't! I would still carry our secret most of my life if needed; we would not go against telling it! In those days I could not imagine the hassle my family would be put through. Thank God, for the many others who have surfaced and made the same choice with telling their stories. I appreciate the many health care workers, doctors, nurses and those who are well known exposing this kind of information by it happening in their own lives.

People who are famous are heard more than those of us who are ordinary people. When they tell of their own events or have written their own experiences people really listen. Putting your personal experience out to the public takes a certain bravery and dedication and there are some of us who charge onward to tell our truth.

A person who has had the experience of death and coming back are the people to believe even if you don't want to believe. We here on Earth have been taught so much that is NOT correct due to the fear of old ways and of the unknown. David and I knew the old books throughout history that were written long ago were not going to be changed. That would create havoc over the world for millions to believe all kind of our information passed down long ago through history could possibly be wrong, and the science of dying wouldn't be changed, at least for now. Thank God for carbon dating, which, has changed so much in our history and can identify the age of anything, such as the ancient people and other finds over the earth. Our information is changing in a new and different way than we ever thought possible, releasing the old ideas.

The Souls Who Reincarnate

There is a new reality of truth of what really happens after death. The next subject we both have experienced is about the choice of reincarnation for those who choose it. Then the next information is the process of how a soul can move on, choosing its own path. And, how the soul has its own choices of heavenly lessons and commitments it wants. Our soul is free to make out its plan but will not be believed by some. Our own free will says it all and we all have this, it is eternal. We each have our Earth school and a Universal Heavenly school. These are among other places to learn from in other worlds. Our Creator created many Beings in other Universes. We are not the only ones created in this vast array of other universal places.

A New Way of Learning

I continued to be fascinated by David's information when he spoke of the ancient wonders of the world, the various customs, new and future space travel, and future discoveries. There would be new medical research coming with more cures, and more miracles, and from Alien beings who want to help us make a better Earth. They are here now and have been since our beginning. There was a storehouse of information coming into us daily. Among all of this information, I was slowly being introduced to what I had known in other life times. By this, I would begin to remember the clear details of why we were here.

The other side and my son were not rushing me by opening me to my own information from them. He knew the timing and knowledge combined with wisdom to teach me. I had not remembered all of our Heavenly bonds and agreements yet at this time, soon I would. The timing was getting closer for the Heavenly Beings to begin my next lessons.

Certain lessons David and our teachers taught me from the other side that lasted for months at a time. It was nearly three years of study on dimensions alone of which I was shown from my Heavenly teachers and Guides. I studied the various ways of Universal travel with Heavenly beings, Spiritual

Alien Beings, and my Spiritual teachers. This is how the work went with us and with our many other commitments.

We both had been given beyond the sixth senses the same gifts; we used to work together in *other worlds*. We received amazing information almost every day from our Divine Source. I knew we were getting closer to a larger secret. We had the best boss in all the Universes over space! How exciting this was to me and to my son. I am sure he watched me with great pleasure in this spiritual learning that he orchestrated for me long ago and everything was going accordingly. My memories had been long forgotten as it was to be for now and slowly returned to me. This was when David had begun teaching me again. When the time was right, he would let me find out more with my own experiences into other dimensions. With being a busy mother in the early years raising my family I was given the extra time to do just that but since then I was growing spiritually faster now here on earth. I knew I would clearly remember where David and I were from in other times. There would be many more visits into other dimensions, universes, star systems, galaxies, and worlds, along with positive Divine Alien Beings of all kind to learn from.

Spiritual Protection

Our spirits would experience many terrifying Beings on some journeys to where we were going. Through this, we were taught to carefully protect ourselves from dark negative forces. The Higher Spiritual Beings and the Archangels told us, "It would be very important to always use their protection around us in times of passing through the underworld." The *underworld* would prove to be a very difficult passage, moving back and forth from our world to other universal places. This was a difficult level to be in. We were among terrible grotesque Beings and Energies I cannot describe! No one would ever want to experience this by choice! Being fully protected in our spiritual travel; when we called for help it was instant! And, for what we were called to do in those times. We both knew to listen well, and that we were being guided by the Angels and Archangel Michael. In certain instances, Archangel Gabriel and Archangel Raphael joined us through our difficult journeys. We had all of these magnificent guardians to call upon protecting us.

There were times when we needed to call them very quickly to help us out of a treacherous part of what we were called to do. There were also selected times we needed to call upon certain Saints in reverence and guidance. This is a part of the complex worlds my son and I have lived in and known. We continued not to be afraid of the *dark* invaders full of evil because of our tremendous spiritual armor. After I felt this protection for a while, we astral traveled and explored. Even though, I did not always see our protectors who accompanied us, when trouble appeared they were always there. There were times I closed my spiritual eye sight for what seemed to be moments. I did not want to see these terrible forces. Leaving and again returning, they are thick and mingle tightly and closely together against us everywhere all around us! This happened as we charged through them in our energy. They were like a living nightmare! We always gave thanks to our protectors from our heart and soul for our safe keeping. There were many days I woke up sore, or with a bruise on myself. Sometimes, I had a tremendous headache for a while. This was due to what had happened in my travel. The "underworld" is something no one could ever forget if they experienced it! This lowest level can't be avoided in Universal travel. It entails a great amount of change in our human molecule structure to travel we were told. The Beings of Light explained to us, that sometimes when we left this place, then later re-entered back to this world with the change, these small injuries can happen. In their beautiful words they would apologize with love and caring to the both of us.

Meditation

We were told to meditate often and become as one with the Universe, and soon many new wonderful events happened to us both. In meditation, one detaches from everyday life and learns to listen for any words. You also may see scenes and pictures, which one receives in the mind. This takes practice, then answers and direction can come. Meditation is a wonderful tool to keep in your life giving great peace and strength to you. Some students learning meditation may meet their Spiritual teachers or someone else they are ready to know by meditating. But, only when the student is ready will the teacher come. No one can rush this or make it happen before the right time. The other side knows when one is ready for any kind of information from your Guide and Spiritual Teachers. It may be a long time getting to know them but they are there. Eventually, we soon knew all of those who were new to us and our older family of them from our beginning.

It takes a great amount of courage to explain our story. Also, in how we worked together and continue to now from his side of the veil. I have no doubt this will seem unbelievable to those who are new to this kind of information and those who have not heard of what the spirit world can do. Our lives were unique, humbling, and extremely complex with our heartfelt agreement.

Chapter 6

David in Heaven's Doorway

Near Death Experiences (NDE)

An important, phenomenal experience both David and I had in common was that each one of us needed to experience death, and near death experiences again in this lifetime. This linked us together for our journey once more. Our experiences connected us, though the experiences had occurred separately in different time spans. This was all orchestrated before we arrived here once again. This was part of the plan. It would quickly change our lives forever in our work together in the spiritual world. David had several amazing death experiences over his years each time returning back from the other world. He was being sent back to tell about each beautiful one! His face would be at peace and glowing with each new phenomenal visit. This was all important to be able to continue the journey. I will start with one particular experience we had with my son coming back to life from a fatal heart attack.

My son lived hundreds of miles away at the time in another state. Like always, we kept in touch daily by phone, so I knew he had not been feeling well. He developed a terrible cough which had continually gotten worse. I urged him to see a doctor. He did, and was told he had emphysema! Information from my spiritual teacher from the other side told me, "No, he has pneumonia, not emphysema!" I quickly called him telling him to go to another doctor, which he had already decided to do. You see, even though we were gifted with our clairvoyance, the other side had an agenda for us we did not always know or remember.

I was anxiously waiting for his return call but my overwhelming feeling told me not to wait! I felt severe panic and a fear for him. I told his father we needed to get to our son quickly! With this emotion I became very weak and almost fainted in the driveway needing to lay down, I knew David was in big trouble!

The next thing I knew the phone was ringing with his best friend, Jane on the other end. She gently said, "You need to come now, David is sick and in the hospital," and gave the directions. She was trying not to alarm me by the way she told me, but I knew better, he was in bad shape! We quickly threw some clothes into a suitcase in record time and left on our way to Oklahoma. Our connection had always been so strong that my son and I each knew when the other one was sick or having a bad time. We quickly decided that it would be faster to drive than try to wait for a plane. I was scared and began a silent conversation with the Beings of Light.

On the way I was told by the familiar Heavenly Beings that David would repair and heal. I then asked for a sign that I had understood the message correctly. We had not traveled far when I looked up into the sky to see brilliant "white crosses" forming in the clouds across it! My heart was beating wildly, I was getting the confirmation I had prayed for! My mind and soul sent my heartfelt thank-you to the Heavenly Beings. My words felt very minimal to express my gratefulness. There aren't words in our language to say how I felt. This is completely understood on the other side. I had newly added strength although I did not know what was happening with my son, but I definitely knew he would make it through this. I also knew that he would have a long hard way to go. He would need to fight for his life to get better and heal. The main thing was I had just been told he would prevail! I heard the familiar loving words, "for he shall be well!"

After we entered the hospital, my son's doctor greeted me quickly as he guided me to the side of the hall. He began explaining how he couldn't believe my son was alive, and to remember he isn't out of the woods yet!" He was a complete miracle the doctor said, and could not explain how my son was still alive for as long as his heart had been stopped! I can still see his doctor shaking his head and then, he suddenly smiled saying he was so relieved that David was alive and fighting against all odds! I saw such a deep compassion in his eyes as he further said, "that with my son being so young, he had so much to live for!" He felt positive that he would pull through after making it this far. Then I was told I could quietly go into his room.

I wasn't prepared for what I would see. I would not have recognized my own son! He was so very thin and gaunt looking. He was connected to oxygen, tubes, and bags of fluid, a machine, and medicines to help keep him alive. This particular time, he was brought in DOA (dead on arrival) by having a fatal heart attack from congestive heart failure and double pneumonia. He was trying to get to his neighbor for help and collapsed in his yard. The neighbor found him and drove him to the emergency room but it was too late. My son had died, drowning in his own fluid!

It was a miracle that a compassionate doctor; who was a leading heart specialist, was in the emergency room and worked on David for a very long time, even after any hope to save him was given up. This doctor didn't give up trying to save him until he got him back! My son had been dead for many minutes! The doctor then told me my son shouldn't be here and hopefully would not have any lasting problems when he healed. This wonderful heart specialist in the ER never gave up on him, thank God! I never believed this specialist just happened to be in the right place at the right time to help my son. I don't believe anything happens by coincidence. There is no such thing as coincidence anyway. That is merely a word used when something can't be explained. I went into David's room slowly and quietly as not to disturb him but his eyes opened slightly and he managed a weak smile, he was so happy to see me! He had sensed that I was there.

In the next few days he told me as best he could what had happened when he passed out of his body to the other side. I wrote everything down as I sat beside his bed. He explained to me with his face glowing what he experienced after leaving his body. He was suddenly moving into a place of beautiful bright light where he was suddenly with the Creator, and with what he was told! I could see in my son that he was completely at peace within and filled with deep love as he spoke to me. He was still in awe of his experience in this magnificent place of light and love. Then he was returned to earth after his blessed visit into the other side. David said jokingly to me, "he knew if he didn't come back I would be coming there to get him," and we laughed happily together as I said, "Yes! I would have come to get you!"

He had experienced an amazing transformation with the Heavenly Creator of Light. I felt strongly he would have stayed on the other side, but wouldn't yet because of his sisters and me. He would be helping us for a long time yet. He was not finished and I thanked God so much for his return. David was sent back after his extraordinary visit of indescribable beauty and heavenly love. He knew the other amazing reasons for this experience which were only for him to know. I was fascinated by his out of body experience and with what happened to him on the other side. With my earlier information telling me, "for he shall be well," I rejoiced with happiness! He spoke of seeing others who were coming back, and those who were passing into the other side in their transition through what we know as the doorways.

Katie's Visit to David

Then he was anxious to tell me the rest of his beautiful visit from a familiar little spirit girl named, Katie Jane, who was present with him this time in his DOA experience. The spirit world is so familiar with both my son and I, knowing that both of us knew Katie well, from when David was a child. She is a happy bubbly little spirit and we call her Angel, and she loves him dearly! In this crucial time of his, she passed him her loving strength. She calls David her brother when she speaks to both of us since we all were always close to one another from another time. He told me how she helped him through his DOA (dead on arrival) experience.

When he became conscious after he had returned from Heaven, Katie was sitting beside him in a chair by his bed. Her tiny little face went into a big smile and she began giggling at him! She was shining full of light! He commented that her front tooth was missing, which couldn't help but make him laugh and feel happy! She kept smiling and swinging her little legs back and forth like any child does. Then, she reached out to him, placing her tiny hand into his, as it lay still on the bed giving him encouragement. Katie was sending her love, energy, and healing to her big Brother.

David said, "I was strengthened in ways beyond what we know of, in our world of healing with Katie's visits." He was very lucid and knew what he was saying about his experiences. Again this relates to the *gifts* he had and his connection to Katie our little Angel of healing. She helped my son not only with her healing and love to him, but David told me her little toothless grin made him smile all the time at her. She would not leave my son until it was time for him to be released and even then Katie stayed nearby to him in all of his years of service on earth. He had died twice this time and told me of the other visit.

We both knew there is a doorway we enter into the other side through, and he experienced it in this way. The Higher Beings of Light had directed him. There are also different doorways there. When we cross over one may experience this by entering a doorway or perhaps called a tunnel of light, and some, such as my son and me, are sent back remembering information we are given. The other side was working with David in the death experience to help him in many ways, he was given the choices to stay or go back.

Our soul always grows in some way after a death experience; this is never forgotten by many people and usually changes lives for the best. This is something one never forgets! Some remember an extraordinary, amazing experience! Some are terrified and remember a bad experience. To have a bad one, it may have to do with teachings of fear growing up and how one lives. One who is afraid of dying often believes the worst scenario. Those who learn from their experiences are usually much happier and change their life by being more appreciative, content, enjoying life more and have more knowledge. It is the most phenomenal thing to happen to a person! They can relay their NDE to others and this helps people everywhere who hear others experiences.

Katie's Story

Here is some history of Katie. The old home we lived in had been her home long ago, and in her world it still is her home. Katie passed over at the age of 5 years and eleven months, in December of 1867! Her small stone is in the local cemetery where we live. She led me to it one day knowing I wanted to find her place. I had no idea of where to go so she took me right to it! She wanted me to know and remember those days. There are no remaining records of Katie on file. Those were destroyed along with others long ago in a fire. I found some information of Katie's in the deed of our home but not her complete family's names.

Shortly after we moved into our old home, Katie made herself known to David and me with her strong presence of sweetness and love. She spent her time moving so much around from place to place. I was busy with the video camera all the time. She would push a small wicker buggy with dolls I had. I have found it in the different rooms including a closet and even on top of the kitchen eating bar! That's how we met Katie in this life time again. She is an absolute love filled spirit who plays like any child. Sometimes others who visit here have heard her small giggle and actually seen her tiny footprint in the carpets.

David and I knew we were all family in other times. We both knew she had been around us for a long time by letting us see her soon after moving into the old house. This was like being reacquainted from long ago; we knew her presence was always of the highest good. Katie is the picture of happiness; and our little Angel is full of sunshine. She stays close to us in times of need. Apparently this is her job passing out her love and healing. She lets herself be known to us in times of trouble, sadness, sickness, happiness, or whatever the occasion. Especially, when David was sick and at Christmas, we can feel Katie's excitement watching all the joy of the season. She feels she is alive with us, being her family too. She had a very hard life when she lived in this home. She must have been such a sad little girl without much love shown to her and because her father had harmed her. This harming of Katie eventually led to her passing away.

Katie was shown the way home to her place in Heaven several years back but wanted to stay here. She wanted to stay longer with the two of us. I had invited a minister and dear friend over to experience her presence when we thought of sending her home years ago to be with her loved ones by showing her the Light. But the minster and our gifted friend, Bev, said she wants to stay with you so let her be here for now. Katie wasn't finished here and she didn't want to go yet.

It was then I felt sure she was on a special mission with us. She had more to do and has helped the both of us in many ways over the years, keeping her bright happiness. I mainly know this because of us being family before. The other side said, "Katie shouldn't be forced against her own free will to leave, no one should do this to anyone by making one do anything against their free will," and we all agreed. Plus, she was a teacher to us in many directions, and her work would take time yet. We were happy she was with us again!

From the beginning, apparently she knew how long she would be here with us and everything that she is here for. This says to me to not judge too quickly when one thinks of a ghost in the house. The presence may be a good positive spirit, a teacher, who has come to help you. This may be their chosen job this time. A Guide may be called a ghost by a person not knowing what is going on and movies for entertainment purposes can be very misleading and scary as to how spirits act. Try not to panic first, unless you know and feel uneasy with a negative force around you. You always have the control to send them on unless one has dabbled into dark territory and don't know what they have. Then you will definitely need special help from someone who can come clear your home, which would normally call for a priest.

I will always remember when I was at home one day feeling rather down, when suddenly I noticed a blue flower beside me on the sofa! At first, I couldn't get a grip on how could this suddenly be here? After investigating, I found the flower came from another room out of an arrangement! I smiled then, knowing Katie wanted to cheer me up in her loving way. She had all of the emotions any earth child does; she is just in a different spirit body now. She is certainly dedicated to her job as our Guide and former loved one. When her work is finished she will leave with her own free will and will be waiting for us.

Soon, I was invited into a past life vision with Katie. There we shared a magical and beautiful visit one night. She wanted me to remember our lives together long ago when it was winter. I found myself outside of the house I live in playing in the snow with her. In this life time I was a grown woman and Katie was my child. She wanted to relive our lives together by taking me back into that happy time we shared together. We both wore long white pretty dresses as in Victorian days, and even though it was winter I felt no coldness at all. Everything outside was so beautiful and reminded me of an old fashioned Christmas card! This was such a time of happiness being together in our magical world and suddenly large soft flakes of snow begun falling, making the night a wonderland of beauty. We were laughing and holding hands together going around in a circle like two children playing our game. I clearly recall we were close to the big tree in the front yard. I felt so free, and this happiness seemed never-ending.

Suddenly, I glanced towards the front of the house which was built in a Victorian period and I noticed a lantern was lit inside the front window. The glowing light, so inviting, spilled out through the tall window panes lighting up the snow. Everything looked like dazzling diamonds sparkling over the snow. I felt like a child and little Katie was calling me mommy. Then I came out of the vision. I have never forgotten this event of our past life time. I knew in my heart this was special to her as well as me. I wondered where my daughters were in this because I felt they were close by. I have also wondered if Katie had returned as one of my daughters in my life today. I can still visualize being in that post card picture in front of my home that I live in today.

Katie was very active in our home most days and did funny things as any small child. There were instances when I found several small dolls that belonged to my daughters and my mother that I had kept, lined up in a row upon my bed or placed throughout the house. David had also experienced these dolls placed in different rooms of the house; and some would be tucked in under my bed covers in my room! She would at times place them in a toy wicker doll carriage and I would find it moved here and there to wherever she left it! I would first see an empty spot where the doll carriage had been; follow the tracks in the carpets until I found the buggy! More than once, the tracks went to a closed closet, and peering inside there it would be! There was the wicker buggy with her babies! I never knew what to expect. David and I would laugh so much and shake our heads trying to grasp all of this. There were the times we both saw Katie with a quick glance, a turn of the head, or out of the corner of our eye.

At night drifting off to sleep I was allowed a longer view of her. Several nights waking from my sleep she was close by me with her big smile, looking as sweet as any child can be. I have drawings of her she somehow etched into the carpet as if by pen. How this is done I couldn't imagine! Some of my friends have been able to see her escapades with the buggy tracks as well. Katie surly felt safe and wanted us to notice her. One drawing we found that we loved has her in a furry winter coat and hat with the figure of a dog with her. Her hands are in a muff of fur and she is a beautiful child with curly hair. I wonder if she shows us this winter picture since she was born in December. It is how we have picked up on this. She has let us know she hid in the small closet by my room from her father which breaks our hearts. The doll buggy sometimes goes into her closet.

All of this information was telling me who we all were to one another in that period of our lives, which is what I had already suspected was true. Yes, I was learning so much, so fast, and I was hungry to know of more things to come. I was very happy by learning in that life Katie was close to all of us today. David and I always held a strong love for little Katie in this current life of ours once more. He too, had no doubt that she had been another one of his sisters in another time period. By the way, even the Bible speaks of reincarnation in several places.

Why Some Spirits Stay

I know without a doubt why Katie and some other spirits seem to linger here or pop back and forth so often from our world and theirs. They also watch over us in many ways but many people would not welcome this. We don't have to understand all of this, just trust that it is not always for us to know. I have learned that some spirits choose this work where they may stay around a long time. They know when we are learning through them and need them. It isn't that they are always stuck some place. This is likely their choice in their contract and free will to do. Even visitors to the house feel that this spirit child is pure love, not a bad energy as some may think. We are not being fooled (as in movies and possession) by a bad energy, we would certainly know from our experiences, and protection we have from the Heavens. As much schooling as we were still being taught, we both would know a *dark* energy very quickly no matter the cover they may choose to appear in as a good entity.

Each person who is tuned into this type of work gets information from their spiritual teachers; or loved ones at times. It is not all the same for everyone. The two of us get our work in an unusual way but we know where it comes from, the Creator who loves all. There is not a certain program for everyone to learn by and there is not supposed to be. An example is going through school with the different levels, one higher than another as one gains more knowledge. You start with Preschool, Kindergarten, Grade school, High school, College, and Universities. This is my example by using our school systems. This is Earth school.

Another Vision during the NDE

The second vision David had while he was still close to death he remembered clearly. A French nun (who looked familiar to him) appeared at the foot of his hospital bed. She was sort of floating in place, clothed in a blue and white habit with a blue cross on it. He knew she was from long ago, another time period and he told me that he thought he had known her before. She spoke loving and healing words to him, reinforcing that he would live. Then she suddenly held out her arms as if to embrace him. She began to slowly come forward, floating higher than the floor. She continually kept a beautiful smile on her face and her arms were still stretched out. Then, right before she slowly faded away she told him, "You shall be well." He was enthralled with everything happening. He had experienced such an amazing visit and was so touched with being bathed in pure love. I could visualize this as he told me of this heavenly visit, and feel the beauty of it reaching my very soul! Oh, how blessed to know he would go on to be here longer with us!

The Aftermath of David's NDE

After some time in the hospital my son was released. I can still see my son's heart specialist shaking his head and with a big smile on how David survived. Through all that happened to him, his doctor still couldn't believe it! It took us awhile to get him home that day his spirits were so lifted because he had his own plan. The first thing he wanted to do was stop to buy a Christmas tree! He managed to find the tallest one they had which made him very happy! Now mind you, just getting released from the hospital he could hardly walk, but he was determined! He always bought the tallest tree he could find, even though the ceilings were too low for it. He always kept that little Charlie Brown or childlike attitude in him and would never lose it.

Early the next day when I got up he was already on a ladder putting it up! I watched him and he was so thin, still needing a large amount of healing to do, but Christmas was his most favorite time of the year in the world, and he seemed to shine like the star on his tree! After days of our special time together we went home and I was so sad to leave him. He was rapidly healing and doing well, and had close friends near him. I knew he would be fine. We continued to visit often and talked every single day, sometimes two or three times a day, which wasn't unusual in all of the years he lived away. A friend soon drove David home for a visit and he looked great. He was his old self once more! He knew my concern for him even though he was doing very well. He would laugh and say "Mom you worry too much, I'm fine!" I don't know if I could ever count the times he said this to me, and he never, ever, complained one time in his many years of suffering.

My personal DOA Experience

My DOA (dead on arrival) experience happened while traveling with my friend, her husband, and their baby son on our way to an air base near San Antonio, Texas. I was about 16 years old and had married very young and was traveling to be with my husband. I had tried very hard not to go to sleep during the trip, but I did in the last 25 miles. I had a strong feeling (my intuition) that I should stay awake, but I was exhausted. It was late at night when a car with two intoxicated service men came over a hill into our lane running into my side of the car. My friend's husband had tried to get on their side of the road to avoid the accident but could not do it, there was not enough time. My head was resting on the car window where I had fallen asleep. Being on the side of the accident, I received the full impact of the crash. I was reported "dead" in this horrific wrack and given up for good. I was DOA when I was found by the ambulance crew. I had been dead quite awhile. I shouldn't be here at all or have any brain function whatsoever.

The next thing I realized I was in a place I didn't know. Everything was covered in bright light yet it did not hurt my eyes. There was an indescribable beautiful Being of Heavenly Light talking to me. The Beings voice was so soothing, and I knew how honored I felt. At that moment, I did not know I was dead, I had no idea! This seemed like a dream at first. I was out of my physical body and dead but not aware of it.

I knew I was being told information that was very important, and to come in my future life. I was also being told how loved I am, more than I could ever know. There are no words to describe the time I was on the other side and I will never forget it. I have remembered this all of my life and how completely loving and glorious the Heavenly Creator is. I was so content, never thinking of how and why this was happening to me. I still didn't give one thought to thinking I was dead. I was surrounded in a special love and willing to stay right there.

After some time went by I was returned to my body, only then did I feel horrible pain! I couldn't understand what had happened; I was fulfilled where I was! I was not thinking I had to return, for I did not understand yet what had happened. I loved where I was! I went into unconsciousness as soon as I was back in my broken body, the pain was so excruciating. Where I had been was so peaceful and I kept repeating "Oh, thank you!" And this seemed so ungrateful. But, there were no right words that I knew in my language to begin to express my thankfulness!

My future work was told to me, but my memory of it would be removed until later and come back at a certain time, when it was the right time in my life. I couldn't process it all now. I had years to grow yet, so I needed to be patient. So much I am not allowed to tell of it. I do guarantee you that where I was, is more than any words can say. The peace, and tremendous love you are in with the Creator, there are no words for. Coming back was not a thought of mine, but my life was just beginning with much to do and souls waiting in the wings to be born as my children. So I was sent back.

I had been brought into the emergency room after being revived and was in very critical condition. Immediately, I was taken into surgery to repair my body. I remember the horrible pain of the injuries while coming to since I could not be sedated. It would have been too dangerous I was later told. I do remember coming too and then passing out from the horrible pain, for that I am grateful. My one eye was thought to have been blinded but despite all the damage and surgery, I have sight in that eye today. I was in a coma like state for some time not knowing what had happened. I thought I was dreaming and I couldn't breathe. Later, I found out I had that sensation because my nose had been crushed and cut from going through the windshield. It was a long period of time for the healing, almost a year before I felt human again.

With each visit to the base hospital a person would take pictures of me, front and side views with my permission. They told me I would be in medical books to study from in the future. These were the pictures that David saw while studying medical practices at Walter Reed hospital for the Air Force. I had never thought of telling my children when they were older about my accident since they had not been born yet when it happened.

At that time I felt so bad I didn't care, with all my injuries I would just nod my head. I was too sick to say anything or ask questions. I should not have been alive, I was dead so long and into the other side. My face had been reconstructed but I looked the same as I had when it healed. I was told I was fortunate to have one of the best surgeons who "just happened" to be there at the right time. There were no pictures of myself to help him see what I had looked like prior to the accident. I was there at the right time and in the right place. Nothing is by coincidence in our lives.

I wish I could thank the airman who took care of me. The day I was discharged my blooded clothes had been sewn up and washed by a female airman so I had them to wear home. How nice of her to do that for me! Maybe she will read my story one day and remember. I thank her so much and have thought of her so often at times.

My new husband at the time told me he was woken up that night of the tragic accident while having a dream of me. In the dream I had died in a car wreck! My dear friends and their baby son were not injured, just banged up some. I thank God that my good friend who was eight months pregnant with their second child was fine. I never knew what hit me for a long time. I was very young but realized when I was better I had had a miracle.

In these true stories I write, I can plainly see how my life and future moved forward in order to have my children, to learn, and grow in my life with all of those I meet. Little did I know my new life was just beginning with huge new changes, and more importantly with a new future endeavor that I would never dream of!

Although my son and I both were DOA in our separate death experiences, occurring to each of us years apart, we both were brought back to complete our agenda here. We both had a visit into the other side; actually David has had many visits. I don't know how a person could not be affected by this unless this memory is quickly taken away for some reason by the other side. We each had a knowing of what we were to do yet in our lives; this journey was not anywhere near completed. We had only just begun. We were both told on these separate occasions that we still had more work left to do on earth and that other important information for each of us to know was given to both David and I. Both of us would never forget our amazing experiences. I recall when I was in the other side it never occurred to me to return. I was in my bliss covered in love. There was Christ surrounding me in his love. I was without time and never thought of going back at all. I felt a non-judgment of anything and…I was not looking back, only to where I was, in complete awe!

Each of our death experiences happened so fast to both of us there was no pain that we each can remember, only the feeling of suddenly being consumed by tremendous love, happiness, and filled with a great peace. Each of our attention spans was solely on the experience, which cannot be fully described or explained. One feels no pain at all, no matter how things look. The soul leaves the body so quickly right before the final pain. I will always remember the Heavenly Christ talking to me, and being surrounded in this unexplainable amazing bright loving Light. I knew I was completely safe! I never recalled seeing myself in a body, I was Light! I knew then my life had a bigger meaning than I could ever have imagined. I had never felt such Divine love. Nothing else mattered as this was taking place, I knew my spirit was totally free, I was weightless! I wanted so much to express how thankful I was, but there were no perfect words, or any words, other than those few I could muster.

Experiencing Joy

Both my son and I agreed by experiencing what we have and with what happened to both of us is the complete truth. And that a person doesn't feel any pain at the end no matter how it appears to loved ones left behind. I have no doubt of this. The other side has confirmed this. Pain leaves with the new transition and the new journey begins. Some souls with manmade fear leave here in confusion or fear but help is there for those who do. There are choices to make when a soul progresses. When a soul leaves they do not suffer as we think regardless of the reason for death: comas, accidents, a long illness etc. The soul is moving into spirit before the last breath. Sometimes weeks, days, even months before death our soul is already moving in and out of the body. Sometimes you may think the one getting ready to die is sleeping, under sedation, even those in a coma who are lifeless, but usually they are out of body in the spirit world. Things are being prepared for the final transition. They are as we say "out and about." They are seeing loved ones, friends, and many others who have passed over before them. They seem to be looking at events going on with their own change and aren't as concerned with what is happening with the living at this point. In this transition the soul is occupied with a new and different energy body, trying to observe what is happening to them. They feel wonder and joy in greeting loved ones, and above all the Infinite Supreme Christ Light.

I clearly recall my spirit was wrapped in such joy that I had the feeling of being totally free in a special magnificent and wonderful place. I was filled with tremendous love that I cannot begin to describe. There are no human words to explain how I felt where I existed when I died. I did not feel the final impact of the accident, just as David said he did not suffer when his heart stopped. Actually, we both wanted to just stay where we were. You feel the same as far as your emotions and your mind, the transition is so amazing, one isn't even thinking of coming back. Perhaps some do when they realize they have left children or loved ones, who they feel still needs them. If it is not their time, they are sent back to finish their mission. But the experience usually changes their life from then on, and that is one way we do a turn around and go back.

Like my son said with his experience of the heart attack and his other death experiences, he didn't even think of coming back until he realized he needed to return back to us here. He wasn't finished, and with his strong love for us he was sent back. Our soul is so happy and free to be where it is then the spirit returns to the body and the pain hits! Some have reported they did want to return for unfinished business of many reasons, perhaps for their children and loved ones. If one is meant to come back they will, but if their time is up on this earth they remain in their new world, because in all reality they are finished on earth with all they were to do. Learning and change comes from this amazing experience and it is very important. On our separate occasions of death my son and I were told that we each still had more to do on earth. Each one of us would never forget our amazing learning experience, which was encoded within our heart, soul, and our DNA.

If someone has never believed in this, and has an experience of leaving their body through a near death experience (NDE), leaving into the unknown, it usually leaves them changed for life. Hopefully erasing the fear of physically dying and knowing the Christ Light has sent them back. Those who have a bad experience terrify some people and view their transition as a horrible Devil, monster type experience! They are filled with fear, afraid of dying, and where they will go. They most likely are fearful because of our human brain conditioning and beliefs of being taught to be afraid and of a burning hell. There are circumstances for each person on this earth.

Life becomes more at peace with a knowing and new understanding inside us, that so much more waits for each person, in a different way in our spirit form. I feel deeply for those who think there is nothing more once they die. The soul can't be buried under dirt in a cemetery, it continues on and on. Energy cannot die, it only changes form and is eternal.

Our Souls Move On

I know not of any kind of understanding in how a decayed body could raise someday; no one's ashes will come back in a physical body we live on in a spirit body. We will know one another in our spirit form when we do not need our solid body any longer. Our soul moves on, there will never be a need again for our solid psychical body. My own belief is that anything may be interpreted in several ways of understanding. Our physical body is only a vehicle we need while living an earthly life, a shell; that we need here on earth, which is all. We will know one another on the other side in another way, being in spirit. I can't help but wonder how much gets misinterpreted, left out, or not inscribed correctly in some of our books. Just be at peace knowing each one of us goes on after we pass over, in our different directions and places, experiencing what we want and need to.

There are many levels on the other side, perhaps meaning the many mansions. We can grow closer to Christ right there. We can move up to higher levels; it's up to each one of us. When we judge color, race, culture, ignorance, poor, or whatever, we are judging ourselves at the same time. God makes no mistakes in his creation. What each soul does with his life is the important part. How we treat one another, having compassion, keeping love within us and sharing it with others is the key.

Going the other way without love or compassion, and using hatred in murderous ways, is not what God planned for us, we used our own free will. He made us whole, and like children, making many mistakes in life so we learn from them, that's why it is earth school. We all have the chance to do our best and treat others the best we can. I admit, in today's world it is good common sense to stay out of the way of those who carry a hardened heart, who are mean, and hateful. Those people will have much to deal with one day.

My son and I both believed that how one is taught, is how we will view where we are on the other side. By this, I mean if one has been conditioned to fear everything and with a hell ingrained in them, they will experience what they believe in. Such as a person who is a loving and forgiving person believing in their higher power, is what they will experience with an open heart and without fear. If you think about it, Christ who is pure love cannot coexist with evil, so Heaven and Hell cannot exist together in anyway. Our heavenly Creator is of love and light.

Manmade rules

The region we lived in is full of wonderful people and is also a large *Bible belt*. There are a few people with ideas that people with *gifts* like ours were from the *devil*. If only they knew I thought that we had received a God given gift in order to do our work for the Heavenly Creator and know what one experienced after we each died. We experienced Christ as we did in our work. The last thing in the world we would ever do was cause harm to anyone or anything. I have found through many that judgment of others is so easy to do.

I strongly feel it is because of man-made fear and how we each are taught. So much of society lives in fear and with negative advice by how one is raised. Bible verses can be turned around in so many different ways, but the thing that is most important is to judge not. Each person's journey is different and only for that person to experience. And we all as humans have done much of this. No one here is perfect, we all are learning on our journey. This is understood on the other side to a point, but we need to learn not to knock people down with words. No one is exempt from making mistakes and one is never too old to learn from them.

Chapter 7

A Long Journey

Believing in Miracles and Beings of Light

He lived with complete positive faith and perseverance as his illness began. He truly believed in miracles because he was one and had experienced many firsthand. He intended to make his time on earth available and make every second count. He didn't waste a second feeling sorry for himself or sitting around doing nothing.

My son knew that the mind is the builder and how one thinks has everything to do with our healing, our every emotion and our lives. David remained as positive as possible and did not give up, which was not an easy task when things were upsetting his life. That is how he came out of being bed ridden to a wheelchair and then off of his crutches. Because of the miracles he experienced, he survived the NDE (near death experiences) and DOA (dead on arrival) experiences and healed so quickly for so long. He wasn't leaving here until the last second like we all do, when it is finally our time to leave.

We were both avid pupils ready to learn as quickly as possible. Several times the Beings of Light gently and graciously told me that I had to wait for a while for me to know, since it was not my time yet. I had not advanced enough yet to know the answer I had asked for. Many times the answers were made clear and signed with love. Everything was in place the way it should be. They explained our human minds are like a glass if you fill it too full it will spill over. We needed time to digest what we were given. Never were our messages anything but of knowledge and great love to us and others.

We both knew to stay around positive minded people, especially when one is sick. When you are around a negative person the effect of them can hit you quickly pulling you down, pulling the energy out of you. Their energy feels like a strong, dark cloud all around you. It looks like tentacles reaching out to others, so stay with positive people and spend your time with those who are uplifting. Those people who can find joy in the meaning of life even when going through their worse times shows the warrior in them! These brave souls still smile and hug, complaining very little if at all. They make their life and others' lives the treasure they are.

Each one of us has our own path when we experience the rough emotion of loss, and it is the hardest place to find peace in. It takes time to want to go on and live our lives without that person. Our world stops and our soul becomes shattered! It feels as if nothing is real anymore, nothing seems to be. It is the least we can eventually do with time on our side, to be able to work on this so our loved one can move on knowing we will be ok.

The Race Home

Going back now to another NDE that turned worse for David, was while he was living in Indiana. It was around 4AM and my phone rang. I did not recognize his voice at first because it was barely a whisper. "Can you come and get me, mom?" I felt the urgency in his weak voice which terrified me! Immediately, I began getting a sick feeling in the pit of my stomach. "Yes! I will be there as soon as possible," I cried out. I was trying to sound as brave and as calm as I could. Something told me I would need to get to him as fast as possible. I didn't ask any questions I just assured him I was coming to get him as quickly as I could!

Knowing my son, I knew he had to be very ill to make this call since he never wanted to worry anyone. I was so afraid when I hung up the phone thinking back to two weeks prior when I stayed to help him for a while because he wasn't feeling well. I knew now he had to be very sick by the tone in his voice and that he needed me. If I had only realized this when I was with him, I would never have left him to come home. I thought so many things, "Why didn't I see that he was getting worse?" Anyway I didn't, and it was far too late now. All I could think of was him home!

I hurried to dress and jumped in the old pickup truck and headed out for a long drive. The hours passed too slowly as I drove as quickly as possible on a 3 hour trip. It seemed like I couldn't go fast enough! When I arrived at his apartment I raced up the four flights of stairs not knowing what to expect. I wasn't prepared to see how deteriorated David had become in such a short time! His door was locked! He didn't have the strength at first to answer the door and I was shocked when he did. He had lost so much weight, his face was sunken in. He had his little dog; Shorty in his arms, both had been lying together on the sofa. He loved her so much with the comfort and love she gave him, and the feeling was mutual.

I was afraid and feeling very emotional when I saw him with his weight loss and face so thin! I tried to hide my shock and my feelings so I didn't panic in front of him knowing he would be worrying about me. I was so happy, yet so sad to see him! A million things were going through my mind. I just couldn't believe the condition he was in. I was planning in my mind to get him to his doctor right then, but he refused saying "he knew he would get better at home and would be ok, and that he had just seen his doctor. And as soon as they knew what was wrong with him we could drive back." I was operating on what my son was telling me.

I knew I must hurry to get him back to our home a couple hundred miles away in another state. There was a strong thunderstorm coming. I wasted no time in asking what all he wanted me to take. He opened his eyes and pointed to some boxes and clothing. Then he nodded, that's all he could do. I told him I would get the truck loaded while he slept.

There were those four flights of stairs to run up and down to load the truck. I was so desperate for help I knocked on a few doors for anybody I could get to help me, but no one answered. I went as fast as I could go, carrying bags and dragging boxes, whatever he had ready. We left all his furnishings, household, more clothing and several of his personal items behind; there was no time to lose. I only wanted to get my beloved son home. I was so afraid for him but went by his amazing intuition. He was positive in his choice so I knew to get going. We would figure the rest out at home. I thought surely the doctor would have admitted him if he thought different, but I didn't know then he had tried. I still would have trusted what David told me. He just wanted to be home.

I think he knew he was close to dying then. It was a very rough trip home for him through a terrible rainstorm. I left so fast I forgot to bring a single pillow for him to rest on, but he managed to sleep some anyway. I questioned him a few times more about what his doctor had said, but wasn't getting much out of him. He was too sick and worn out. I would have to wait. His voice was only a whisper when he spoke. David again said that he knew he would get well at home. I hoped with his gift of knowing future events he would definitely get better at home. I also knew it would be very hard for him. He said, "You will make me well." This was a huge order and I prayed this would happen quickly with the Creator's healing and the divine healing energy work.

I made him a bed downstairs so he would be closer to me at all times. He needed help to rise up and walk and was too weak to talk or eat. He liked being on the sofa in the day and at night I took him to his room. I don't feel as if I ever slept. I was so afraid and checked on him all the time. Even though my room was near to his, he was so very sick and I helped him all I could 24/7. As long as Shorty was in his arms he tried sleeping. Soon, I found out David weighed only 97 pounds and at almost 6ft 4inches tall you can imagine how wasted away he was! I would prop him up on pillows like a little baby; his whole body was in so much pain. That was because he had no padding with his bones protruding out! I was just beside myself about the situation.

I called his doctor again but really had nothing to go on after the call. His doctor was evasive to me because of the HIPPA Law, which means a person's medical information cannot be given out to anyone. I could get nothing out of his doctor even though I said, "I am his mother I need to know what to do!" The doctor only went around the conversation. Something was really wrong! I wanted so much to admit him but he pleaded to wait because he would get better. I was heartbroken and wracking my brain on what to do. I had to get my son to agree to go to a doctor where I lived. I couldn't wait any longer; I ended up taking him back to his doctor in Indiana where he was hospitalized immediately.

I slept in his room on a cot for many days. I wouldn't have left him for anything in this world! He was critical but we gave each other strength without a word. I held his hands and rubbed his feet passing the healing energy into him most of the time because he was so weak. He was peaceful knowing I was right beside him, he always told me. He was still my little boy and always would be. He had given his total love and joy to me and his family and now was lying in that bed. He looked so small and thin with his severe weight loss. The doctor told me that David had many blood transfusions and medications by now and they were doing more tests on him.

I never quit praying for his healing to come. I felt sure my son was dying and the doctor would not tell me much by David's orders in private. I believed 100% in what David said to me, that he would recover and mend. I knew he had superior gifts, but I was also confused and scared! The thing he always kept was his beautiful smile and his fight to live with a positive calmness within.

I needed a sign now for me from our heavenly Beings of Light that he would live. I needed to be lifted with a strong confirmation of this. I prayed and I was heard. I knew in my heart our prayers were always heard. His change happened the next night for his turn around with his Angel close by.

She made her presence known to him.

An Angel Appeared

In another instance with David, it was around midnight and he was still in poor condition at the hospital when a nurse in a white uniform came into his room just as he opened his eyes. She carried a vase of beautiful red roses for him. She spoke softly and told him with a radiant smile, "that he would be well!" Carefully, she then placed the roses on his bedside table still smiling at him with her love and then left. When morning came he told me about her visit while I had been asleep. He asked the day shift about this kind nurse. He wanted to thank her for bringing him the beautiful roses and he needed to know her name. He continued on about "how grateful he was for her visit. She was so kind to him and brought him the roses." He knew himself then there was something special about her. He needed to describe her, they said. David looked puzzled but then described her.

He told the story of the roses once more as he pointed to the nightstand table beside his bed. "She was African American in a white nurse's uniform when she came into his room with the flowers." The main day nurse looked completely baffled and surprised, "no one worked the night shift that was African American last night!" This was a very small hospital with a small staff so the nurse knew who worked each shift and this nurse wasn't on hers. No one from the other two floors knew who it possibly could have been that night.

I had been sleeping when the phantom nurse made her visit to my son. He said "he was only awake those moments she appeared in his room." I slept on a cot in his room and the roses said it all, it had happened! We quickly knew this was a Divine presence; this beautiful experience was for him only. The nurse couldn't just disappear or totally be unknown if she worked there. David knew she was a Divine Being he said, but checked with this nurse to finalize his feelings. This, along with her beautiful presences, was a gift to him. A messenger of God bringing life to him, and for me to know he would live and be well again. Another miracle had taken place with this beautiful message from the *Angel* in disguise! We were more than overwhelmed with happiness!

A Dream Vision

All of what happened that evening triggered my memory recalling an earlier dream vision I had right before David called me to come and get him to bring him home. In my vision experience, I was being told ahead in the future, something about me, a hospital, and a flag with the name Saint Anthony's. The following day after the *Angel nurse* had made the visit to my son I suddenly felt compelled, or was led in some way, to walk down the hall. I thought I would feel better to walk and stretch my legs. I entered a large waiting room and walked across to the windows. Then I turned to look out of a window to check the weather. Looking outside of the window I saw a flag blowing around in a strong wind that somehow looked familiar. When the flag settled down it had Saint Anthony's in large letters the same exact flag as in my vision! There was my answer right in front of me; I had been shown the future we were living now! For a few moments I felt as if I were in some kind of unexplainable place other than on Earth knowing more of why we were here now. It was so extraordinary! I was stunned for awhile and stood staring at the flag until I could ground myself once more.

I cannot describe the gratefulness and happiness inside of me. My son would continue to live. We had experienced in these phenomenal steps what we knew as a miracle! He slowly became better, improved, and at last was discharged to go home. This had been a very close call once more. We thanked God for the Divine Angel messenger sent that night to help him and for her healing words. She would never be forgotten by us both and I felt positive we would see her again!

The Next Miracle

In the coming months I went into the city not far from my home where I talked with a friend of mine who is also psychic. He asked me several times if I was going to Paris. He kept getting the names L. and Paris. Not that I know of, I responded laughing, "but one never knows what may happen in this world." My son and I had experienced so much; we knew nothing was impossible to happen to anyone. Were we going to Paris? I wasn't getting that we were, but things can happen when you least expect it.

Later on, this information came to pass. David's lungs were now failing and he was in very serious condition. His lungs began tearing with holes in them. He was in great danger! He told me he found a Specialist in another area of the city with whom to make an appointment. He was spitting up blood and his condition was becoming critical. He let his intuition help him find the right doctor. He had simply ran his finger down a list of doctors in his telephone book stopping on one he felt good about, which said Dr. L. E.

Paris! David knew nothing about my psychic friend asking me some time back about the names L. and Paris, and I had forgotten about it! By living apart at this time I didn't always know when my son was getting sick. He kept so much hidden until he needed to tell me or until I picked up through my intuition. With this news I knew he had another large battle to win. I soon realized my friend's message had been so true concerning the future of my son. I told David about the message to me from my friend, and we knew for sure he was being divinely guided to Dr. Paris, he was the right one! We were going to Paris but not the one in France.

The doctor knew David wouldn't live long enough to get lung transplants. He had 12 torn places combined in both lungs, and one was very large! Another serious problem he had was that his lungs were filling with blood, which was much more dangerous than fluid because of infection. This had to be stopped! We felt with the amazing way he was directed to Dr. Paris that this had to work! The doctor said, "David was too young to not have a chance to live, and it would be too long waiting for someone's lungs. He couldn't wait any length of time now!" The doctor asked him about trying a new product that had just come out. This material was for the human body to seal places; it was new, but could possibly help him. Dr. Paris had only used it once on a man who had only one small tear in his lung. David knew when he found this doctor's name it wasn't by chance, this would work! The specialist wasted no time and began a series of repairs.

I will attempt to explain how this was done in layman terms. An instrument was passed down my son's esophagus finding a way into his lungs, and then the doctor started a series of repairs which took some time to do working on one tear at a time. David, by his choice endured the repairs without being put under, even with the pain involved. The largest and last place to be done was reinforced with a mesh material and was the only one to break loose later on and was redone. All of the rest stayed sealed, it was a big success! The places repaired were still holding all of the rest of the years he lived without any problems.

There is no explanation of how this all happened except starting with my friend's information to me. Then, with my son intuitively pointing out the correct specialist with the last name of Paris in a telephone book, which saved his life! There is no explaining how all of this fell together except as another miracle! There are no human words to explain a miracle, because a miracle is something that can't be explained in human language. One more interesting thing is this new material had just been released for use at that exact time. Everything was perfect timing, this helped my son's life to go on! All the information we received from beginning to end was perfect! I treasured the beautiful words given to me once more, "for he shall be well," as he went through the lung procedures. We were so thankful!

David quickly recuperated as his lungs healed and soon he was like new. He knew a Divine presence had stayed with him continually. The good news was as the Angel nurse had told him when he was in Saint Anthony "that he would be well!" And now, he felt positive she would be with him again in the future. He had been guided to the right doctor with the angel nurse leading his thoughts and intuition. He was released to go home with me and checkups were to be made in a couple of weeks. He had had another miracle and the phantom nurse was definitely his guardian Angel. She was an Angel in disguise; this Heavenly being had come to help rescue him again. The Angel told him he would be here longer in order to help others on their path. The Angels were still guiding his journey!

Thinking back, I always wished I had been awake to experience the angel nurse who brought the roses to my son. I believe the amazing miracle was only for him to experience and no one else. Like I said, the roses proved it all, and the nurse who brought them to him didn't exist in our world. There would be yet another time coming when he would meet his Angel again.

A Familiar Angel

The next experience was not too long into the future. This happened one day while coming home from a nearby hospital with my son. We had become lost and met up with our familiar Angel. In this experience and dilemma we were certainly in a time of need. David was released unexpectedly from the hospital. I had not driven that day and came by the Metro train just to relax. I had been driving so much for so long I thought it would be nice to take the train. He was doing well so I had hurried home to change clothes and was returning. I recall the first thing he said as I was leaving to go home was, not to ride the Metro coming back. When I returned, and was walking into his room he said, "You didn't come back on the train did you?" "Yes," I said, I wanted him to know I knew how to get around on the trains and for him not to worry. As soon as I said yes, I knew he had been released unexpectedly! I realized I should have listened to him. I was so happy he was released, but my next thought was how to get him on the Metro! He was still unsteady plus, I had brought him in as an emergency without his shoes or a change of clothes! I had to get my thoughts together with a plan. How would I manage to do this without him becoming sick again? He was barely able to walk! Why didn't I listen and drive the car here? He was determined to get out and go home now.

That's how we started our important journey that day. I was loaned a wheel chair to take him to the Metro station which was across the street. I had to leave him there to return it. He had green scrubs and a white t shirt on with the hospital socks he was given when he was admitted. I ran as fast as possible to return the chair while he waited alone on the train platform and at anyone's mercy. Being a mother, I was afraid he could be mugged or worse. I felt a big sigh of relief when I returned to see him sitting there safe and sound. He was holding his three pillows and a bag of items I had previously taken to him. When I told him how scared I was to leave him he burst out laughing! David said, "Mom, I look like I'm homeless. Who would bother with me?" We both were laughing then because of the clothing he wore and especially that he had no shoes. I felt bad that I hadn't listened to him about using the Metro. But he did paint a picture of homelessness. I knew then how silly I worried about him the minutes I was gone but hey, I'm a devoted Mom! We had to take the Metro train part way then get a bus to where I left my car.

I held the pillows, bag, and my purse, plus I held onto my son as we left the train walking a short distance to the bus stop. I was very concerned about him. He was still weak and tired easily. There were items and small shards of glass here and there on the train platform that I carefully steered him around.

Finally, the bus arrived with its sign on to the location where the car was parked. Everyone got off of the bus as we stayed out of the way in the crowd of people; then we boarded. I had clearly seen the sign on front of the bus to our destination, making sure of where it was going. But this was going to be a big mistake! We had ridden a very long way and I became upset to see unfamiliar places; nothing looked right but I said nothing. Then the bus suddenly stopped and the driver called out loudly, "END OF THE LINE!" I told the driver, "This isn't the right stop." "NO! This is as far as I go," she said briskly. Then the driver called out loudly once more, "END OF THE LINE!" We both were stunned; her sign had had the name of our stop. On her way off the bus she confessed she had forgotten to change her sign! Lucky for most others they had gotten off of the bus at previous stops. I had us in a difficult spot and didn't know what to do! I figured we were about

60 miles from home!

We had no choice but to get off the bus. I didn't know what to do; we were also several miles from where the car was parked. David was very tired and too weak to walk by then. I would never forgive myself if he ended up back in the hospital! I held on to help him and our other items as we walked to a bench. I looked around for the driver to ask where to get another bus to our stop but she was long gone. I didn't have a cell phone at that time and we were out in the middle of an unknown area. My son was calmly depending on me and I knew we needed help in the worse way.

There was a lone couple who sat down beside him on the bench to chat so I checked with them. "Will there be another bus today?" I was confirming what the driver had told us. Again, I got "No, it was the last one today." I turned to David getting him up not knowing where to go or what to do. Where can I take him to rest and call someone? I was thinking. I felt so helpless and defeated looking around. There was no one else to ask where we were or what could I do to get him to safety? We seemed to be in a pretty bad area on top of this. No one else was around anywhere. The couple had left walking off in another direction.

It was after we took a few steps forward we both heard a voice right behind us where no one had been a second before. "Come; follow me I will show you the way home." We both turned to see who said this. Right beside us stood a young African American woman in a green checked dress facing the two of us. She was holding out both of her hands motioning for us to come and follow her. Again she said, "Come follow me I will show you the way home!" She was very direct, somehow knowing we needed her help! We followed her without thinking at all; this was like being in some kind of a dream! She walked slowly backwards motioning us to follow her. We only went a short way as she continued telling us to follow her, she would show us the way home! Suddenly, she was pointing to another direction, we looked over to where she pointed and there sat a bus! We had heard no noise, nothing, but her voice! Where did this bus come from? Our kind stranger continued, "Get on that bus, it will take you home!" She was definite, and walked beside us to the steps of the bus. We were following everything she said to do. How could she know where home even was?

This young lady held no purse or ticket, nothing in her hands. My thoughts were beginning to work now. How can she know where we were going? How would she know this bus, which hadn't been there a minute ago, would take us home? Where did she and the bus come from, out of thin air! She was not on the other bus we had been on, nor had we ever seen her until now! She just appeared! Still, in this dream state I did just what she said, I started helping my son by placing him in front of me to help him up the steps into the bus. She stood closely beside us both by the bus door. With my foot on the first step I quickly turned to thank her. As I turned I was already saying, thank-you, Angel. I started to say Angel somehow without thinking of that word! I just knew then she was an Angel! My quick turnaround had been no more than tenth of a second but she had vanished! There was no one anywhere around any place.

There was a high wire fence close to the side of the bus and a dead end a short way in front of it. She couldn't have disappeared, but she had in that split second! I looked everywhere around quickly, then we both knew for sure what had happened once again. We had experienced Divine help once more! At that moment David and I knew we had just experienced our Angel once again in our time of need! Our Angel protector appeared once again as a human, a young woman in a simple green checked dress. We were lifted up feeling perfectly safe now and very relieved to meet our Angel guardian once more in solid form. She was sent to us in time of great need and she had watched over us.

There would be even more times she would help my son. I had finally got to meet this Angel in a solid form as a human. This proves without a doubt that she is our guardian Angel! We were allowed to meet her once more in our desperate time of help! David seemed to be revived the rest of the trip to the car and to home, and so was I! We talked of our magical and amazing trip for days. This again was a miracle which cannot be explained! We both were being closely watched over in this way and being kept safe once again. I did not know then the complete story of our spiritual work, nor how this powerful and planned experience continued to bring such great meaning into our lives. I believe we were meant to do everything as it happened that day in order to experience everything we did. It was to be that we would get on the wrong bus! In this way I met her in a solid looking way too. My son and I talked about our angel for days and what it all meant!

I was urged to write our story of that day coming home from the hospital. My daughter helped me do this. This was the story I sent to *Guideposts Angels on Earth*, which I earlier mentioned with the Angel drawings imprinted in the carpet. It was published and put into their wonderful magazine. What we considered a mistake by getting on the wrong bus was anything but. We were meant to have another extraordinary experience we would never forget! Our guardian Angel came to our aid to help us home with the guidance we needed. We gained more inner strength from this amazing trip. We knew the Angel helped us along our journey. We understood without a doubt how they can humanly appear and walk among us here on Earth. The Angels message was clear once more, "for you shall be well."

We knew our lessons were directed for us to teach and tell everyone we could. There are Angels who walk among us in human form on this earth right beside us at times and we are not meant to know who they are. There are Angels who have saved lives and are with us in times of need and who help us as Guardians. We have Angels of every kind who can come to our aid. Angels of healing, Angels who can make miracles happen, those who come as a teacher in spirit. Angels who appear as humans, all kind of blessed Angels who come to help in times of need and make things happen. People can't explain how a stranger came to them in a blizzard to help, or they would have died, realizing later this was an Angel in disguise and called a miracle.

We have other worlds and other Beings in our many Universes. We would have to be rather conceited to think only Earth was created. I would not put these words in print without instruction from the Beings of Light who have taught me and my son in order to tell others how it really is. Sometimes our task was almost more than we could do. They advised us it is near to time for the truth to be told. And I will always be grateful for this. Our tasks would become more often and we embraced them all with gratitude.

The Guardian Who Helped David Home

The telephone was ringing as I came in the door with my groceries. It was David; he sounded quite hoarse and was coughing badly. He lived in Oklahoma at the time and said, "he was coming home," as I had asked him to do until he was better. I was so glad to hear this because I knew something was terribly wrong with him. He would be leaving the next day with a U-Haul packed full of his belongings and his little dog, Shorty. I was relieved, but very concerned of how he could manage a move like this being so sick. I asked to let me come to help him. He put me at ease telling me his neighbor, Jane, was helping him pack the U-Haul. I asked, "Can you drive home without help?" "Yes," he assured me he could, but I was frantic inside because I felt he was more than just sick.

I tossed and turned throughout the long night. Finally, I dozed off and went into a "vision" where I met an elderly lady who was a Protector and Guardian. She told me, "Your son will be all right coming home to you. Do not worry he will be fine." I recall in the vision that we were close to the highway on the same route he would be driving home. With that wonderful message I came out of the vision and wrote her message down while feeling a great sigh of relief! I knew this was indeed our spiritual Guardian speaking to me. She had come to relieve my mind because I was so worried about him.

When he pulled into the driveway the next day he barely made it out of the truck with his little dog; he was so terribly sick. God only knows how he drove the distance! I got him right to bed and we unloaded the truck.

Months later he became well, although this took him quite a while with doctors' care and Reiki healing energy. He always came home when he was seriously ill where he knew he needed to be. He had been home recovering for some time now and it was great to have him here once again! He had fought a hard battle once more. I knew for him to have the strength to get here he had the Angels' help! Once again he was spared, thank God. David's heart and soul was always here with me no matter how far away he was. I felt just the same as he did and this was because of our promise and covenant.

Someone's at the Door

Before long it was spring and it was a sunny and beautiful day when I heard the door bell ringing early one morning. I was still in my pajamas so I didn't open the door but I peered out through the curtains to see who it was. I saw a small elderly woman with curly short white hair dressed in an old fashion dress and full apron. The apron was the old fashioned kind that goes over your head to cover most of the dress like my grandmother wore. Her dress had a pattern of small pink flowers with a dark background. She was either nervous or she had a habit of moving her mouth in a certain way. She even looked like my late grandmother or someone out from a long ago period.

I felt badly I had not opened the door, so I quickly did. It only took a second to unlock the door and pull it open, but when I did, no one was there! I went outside looked down the street, walked across the porch and around my home, no one was there she had vanished! There had not been a car in front of my home, in the driveway, or on the street! My wrap around front porch is large so I checked again, but she was nowhere to be seen! I have a high privacy fence all around the sides and back of my home so I knew she didn't go that way.

It dawned on me to ask the other side, "Who was this lady?" I was given the answer, "Guardian!" I thought, could this be the Protector/Guardian who helped my son get home from Oklahoma who told me he would be ok? This, I believe, was the same lady in my vision who gave me peace the night my son drove home sick from Oklahoma. She was letting me know he would get here safely. Apparently she had always watched over the both of us. It was time she wanted me to see her and to know who she is. I knew then I was meant to meet her in the quick visit to my home that day. The other side also had let me know she was someone I knew from long ago. I appreciated her so much with her short visit and to see her in human form. This was the start to a wonderful day!

We continued our doctor trips back and forth, but I still could never get much information or a plan of what I needed to do from the doctor to help my son. He was hiding something from me. I knew by then I wasn't getting told nearly everything. But, I still couldn't get any more information other than they wanted to remove his gallbladder because it could be involved with his illness. I didn't buy these diagnoses and by now felt absolutely sure my son wasn't LETTING the doctors tell me everything because he did not want me to worry. The gallbladder idea was a true diagnosis, but I would soon find out I was right on my information too. My son wasn't letting the doctor tell me all of his condition so the doctor had no choice. That is because David was so protective of me all of his life.

It wasn't long before I was told at a new hospital, which was closer to home, that my son needed another surgery done. David told me he felt too weak for surgery and the other side told him to refuse it that he was too weak and he wouldn't live. With this, he would not agree to it at that time. His refusing didn't go over too well with his doctor, but that was his decision and I backed him up since I was getting the same thing. Later testing revealed that David's refusal of the surgery turned out to be a good decision after all. Thank God again for his gift which very likely saved his life once more. We always went by what the Heavenly Beings told us. They know and were never wrong.

Back at home he soon couldn't keep his food down and had no appetite. Only with my encouragement would he try. A spoon full was all he could do many times. He was in so much pain and tried to hide it from everyone. I was relieved to see him hold the tiniest amount of food; it was a start and hopefully he would begin to hold more. He became so thin his face was actually sunken in. I panicked seeing his weight drop. We both held onto our strong faith and belief in the phantom nurse's message to him, that he would get better and better as he had before. We believed 100% without a doubt and we understood what was happening from the other side. It did not matter if anyone else did or not, as long as we kept our belief and faith we would make it through this. We never gave up on our Divine help; we knew it was there for us.

Many times things got much worse before they got better, and sometimes turned worse again. Through this, we each helped one another together with our strong heavenly belief. I was afraid for him as his mother, and the other side understood I needed more of their support. They gave us both the strength we needed. This was given through their words, visions, signs and feeling the love they sent to us both that got us through.

I will never forget one of the later trips of taking my son back to his old doctor when he became very sick. He wanted to go back to Indiana and see him. I managed to get him in the car and drove as fast as possible. David wanted me to take him, not an ambulance, convincing me he would be okay to make the trip. I called for one anyway to take him to the hospital several miles away, but was told they didn't have a carrier available for that long of a trip. I didn't dare wait any longer; it was quicker for me to get in the car and go! I had done this so many times through the years by now I knew just where to go.

My heart was broken as I watched him throwing up all the way without one complaint. He was so weak I was sure he needed more blood transfusions. On the way to the hospital we had to stop so he could go to the restroom. I saw a fast food place, pulled in, parked, and opened the door for him. Before I could help him he fell out of the car onto the hot blacktop. His head was on the ground. I took his arm trying to gently help him back up. "No! Mom, please don't try to help me I just need a few moments to get up," he said. I watched my brave son with his ribs showing through his tee shirt and his sweat pants so big he held onto them when he walked. He lay there in the hot sun. My mind was swimming with thoughts on how to let go of him to get help. I looked around for someone for help. What I did see soon was people with nothing but looks of disgust on some of their faces. I knew they thought of drugs, alcohol, and the worst and they quickly moved on their way! I wanted to scream out at them to help me! There was no one to help us! I was then able to raise David up and back into the car.

After a moment, he weakly asked me to drive him across the highway to try again at another place. This time I got him out of the car with my arms around him helping him into the Gas Mart. I sort of walked him to the men's restroom door. I was scared to let him go on in alone. He said to let him go and wait there for him. Even sick, he was very independent. I waited outside praying he didn't fall, pass out, or hurt himself. He didn't come out for a long time, and just as I was getting ready to stop a man going in, he came out of the door. He was holding on to the door frame and I grabbed him falling into my arms, then slowly together we made it back to the car. He was completely exhausted to no end, and I wished so hard I could take his place; if I could only see him healthy again and living his young life. But I knew it was futile for now. I always did what he asked me to do, knowing he knew best. He said he had passed out in the restroom and no one stopped to help him, so he lay on the floor until he could get the strength to get up. I was so horribly stunned that the men going in and out let him lay on a cold bathroom floor! I was sick to my stomach picturing all of what he endured. How can some people look in the mirror? How can they not help a person?

When we got to the hospital I was surprised the doctor didn't admit him. He was taken to the ER, given blood transfusions, fluids, and treatment only to send him back home! It was then I knew they had no hope for him and it was just a matter of time to them. David would not tell me any news of what was wrong. He barely felt like talking but mentioned tests were taken, blood transfusions given and not to worry. He didn't want me in the emergency room; he knew I would question everyone I could. Inside myself, I was torn up and a wreck, but I did not let him ever see me like this. I vowed he wouldn't ever see me the way I felt. That would put more stress on him. I could always be strong for him; he had enough on his young mind. I know how ones reactions can devastate a sick person. Even a look can say so much to let someone know how you feel. He was sent back home with me once more.

When he had come home in the very beginning being extremely sick and his life force was shutting down completely. With him being released like he was I am positive his doctor could see no hope for him to live even then.

I think they expected he had but a few days at the most. He could only whisper for almost three months. His life force was shutting down getting ready to leave his body. Even though he was bed ridden, I kept him with me in the family room so he could see the TV or just listen to it. I stayed right beside him at the foot of the sofa always rubbing his feet and hands, they hurt him so much. He had neuropathy with everything else and the pain was so bad he couldn't stand a sheet or anything to touch his feet. But, when I gently rubbed his feet the energy passed into them and he said he had no pain, it would quit and soon he easily went to sleep. He had relief for a while and most of the time he was on the edge of two places; trying to survive here and close into the other side. He was just content to be alive and told me he knew he would get well at home, that I would help him get well. Anything I could do for him would never be too big. I would do anything for him if it took me a million years, again and again! He had such faith in me as I did him.

Our lives were unsettled each day with doctor and hospital stays, tests, and treatments. Our home was very busy with his nurses, and others, but things changed for the better with our new growth from the other side. I didn't talk to others about our Heavenly teachers since it was not time yet, and most others would not understand our work. We continued to use our energy for his healing and to learn more.

My son and I would discuss all our wonderful spiritual events and teachers, and we had to figure out many of their messages. The other side seems to want us to figure out some things by ourselves to sharpen our skills, they would tell us. This was a special learning school for us that we loved. All of this happening at the same time held our focus helping both of us to get though the critical times. We knew we were never alone in this the Christ Light Beings were with us.

The house continued to be crowded, like Grand Central Station, with medical people the first several years. There were few private times for the family, but we were grateful for these people who helped my son. We had some wonderful caring people who truly cared about him and became best friends to us. Several were taken with him, his humor, and gift of reading for them. He helped several who helped him they cared about him and wanted to see him better. I felt we were blessed to have these wonderful people in our lives. He was bed ridden for some time and then he graduated to a wheelchair later on.

After he regained some of his strength back, one day he called out to me from his room. As I entered his room, he surprised me! He was standing on his own! He was so happy, he had such a proud look on his smiling face and then he told me that he would not be in that wheelchair again.

The spiritual teacher will come when the student is ready for one to elevate on their journey. If this is not accomplished this time, or whatever one's agenda is about, one may choose to start over and complete this another time until it is right. Then we grow closer to Christ and our Creator. Every individual's work is different in life. We can help others in so many ways that are very important, even by small gestures such as sharing our kindness.

Once in a while, an important lesson comes along and we learn the needed lesson to keep our distance from a very negative or troublesome person. Unfortunately, they will try to drag you down, taking your energy and will hurt who they can in some way for their own means.

David and I could see the *dark* ones so we knew to use good common sense in our world today. There were occasions we were instructed to work with the negative forces which could be very unpleasant, but there was always hope they would see the light someday to ease their soul. Sometimes, the start of this only takes a hug, a good word, not judging, or showing love or compassion in place of anger, malice, fighting and so on.

When it was our time to move on from this part of our lesson we moved forward to use our energy in other directions. Also, it is a plus to remember that everyone won't like you and you can't make them. But, you can help them with positive thoughts that they find their way with good intent.

This is a simple and powerful way to send love and to also protect one's self. A person may reach a negative soul in this way and soften their heart, into an unknown joy and peace waiting for them. We are all teachers in some way, good and bad, and change can always come into your life with your desire.

We both looked at our way of life as the great responsibility it is. We lovingly agreed to it in another time and place, with our promise using God's gifts to us. These precious gifts we treasured. One day, I would know much more, even the end result of completely why we both had chosen our work. I defiantly knew that out of love we decided to merge together once more this time around to complete our work. Eventually, I would slowly begin to remember more and more about the promise I made. There would be so much to learn through my life, and through David's tender heart and soul. He knew we only have control over ourselves and yet, I could tell he was thinking of other things within him that he hoped to be sure and accomplish.

Mentally, I knew he was sending his love and thoughts to the Creator along with his direction to keep on track. I knew the answer to "Who was he the most part of, this world, or the other?" He was, as he told me once, that he was NOT of this world, he was something else from the other side, and he was not from this dimension at all. I was remembering that underneath, I knew we were the same!

We both worked hard trying to balance both sides and other worlds we were in, and in time it seemed pretty well normal. It was hard to keep a balance at times because of the human side. It comes out most because we are here as a human, living an earthly life. I felt at times we also wore a "secret" cloak to keep our strange life and worlds hidden from others. For now, it had to be that way under the circumstances.

It has been such a freedom in these last years to reveal some of our true thoughts, teachings, and spiritual life, with a new happiness hard to explain. We both felt more than honored to be here with our loved ones again to share all of our lives together once more as the family we are.

One wonderful thing is people have been becoming more open to the paranormal world. Others are sharing their true events that are written into books and even made into movies. By those writing and reporting their experiences and stories, it opens up more people everywhere to accepting and understanding this other world. Many of these paranormal events are found to be linked around the world, and voiced by all cultures and ages which include, doctors, scientists, husbands, wives, children, ministers, and friends and from all walks of life everywhere.

Ask yourself, is each one of these people lying just to ruin their reputations, and doing this for no reason? I know they are not; we are all sharing experiences, which cannot always be explained! There are many of us who are like the pioneers, sent for centuries, to carry our truth out into the world. My son and I view our agreement and our way of life as the great responsibility it is. We both and others throughout this world have agreed to do this in whatever it takes. My son and I know where all of this comes from to us with having majestic and magnificent heavenly teachers and our Creator guiding us.

Our lives changed drastically for all of us and for a long time to come. It may sound strange, but those years were the best times for us. We as a family became even closer together. We had not had time like this to talk and enjoy one another since before David went into the service. All of us had so much to catch up on when he was better. And with our studies from the other side our bond was stronger than ever before. It increased more with every day. We shared our strange life together feeling blessed. We knew our lives were dedicated in complete trust and faith in our Universal Creator. We had so much to be thankful for with the Heavenly teachings. Our faith was 100% and nothing could have ever shaken it. This was a main part of my son getting well over and over and in our plan coming back.

Chapter 8

Reiki, the Energy Healer

Reiki

I have been a Reiki Master for several years which means I work in energy healing. You may call this laying of hands if you like, because it is hands on. This, for me, is a very spiritual way of sending out energy to help others. Reiki energy goes hand in hand with a doctor's medical care. One compliments the other when combined.

Reiki (ray-ki) is a Japanese concept which simply means Universal energy and is available for those who are sincere and want to learn. Reiki was already in my son and me from long ago built into of our DNA. We are all energy and can be taught how to utilize it. Every living thing is energy. This spiritual energy works hand in hand with medical. A person who uses Reiki never recommends even over the counter medicine or tries to be a doctor in anyway. Combined with medical practices it can be amazing at times for faster healing, stopping pain, helping one to have an easier passing, and used in many other healing ways. Now, years later it is used more and more over the world. This spiritual energy way is available to anyone who wants to learn, achieve and use this healing art. A Reiki practitioner also never gives any kind of medical advice, we only send healing energy. That would be forbidden in Reiki.

Our bodies are complete energy and we have to have energy to be alive. When one is sick, the energy has been lost in that area of the body causing problems or disease. That's where Reiki comes in and supplies the energy to open the path where the blockage is. One never knows how much the Universe will pass to each individual, but it is always working for the better good.

I continued working with David many times a day using healing energy on him. It relieved his pain more and more. He loved how it relaxed him to sleep. He would lie on the massage table outside on the patio with soothing soft music playing as I sent the healing through to him. He could get the fresh air, sunshine, and listen to the birds' singing. I knew he needed that. The other side told me that "he needed the sun and fresh air as another part of his healing." It wasn't long before I was getting him outside for drives. Even when he tired quickly this made him feel much better. He also was given warnings of events to come through nature in the future from his protectors. I took this to mean hurricanes, dry spells, insect problems, tornados, winds, and floods. Now we are experiencing these problems.

He was very interested in the Reiki spiritual way of healing and so was his doctor. The doctor said, "I want to know more about this Reiki energy, he has improved so much!" Keep doing whatever it is, he is doing better and better!"

One day my son's next miracle was completed. His combined healing really took hold, he began walking! He had graduated from being bedridden for many long months, and now after a lengthy time he was released from a wheelchair! One day, with a mischievous look in his eyes, he super surprised me. He looked at me grinning and simply said, "Mom, I'm never going back in this wheelchair again." He rose up on his own and out of his chair! He walked from then on without his wheel chair and went on with his life! I was so excited; this was another blessing, a miracle! If his mind was made up he knew inside of himself that he could do it! This was fantastic!

David had made a recovery time after time, surviving his (NDE) near death experiences. He was now walking in his normal way and everyone was happy! His sisters and I were thrilled to see him getting better and better. As the weeks went by, he was gaining back his weight and strength. He was on his way now blooming more all the time, he looked great! The first food he ate and held down in a long time were tacos and a crème puff each day! I was so excited to see him eat this much food I didn't care what it was and neither did his doctor! I thought it was the strangest combo of foods to start out with. He had gotten his food list from the other side to eat this; they sure knew what they were doing! Every day I was at the bakery early and then to Taco Bell! As thin as he was, I suppose these foods was what he needed because they sure worked; the other side gives the true answers.

The doctors were quite astounded to see this happen; it was something they had no answer for! David was defying the odds each time. The Reiki energy helped sustain him with his doctors' medical care for years. Before this "miracle" we were at the hospital sometimes three days a week for chemo, meds, tests, blood transfusions, and so on. The other weekdays the house was busy with a nurse coming by to hook him up to chemo. Those years were so busy with hardly a moment for the both of us. Except at night when things slowed down. We were very grateful for these helpers.

It is not unusual for the Reiki energy to begin to show progress. It is always working but it can happen fast or slow in healing. Everyone is different. When he was so sick each time the Reiki energy gave him healing after healing. It helped bring him through the DOA's, NDE and the "miracles" he had, along with his doctor's care. Even they could not understand how he kept living with a good quality of life. It was the hard times when he was not in remission that were so bad. Remember, it is our Divine Creator who sends the energy, a practitioner such as us only passes it. This was a very spiritual way of life that we loved and shared with whoever we could.

He had many emergencies and hospital stays over the years. I cannot begin to count them. Everything had changed now, finally turning David around to being like his old self and he continued to soar. Unfortunately, his body had a great amount of internal damage from his illness and continued harsh treatments. The chemo and some medicines destroyed his good organs. He never complained about the sickness or being in the chair for three hours each time he needed a chemo treatment. He was busy talking to the nurses and laughing with them. There he was with his big grin saying "the treatment was a "piece of cake" which I knew it wasn't. He had the old type of strong chemo in those years, which is known to be much harder on a person than today's. I know none of it is pleasant, far from it. He was simply grateful to be alive and see each day. My life was completely focused on getting my son well, and being with my family. I was committed and honored to be doing this with him.

Each time this happened his doctor asked more and if he could "learn about Reiki energy work." David and I were stunned and impressed just to know his doctor wanted to learn the spiritual part of healing. He was seeing unbelievable results along with the medical. He knew something was happening he couldn't understand and he wanted to know what it was. How does this energy work? Doctors were amazed at what happened with him all through his life.

I wasn't surprised when David mentioned that as soon as he could travel very far he wanted to learn Reiki energy healing techniques. He wanted to go to my Reiki teacher. He knew it was time for him to go back into his healing work as in his life before.

Our Reiki and Spiritual Teachers

I had begun learning Reiki a couple of years before David came home to stay and during the short time periods that we were together before he came home I would apply my new found energy healing methods on him. This spiritual healing interested him and he too wanted to learn more about Reiki. When he came home, we decided that we would begin learning Reiki in great earnest together and asked for additional guidance from our Christ Light Being Guides.

I took David to my Reiki teacher where I had studied energy healing; he is an old time Reiki Master teacher. He only taught the ancient and first original way of Reiki from when the secrets were found hidden centuries ago. There were only three people in the very beginning of Reiki who carried on the original healing techniques for many years and taught those only to a few others. This is the true Universal way of healing from the beginning of time. After we settled in, our Master teacher told us his story. This was how he began his journey into Universal healing.

He told us that he and his brother were pretty wild young men. There was almost nothing they hadn't done or tried. Both were on motorcycles one day speeding through an intersection against a red light. Bam! Our Reiki Master's motorcycle was hit by a car! He remembered flying up in the air then falling back down toward the cement highway. He instantly knew his head would be split open! Right before he would have hit the road he suddenly saw an Angel figure! He said, "The Angel cradled my head to keep it from hitting the cement!" He didn't wear a helmet in those days so you can imagine what would have happened!

In the emergency room there were two nurses attending to him. One was positive minded and the other was negative in attitude. He was semi-conscious and going on about the Angel who saved him. The positive nurse was in awe and gently said, "He saw an Angel!" The other scoffed and replied, "Yeah, he saw an Angel alright!" One was a believer and the other was non-believer. It didn't matter to him about the one with the negative remark; he was a 100% changed man.

As he healed he immediately gave up his wild life in order to help others. He understood he had been given a chance to do something good with his life. He began to study the Universal way of healing, about the spiritual, emotional, mental, and physical body. He dedicated his life to helping others with Reiki healing because now he was led by his heart and spiritual soul. Over the years, he became a Master teacher of Reiki, traveling to teach others.

As we had begun learning Reiki, to our astonishment we received messages that we were to have two spirits also help teach us. We soon found that one of these spirits was an Eastern Sage from a long ago dynasty and the other spirit had lived more recently on earth and was named Edgar Cayce. We were delighted to have these spirits as our teachers with their abilities to teach us in the original ways of Reiki that were created in the beginning.

The second of our teachers was from the Ancient Han Dynasty. He had been an ancient philosopher and a Sage in his time named Han Tai Chen Su. He taught the true ancient way and has been with the both of us all of our lives. He and our third spiritual teacher stay with us guiding our hands when we work on the sick.

The third teacher is a man named Edgar Cayce, who crossed over in 1945. He was often called *The Sleeping Prophet*. Edgar also stays near us in our work. It was he who taught us some of his other gifts in healing and the trance states. Edgar was a wonderful person on this earth who gave until he had no more life to give, helping others. He crossed over from wearing his body out too soon from helping all he could. We felt so humbled that he was our teacher and came to work with us throughout our lives.

The following information about Cayce comes from the book, *There Is a River,* by Thomas Sugrue. His life was not easy and he was many times treated wrongly by others in his years of healing work. He was born very poor and while growing up he taught Sunday school in his church, starting as a very young boy. He read his Bible once through every year all his life. When he was around 12 he was in his *secret* place in the woods reading his daily Bible when suddenly an Angel appeared! The Angel asked Edgar what he desired most. Without thought, he replied "to help others!" This gift was granted! From then on his young life changed. But, because of his gifts of intuitiveness to help others he was turned away by many in his life. At one point his church made him leave because of his gifts from God, which broke Edgar's heart. The church could not condone his gifts thinking this was bad!

Edgar never gave up his blessed work and in his later years he made his dream come true. He dreamt of having his own hospital built in Virginia Beach. The hospital would be for the poor, they deserved care like anyone else. This took years before it could be made possible but he persevered. A close friend of Edgar's donated the money to build the hospital. He too, was a believer in Cayce and had known him for years. He had seen phenomenal results from Edgar's healing work. The hospital offered the best treatment available from good doctors even though the patients had nothing to pay with. Today, it is still extremely famous and it is called the A.R.E. (Area of Research and Enlightenment) located in Virginia Beach, Virginia.

There are many books on Edgar Cayce filled with cases of his wonderful healings. He was a kind man who had never gone to medical school. He baffled specialists and other doctors. He was given the gifts of healing and prophecy when he was a small boy. Edgar was born poor and mostly remained this way throughout his life. He was a clairvoyant and a healer. Even when doctors gave up, he could heal. Some doctors would send their patients to Edgar when they did not know what else to do with them!

Edgar was torn apart by the press and went through hard times by many people for the gifted life he had, but he always persevered. He over did his spiritual work dying of exhaustion and a stroke by helping others as long as he could. It was war time and his work load increased. The other side told him, "he had to stop or he would die soon," but he couldn't let people down. In fact, he worked more than ever until a stroke took him down. Edgar did show us of our connected lives together in the beginning. We had our memories of this, he was our spiritual teacher this time once more and we all worked together. He is always present in the healing work we do.

How happy and proud my son and I have been to have Edgar Cayce come to us as one of our spiritual teachers! He has taught us so much that included the beauty of life and in other areas such as with trance states and in different medicine cures he used. He is love and wisdom and his legacy shall go on forever.

The A.R.E. is very active today; people come there to visit from all over the world. Some take classes and to meet one another and some are learning the arts of energy work. David and I always planned to go there and visit the A.R. E. One day, I will go for the both of us and complete our dream and experience this wonderful place.

Sending Reiki to Others

Our spiritual teachers I mentioned above would come to work with me as I worked on my son and vice-versa. They would, at times, advise us as we worked where to lay our hands to send the energy and for how long. From the beginning we each could hear and see them. We felt the pain and emotion in people through our hands and minds of the person's mental, emotional, physical and spiritual well being. Often times we were to use different hand placements' where needed. We were taught how to send the energy to other places. Even far away to where a sick person lived, distance is never a barrier. We always had Divine Company beside us. It was normal for us to have an invisible crowd around our client. Some of these invisible crowd members were their passed over loved one's.

One time a man's Indian Shaman was working in his healing way combined with ours. The Shaman went through quite a ceremony all around our client. The client had no idea, since this was not anything he could see. The Shaman spirit and both of us worked well together. After this treatment the man became better. We felt proud the Shaman worked with us like he did. In healing we seem to all be as one. The energy is so very strong and the client usually falls asleep then wakes when we are finished. They say they feel so relaxed and wonderful. Then they sleep very well that night.

One amazing time while sending healing energy to a client, my son and I could both see the spirit of the man's passed over grandmother in the corner of the room waiting. She wanted us to give a message to her grandson who was lying on the table. We told him his "grandmother was there and she had a message for him." With that, a woman's voice came from where her spirit was in the room! The man was so startled by hearing his grandmother trying to make words that he shot up off of the table! They had a close bond in life and she had raised him as a child. We were able to tell him what his grandmother had to say in her loving message. Everything she said to him through us he verified. There was no doubt this was her and he cried out in happiness!

This man had brought his friend along who also experienced this moment and had been a non-believer, but not anymore, he said! These are our rewards; to see someone be relieved of pain and to know their loved ones watch over them. Love is the strongest emotion there is. Love can move mountains.

My son and I experienced many good results on patients and burn victims. Their healing was usually always quick and the horrible pain was taken away. One never knows what our Creator has in store for us. A practitioner never knows the end result, how fast, or how much energy will be sent to them from the Creator. Regardless, it is always working. Sometimes in a grave illness there may need to be repeated sessions helping to move it on. Never lose hope that it is not doing its job. It always keeps working even if you think it is not. People who are going to be passing on who receive the energy are known to have an easier peaceful passing. First the universal energy must pass through the practitioner first starting at the crown, moving down into the heart and arms and then into the hands. The practitioner's hands then pass the energy to the client/person. Reiki may only be used in a good and positive way. This spiritual energy can never be used for negative, it will return back to the one trying to send it. It does not change anyone's time to go but helps in the process of dying.

In other experiences of energy work even a broken bone can mend or pop back into place. This happened with my small baby granddaughter when the tip of her finger was torn off in an accident. She was quickly taken to a hospital and we began sending energy healing to her. In about an hour I was called by my daughter telling us to stop sending! Her finger had begun to heal with new skin too fast she was going into surgery to have the tip reattached! As you see Reiki (universal) energy works in many different concepts for each individual. The doctor couldn't understand why her finger was healing.

By working in this way we both experienced many Angel Beings who also would at times work through our hands in healing and in some divine instances, we witnessed Jesus Christ and were more than completely humbled! There are no words expressing the emotions of joy! In one of these times our friend, a doctor, lost his sight in one eye. He had taken Reiki energy healing in my class out of curiosity wanting to know what Reiki energy was about and how it worked in healing. David and I became friends with the doctor and his lovely wife. After the classes were completed I gave them their final attunements.

One day he called asking to see us for a healing and we were happy to do so. A few days later he came to the house with his wife for my son and me to work on his eye. He had been to the best eye doctors but nothing could be done to help him. The healing he had when we worked with him was more than breathtaking! The energy was so strong that suddenly a small Light began to appear and come to us, growing larger as it came closer and then it happened! The Light changed into its complete form, the figure of Jesus Christ!

Christ's arms and hands melted into David's and mine and we knew this was a miracle healing we were witness to! The healing energy was so strong I felt I would not be able to stand long. We were so excited and humbled but we didn't tell our dear friend, the doctor, and his wife that day what we saw.

I did tell him he had a miraculous healing! I felt renewed and so happy I wanted to sink to my knees giving my heartfelt thanks for this blessing to our dear friend. David and I knew he was being healed and it would show quickly. This was on a Friday and by Sunday the doctor and his wife called us on separate telephone extensions so excited to tell us he could see again, even to drive that day! Most of his sight had been restored! His wife, Angelia, had been driving him everywhere and at home he couldn't see to do anything with the eye condition he had. They were ecstatic and in a couple more days all of his sight was restored to 20/20! This was about 8 years ago now or perhaps longer and his sight is still perfect!

David and I only passed the healing energy that Jesus Christ flowed through us to the doctor healing his sight! Healing does not always happen so fast in this way, but it always helps the person in some way. We never know how the outcome will be with anyone except when we have experienced the Heavenly Christ and then we know the healing will happen quickly in some divine way.

Our friend, the kind doctor and his wife came to my workshops later on as a speaker where he would tell his amazing story of healing. He told us his way of healing now would be changed. He combined Reiki energy and his medical knowledge. Combining the spiritual energy and medical knowledge compliments each other. David and I were very happy that the doctor knew he had experienced something unexplainable and wonderful with his eye through Christ.

They drove a long way to be present at my son's celebration of life and the doctor expressed to me his eye was still perfect! I am still in touch with this couple and they speak of my son with their love. They will always be an important part of both of our lives.

Our Honored Work

We stayed alert and busy in Reiki and spiritual healing. We worked on my clients with AIDS and others with any kind of illness at a clinic not too far from my home and sometimes we would go to other locations to help. We both loved all of our clients as a second family. We felt badly of how the aids people were treated by others. They are humans just like anyone else, but with a different type of terminal disease. Unfortunately, they are condemned greatly. Neither of us could ever understand why people do this to them, even some churches!

They suffer beyond what you can imagine in life. No one deserves a terrible way to die. They come here as the soldiers they are, if you only think about this. Have you ever thought of how this may be? What if they are teachers for you to learn by to see if you have compassion in life? David and I knew many AIDS patients were teachers here for others to learn from by going through their pain. You never know what we each chose to do here on earth as a human so be careful of judging others. Would Jesus Christ turn himself away from them? Not the loving Jesus we know.

In the energy work that David and I did together we were able to see many loved ones in spirit, and higher up spiritual beings attending us. Mostly they gave messages to us for the one we worked on. It was giving the client healing energy, and an unexpected reading combined! We always thanked the spirits of loved ones and the spirit healers for doing this. This is also an emotional experience for both of us that we always give thanks for.

My son and I both became Reiki Master Teachers and Ministers of healing as we promised to do in this life. We took our work and the responsibly very seriously. By being the first two Reiki practitioners in the middle and southern part of our state, it wasn't easy getting started.

The main question we always seemed to hear was, "Do you go to church?" I couldn't believe people wouldn't know this was a very spiritual thing, and that we had the best BOSS they could EVER imagine! Our energy came from the Universal Creator for our work, we only passed it on.

After some time, we were led by the other side to a nearby college by our spiritual teachers where I had been told I was to teach Reiki. How this came about was one evening I sat down on my bed and heard a heavenly voice call out to me "what does thou seek most?" Never hesitating I called out "to help others!" The next day I was told by my spiritual teachers I would go into a healing Ministry! I thought how would a wife with four children ever do this?

I was quickly shown the way by the spiritual teachers as they opened the right doors for me. Talking to the right people at a college and showing them my syllabus they wanted me to teach at their college! Just as the other side had said I would be doing. This was a new subject to them and they were so interested in Reiki it was quickly accepted. I immediately began in the new semester to teach it there! My classes began filling up until I had to make room for more classes. The other side had told me it would be greatly accepted and it certainly was.

After I had taught for some time and was driving many miles to school and back, the other side said, "I needed to rest; my energy had become low by teaching so many back to back classes." I am happy to say, most of my students have continued using Reiki over large areas to this day. In the study of this healing art one learns about everything it is and how to use it. In this way the art of healing energy will never be lost.

After teaching, conducting workshops, and speaking engagements, both my son and I experienced amazing results through the Universal energy work. After my resting period I wanted to share and teach others who were close around me in my area. Immediately with that thought I was told by the Christ like Beings that the timing was not quite right, to wait until the people here were more ready. I knew in my heart I should listen to my spiritual teacher they knew and guided us both. I always had before, but this time I bypassed the advice without asking them to let me try. I was so committed and I thought I was ready to start now.

Learning to Listen Better

Of course, this proved to be the wrong thing to do. Not long after my answer to wait from the spiritual beings I had a vision in the night. The vision was plainly showing me to put a hold on doing this! In the vision I was with one of my spiritual Guides who came to me. We seemed to be very high up looking over the town and the place where I would be using Reiki. I was shown an enormous dark cloud spreading over the location that I would be in, and the entire area. I was being told again to wait; things weren't ready yet, people would not understand what it was.

I had already secured my place and made arrangements to move my things in. I figured if I would be able to help even one person it would be a start. Then, by word of mouth hopefully others would come. I was being very positive and forging right ahead with that thought, just like some child who doesn't listen. I had never done this before when I was told "to wait, that it was too soon!" I learned my lesson very quickly, not one person came in and needless to say, "I told you so" was ringing in my ears as I moved out! I have never again moved on with a plan of my own when told not to by the other side. I had a hard lesson and I needed it.

My son never interfered with any of my free will to do this; he knew this was something I needed to learn when told to wait. He let me learn as he stood aside. He had helped move me in, and helped me move out, and never said a word about it. The old advanced soul that he is stepped back and let me the "student" learn from my mistakes. After this, my son and I practiced

Reiki together as usual.

For many years I had worked for the state that I live in. The clients were people with AIDS and we were honored to be able to share this important work with them. This was something important that we were here to do. We both loved helping any sick people all that we could. Whatever their health problem never made a difference to how we treated them. They were all special and like a second family to us. Every person and with any illness we were happy and honored to assist with Reiki.

The next time I wanted to try teaching the healing process to others in our area I received a go forward from the other side and I was told that people would begin to be receptive. I rented a different place which had a nice room to resume my work and to teach workshops. I knew it was okay being the right time and place, and I had the other side's blessing. The owner had no objection to my teaching these techniques. I still kidded him asking, "Do you have a back door?" "Oh yes" he responded looking a little confused, "if you see a large group of people coming down the middle of Main Street with torches let me know!" We both began to laugh at my joke and it broke the ice. This man had an open mind and heart, and wasn't afraid of our work. He understood it was for the goodness to others. The workshop was a great success! I could hear the words from my teachers, "See how this works for you when you listen," and then I heard the most humorous laughter from the other side. I was learning, and I would NEVER forget this. My enthusiasm in the beginning was good to have but I learned to listen well!

Chapter 9

Building His Rose Garden in Life

A Positive Soul

While David was still here, we continued to hold on to our strong belief, that not to talk about his illness would help to be positive; we did not want to focus on the negative. With this, he stayed the most positive person I have ever met or known. He never talked or complained about his illness, and he knew how he wanted to live out his life. He went to his doctors and did what they said, and we did the rest with Reiki energy. We both knew that "the mind is the builder" as Cayce taught us and how one thinks has so much to do with getting well, plus to stay as positive as possible. His illness was a very personal thing to him; that's why he didn't talk about it. There are others who feel the same way.

We always knew without a doubt in our hearts that God was sending healing energy. The energy was being passed to David going to where it would be guided and needed, and for as long as it was supposed to. As I worked on him through the days, evenings, and all the years I listened for guided words from the other side. I was being guided in applying the energy, and combined with my clairvoyance, this is how it worked. I was told specific ways to use the energy, and for how long, soon he would feel better. I was following the words I was given and passing what God sent to him. He still had much to do yet.

He always received the healing energy like a sponge absorbing every atom into his body with happiness. He gave himself healing with Reiki energy, knowing we can work on others and ourselves. With both of us using this powerful energy he was receiving two times the amount of energy into his body. The Reiki way is for anyone who wants to learn and is a gift that anyone can attain by learning from a qualified teacher who has worked a long time to develop the skills. Those who truly want to do well for those they work on need to study and learn from experience. It takes time to learn and develop the skills from experience.

Never Another Crutch

Life had been going quite well for a while now, but one summer day an unusual thing happened to David. He bent down on his knee to pick something up and sharp pain shot through his knee hurting him badly. He rubbed his hand over it and discovered a large mass protruding outward. He told me his intuition was telling him we needed to waste no time getting to a doctor. This large mass had appeared nearly overnight! I looked to see a large swollen place on his knee and quickly made the appointment. He was seen right away when we arrived. It was called a "Giant cell tumor." The doctor said, "The tumor had eaten part of his knee cap away very quickly. They couldn't tell us much more until they got into it."

We arrived early at the hospital the next morning for surgery. He was smiling and teasing the nurses that day as usual and telling me not to worry. We had been given information from the other side, "that he would get through it alright, that he would be well." We were confident he would be okay, but as his mother I always worried and prayed his leg would be spared. We can be told the outcome but not always what will happen in between to get there. Would he keep his leg, I could only pray he would. Did he know if he would? If not, he would not have told me. The main thing was he would still be alive and that's all that mattered! I knew he would make his life as normal as possible.

The wait seemed forever to me while his surgery was going on. When everything was over I was told to come in, that I could see him now in recovery. I saw big smiles all around him, and was told his surgery was successful! His knee had been replaced with cadaver bone and his leg would be fine the doctor said. We had believed in our Divine source as always and with the surgeons' gift to operate on him!

This was a great day for all of us! He was to be on crutches eight weeks and later that day I had him home. I helped him out of the car with his crutches and as I did he looked at me smiling with a twinkle in his eyes. He said, "Mom, I'll be off of these by tomorrow." And he was he never used the crutches again! His knee healed overnight and he was never bothered by it again! I put his crutches away for good. His amazing healing really shocked his doctor when we went back for his check up! He was completely baffled! David had an extraordinary and phenomenal recovery!

Storing Memories of David

I found out there would be many more things that can crop up and can happen to a person fighting to live over the years. So I made sure to soak in every minute of him with storing precious memories in my mind forever and this was never enough. It would never be long enough. I knew someday he would be called home. It was sometimes hard to know or tell how he felt for sure; he was a master at blocking my thoughts when he wanted to. I knew him better than anyone so I knew when he was hiding his thoughts from me the days he felt really bad. I believe most parents can feel their child's pain or the adults who they are close to. We each learn about every emotion a human has.

I realized how much forgiveness, and patience with others goes along with one's illness as people could be very cruel at times to him and not tolerant of his medical condition. He was so healthy looking we would be criticized at times for parking in handicapped places, though he still needed my help getting out of the car to walk a longer distance. Because he was young, he was quickly judged by older people who gave him hard remarks. Even at the doctor's office, "What are you doing in here?" they would ask him. If they only knew, I would think. He knew what they were thinking because of his young age and of course he would simply let it pass with a smile to them. I was learning so much that goes along with someone who fights to stay alive I would never have thought of.

He could go down so fast and into an emergency with little time to get him to the hospital and most of those times he was critical going straight into the ER. Later, when the danger was under control he was hospitalized when they dared move him. This happened over and over again throughout the years. I would try to rest in the late night on the floor, in a chair, anyplace, to always be close to him. When he was in ICU, I would lay on the floor outside the doors by a wall or in a small area as close as I could get. I wasn't going to be apart from him no matter where he was. On the many trips when this happened I drove as fast as possible hoping I would get stopped so the police could help lead us safely to the hospital. Not one time did this happen.

Through the years of emergencies, there was only one time I caught his look of sadness for a second. I have kept in my memories of how his face still looked like a child when he finally fell asleep. I thought of how he loved chocolate and being so tall and slim he could eat all he wanted. I stored my thoughts away each day, and later my daughters told me they had done the same with their brother. We continued storing him in our minds like our own special library and computer. We would always keep him alive with our words and stories of his humor, his kindness, and all he did.

David in his ball cap with his nephew Daniel

It would be hard not to notice how he would straighten his ball cap just right every time when he put it on. I would find myself thinking of those times and put on a little smile. Today, his Cardinal cap hangs on my coat rack just like always. I have never washed it. I can still smell him and I don't want to lose his fragrance. I keep it like it was. It is strange how we try to keep what we can of our loved ones when they are gone. I suppose most of us have our comfort in that way.

I would often wear his heavy Levi coat to go outside in the winter; it would keep me nice and cozy. It is important how we grieve; it takes each person a certain amount of time to work things out to the best they can.

Having some of their things around us makes one feel better we pick up on their energy from those items. It's more than okay to do what one needs to if it is forever.

I remember one day some time back after I got up he sheepishly told me "Mom, I need to tell you what I did this morning. I got the old truck out and drove it to the store." He still had some sight left then; I couldn't help but smile as he finished saying he went early before traffic and that he did just fine. I wouldn't have taken that precious trip away from him for anything. Not to mention we only lived two blocks from the store. I believe this was the last drive he ever made. When I sold the old truck years later after he had passed over I was very sad. That old truck had a lot of memories over those years with us going everywhere we needed to most of the time.

It can be quite devastating when everything changes in one's life when it has to do with loss. You want to take those things and never let go of them. We can't seem to let them go. I still can't believe some days David is in another time and place even with his visits to me. I can hear his words to me each early morning, and I say, "Thank you my son for being with me." As we both said, always together, we promised one another and that's how it will always be for us. My daughters feel the same terrible loneliness for him and will always miss their brother as much as I do. It will never be any different for us and all those who have a loss. I only use the word loss because that is how we talk to one another here on earth. We never lose anyone; they are still alive in spirit. Another thing to point out is no one is ever taken. When it is our time to leave, we are finished with why we came here, it does not matter what age you are, some lives are short and some are long.

The Jokes We Played

Now, I will tell you how we made life happy together the best we could with our humorous times. When I returned home one summer afternoon I looked out my kitchen window to check out my garden and to my shock, I saw a nude woman! I raced outside looked and burst out laughing so hard I couldn't stop! David had put a life-sized mannequin in the garden and draped my morning glories around the body of it! This looked as if she had a two piece swimsuit on. I had to take pictures of her and of course he was nowhere to be seen. I figured he was somewhere nearby hiding, watching me gasp with laughter. I left her there quite some time until one day when the rain was coming. I thought I better keep her dry so I took her to safety in the garage. It was so funny because the neighbors at first thought she was real! They would drive up and down the alley looking at her until they figured the joke out. I never said a word to them about the mysterious woman in my garden.

The next joke we both played was on his sister, Pam. She lives out in the boonies as David would say. While she was at work, we took one leg of the mannequin and put a red high heel on it. Then we planted it upside down in her tomatoes and waited for the phone to ring when she returned home. That was really a good one! She said, "She glanced out the window of her kitchen and it scared her to death! She could not imagine what it was at first! And it didn't take long for her to figure out who did it," she said. I am so glad he kept the kid in him and in us no matter what happened. David always called his sister "Petunia or Ellie Mae."

Another funny thing we did to Petunia was David made an exact double of a leg lamp like the one in the movie *A Christmas Story* (one of his favorite movies). The lamp was life size but exact! Pam had gone to work as an assistant manager in a large store. We went into her office the back way and quietly sat it up on her desk. It was trimmed out with a red high heel and mom's lamp shade on top of the leg lamp! He had made a masterpiece! It had several small Christmas lights around the shade so he turned it on. Quickly employees were darting in and out loving it! She finally returned from working up front and went into her office. A second later we heard her laughing so hard! We had hidden behind some boxes to see the expression on her face, it was great. Even her manager loved her new leg lamp! Pam had recently lost her young husband and this funny surprise really helped to cheer her up at Christmas time. This joke made her laugh and tears rolled down her face and we felt well, mission completed!

Another time, David had these little plastic monkey hands (who knows where they came from). We went to the local restaurant where the manager was a good friend of ours. After she took our orders and money she whirled around to give him his change. Meanwhile, he had slid the little hands out of his sleeves holding out the miniature hands for the change. She was stunned and let out a big scream! All the customers heard her screaming all over the place dropping the change everywhere! Our friend realized the joke then she laughed so hard it made her day! Over the following years she would still laugh about that day. Everything we did was harmless and helped keep the "child" in him instead of him stuck in a bed. I know though he had to have his sad days in private knowing he couldn't be with us much longer but he kept it to himself. He never gave up though! One day parking at the coffee shop David asked me to back in to park. I thought that was odd to say. I asked why? He muttered something about the hot sun coming in the other direction. I should have known...People were soon going to the windows pointing to my truck! I looked out to see a monstrous sized bug on the front of the truck grill! It Looked like Jurassic Park!

The next time we got into mischief was with my other daughter, Robin. We found a stuffed toy black bird in a store and the light bulb went off in David's head with a great idea! He took a small box, lined it nicely and laid the bird inside on its back. He had me write a small message tied it to the feet and put the lid on. We waited until dark, parked my car two blocks away, and then I helped him to walk to her driveway in the dark night. I prayed she forgot to lock her car door and bingo, it was unlocked. We put the gift inside on her front seat and left in a hurry. The fun of this was how we always denied knowing a thing about the bird, and his sisters sometimes never really knew who did the joke. We would stick to our story. This tiny bird was the ending of a joke she had done to us. The next object we took to my same daughter's house he put in her boyfriend's car. We hung a rubber bat on the mirror so it had movement. When he got into his car he saw a bat moving! He wasted no time in making a quick getaway out of his car! The best part was he never knew who really did it; he also had a good sense of humor. The boyfriend had funny jokes he played on us too. We all kept the child alive inside of us, keeping our spirits lifted highly. All of us had a good sense of humor. You need humor to keep going and we used it anytime in anyplace.

This gives you an idea of how we made life more fun taking away the serious part of his terminal illness. We were always busy thinking up some kind of funny situation. We got our share of pranks back from his sisters by catching us off guard at times too. It was wonderful to see him light up with funny, harmless ideas which made him feel extra good again. He was in continued pain and sick so many times, but he would never have said so. He knew what it took for him to keep going and how to use his energy wisely. He took no pain medication at all through the many years. At night I slowed down but my mind couldn't stop thinking that his life was slipping away from us. My thoughts couldn't shut down. Finally with exhaustion I fell asleep. I was sad and afraid of time getting closer when he would have to leave! I released my sorrow by talking with the Beings of Light for comfort.

I am sure he did the same thing; he was so close in spirit to the Creator.

Divine Presence

As time passed over the years there were some very serious times when I was led out of his hospital room into the hall. I was told from his doctor, "that he wouldn't live out the day!" I can't really describe my shock to you. I can share this now with the thousands of others who have been in my place and went through these horrors. I nodded my head that I understood what the doctor was saying, but even in those worse times I never believed him/her. Call it denial, but as long as I heard the familiar Christ Light Beings saying, "For he shall be well," I made it through and waited patiently for his turn around. As long as I was given those loving words by the Heavenly messenger I knew he would pull through and I never doubted it!

We both kept our humility and complete faith yet my heart still shattered as a mother, a human being, watching my son suffer and stay strong, over and over, we survived on one another's strength. He always smiled at me with a certain shining radiance around him and speaking softly he mustered the energy to tell me, "not to worry that he would be well." I believed this with all my heart! He made his amazing turn around that particular evening and slowly began getting better! We never doubted for one second that his work was finished yet. We were together in this fight for his life along with our loved ones.

When the terrible times were happening to my son there would appear the most beautiful bright light as far as I could see in his hospital room. It was as if there were no walls or ceiling anywhere. I knew a Divine presence was with us and it was not his time to leave just yet. I knew that a miracle was happening right in front of me! As a mother and believer I would never think a negative thought with the messages given to us from our Heavenly source. Why would I? They were Divine and we were humbling. We had been given another amazing and glorious gift! We would never quit believing what our Heavenly Beings said to us. Only a fool would not believe. But as a mother my heart hurt watching what he had to go through daily all of those years. How easy it would have been for him to have just given up. Thank God he was a pillar of strength and Light who came here to accomplish many things.

A mother knows her children better than anyone on earth and even with the powerful messages we received it was still very hard to watch his battle.

As long as we both heard the voices and could see the beautiful Beings of Light; we knew as God's messengers we were strong. I stayed right beside my son holding back my tears. He would say to me often, "It's ok mom, you worry too much," smiling at me and then he would give me a big hug.

We both continued to receive the blessed Angels of healing supplying our energy. The comfort of that alone was a knowing we were being watched over and guided. I clung to my worlds of knowledge yet felt I stood close to the edge of a cliff. I knew I would fall when everything was over for us. I would fall so deep; I would need all of my strength for an immeasurable amount of time in order to crawl back up and out to begin my life once more. I knew my girls would help pull me to the top when I needed help and David would be pushing them giving them the strength. He would help us all survive!

My son and I thanked God so much for giving us the gifts of clairvoyance and more, and to follow what we were told by the Heavenly voices. We felt we were going through many tests of faith, belief, and trust. We would be reminded again by our spiritual teachers and Indian Shaman that, "a believer continues to learn and grow, non-believers learn nothing." A living Shaman also said to us, "Negative souls go up like a puff of smoke showing nothing at the end of their lives."

Our Spiritual Native American Shaman

In those last years I was given much of my courage from our spiritual Shaman teacher and my dear Indian friend, Alex. He taught me how to use sweet grass and sage, and told me of many other techniques which was important to me and my son. He has a terrific sense of humor and has kept me going through these many years as my dear and good friend. I am honored to know him again in this lifetime. He is a healer in many ways to others and is a well-known artist. He creates the most beautiful art work which shows the history of his ancient people and the old hidden places where some lived. This is where his people lived long ago in the canyons and other territories in the Southwest. He also teaches the younger Indian people the truth of the Ancient Indian history so they can learn and know their forefather's history. Those people can pass this information onto the next younger generation and others before it is lost.

Life has changed so much for them since the white man came to destroy them and take their land. Now many live in the worst conditions; they seem to have no hope for a future. How can they, when they are offered nothing?

They are a nation who is suffering and proud to be the souls they are. They deserve to know the truth and their ancestors' history. The white man took everything from them long ago. I feel ashamed of what our ancestors have done and destroyed in their crude way then, and now. The killings and loss of their land pushed them into slavery by the white man who tried to change all of their ways.

Alex has helped me grow and learn with his teachings, and has been a protector to me in many ways. He loved my son although he never met him but wanted to. My son and I planned to meet with Alex that last year in the summer, but David passed a short time before. My son said, "He knew when Alex came to visit him in astral (soul) travel in his spirit and he liked his essence very much looking forward to meeting him too." He probably knew they would never get to meet in this life but always knew when Alex was near to him.

Alex brought me through some of my worst times after my son crossed over. I used the strength he passed to me to recover. I will have him in my heart forever. We had shared life times before and we both had remembered one another in this one. Thank you my dear companion from our other times. After I began writing David's story, my beloved Alex crossed over and I felt so empty with him gone now too. He has come with my son in spirit several times since and at times by himself to visit with me in our way. He has happiness and peace, still kidding me and calling me a nick name he teased me with, Collard Green!

Angels and the Transition of Love

An Angel once brought a treasure to my son and me in these words. The Angel told us, "My son and I were both full of love for others; to pass this gift of love on to them for those to pass on again and in this way the love continues on." With that, David more than earned his crown and wings with flying colors over and over! That's what he was about giving his love to others and passing it on.

I was told more than once by the other side to write David's story and what happened to him in his life here to help others. This was to give others hope, faith, trust, perseverance, and to know miracles happen every day somewhere. We learn by mustering our faith, trust, hope, and belief, to persevere and keep humility. When it is your time and your soul is tired and has done everything you came here to do you will pass into the other world, your heaven. Life does not go in a certain order in how we think it should. We think the first to go should be the grandparents, then parents, then children and so on.

Another important thing we each were taught about living earth life was each person can either make their life a rose garden or a thorn garden; we each make our own choice. We make that choice every single day we live. We design every single day we live. We often get mad at ourselves by making the wrong choices but that is the major learning part of earth school. I have often thought of how much strength David and others like him used to battle the tribulations of life on earth, yet choose a rose garden knowing their end is near with the Grace of God.

Small children and some adults adapt to death in amazing ways of acceptance and seem to sense when they will be leaving. They make their lives a natural rose garden. Their lives leave us with their legacy of being our child/ loved one with beautiful stories, memories, and lessons they have given to us. We have those as our treasures to keep with us forever. That can never be taken from us by anyone. There are small children who have a NDE (near death experience) coming back to tell about it. Small children do not make up stories such as this. They have helped to bring the truth of dying into realization along with thousands of others. Perhaps this is a large part of their journey to tell adults there are such things as heaven by returning to tell about it! We don't know any one's agenda, even our own, and we are not meant to know.

One other particular time when David was very close to death and his heart was again failing. I barely got him to the hospital in time! He was in and out of both worlds through the day and night, it was touch and go. In the ER I was told his heart looked like a wadded up piece of paper! I couldn't imagine how he was still breathing, and I was very frightened for him! I reluctantly had to step out of the treatment room often while he was being worked on.

Finally, after all day and into the night he could be moved quickly to the Intensive Care Unit on another floor. It was a chance they had to take now. I have never seen attendants run as fast as they did from the ER pushing his bed to a nearby back elevator and up to the Intensive Care Unit. I had been praying over and over for him and although I didn't hear the Heavenly words given to me of a healing, I had an amazing and beautiful experience in place of them!

After he was settled in the ICU I was allowed to go in his room for just a few moments. As I stood by him he was completely white and unconscious! He was out and sedated along with oxygen and medicines going into his body. Suddenly, I realized we weren't alone! I began to see his room light up in a bright glow of golden light and the walls seemed to disappear! Then I saw the most amazing site, there were hundreds of Angels in a soft but yet brighter white and gold and all of their light surrounded him as far as I could see! With that sign I knew he would be healed again! There was my answer in this glorious wonder of beautiful Angels! I didn't want to leave him when the vision ended! Everything happened to let me know he would be fine.

Through this phenomenal miracle my answer had been made clear in those few precious minutes! Seeing this amazing vision I was at peace, but I didn't go far, I wasn't about to. I slept in the hall on the floor by the entrance to ICU that night.

He had a long way to go before he could be moved to a room. I had seen the Angels come to help him and to give me the peace that, "he would be healed." I was calm and content now knowing he would live once more! With each heavenly experience I have never forgotten any of them! I would run each one as they happened over and over in my mind in these critical times. They knew the relief it gave us letting us know that they would be close beside us until our journey and promise was completed here.

A Magnificent Physician

Days later David was moved to a single room and a leading heart specialist named Dr. W. came in to meet my son. First, he explained who he was in his greeting to David and said, "I have read only a few pages of your chart (which he commented it looked like a telephone book) and I can't believe what all you have been through so young! I wanted to meet you in person, David, and I want to shake your hand." He continued on, "Even though I have only read these few pages I plan to read all of your history. I heard about you when you were down in ER for all of that time. I couldn't believe what shape you were in and made it through! I had to see for myself!"

Dr. W. had brought several colleagues/ medical people in with him that were standing all around his bed. They were all observing, looking at my son and soaking in everything the doctor said. This was such a wonderful and kind expression of caring from the heart for Dr. W. to do. David again was an unexplained "miracle" with the odds all against him! He never worried about the odds, he lived in the moment. The doctor couldn't see how David had survived all he had went through and lived with his heart looking as it did! Dr. W. the noted heart specialist, who was talking to my son, has a brother who is also a doctor.

His brother Dr. B. W. took care of and attended to my mother's illness that happened to her many years ago. He was the one who was able to diagnose what was wrong with her. A type of disease called cerebellum spinal degeneration. Here is the way I found out both doctors were related. My mother's sister, my Aunt Mary, who lived in New Mexico, said she found an old letter from me many years ago when this strange sickness happened to my mother. In the letter I sent to her when Mom became sick I told her the name of the nice young doctor who diagnosed her was Dr. B.W. I would never have known and made the connection between the two doctors as brothers if she had not reminded me of my old letter. We were really excited to find out this connection!

Before my Aunt found the old letter I happened to tell her about this wonderful Dr. B.W. and give her the gift of a book written by him. I am very interested in all of his wonderful books. I feel we both are connected with many of the same ideas and each one's work, but yet in our own way. I also admired that he put his career on the line by exposing his experiences to others while being a doctor. He writes about NDE, near death experiences, and past lives of patients he has had and others who go under his hypnosis.

The doctor said "it took him four years to start writing because he knew he could lose everything, including his position as a qualified doctor, plus his credibility that would change his very life." He had to choose to tell the experiences in his books of those who had them. His colleagues supported him in his work doing regressions of past lives and he is highly admired by many people in his work. Thank goodness he persevered and wrote his wonderful books. He is still a renowned doctor, famous writer and speaker today and his work has been wonderfully received over the world! The connection I had with him started those many years ago.

My Aunt and I were very surprised to say the least! Although this was years ago, I certainly thank both of them. They both have been a wonderful part of our lives. We thought it was amazing that Dr. B.W. brother, the Heart specialist, was now meeting my son, David, many years later. Nothing is by coincidence. My son and I appreciated the doctor's gracious visit to him and I certainly appreciated his brother years ago for helping my mother. Isn't it strange how things go full circle? Now with my son having the heart specialist and in earlier years my mother having his brother for her illness is an example of how our lives can mingle together in mysterious ways.

Through David's remaining years he kept the most powerful inner strength and mind that I have ever seen. His doctors were very happy to see his continued amazing progress and to experience David's friendship. They thought very highly of him with his positive attitude and personality, they said he was a joy to see! In his gratitude for them he brought homemade snacks, candy, chocolates, and fresh baked bread and cookies at Christmas. He loved doing this to let them know how important they were to him, he was still able to show his appreciation in this way and be joyful

Chapter 10

Charley's Spirit Returns at Christmas

Spirits and Toy Soldiers

On the night before Christmas I was missing my tape recorder. David and I knew someone from the other side had taken it for some reason earlier that day. This was happening because in November my daughter, Pam, had lost her young husband, Charley, to over a year of illness. He passed over right before his thirty-first birthday in November. This was an extremely hard time for her and she was devastated! So were we and the whole family and now it was almost Christmas. My daughter said she would come over the next day, that on this special night of Christmas Eve she needed to be alone at home. We understood this.

That same evening I started to turn in and as I was putting my foot on the first step to go upstairs to bed I heard it; I could faintly hear Charley's song that he had been playing the night he died! The music was coming from the top of the stairs, *No More Tears in Heaven*! This had also been used at his funeral.

I called out to David to come quickly, "let's see what was going on!" We slowly went up the dark stairs to the top landing stopping suddenly. In the faint light, placed on the floor was my tape recorder with his song playing! Then it stopped and his voice was talking. We made out the words, "Tell Pam I love her!" How excited we both were for my daughter! We were very sad but also happy with Charley's Christmas message to her! David and I were choked up with our tears knowing how much this meant to the both of them.

The next day I was up early and getting ready to go downstairs. Getting close to the staircase I could see objects on each step of it. Looking closer, I saw our entire collection of toy soldiers that I had put around the tree were lined up with one on each step on down to the bottom! I knew Charley had arranged this surprise and was saying to Pam, "I love you" and "Try to be a brave little soldier for me, I am with you and I love you!" How amazing it was that he had managed to do these things for her at Christmas and trying to help her through his leaving with the holidays they had shared together. His spirit energy did this, moving the soldiers and placing them on the stairs, proving the power of love he had for her! This would not be the finish; there were many experiences he orchestrated over time for her. He wanted her to know he was with her. She was not alone.

Another clever thing Charley did that Christmas morning was he had moved every gift from under the tree! He had arranged them almost like a tall tower on the coffee table perfectly. How they stayed balanced I don't know, but they did. He made sure she knew it was what he had done. He had learned how to make visual contact, make his voice heard and move objects very quickly. He wanted to comfort her all he could.

While I stayed with my daughter at their home his presence was strong in every room, mainly where he had collapsed and died. In the spare bedroom where I was at night I could see his form in blue sparkles and I could hear and see him in spirit. He told me he had no idea it was himself lying on the living room floor when he died. There was so much commotion going on with the rescue people. He began to realize he was floating up over them. Then he took a better look to see what was going on. To his horror, he saw a body lying there with his face and to his shock it was him, he realized that he had died! But, this was very hard for him to accept and to believe it! He felt more alive than ever! He was having a difficult time knowing now he was in spirit.

In the days and months to come, many other things would happen to prove Charley was still with her. The next day we went to make his arrangements at the funeral home and I saw Pam suddenly freeze up when she opened her purse to get her car keys. I asked, what was wrong?" but she couldn't speak! I looked inside of her purse to where she focused and there were three small blocks. They had sat on top of the television in the living room since they bought their new home! They said, Home Sweet Home! How did they get into her purse? Only Charley knew. This was their first home they had waited so long to buy. It had only been five months earlier they had bought it. Charley continued to make contact.

Some months later I plainly recalled when my granddaughter was house sitting for my daughter while she worked out of town. She would come out to feed her cats and dog, check out the house and stay overnight. The first day she got up was a sunny beautiful one. She walked out onto the front porch and noticed a coffee cup with warm coffee in it! That really scared her, it was Charley's cup! No one else was there and she didn't drink coffee! This was Charley's chair on the porch where he sat having his coffee early each day before work!

Apparently, he still could make this happen in his way to be noticed that he was there. This was his sign, his symbol of saying to Pam, "I am still here with you where I love to be!" He knew my granddaughter would tell her about finding his cup. I always knew in my heart both Charley and David would pass over young, but I didn't know which one would be first. This was excruciating to know for years.

I remember once while Charley was still alive, he mentioned to me that "all he and Pam needed now was a couple of kids!" Sometime later he passed on with no children in sight. In time my daughter remarried and something astounding happened! There came to be in the future a gift Charley brought to Pam, and actually it was a wonderful message he brought to her in a miracle way! I went to take flowers to the cemetery one beautiful sunny day and what I found was absolutely shocking! On Charley's stone ledge sat the figure of an Angel! The Angel had a small boy on one side and smaller little girl on the other side. It had each wing around each one of the two children as if protecting them and bringing them forth to her. I called my daughter as fast as I could! I told her what I found; this was a sign Charley had left for her! He was letting her know she would have two beautiful healthy children in the near future.

We still called around to others who knew him to no avail! His family all lived miles away and he had been gone for some time. To make the story short she became pregnant, and first had a little boy. A short time later she had a little girl and they are as healthy as can be! We know what Charley did to bring her this most welcomed news! If only people knew what can be arranged from Heaven showing that anything is possible!

The Amazing 4th of July and Becoming a Healer

It was the 4th of July soon and the family gathered together at my daughter, Pam's, home. She had purchased all kind of fireworks to set off in the evening. David loved them, and he felt like a kid! As the family began setting off the fireworks he slowly stood up on the porch. I saw him pausing a minute as if deciding something, or sizing up the situation.

Then unexpectedly and slowly he began walking towards the fireworks. I couldn't believe my eyes; when he broke into an amazing run! I had not seen him run in years! Then he joined in setting the fireworks off too! We couldn't believe he could have the stamina to do this! Even though he was walking fine and starting to improve each day. I felt my heart leap into my throat, afraid he would fall when going up the small hill to join in. Now, most everyone had risen up out of their chairs cheering him on! There was much clapping and laughing, we were so happy! It was if there was another person in his body laughing and having fun. I couldn't help but think that my late son in law, Charley, was somehow helping my son. I felt his energy was combined with David's!

Something sure happened that night in an unexplainable and wonderful way. This was not a normal thing; we all felt David had Charley's extra help! This place had been my son in law's first home with my daughter and he loved it! I am sure he was attending the celebration in this way. My son later said, "That's what had happened; he was given strength and energy in that way." It takes a great amount of energy to run like he did that night. From that night on he ate better, and ran with a new energy like anyone.

Charley loved July 4th it was a special and favorite night he enjoyed so much. He had loved setting off the fireworks on these gatherings. This was how he was again able to enjoy this!

Bicycling

Soon another test came for him. I love bike riding and so did David. He felt so good he wanted to try his old skills on a bicycle. He would be able to ride with my daughter and I like old times. The first time he rode his bike leading the way; it had been years since he had done this! His energy had somehow been restored in a wonderful Divine way that night with Charley. I will never forget this and no one else who was there will ever forget this either. I recall how we all cheered him on and I could see "the little boy" in him was having such a good time.

Yes, the Angel nurse had told us it would happen more, for he shall be well, was now in force! I thought to myself, his doctor won't believe this one! By this time his doctor loved hearing about all the things he could do once more! Things were really looking up!

A Somber Reality

Then, on one peculiar day David became very serious with a deep sadness and with great difficulty, he told me of his terminal illness. He was on the sofa and asked me to come and sit down beside of him; he struggled awhile to tell me what had happened to him. That he would die one day, and why he had kept it hidden for so long. I hugged him and we cried together holding one another tightly. I could only think of how brave and strong he was because he did not want us to be sad in any way. What a burden he had carried for so long by himself! What a relief that he wanted to confide in me at last so I finally understood. I know by him telling me it helped to lift a heavy weight off of his shoulders and mine. He only thought of others, never himself. We were not only mother and son, but the best of friends. We were a team in this world with a unique and unheard of unbroken bond.

Finally, the excuses he had for every illness had just been explained to me. How did he manage this long? His inner strength and spirit was so strong. I was devastated, knowing when he told us as a small child he would die young; it was probably not too long away now. How have you carried this weight so long, I thought? Now we could share whatever he wanted together. He had protected us as long as possible. I always hoped what he said as a child would change in some remarkable way for him.

Those nights I silently cried my heart out and held onto my promise not to tell the rest of the family yet, to save them from the worry they would go through. He explained he would tell them later on. Through the years I had to cover for him with family questions about his health and each time he was in the hospital which was often. I had tons of stress to carry, but for him I would have carried the world if needed!

He always knew I was his loyal supporter and I had made him a promise. He knew I would never tell any of the others until he did. That was the very least I could do for him. I prayed for him to be here as long as possible and I would not put any extra stress on him. I wanted to tell my daughters so much, so they could give him the extra support he could use. I never lied to them about what the doctors did for him. And somehow, even with all the questions from the family it all worked out. Looking back, I wonder how we did it with so many things that happened through the years. How did he manage it, is the unbelievable thing! What courage it must have taken.

I watched his total faith knowing that miracles had happened to him time after time. I never thought he would run out of them. I knew his work with others on earth would take time and I prayed for the extra time for him and for our family to be together. There would soon come a time when the whole family would know about the fight for his life. My son was like a brave Warrior trying to protect us and we had Indian in our blood from my mother's side which I could see in him.

Being believers, David and I discussed the Bible often, which clearly states there will be miracles. This we certainly had seen many times over and believed were 100% true. Someday I wanted others to know what he had experienced to give them hope, to keep on fighting, and never give up! There are many other people on this earth that have had all kinds of experiences, they are everywhere. So please keep your hope, faith and the belief in your life and never give up even at the end because there is no END! We go on and on evolving we are energy and energy never dies. Every moment of one's' life has meaning.

For our part in this we were doing what we were sent here for. My son and I knew there is only one Supreme Being, our Creator, who is an Absolute Infinite Intelligence over all Universes and Worlds. This is an unseen force that created everything there is. There are many different names that are used to describe this force, God, Buddha, Tunkashila (American Indian) and many others depending on culture. We are all working to get to the same place in the end, just in many different ways.

My son had his good days and bad days, took his chemo and medicines, but never laid in bed waiting in all the years to come. He said, "He wouldn't waste time; he wanted to be up doing everything he could, no lying in bed for him." He knew how to make each moment of life count and it wasn't going to be by complaining. Someone asked him once why he never complained, he said "complaining never changes anything. It's a waste of time."

At night he rested in a recliner so he could breathe better by sitting upright. He slept very little; if he laid down flat he would be very sick at his stomach all night. He slept perhaps two to three hours then would get up for the day which was usually around 3 AM and would usually go out into the yard. There he tended to his plants and made sure his house was secure. He sometimes couldn't get his breath inside and needed the cooler air to breathe better. But with all of his health problems he wanted to stay motivated and healthy for as long as possible.

Some days were full of unexpected surprises for the both of us. I would call those hurdles, along with the manmade rules that you would never imagine, making it harder to try to stay healthy and alive to enjoy what life one has left. Some of these rules can make a person's life even more difficult for those people who are sick.

David wanted to stay as healthy and strong as he could considering all he had to face. By wanting to do this he was upbeat about this idea. I took him to a nearby recreation center facility to sign up, and dropped him off for a few minutes. When I came back to pick him up, he had a look of being deeply defeated. He told me he would not be allowed to use the facility because of his hat! I was as shocked, as he was hurt! All he wanted to accomplish was to work out and walk to keep his strength up, but he was turned away! I was absolutely shattered when he told me this. He said, "It was because he wanted to keep his Cardinal's Ball cap on." I asked. "What were they thinking to turn someone down because they wore a baseball cap?"

It was because of gangs who wore their different colors and hats to express who they were to other gangs. I tried to get the people at the center to understand why some people feel the need to wear a hat. Some lost their hair with treatments and others were cold. Chemo burns a person from the inside out which made his head cold. They needed exercise the same as anyone. Sadly, my talking did no good. If these rules were made to keep the good people out, they worked.

First it was the church woman I mentioned earlier, and then the recreation center. He certainly didn't look like any member of a gang in simple Levis, fitted properly with a simple shirt. He was clean cut with short hair and manners. There really needed to be a way to fix this problem so sick people could have this kind of enjoyment in their lives and a safe place to exercise helps to keep moral up. Rules can be easily changed for certain exceptions such as those who are sick. I wonder if the people who make the rules haven't had to watch a loved one go down in health so they have no clue how important this can be.

Something so simple can help make a sick person want to stay in the best of health they can. This is such a small thing, but very meaningful to those who are ill. I will never forget how sad he looked by being refused. He looked completely broken and defeated. I noticed he lost his up-beat attitude for a while.

I later sent a letter to the office which never replied back. After that he seemed to weaken some for a while. There is an easy way to fix this problem. Have the sick person wear a simple sticker on their shirt with a medical emblem on it or on their hat. Their names can be kept in a book and check it off when they come in to work out. And here is one of the simplest ways of all bring a doctors slip with them each time they come in! Don't keep them from having this small amount of enjoyment in their short lives.

During the next couple of years he was getting stronger again and we had the best heart-warming talks and laughter ever. He was so funny we laughed so hard until the tears rolled down our faces. My son always said, "I was his eyes and he was my ears." That was true. His sight was leaving and I had a slight hearing loss from an old job. We were even a team in this way too.

But no matter to us was he made life fantastic and was alive! To see him walk, eat, and still hold his food down I was overjoyed! He looked like his old self again from long ago. No wonder every one of us was so happy with lots of laughter in the house. In the early years of his illness his bed was on the sofa so he didn't have the stairs to contend with so much, but things had been different for a long time now.

Before I knew it, his childhood name of Flash had returned! He could be at the top of the stairs in record time just like he did as a child going up to his old room! These are ordinary things that most people do not think about if one has been healthy, but this meant everything to us. I know there are others who are grateful and have watched a loved lose their normal abilities in life. We are a circle of people having this connection along with compassion in common. This helps hold us together with love and understanding in this world of ours.

David never hurt anyone in his life. He was gentle, loved flowers and gardening, and enjoyed his photography. He had a wonderful talent to create and build things. I always said, "He could take something a person threw out as junk and make something beautiful out of it." He enjoyed decorating his home and landscaped our yards which kept him busy when he felt up to it, and even when he didn't feel well. He had to go slowly and worked hard at anything he did.

I will never forget the day he could move into his own home, he was so thrilled to see his dream finally come true! He had made it happen and his dreams had kept him going. I was sad to see him move, even though it was only a few blocks away from me. I would still be at his side but I would have to let go a little, just a little now, and let him enjoy his own home. We were still together each day and evening, in our work, and with my care for him.

Chapter 11

Living In a Broken Body
St. Odilia Heals His Eyes

David Carries on in a Broken Body

I was now on another level of my future and processing my thoughts back to the day of my son's appointment with a new Specialist he had never seen before. My son and I were in the waiting room when his new doctor came in. He looked very surprised to see my son who he had never met. "I came in here expecting to see a young man looking like an old man, and here is this young guy with the biggest smile looking so young and healthy!" The specialist was quite shocked to see how good my son looked and yet was so terminally ill at the same time. David gave him his biggest grin liking this doctor immediately.

After his tests we found out David was in more trouble with his Adrenal glands than we knew. This had been a growing and serious problem for years and now with all his other problems combined. His skeletal bones were much worse now than we knew. They had long lost the inside hard filler they needed. His bones were very thin, soft, and breaking more often. He again didn't want me to come inside with him so I never asked. I respected his wish. Maybe I was too afraid to hear the truth by now because I know he was going down faster now. I was so relieved to see him each and every time. Time was getting shorter and I pretended to be as upbeat as usual.

I was overjoyed to see him come out of the office smiling so big. Each time he was gone even a short time it scared me more. Now suddenly he was coming towards me to go home. He was my son who was still with me and was loved so much! He knew he was getting closer and he walked so straight to me as if nothing was wrong and he kept smiling at me. His posture was always perfect in how he carried himself and no matter what he went through he never slumped over.

I found out what the doctor said by asking questions. David shook the doctor's hand and flashed him another big grin. The doctor said, "David had enough steroids in his body for 10 men, which upset me and the doctor greatly!" He had been on steroids a very long time to help control his

Adrenal Glands. He had been in a catch 22; the steroid medicine had been increased too much over time to keep him going. If it were stopped he would die. He couldn't go on with all that was in his body now. The doctor quickly told him how to start slowing down on the medication, a little at a time to a much lower level, because of his immediate danger to the amount in him. David had way too much in his system!

At this same time it was soon discovered that my son had three more cancer places on his back that were later removed by another doctor. When David came out of his office he seemed just fine, no dreary or sad look, and in his usual way of "everything will be all right mom, don't worry."

He was a Master of disguise at trying to make things sound better than they were. Later I thought of how strong he must think he needed to be again and again all through his life. As long as I could see him smiling and seemingly normal I tried only to think positive. He had the spiritual healers helping him with energy.

I knew his healing could develop in two different ways: to keep him going longer, or to help him come home to his Heaven. There would be only two ways to heal him. A parent often stands by helplessly by watching a loved one slowly die with the feeling of being unable to do anything just tearing you apart! He was much further along now in his journey. I knew in my heart his body could not take much more. All of his "miracles" were nearly over.

He was tired, and I could see this in his soul. Even the trips were becoming harder on him now. He tried to hide this but I was completely in tune with him, being the other half of our creation as one soul in the beginning. I could only forget for a short while by putting his condition out of my mind when I could sleep. Even if it was only for a few moments waking it was too unbearable! Just a few weeks later my sweet, wonderful, strong son, David, would be dead!

The Passing Years

During his critical times in the hospital my son had difficulty talking and only a whisper could be heard from him. He was so tired and weak using all of his strength to go on. The nurses just loved him, and they said it was so unusual to have a patient so sick with such good humor and he made their day. Even a few of the nurses, at times, would come into his room late at night and tell him of their troubles. Somehow they were drawn to him and seemed to know it was safe to tell their problems to him. He respected them and kept their private life private.

Some of the nurses were so glad to see David and in his passing by them they would call out to him as we went on and off the various floors of the hospital over the years. Hi David, Hi David! They were good friends to us without him knowing most of their names. We appreciated all of them so much. Those friendships make a world of difference when someone is in the hospital and needs caring and compassionate people around them.

Among other things he continued to do was to still bring treats to his doctors and nurses from time to time. His doctors and the nurses enjoyed the treats he brought around the holidays. Sometimes on his regular appointments he would have a platter of cookies, candy, anything sweet for them. It was so funny when I heard one of his doctors ask my son, "What have you got in there (his back pack) today?" As if waiting to check out the supply of goodies. The doctor said, "Come on back into the hall he needed something to eat, he hadn't eaten all day, they had been so busy!" I could hear a lot of laughing coming from them in the hall! I was totally happy to know the great bond they had over the years, that is so important. His one doctor even gave him some kind of special ordered tomato plants one time when they were both planting a garden. David was so happy with his plants we went home and he planted them right away. How wonderful his doctors were to him, and David thought the world of them.

David and his doctor had much in common. One doctor was trying to save the small amount of eye sight that David had left and we saw this doctor often because he did many surgeries and laser surgeries over time on his eyes. He had such a caring attitude for my son and they had built a great respect for one another. They laughed and enjoyed the appointment time together. I believe they empowered one another with their great attitudes.

David and I spent most of our time over many years in the hospitals. Despite their lists of tests, blood transfusions, chemo, surgeries, seeing all kind of doctors and nurses, David always made it a good and positive experience. But I could see the tiredness in his eyes, though he tried to hide it from me.

I was still hearing the words from the other side for he shall be well, and I know David always knew how things were going to go with him. I did Reiki spiritual energy healing on him at home and every trip as he lay in his hospital bed. He loved it and was always so relaxed. It put him to sleep and out of pain, then he finally rested and would get better.

Saint Odilia

A Heavenly surprise was waiting for my son and I one day at home in the most unusual way of delivery. I found a small card out in the middle of the carpet with the picture of Saint Odilia on the front side of it! I had no idea who or what the Saint represented, or where her card had come from, but there it was lying out in the open! After I read the card I knew it was put here for a certain reason for my son. I was very excited knowing this was special for him to know without a doubt to continue on keeping his courage! This sign from Saint Odilia gave great hope for him appearing in this way. By finding this Heavenly card (special delivery) we both knew it was put there, and delivered by Saint Odilia! She is known as the Saint for vision, blindness, and healing of the eyes!

I read the prayer out loud and knew without a doubt this was "given" to us both for a good reason. How else could this unfamiliar prayer card appear in my home? We had not had company, nor had we ever seen this card anywhere ever before. This Saint was letting us know she was here to help him all she could! We had noticed the card looked old and we had no other clue as to how the card was placed here except by our Heavenly source. This was the positive help we needed at this time with his eyes.

David and I became so excited we memorized the prayer immediately! We agreed we were to pray every day for his sight to get better with this prayer to her. We both stayed faithful each day and night for this gift she had brought to us. We would forever be grateful for her help. Here is her prayer. Perhaps it will benefit you as it did David and myself.

PRAYER TO ST. ODILIA

O God, who in your kindness did give us St. Odilia, Virgin and Martyr, as the Protectress of the

Order of the Holy Cross and the Patroness of the eyes and the afflicted, grant us we humbly

Beseech you to protect through her intercession, from the darkness of ignorance and sin and to

be cured from the blindness of the eyes and other bodily infirmities. Through him who it the

Light and Life of the World. Jesus Christ Our Lord.

The Story of David

The Miracle of Sight

Now, I want to share the most beautiful story, which happened after this card was mysteriously brought to us. David experienced a miracle with his eye that occurred before a scheduled surgery. When I say miracle those of us knew it was, but his such as this, were never declared as "miracles" by a church. We never told a church of these things over all of the years they happened. They could not be explained by doctors or anyone else. They knew something greater than they could ever understand had happened to him with the many years he lived and the unexplained healings he had. The NDE's and the DOA's he had survived through were against all odds! How else could he still be here after dying several times? I was told more than once by his doctor they planned to see he was put in the Medical books for others to learn from.

I knew this was a big part of why he was here; this would be such an honor to help others to never give up! The Universe continues to have mysterious plans for all of us which we can't begin to understand or imagine, working in our behalf that we don't have a clue of.

Both of us had been learning hypnosis in a nearby college and the date to have his eye surgery was near. His eyes were not very good at all by now and were worsening. They were not expected to ever get better. Our hypnosis teacher, Mr. B., put my son into a trance a few nights before his surgery was to be done. The suggestion to him was that his eye would be healed. David was as deep as one can go; he was easy to be put under hypnosis.

Each night we continued to say our prayer to Saint Odilia. We arrived early and reported for surgery on the following day. His Doctor was prepared to do laser surgery but after checking my son's eye he told us he didn't know how to explain what had happened to it! The thick covering he was going to remove had disappeared! It was gone! Needless to say, his doctor was very happy but at the same time baffled and at a loss, he could not explain what happened! Other Doctors were called in to look at his eye. One came out in tears saying to the nurse, Mr. Friend can see! He had seen David only a few days before to set up his surgery and make the arrangements. Now this was right before the Saint's card appeared in my home and the hypnosis with Mr. B.! This was another miracle! All we could think in our happiness was, Thank-you Saint Odilia! We both continued to pray to her each night giving our thanks, and we couldn't get the enormous smiles off of our faces!

During the next class, David told our hypnosis teacher about finding the Saint's card and what had happened and he was stunned! For a long time Mr. B. told about David's miracles to other students, and he may still be telling his story. I am not saying hypnosis will heal people in this way, but I believe between our strong faith, hypnosis, Saint Odilia, along with our prayers, that is what happened to my son. This was another true healing for all of us to experience happening to my son and granted to him by our Creator.

David and I carry no specific title of religion if we are protestant or whatever, but our hearts are completely merged with our Universal Creator. We never forgot when we were told by the Christ that labels do not matter, it's all about love! The titles cannot get one into heaven it is the love we give out to others. After my son crossed over I saw he still kept the Saint Odilia prayer card right beside his bed on the night stand. I knew he still prayed to her every night as I did. I have continued to pray to her and Mother Mary for all they have done to help us.

Past Life Regression

Back to our hypnosis class with Mr. B, our teacher. David was a good student and would go into a deep trance easily. One evening he was put into a past life regression, something we were all working on in class. The first thing he was asked by our teacher was, "Where are you?" He answered, "In the dessert." "What do you have on?" "I have on a brown colored robe with some kind of sandals on my feet." "What are you doing there?" "Herding my sheep." Mr. B said, "Ok, let us move further into your later years there. "What are you doing now?" David replied, "I am in the water." What are you doing there?" Mr. B asked. David responded, "I am baptizing people". "Do you know your name?" "Yes, it is John." Our teacher paused and looked confused, or I should describe shocked! He is a very religious man. There was a hush over the class and Mr. B. brought him out of the trance.

A professional such as Mr. B. with over 40 something years can tell if a person is not in a trance easily. A good hypnotist will see the sign if a person tries to fake it. You can't fake this and not show it. Mr. B. had a wonderful open mind, was intelligent, and is a good man; he saw inside of my son's soul and knew him to be a good and spiritual young man. He was amazed at what he had just experienced!

David's gift was so strong he would teach me many things each day, just by his everyday actions. I watched his strength and the spiritual teacher he was. We both grew more and closer to our Creator and our phenomenal connection to the spiritual world. When I began to use my teachings more he would begin to explain what was happening, as if I was confused. We also learned to completely believe without explanations from our Spiritual teachers and by using our inner strength. We needed to be strong so we could continue to help more people and our beloved family. Especially, with coming events and the daily *dark* ones we passed each day in some way. The *dark o*nes walk among us as the Angels of Light do. They are also everywhere and appearing in your life, most times without ones awareness.

I am not concerned about the people who do not understand the subjects we offered to pass along, and a few we confided in who thought we were out there. But, the seekers outnumbered the non-believers who wanted to learn all they could. Everyone is different in some way, and that is how it should be. People around us still didn't know of our other life in the other worlds but they soon would. We tried to always remember there is only one person you can control, which is yourself. Never bother to try and control others' lives with your ideas. We met others in spiritual groups who wanted to tell of their experiences. So everyone shared what they wanted to without being afraid of what anyone would say.

Fear, is something we learn from childhood. I hope that all of this will change more and more as time passes. There are others across the World who have had unexplainable experiences, dreams states, and visions. There are many strange things happening in our world that may never be explained. It is like Mythology, who some people think are only stories, but I believe without a doubt these creatures existed. I also believe many things happened similar to those stories. We are creatures who seem to want to believe something only if we have seen it. There is so much we don't begin to know and live from being taught not to believe it if you can't see it!

Things to Think About in Our World

There is a beautiful book for all ages called, *The Fairies*. It may be found in libraries and on DVD. This is a true story documented long ago that I wish everyone could read. The Fairy pictures taken and used in the book were declared authentic and verified by leading people in the world who specialize in this. It is a beautiful story which can introduce you to strange events which did happen. You will be amazed! Check it out. Nothing is impossible!

Which Leads to the Next Part of Our Story

We had been holding back for years to tell of our strange world to the public. We had been private about our strange life for a long time until I was ready to teach the college classes. I knew then we were close to being told to share our work! We would not hide it much longer. I was led into teaching at a wonderful college by my spiritual teachers as I mentioned earlier. The first clue I was given before I went to teach at the college was a sign I found in the carpet on the stair landing. A large symbol had been drawn into the carpet with four arrows clearly showing the four directions. In my beginning early on I had been told the four directions were my sign.

Soon after this our ancient Eastern spiritual healer, Han Tai Chen Su, said, "We were to go south; he would lead us to teach the Reiki Energy Healing techniques." He also assured us that Reiki would be well received by many. I knew then I had been given a gift to cherish, not to be hiding it. With this beginning, we were presently involved with the ARE, Edgar Cayce's classes, and I never dreamt I would be teaching.

It wasn't long until everything unfolded for us both in such a clever way, and we were led to a wonderful college with his guidance. At this college I had an appointment where I presented my credentials and syllabus to the administrator. This subject had never been taught there before or heard of he said. I explained what it was and how it worked. He was very receptive to the technique and art of energy healing and my classes were set up. The door had been opened just as we had been told it would be! I could now teach our beloved Reiki plus added discussions on other topics. This was something we had been given to use in a good way to help others and ourselves from our Creator. Only a fool would not want their path with blessings. So, armored up with what we had been given, we went forth on our new journey.

The night before my first class started, I had a visitor. I awoke suddenly, like I do when a spirit of some kind is waiting for me to acknowledge them. It began to form near my bed, that's when I became in complete awe! The one who came to see me had on a white suit jacket, black string tie, white/gray messy hair and mustache. I knew quickly who he was and I couldn't believe it! I won't say his name, but he was a great scientist. He told me, not to worry that he would be with me to help me, all the way through my classes. That I would do fine and the classes would be very highly accepted.

And they were. So many came I split classes and doubled up.

I loved the work of teaching and had many students who were proud to learn. There were all ages and professions with students from all over. David worked beside me showing how to apply the energy and where it would go to. I began first with the ancient history of Reiki Universal energy from the beginning of time. We supplied all the important parts of what a student needed to begin with, and worked with the hands on placements. After the 1st level they could continue to higher levels if they wanted. When each one completed a level with total understanding, which took time to use it thoroughly, the class graduated with spiritual attunements. This was all a sacred part of becoming a practitioner. All of the attunements, symbols, and information are sacred.

I taught for some time there. I loved the people and the teaching. David was at my side and many times he was asked to speak in other classes. We knew how important this was on our path. Reiki would continue on and on as the other side wanted. New energy would also begin with others called "touch" healing and so on. This is about people helping people.

Eventually, I had to leave that part of my teaching a few years later when many things changed in my life and my work was done there. I was told I had other things waiting now for David and me. Most all of the students now were using Reiki in some way. It was hard to leave the teaching behind, but I knew I would continue to teach and we would use it in all our lives, it was in our promise! Reiki was woven into our DNA, our hearts and souls forever. We came here with this as a huge part of our mission so this technique would never be lost. So when our spiritual teachers said, "it was time to go to other things now, that I would need my energy more than ever in a different way, and my body was tired." I left that part of my life.

I still miss the students and teaching at this college to this day and I will never give up Reiki. Reiki is a part of me as it was with David, a main part of our dedication in this life. David and I continued to use Reiki every day on him and others sending spiritual healing out to those who need it no matter where they were. With experience, distance makes no difference. It can be sent with certain symbols/techniques and guided methods that one must know and understand. Distance is never a barrier. Reiki can NEVER be used in negative ways. If one tries it will simply go back to the one sending it.

My son always said that is why he would get well when I applied Reiki to him and he recovered many times, with this powerful energy healing from our Creator along with his doctors. Even though some do not use the energy as a spiritual energy such as this, we always have. This is the way we were taught and recognize where it is coming from in the universe.

We work with other spiritual healers, Angels, and passed over loved ones sometimes beside of us. Jesus Christ has appeared to us at times as we send energy into a person who is very ill. This is always a very powerful session! I would be so in awe and I sometimes sank to my knees. We were happy and proud to be Reiki Masters to serve others. My son was a true healer and very aware that when our time comes we will leave here moving into a perfect spirit form. A soul has the opportunity to learning more there and continuing to advance as they choose growing to other levels.

Even though we were no longer teaching, we continually used the Reiki technique on every type of illness we came across and on whom we could. The AIDS patients desperately needed our services and we felt honored to help do everything we could for them the same as any other illness. We both worked alongside one another so the client received a double amount of Reiki energy. We sincerely and greatly appreciated the energy we could pass to these people.

We used Reiki on any walk of life, without ever holding prejudice because of color, culture, country, rich or poor, straight or gay, it never made any difference. All that we hoped for was to be able to extend their lives as long as possible, and help them out of pain and/or give them a peaceful passing. It is a disgrace how those with AIDS have been publically been treated so badly because of others' ignorance. They are human beings with much to offer society, not lepers as some are treated, even by their family. When we both met our "family" of AIDS clients we naturally hugged each one. I will never forget those who exclaimed, "They touched me!" This staggered my own mind realizing how horrible these people are so often judged and treated in our society. Their comment melted both our hearts and souls.

I once read of a church that taught to condemn people with AIDS! We realized those who do this terrible thing need to beg for forgiveness for themselves. Do they actually think Jesus would turn his back on those with AIDS? If so, they better not cast the first stone. David and I told our AIDS patients they are special human beings who are loved the same as anyone by God. They have come here to teach through their suffering of illness and death for the ignorance of the many people who judge them. It is unbelievable how cruel people can be to others and to one another.

Times never seem to change when it comes to fear and ignorance. I wonder if those have heard God's law, "Love one another." This is sometimes impossible for some to do because their heart is like concrete! But, one can be truly sorry and ask forgiveness from a pure heart and it be granted. The heart does not lie so God knows when we are sincere. We all do things in life we don't really mean too. Our human emotions tend to get us into trouble. I hope I can make up any mistakes I have made and leave with a clean chart when I go. If I haven't, I will work on those on the other side. Life is full of mistakes to learn by and we need every one of them to do this.

Our dear friend Bev told us of a man with Aids who became her friend and had no one to turn to. She heard about this young man and even his parents turned him away; their own son! He had no one but a sister who came by to see him once in a while. He lived in a small room in the city all alone and was dying. When Bev found out about him she came to see him, bringing food and clothing that she hoped he could use. She first had to get him to hold down his food a spoon at a time.

Each visit she talked with him about his importance as a human. He needed to understand he was as important as any other human on this earth. Because he had lived in a different way he was not judged, his connection to God was solid. He was afraid he was nothing and had a great fear of death.

The day came when she knew he was dying, nothing more could be done for him. Bev knew he would pass over soon and she had come to be with him. He was shivering, cold, and afraid. She lovingly climbed into his bed putting her arms around his thin body to hold him to keep him warm, continuing to tell him how much he is loved by God. She said the precious words he needed to hear. Bev was a healer too, and shared her healing with others.

I cried, when she told me about her friend, this lonely and scared young man who had been abandoned by family and friends. How terrible that he had to suffer so much because of others' ignorance. I was humbled and proud of her, as my son was. If ever there were Saints she was one of them, and I truly believe in Saints. She did what Jesus Christ would do. She walked with beauty, grace, and love; I called her our little earth Angel.

One year after my son died, so did Bev. Her rare liver disease had been terminal for many years. She too, out lived her time by years because her healing work was not done until after David's. She will be remembered by many people with her love and kindness. No matter how sick she became she continued to help others. I miss her terribly and I know David and Bev are together in their heavenly world. I have seen both together at times when they come to see me.

I knew from the very beginning she was special and needed in this cruel world. I have always loved her since we met long ago; she helped me survive after my son left here. She loved him dearly and when she passed over it was another deep void and sadness in my life with my beloved friend gone too. I see her in my visions where we visit from time to time and David is sometimes with her, that's a big bonus! She is always happy and laughing as she was on earth. We three were the same in our work; we each understood our path together, we laughed and giggled at times like kids. Now, I was the one left behind and had work to accomplish here.

One particular time she told me before David ever left here that in a vision she had in the night they were together. They had this beautiful blue mist of color all around them with silver sparkles traveling through the Universe. She explained their experience with such joy her face lit up and so did mine!

Because someone is different doesn't make them bad in any way, everyone is unique and different. We, by our choice, worked in our worlds guided by Christ and the Heavenly Beings. And, for us it is a blessing and honor. There are many people similar to us working on different levels in this world. I feel we are a network of spiritual Light workers all over the world. These people are also on their chosen agenda, and we are in this connection as Light workers, we are all a part of this intertwined together. I felt sorry that some people couldn't be more open and understanding, but as David said, "they are not ready yet, and may never be. It is not time yet for those and we are each are on a certain level and each growing in our own way."

I know each person has his or her own journey so it is best to try and not push ones belief off onto another person. It is Universal law as said; "When the pupil is ready, the teacher will come." We also remembered "Forgive them Father for they know not what they do" in judgment of others, who they do not understand. The both of us were learning as fast as we could. David and I knew we would always be well guided by whom God guides. We also knew few would ever understand our part in this world. Above all, we knew there was nothing really to fear but the fear we put on ourselves. We had opened our souls to God's light since birth, by which we could receive messages in words not audible to others, but clearly intelligent to our soul.

A human who is attuned to the universe is a rich soul who doesn't need wealth; my son was happy within and rich in spirit! Many brave souls here on earth are living in poverty that are looked down upon, who are "brave soldiers" by the other side. They are the ones who kept their hearts and souls open in the worst of times, keeping hope and love within themselves, no matter their conditions.

Chapter 12

David's Suffering and a Praying Mantis

A Compassionate Heart and His Love for Shorty

I don't know how many times I have seen such a deep love and compassion in David's eyes while taking hold of someone's hand and/or giving them a big hug letting them know he cared about them, that he understood their pain, and he cared as a friend. He didn't preach to anyone or make a person feel as if they were not living right; he empowered them as a human being. He took those who needed understanding under his wing and sometimes this is all one needs to know, is that someone cares. A person, who will patiently give their time to listen to the troubles that are bothering another person so they can get things out, can certainly make a big difference. Above all, it is so important for one to know they are being listened to and are really cared about by those who are not in judgment of them. It is so easy for people to judge and tear others down it seems.

David had dedicated his life to Christ before his birth and again as a small child, loving God his Creator with all of his heart. I could not have special ordered a sweeter and more good hearted son. Sometimes when he watched certain movies that tugged at his heart strings I would see tears roll silently down his face and he would say, "I'm being a big baby but I can't help it." I could always get him laughing and then we were both laughing together.

There is never anything to apologize about for having a big heart, that's a blessing! His sisters did the same thing with him, and they would begin laughing together in this way, making our sadness go away. His heart was so tender he felt others pain and joy to even taking on the very symptoms of those he was near to with their sickness and so on. Sometimes this happens to a healer and you have to learn how to protect yourself so you can continue to help others. He was always ready to help anyone, even when he took on their pain and sadness. Both of us did this many times but had to let it go eventually, ending up in trouble with our own health which happened every now and then. We were helping the sick and dying as much as possible most of our time working together. When we feel the symptoms of others even though we are protected by the spiritual world we must still be careful to not lose our own energy. I was very careful to not bring anything into my son's life that could pull his energy and life force down. I always tried to only work to empower him.

Each time my son was out of the hospital and at home, he was back helping those who needed clothing and giving his food to someone who had very little or none. One time around Christmas he bought a nice stove to give to a young father with two young children who had none. He would spend what he had to help people in need and he loved to help animals in need of a good home.

He managed to find heaters for an older sick lady to stay warm; along with some warm winter clothing. He managed to take her to the hospital when she became sick with cancer, something her own family who should have been helping her, didn't do. He didn't have money or cars, but his heart was in the perfect place by giving what he had. He didn't worry about money, he was rich within.

He counseled and uplifted those who needed it most, giving the gift of time to them. He would drop off needy items for those who society sometimes shuns. He never told what all he did or what he was doing, but I knew and saw the many things he did. And after he crossed over many people told me what he did for them. He was very humble and needed no praise for anything he did; he was genuine and happy to help.

Once he asked a Minister to help him with a mother and her grown son who needed more heaters to stay warm. The Minister went to the home which was in terrible shape, and would not enter nor offer to help, needless to say we were disappointed. The son was mentally handicapped and the mother had health problems and couldn't work, they lived in a terrible place. We both managed to get the heaters for them so it worked out.

The point of my story is that this reminds me of the Lepers in Bible days. I recall the Bible saying how Jesus mingled with the cast offs, that's where he did his good works, and that is how David felt about the people who were sometimes cast away from society. That's where he spent his time, even the days he felt so bad he could hardly walk. He understood how to help those who no one wanted to be near, and he did not judge them. All of his hours were filled and this took a big toll on him. He ended up in the hospital more than once because of helping others in a weakened state. I am so proud of how he lived his life. He didn't know the word No, and if he could of healed the world he would have. He showed love to everyone he met with his kindness.

One mother and son he helped long ago when he could still drive often wanted to ride in the back of the truck. They preferred to ride in the vehicle that way. I had to laugh since it looked so strange, and David smiled about it too. I kidded him that they reminded me of the Beverly Hillbillies, only joking. We all would laugh and we were their friends and they kidded us too.

I watched him as well as I could because he needed more and more rest and wasn't getting it. I could see all his life that to help others was his livelihood. My hands were tied for to take away what he was driven to was at a great cost to him. This was a big part of what he lived for. Several more times he ended up in the hospital from exhaustion and was very sick. It was all I could do to not try to stop him, and for me not to interfere, although I did my best when I saw how weary he was. It did no good; I could see he was determined in his heart and soul to keep on. I also understood he wanted this, by choosing to come here and do his work no matter the cost to him.

I personally believe it is important to let a terminal person continue their dream if at all possible; it is their Bucket list. A sick person needs a focal point to feel useful each day to the best they can. Sometimes this breaks your heart knowing how hard it is for them. In their heart and thinking they need to do what matters and counts to them.

There were some negative people who used David regardless, knowing he shouldn't be in the heat or extreme cold, which was dangerous for him. Even so, he still seemed driven to continue and be full of kindness to them. It is my opinion that sometimes a sick person survives longer by keeping focused and feeling useful than to give up and go to bed, unless they just can't be up. There is no specific way for each person since we all are different. I can only go by what I have experienced with loved ones.

Ministers of Healing

My son and I became Ministers of Healing in his life, which he and I were so proud of. We felt this was our highest honor and very proud to accomplish our dream come true. On a special day we were ordained in a special Heavenly way from the Christ, and other Beings of Light. This was an extremely important event for us in our lives which I cannot describe and that no one can ever take away. David also earned his Minister's papers thus working on his dream to have a church to help others by making it a place for abused women and children. He also wanted a shelter for those who are homeless, need food and clothing, and a roof over their head. He also envisioned a soup kitchen to help others who need a hand. This was his dream if we ever had the money to build it.

Before David crossed over and was still doing fine, I watched him as he continued to go everyday like a ball of fire. I knew he crammed all he could into each minute of every day never wasting a minute. He continued doing all he could because he knew he only had a short time. I had to bite my tongue by not telling him what he could or couldn't do, so I never did. I couldn't choose what he wanted to finish and slow him down too much. I knew he had to feel like a human being to have his own self-worth. In all, he touched some pretty hard hearts with his love and caring, especially those who had probably never felt love before. What a terrible thought to have never known love! He showed those souls he met kindness, his trust, and that they counted as much as you or I. He had come to earth to plant the seeds of goodness in others so those who were hard hearted were who he was drawn to. He never told them to take any certain road in life.

One day he hoped they would learn to do better in life. He hoped for them to travel the right road, but always with their choice. No one should tamper with another human's free will. I pray many people will remember what he taught them and I believe some will. His work was never in vain. His words may still ring in their hearts of how he cared for them if no one else did.

I am reminded now of a lady ringing the bell at Christmas time for the Salvation Army. She stood outside of a store that my son and I had been shopping in one cold night. We exchanged a Merry Christmas with her after coming out of the store and walked a few steps away. David said "just a minute, Mom" and went back to her. He put more money in her kettle and gave her the biggest hug with another big Merry Christmas! I knew this kind lady but he didn't. His hug just lifted her up out of the sadness within her. He could see this in her and with his big smile he wished her once more a Merry Christmas!

After he passed away months later I ran into her. She stopped to tell me how he touched her heart so much that night; no one had ever done what he did with his kindness and that big hug! She had tears in her eyes and said, "She would always remember him." I remembered David telling me that cold night she needed a hug because he saw that she was sad, he could see this in her soul.

Christmas time was really a scary time for me. I watched David getting on the roof to decorate for Christmas! I was a nervous wreck and had to go in the house and be quiet. He didn't have much sight left at all then, but he sure had his gift of intuition and the house never looked more beautiful with lights everywhere. I told him the house looked like the movie with Chevy Chase at Christmas time and it was close, believe me! It was times such as these I thought he would get to be here until he was old, that was my wish, I wouldn't let go of. Yes, I could tell he took pride in still being able to do things that gave happiness. I had to just let him go and do what he wanted. I am so glad I didn't take his world away from him. I knew he went by his wonderful intuition which always guided him safely and gave him great comfort.

All Creatures Great and Small

Soon it was spring time again and I had driven David to his house to putter around awhile. After I was home a short time I felt I needed to go back and see about him. He was sitting on his back steps close to his back door looking intently at something. I walked to him and asked what he was looking at. When he turned to me I could see the tears in his eyes as he explained there was a Praying Mantis on the storm door, it was dying and he couldn't save it! I knew his love for all creatures large or small, especially little butterflies, and dragon flies; they are symbols of love and goodness to us. I felt such deep compassion for him and this Heavenly created creature. I told him how sorry I was. His heart was so tender he felt into the Praying Mantis with his heart into its suffering, that's how attuned to the Universe my son was. He loved so much, and this world was a hard one for both of us as it is for many others.

The next occurrence was with one of God's creatures that summer when a friend called to ask him for help with her horse, Precious. She had raised this beautiful horse from a small colt. The horse had hurt itself going into the barn stall. Somehow, it had gotten a bad gash and other facial cuts on the stall door frame and was in shock. Suddenly the horse seemed to give up and lay down. The horse was in such a state of pain it just gave up and couldn't get up at all, she said.

David's friend asked him to come and do a healing on Precious so he did. He began working on her injured horse steadily. He knew how to talk in a soft voice and stayed with the horse for hours working on it with healing energy. Later the healing was completed by evening, and suddenly Precious raised up, stood and soon began to eat! Precious continued to make progress and was healthy once more. The owner knew as hurt as Precious was to lie down, the horse was giving up to die, so she was extremely happy now! Her horse was fine from then on. David put his healing love into her horse and the two of them healed together.

The love for animals my son had was amazing! He rescued them when they needed help. This was a mission he felt strongly. I know of times when an animal was being treated cruelly, not watered, fed or loved and he would take food and water to the animal. At first chance, he would take the animal away in the night and get it to a good home so the animal would be able to live. He always figured out how to help the helpless and abused animals. I was so proud that he did. Together at times we found several good homes for lost and abused pets to give them a new and better life with humane treatment and lots of love. A pattern seemed to be developed within these people, who had not cared about the life of their pet or any pet. They would usually replace one with another and the abuse started over again and again. A cruel owner should never have a pet in the first place, but sadly they do.

It always grieves me and I question, why do some people torture the helpless; does this give them a good feeling? Are they just crazy? Were they treated this way themselves? Do they enjoy the sadistic feeling they get? One never really knows, but they are the biggest COWARDS ever! When an adult has to pick on a helpless animal or child this shows who they really are. They will get to feel and know how cruel they were when they cross over.

I shall always remember when the Christ like Beings on the other side said, "Tell others that our pets were given to us as Gods gifts, to help us through our lives in the good and hard times. To learn to respect this gift and give animals the loving care they more than deserve!" They will give their unconditional love no matter the circumstances.

David's Heartbreak with Little Shorty Crossing Over

Then the terrible time came for Shorty, David's little Angel to return back to her heavenly home. This tore out David's heart and he was not the same after. He took this very hard she had helped to pull him through for years. The loss of her going back made him want to go more than ever I believe.

David's little companion Shorty

One of the greatest gifts he loved with all of his heart was his beloved companion his little 4 pound Yorkie dog with an attitude! I will never forget when I first met Shorty. My son was still living away and came home for one of his many visits. When I opened the door he had the biggest grin, gave me a big hug and said, "Mom I know you don't have dogs in the house but I have something to ask you." He unzipped his Air Force jacket and out popped the cutest little face I ever saw! I immediately fell head over heels in love with this tiny precious little Angel. David said, "He already had another place to keep her if I didn't want her to stay in the house." In less than a moment I knew she was a God given gift to him and to me, needless to say I wanted her to be with us for always and in the house! I loved her completely! All four pounds of cuteness!

Shorty was a blessing to us and a dream come true and made our lives full of love, laughs, and comfort. She would lie on David's chest in all of the years that he was well or down and sick. She knew when he was sick and wouldn't leave his side. I took her outside when needed, fed her quickly and then she was snuggled up again with him. I could see the deep love and connection they had. She had quite a personality, such as our pets each do, that made us laugh so much. I loved her head over heels. They understand our moods, sadness, worry, and happiness, much more than any human can. Our pets know so much and are healers themselves to us. I loved all my pets but not quite like Shorty. She was very special in her own amazing way. As time went by I found out just how special she was.

The other side came to me more than once to explain to me that, Shorty would cross over before my son when he began to have more remissions and was feeling better, then she would need to return back to the spiritual world. Just as they told me, Shorty crossed over before him, which was a very hard time for both of us. It was our saddest day and we both were not the same for a long time. We adored her and I always claimed her as mine too. Shorty's spirit was still with us after she passed over. I think she had no idea she wasn't in this world and was still with us. I would see her go up the stairs to his room and David would hear her bark at him to get his attention, then turning around he would see her! She wanted his attention just like old times. In his loss of her this affected him greatly and he couldn't mention her at all, and never did but very little again. I know so many of you know what I mean. Pets are the ultimate blessed gift and a huge part of the family. Their eyes show every concern and emotion we have. They know.

When she lived here for those years there was a certain place she took her daily naps, in David's old upstairs bedroom. Right after she passed over I walked into his old room and was shocked to see the deep outline of her in the carpet after I had just vacuumed! There was her imprint as clear as could be! She would lie in the warm sun there by the south window to take her daytime nap before my son moved into his house! I stood there a few moments taking this all in then took pictures of her imprint to always have. Don't ask me to explain this. I have seen so much the spirit world can do, and I am still always amazed! I just know Shorty was here in spirit sticking around her Master and me. She in her spirit world apparently was sleeping in the sun the day I found her imprint in his room. My opinion is that she was still definitely with us in spirit and I doubt she knew she was any different than in life here. David said, "He also felt her beside him at night on his bed and in his home." We both had contact with her and knew she came to both places which were home to her.

Right after she passed and the day came to bury her body was the saddest for him and me. I was truly worried about my son because she was with him so long. He packed her little collar; comb, brush, and toys in a small heavy rubber tub, lining it with her puppy blanket and Angel wings. She was so cute and beautiful to us and meant so much and was such a big part of David's many healings. He held her in his hands brushing her hair so gently like he did every day. I could hardly bare to watch as he spoke quietly to her with his love while brushing her. He had his back to me but I knew he was devastated! He was hurting so much for his little loving companion and asked me for some time with her alone, so I left for a long time. When I came back he had buried her under the peach tree with my old dog, Lucky, of long ago that I loved so much. I have never loved dogs like Lucky and Shorty. Both of them were more than just dogs, they were everything to us. I can still picture David holding her and tenderly talking to her with his heart broken. That was the saddest thing to see, I cried for weeks off and on when I was alone because his companion we both loved was gone. I cried for my son who never asked for anything and loved her so much.

I see her in my visions at times and I am so happy to see her in these visits. She was letting me know she will always be with us. After David crossed over I have seen them both together; my son has her with him where he is now. When he passed I saw her as she came running to greet him with all her love. Later on, David came in one of his visits holding out Shorty to me. David said, "He was "arranging and working on sending her back home to me, that I needed her in my life." I know I will see her again; I am not trying to find her or make it happen because I know it will. Shorty may be a 100 pound dog this time, I have no idea, but she will find me without any trouble and I will know it is her.

In some cases when a soul is so afraid to move forward after death, a former pet they loved or know will come to help them. This seems to work well and the soul feels they are not alone now. David and I have seen many animals that come to help their former owners they had on earth. Animals can be sent to help a new soul who never knew the animal. They are pure love and they are also healers in their own way. And, our pets do have a SOUL and this comes from the heavenly realm.

I have a story to share with you showing the magnificent souls animals have. Buck is a beautiful tan and white pit bull dog. Buck is like a big baby, sweet and gentle. About two years ago another pit bull named Luna came to live with the same family at my granddaughters. It was love at first sight for the two of them. Buck loved her and Luna loved him. There was no jealousy; they played together as if they had been raised together.

Sometime later Buck became very sick with multiple cancerous tumors in many places over his body. Luna knew he was sick, and was always licking his knots and bumps which had continued to spread. Later, it was noticed that Bucks growths were getting smaller and actually disappearing! Luna was healing him! He now weighed 91 pounds up from 73 and was back filled with new energy and a shiny new coat. Nearly all the tumors vanished except for two small ones!

The other side has proved and taught us both nothing is impossible and they on the other side can and do arrange so many things on earth for us. They also can supply us with thoughts and ideas which we think are our own helping us in our life.

I had been learning so much about sickness for many years now on people and pets and how to utilize energy. We were dedicated to doing what we could for those we did energy healing on along with our friends and family. I had also enjoyed teaching Reiki very much at the college with my son at my side. It was very successful and many people came to learn this way of spiritual energy healing. This meant my goal that Reiki would go on and on. I met all walks of life, from different countries, cultures and races. I also gave advice on things to do for an ill person that may help those depressed.

The Last Two Years

The days were going by too fast as time went on. I could sadly see my son going down more and more, but he still stayed determined in his mind to make it the best. I would tell him daily how just the sound of his voice made me feel good. He had a calming, uplifting effect on me and gave me inner strength. We were never apart for long at any given time even when he was better, most of the years we were always together 24-7. If I had to run someplace I called him and he would check on me. I was so uneasy if I was apart from him very long at all, shopping or whatever. I would always stay close to him and take the best care of him.

I tried to savor his voice for the day when I would not hear him in the same way anymore. This hurt so much to even think of. I blocked this as much as I could because I never thought he would ever really leave us. A parent will do many things in this kind of deep sadness, even to trick ourselves and block the pain we are in, by refusing to believe the truth. You live in a different world to survive, which was what was happening.

In my mind, I thought my son's miracles would continue on until he was old, but in the last two years things had worsened quickly. It was the knowing in my heart every day that he was getting closer to leaving us. I tried to savor everything about him more than ever, if that was possible. It was easy to see the tiredness in his eyes and body, but he continued to work on projects and help people.

All of us who have had a child go first handle this in a different way, and so do the children. David's way was that he never talked about his sickness except when the appointments were due and so on. This was the only way he did things and I know it was for us. Regardless, each one of us was suffering in our own way to hold onto him.

There were certain negative people who still wouldn't leave him alone. They wanted what they wanted regardless of his condition. One was almost hounding him to do this and that, and David never said no. He kept doing all he could, but some people continued to take advantage of him knowing how sick he was. His eye sight was all but gone, but they did not care, it was all about what they wanted from him. I couldn't stop him, he said, "its ok, mom," Why did he push himself so much I thought. He could not quit his contact with them because he had given his word. I was really upset inside, even though this was his choice.

He had to stay busy and continued on instead of getting his much needed rest. His sisters were very worried; they too were frightened and saddened knowing he was much worse and still doing too much. I am sure he wanted to make each minute count in some way other than in bed because he knew what was going to be his final ending. Again this was what he wanted to accomplish for himself, knowing he had to stay busy as long as he could. He felt if he stopped he would not be able to get back on his feet. We all hurt more than ever watching his struggles increase.

We kept our trust and faith which carried us through each and every time he was back in the hospital. His body and bones were in much worse shape; his bones were hollow and still breaking. His adrenal glands were worsening sending him back to the hospital with more frequent and serious trips. He was going into adrenal gland failure quite often now, which was extremely dangerous. His stomach was very swollen. He would tell me, "Mom, I look like a starving refugee" and I always replied, "No, you don't!" Then we both smiled at one another to try and lighten the moment. I worried, I knew this was a big concern about his adrenals and all the rest of what was wrong inside his body. I couldn't face this thought more than a few minutes. I knew the last stage of this disease was when the stomach enlarged. He had been this way for a long time now. That's as close to him ever complaining, which wasn't much of a complaint with all he suffered. Then he was back kidding around.

It was a comfort and yet so very sad to know how David suffered to have extra time here with us, his loved ones. The one leaving feels such guilt that they are leaving us and they are concerned about how their loved ones will do without them! They may be more than ready to go on, but have regrets about leaving us as my son did. I can't imagine what a person thinks each day when time passes so quickly, trying to make each day count, and knowing their days are numbered. I do know how I handled being a parent hurting so much inside not wanting to believe it would happen. I knew I couldn't change a thing for now, but I would always stay close to my son David and take the best care of him. And even with my denial, my son gave and taught me more strength, faith; hope, to believe, and to never give up! To always keep going forward with perseverance and humility.

I felt so helpless except in one important way, to pray and we all continued praying for him with our love. I cried and asked for his healing and prayed most of the time as any parent would. At a time like this, one reaches out more and more to our highest power. How utterly helpless I felt but safe in our spiritual world. This has only been my true place of safety. I knew when his time came Jesus Christ, my parents, the Christ like Beings and I would help him home. My loved ones and others were already waiting for him.

Every time I asked the Divine Creator, "What more can I do?" the answer was the same, "Always stay close to him," which I had always had and always would. Nothing could ever pry me away from taking being there for him. I would under no circumstance ever leave him; we always knew this! We were a team who always stayed together. I was ready to do anything I could to make his life better. He always said, "I will never leave you" and I always told him the same. This had been the bond we made in our very beginning of our creation.

Our Plan and Our Creation

I was told long ago in the night hours in an amazing experience from a beautiful Christ Being of pure Light the most wonderful story of how David and I were created as one soul and we had made a Covenant for eternity. I was directly told, "You see, in the very beginning you both were created as one soul then later divided into two souls. From the beginning of our existence we would always do our spiritual work together through our lifetimes! We were a part of one another for eternity and would always be together with our promise and the Covenant we made.

I don't know how else to explain this other than how I have been told, and this is our truth and I knew it was. The other side has a way of orchestrating circumstances in the correct manner. In other words, this time I was born first as the mother, later my two daughters, my son, and another daughter came into this world to become my children by their own choice. We had all made this plan together, even though David and I would be the only ones to remember this. I somehow knew this was what happened in the very beginning of this life time. My memory was allowed to surface more after the car accident in which I died. Later, as I went ahead in my life, I remembered our Covenant little by little. The Creator and Council confirmed what we both knew when it was time for me.

I know the other side and this one are mingled closely together. Both dimensions are simultaneously combined, we were told this by the Heavenly Beings and we traveled in and out of these dimensions often. When one gets a glimpse into the other side, you see the Spiritual dimension into the other world, if your vibrations are high and fast enough. In life here on earth, the vibrations are too slow for most to see into the other worlds and places to experience this.

Try to remember, we don't have to know all the answers of the how and why, it's not for us to know now. One day we will know and understand many things our human mind questions and thinks about. I doubt it will seem very important any longer then, we will be past our lives as a human. By our soul being set free we will be happy to leave this darkened world which is cruel, and filled full of hard lessons. Yet, we will feel blessed to have seen and been with loved ones again along with all the beauty that was created for us here on earth.

Shared Experiences

David, his sister's and I will always stay together with our blessed bond. Our family has stayed together in a different order in other lives and through our evolving again and again together. Entire families stay together in all kinds of orders. We tend to stay in groups each time but some return in a different order. It is all by choice. Some never return back to earth and go someplace else in the vast Universal world.

To understand this more I suggest you read good positive book's written by well-known authors on reincarnation and dimensions. Hopefully, this will make sense to you who are not familiar with my terms on this subject. Excellent books to read are written by Doctor Brian Weiss MD, Arthur Ford, Edgar Cayce, and Ruth Montgomery for starters. There are many positive books to learn from. I have always been drawn to certain books.

One particular book I have read about Chuck Norris turned out to be quite amazing. Each week my friend and I did Tai Chi at a church in the basement. I called my friend on meeting night asking if she wanted to read his book. We both were into Martial Arts which teach the art of energy and mind control and we have a strong connection to it. She asked me to bring the book to the meeting that evening. I laid the book by the door so I would not forget it, but when David and I were ready to leave, the book was gone! We knew for sure it had been there and looked everywhere to no avail. We both felt it would be some place near our friend at the church for some reason.

We arrived first waiting in the car since we had no key to get in. Soon our friend J. arrived and opened the door for us. I told her, "I was bringing the book for you to read and it disappeared!" She looked stunned at first, and then David said, "We feel it's here in the church or close by outside." We three began to look around in the church downstairs. David's guide then told him it was close by the church outside. His spiritual guide led him along with the two of us following outside and to our friend's car, which she had locked. David said, "It's in your car unlock the door it's in the front floor." My word! She exclaimed, but got her key and unlocked the car. She reached down to the floor, and under a towel there was the book! She had locked her car as soon as she arrived, and had been with us every moment in the church.

After she calmed down we did our Tai Chi, then she took the book home to read. There was a reason for this and in reading the book she found out her brother had worked at the same place years ago in Oklahoma where Chuck Norris worked when he was young! There was a link there for her. David and I felt we had some kind of a deep connection to Chuck Norris through our work.

I had encountered Chuck Norris many times in my astral travel experiences which I can't explain. We seem to share universal information with one another. I often thought did he remember any of this or who we may have been in relation to one another? We know him to certainly be a very good spiritual person. These are our own personal thoughts and feelings, and with what took place with his book and at the church with our friend.

Our Close Friend Deenie

And then, there was Deenie, our dear friend, who had been a school teacher and was now retired. We were all close friends! She had become very sick and was now dying in a large hospital in St. Louis, Mo. David and I went to see her because we knew her time was short. The spirit world had let us know it was time for us to go to her.

On the way David went into a shop to get her some flowers. It was a very cold and dreary day. Soon he came out with a BUCKET size container full of beautiful spring flowers in all colors. We would bring spring to her one last time; she would be gone in a day. Intuitively we knew she was waiting for us to come, and then she would release and go home to her Heaven.

When we arrived her husband was in the hall with tears running down his face and with a hug we greeted one another. He said, "She was in a coma and asleep with no response." As soon as David and I stepped inside the room her eyes flew open, and she had the biggest smile across her face! We each sat down on a side of her bed hugging her and telling her we loved her, we were so happy to see her! The flowers he showed her, with all of the beautiful colors, reminded her of spring. She loved them and her spirit lifted. It seemed that all too soon it was sadly time to go; she had smiled and stayed awake the whole time for us. We each had our own words to say to her. With a kiss on her cheek and big hug I said, "I will see you soon, Deenie, I love you," and smiled at her. She said, "Yes I know" and we hugged one last time. My son had his own loving personal words for her too with a big hug. She told us she had waited for us to come and she would see us soon and then she gave us another smile. This is how we would always remember our dear friend. We all knew what we meant, that we would meet again in Heaven. It was hard to walk out the door knowing this was all of our earth life together as best friends.

That evening she crossed over, and our dear beloved friend is close by us, she was a special being of goodness all her life. We were honored to know her and to meet one another again in this life. I have missed her here very much. At times I can mentally and spiritually picture David and Deenie when they greeted one another after he passed over, in their joy with the biggest smiles being so happy to see one another, and with those great big hugs we all shared together!

David and I being created the way we were and thinking with the same mind, and living in our unique way, made our beloved work such a joy. This story explains why we thought alike and combined our spiritual work and our lives. I have no doubt David always had his total memory from his first existence of being the other half and that's why he once said to me, "Mom we know who we are don't we?" "Yes, yes we do!"

We had one another to share our experiences with together, and with my son's help and answers to my many questions of the other worlds. I thank God we planned our lives together or I would have felt lost by not being able to share our experiences. And who would believe them? It was hard for me to believe our experiences as I experienced them myself!

One thing I am especially grateful for is that I did not know my son would have to suffer most all of his life. This was a kindness in not knowing for some time of what was to come in the future. Not knowing some things is actually a gift.

It wasn't long again, that I begged and pleaded as I prayed to let me go first instead of him. I wanted so much to take his place. He was getting in very bad shape then. His sister was thinking the same thing she told me later. Suddenly, one evening after I prayed and asked to trade, a Heavenly Being of Light spoke to me. This Being of Light knew how distressed I was. In complete gentleness and love the understanding voice said, "There are no trades for thy son, do not ask again as each one has their own journey that cannot be changed." Sadly, I knew not to ask again, there would be no trades. There would never be a trade.

I would have given my life so eagerly to go first instead of David, he was a young man who had so much to give and teach others. I was devastated that I could not help in this way, but I also understood the best I could. I had to try and not to ask again. Could I keep my word? I knew I would try again. My heart hurt so much I was deeply wounded over what else could I do for my son? I would always be by his side, but this wasn't enough for me to give much peace to my heart. The eye of my heart could see the journey coming to the end of our lives here together. I would have to wait and let my son go on one day. This was how it had been written in the other world with our choices. We couldn't go back and change any part of it.

Chapter 13

Mother Mary, the Miracle Healing

She Lift's Our Hearts

One evening after I had soon gone to bed I could not get to sleep I was worried about my son and was tossing and turning. I suddenly felt a very strong presence in the room close by me. I gazed over to where I knew this presence would be to see the most beautiful amazing sight! It took me a moment, not believing my eyes to realize who my visitor was! I still couldn't believe what my eyes were fixed upon! It was MOTHER MARY, the most phenomenal being you could ever dream of!

She was in beautiful soft blue with glowing white all around her. I realized she had come to help me and she began to speak to me in her loving voice. She began by saying, "I come to you as a mother to a mother." I can't tell you all of her message, but she spoke of how she understood the pain for my son as he suffered as her son, Jesus, did when he suffered on the cross. She understood the pain of all of this, and she came to give me strength to get me through this critical time in my life as a mother, and that she would always be with me.

There were many more words in her message that she said, but they are personal and I cannot reveal them. This was the greatest thing happening at that point in my life! I needed her so much and she gave me the extra strength I needed. I have been in complete awe ever since when I think of that night. I have thought of these moments so many times knowing Mother Mary also came to give me her blessing. She knew my struggle and heard my prayers. This was the third time in these years of my son's illness she had come to help me.

I am not Catholic, but as the Christ Light Beings have said, "It is not about the label one wears, it is all about the love in one's heart." I have believed in her throughout my life.

Mother Mary was full of love for my son and me. She saw no difference in what religion we were or not. Those things, our labels, do not matter to our Creator. Her message was about the love in one's heart is what counts. This was a revelation and her love poured forth to me. She was a brilliant light of glorious love. I was completely ecstatic and yet humbled. She stays in my mind daily that we are in her care. I know she watches over us and has helped me since my beginning. I believe Mother Mary is with all of those who need her and that she hears our prayers to her.

I found out long ago that all the religious labels in the world, Protestant, Catholic, Jewish, on and on, don't really matter in the end. It all boils down to the love you give out to others and living the best one can. The labels we carry are not what gets us to our Heaven, and this information comes from the other side. It is how you live your life, what you learn, and love is the main key to it all. We are like babies in this world wandering, falling down and getting back up, looking for answers and hopefully learning.

Healed Completely

In another experience from the other side, I was told that in 2007 David would be healed completely! I was absolutely thrilled with this message; my son had had so many miracles over many years I thought this time he would receive a huge Spiritual final healing! I prayed this meant that he would get to live longer and have more time to be with us for many years to come! But something felt wrong; my intuition was not feeling good and positive about this new miracle I had in my mind. In my heart I knew something was off, and pushed back the fact that the message could be a two-way message. Meaning, he may be going home in 2007 into his perfect spirit body. No! I wasn't going to think that I told myself! He would have the most amazing healing he ever had, one more time to live on into old age! But underneath, I knew what it might also mean, that he could slip into the other side! No! I would not dare to think the message meant anything else, except that he would be healed!

I continually had this enormous battle going on inside myself. I knew in my soul this message may mean it could be for the final part of our lives here together. With my intuition and the messages from our Higher Beings of Light, I knew they were always correct and may be preparing me.

David and I continued more to talk of our bond often, saying to one another, I don't know what I would do without you. We had so much to do yet. I felt we would continue on, and I thought that perhaps we both would leave here close to the same time that's because I CHOSE to believe he would be healed into old age. He never went that far, he didn't commit. He only let on that, "It would be awhile yet." I know now he knew much more but would never have told me. He knew the promise he made long ago of when he would need to return home. There would be some time yet, but never what I thought it would be before he crossed over. The Divine ones would return to me soon with the rest of their messages. There would be more about his healing and I would later understand why I wasn't given the entire information now. I knew to always take what the other side gave us without questions; I will know the rest when the time is right.

Hollow Bones

I knew my son's body was worn out and tired now. His bone structure continued to become much weaker. The last few years David's bones had become extremely thin, breaking and collapsing from his illness. This didn't slow him down much and he still did so many things every day. He sneezed one day and broke three ribs they were so brittle. He turned over in bed and soon broke another rib, but this did not stop him, he would soon be doing some kind of work around the house and sometimes on the same day. His pain tolerance was high as was his attitude and mind control to continue on.

Needless to say we were going to the doctor to have bone test scans and other testing often. I had more knowledge now of how serious this was; we had to find something to help him! Soon I took him to a foot doctor at a special clinic we were referred too hoping he could do something for him. At home I worked on his feet every day and feelings ran through me of how his bones were getting much worse. They never felt normal unless he had several bags of fluid put into him at the hospital that he needed which was short lived, the fluids filled him out but not for long.

My son's feet had been paper thin for ages and he began having break after break. He was wearing a support boot now. He never let me come in to see his doctor or his x-rays and I knew why. This last time we went his feet had several breaks, eight in one, and three in the other! The doctor that day asked me to come in to show me the x-rays of his feet. The doctor exclaimed to David, "You should be in excruciating pain! How can you walk on your feet like that? One fracture would be extremely painful!" No doctor ever understood how he did what he could do, and still keep his humor. I hid my shock; one foot was almost broken off from his ankle! At home he was on his feet all of the time without a limp or showing any pain. He did not take pain pills, he wouldn't, and he never did saying he didn't want to lay around not knowing what was going on. I was sick at my stomach for what he was enduring and I couldn't help him. David stayed very quiet as his doctor talked to me about a steel plate he was ordering to insert into special shoes for him to hold his foot together in the shoes. His instep on both feet had also slid over to the sides of his feet! My heart crumbled into pieces! I knew he couldn't keep going much longer like this yet he didn't show his emotion.

All of his bones were now seriously giving away. We didn't talk about this on the way home except about the brace and shoes he would be getting. We both felt a loss for words, he knew then I knew the whole situation. I finally had to face things. I had just witnessed my son's broken feet along with his entire body that day. He had a hard time, especially in his last year when he needed to wear a big boot cast on his foot and his leg both.

One day a man he knew came up to him in a restaurant asking, "What in the world happened to you?" David said, "He had some breaks." "Well, how did you get them, what happened?" David grinned so big and replied, "I've been blessed!" The man was so surprised at his answer it threw him off and stunned him at the same time! Then they both laughed, we all laughed, and the man left shaking his head. I think the man expected a big long story as to what happened to him, but that would never happen with David. He let it be a blessing in his way of accepting whatever came his way.

I knew my son was almost blind now and with his bones collapsing, the after effects on his body of medications and chemo, his body was shutting down, he was struggling! But nothing could shake his wonderful spirit which was as strong as ever! I know he had to have hidden so much and worried about all of us. He always felt so responsible for all of us. He was suffering quietly, and to me he was still my little boy; and he would always be my little boy who never hurt anyone.

I hurt from holding so much pain inside it was unbearable, and my girls' hearts were the same hurting for their brother. We were afraid and helpless; his sisters knew their brother was long worn out not wanting to give in. He wasn't ready to leave us no matter what. We had one another to stay strong, and his sisters were very brave. We loved every second when we could be all together. You wish you could take time and tuck it away like putting things in a safe to save it, but it passes too quickly and it's gone. No one is ever ready to give their loved one up! We made the days happier all we could for all of us to share each moment together even though everything was coming apart at the seams now.

Around this same time a lady who teaches the blind began training David for his blindness. I will never forget when I first saw him walking with his new white cane. I was stunned because it meant it was the time for that to happen. This made me realize more that my son was nearly completely blind now. His sight would never return and his life span was extremely narrowed down, but never his spirit! Just so he remained longer, we could handle the blindness as others do. He was more than willing to learn what he needed, to help care for himself and keep his independence I knew we could do this together and I would be with him all the way. Still again, he never complained and complimented the lady who was training him. All of what was happening now no one could stop, but our heavenly Creator. I had to wait now until I received more information from the other side. I prayed and prayed to God all through the nights about what could I do more in order to help him. Always stay close by to him, was my answer each time.

Before he was sick he had more than excellent eyesight, and the most he missed in these last several years was reading and driving the old truck. His independence was completely past gone now but he still fought for it. By just looking at his bright blue eyes, they looked great, and were still so beautiful, a crystal blue. I wished so much he could have my eyes. Then my mind would jump to the fact that even if I could, this would not help him long because his body was tired. But I would easily do it for him for any length of time so he could see once more before he left. I wanted to give him my life.

The Promised Healing

It was Christmas now nearly the end of 2007 and I pondered over a major question that I talked to my son about. I wonder what is happening, the other side said you are to be healed in 2007 and it is almost the end of December? He seemed to take this okay, but in my mind the feeling I got frightened me. He didn't respond too much about it. I could tell he was thinking on how to answer my question. Did he know anything, or was he trying to figure out an answer back without saying too much? I don't know what he thought for sure, he could block me at times from his thoughts and I only wanted to believe my own thoughts – he would be healed completely. It was what he told me later, that I have thought back on so many times. I knew the other side was always in absolute truth to us so I tried to make myself think that the timing was somehow off for his healing. After all, it wasn't the end of this year yet, it was still December, and he reminded me of this.

Now it was January of 2008, and I was told from the other side once more that David would be completely healed, although the time had been changed. I excitedly talked with him about this new message and his response was shocking! "I have already been healed, mom," he said. I replied, what! When did they tell you this? He was so calm sounding and very definite about it saying, I just know! I was so excited and so happy, I told him, I was thrilled! He seemed just fine with a big relief sounding happy too! I was in awe about his miracle to happen; he could go on and live! He never did elaborate anymore on this. It was later on I wondered, after he was gone, how could he tell me more if he knew, and what all was in his mind then? Every day, I hoped would be the day I would see this miracle happen to him. This was our greatest wish for him to be completely well! He could be here with us until his old age! This is all that I allowed myself to think.

I had questioned him more the next day; did the other side just tell you this? He answered yes, and reassured me he just knew. His voice sounded happy, but we were on the phone and I couldn't see his face or his expression. I feel now he knew it was getting time to cross-over but couldn't tell me, trying to spare me. He would have hoped that I didn't intuitively pick up more on this. I wonder if a big part of him was so ready to be out of pain that he sounded happy, and the other part of him I know, was not ready to leave here I only knew he had no choice, since everything was in the promise, and our covenant to the Creator. We both designed our spiritual work here and had chosen each one's time. I was not to recall mine yet, but it would come as the end of my life comes near.

I refused to let my mind think any other way than that he would be well again in the way I wanted. But I just couldn't shake that dark shadow that stayed over me. I know that he had to have known when, by the remark he made about, "he had been healed." I wondered if he prayed to move the date once more after it was moved into 2008. He wouldn't have lied but maybe the other side had only told him his healing was very near now and to be ready? These were my thoughts that have stayed with me. I don't dwell on this, but have my own thoughts on it. He knew I would understand one day after he was gone why he had to tell me in this way. I decided that I was trying to re-examine this too much with wanting to know the answer. Everything had fallen into place as we both chose, it couldn't be changed.

Apparently, he was being healed and getting ready for his transition. I know that somehow he was given precious extra time into 2008 to complete some important things. He had to have believed by the extension of his life, everything was in place for him. He wouldn't have lied to me of what he heard. One day, I will know the entire Master life plan we made completely. Some day in all the bliss and joy of us all being united together once more on the other side, I doubt any of us will ever care anymore or look back. Why would we, it's over!

It was with his next check-up the doctor found three more cancer places, one on his shoulder and two on his back. This was in Feb of 2008, and the cancers were removed. David said, "He would be ok, and felt they got it all." I think I was starting to shut my thoughts down and went into some kind of hidden depressed state because, I knew his energy was shutting down further.

For many years now I had taken care of my son and was so blessed to do this, what an honor to have him for my son! We both had a cute way to express our feelings to one another. David would smile so big and said, "I am so honored to have you for my mother." I responded back, "and I am so honored to have you for my son!" Then we would bow to one another as the eastern people do. And, he was so honored to have his sisters as I am honored to have them for my daughters. We all felt honored to be together, we knew how important it was.

A day never passed without us all saying; I love you, to one another. We made the time count all we could. We knew how important it is to express love to one another. His sisters were so dedicated to their brother they were hurting with seeing him getting weaker in body as I was. We knew how precious life is no matter how it goes, it is our greatest gift and life passes us by too quickly.

I noticed immediately how the long trips home from the hospital were too tiring for him anymore. He couldn't stay awake, he was so exhausted going to sleep as I drove. In all the years before he wanted to be awake and talk going home, even when he had had a very difficult ER experience and/or was hospitalized for a while. He knew how to talk his way out early each time at the hospital with his charm and humor.

At home, when I checked on him for a few seconds I watched him sleeping. I was thinking of how much he had gone through so young. He had to be worn out and this scared me so badly. I had to hold myself together; I would go back and forth with these thoughts. It is the hardest thing to watch your child die a little each day and stand by completely helpless.

David was the strongest man I have ever met in my life. He had his way to shield us from any hurt. I know in my heart he was ready and started to accept that he was going home to be with our loved ones and his Creator. He knew he was worn out better than anyone. He was worried about all of us and I knew he would hold on up to the last moment. I was still praying for another miracle! I had to know I could make it through all of this regardless of what the future held. I knew I would have God's strength, but past that I couldn't think any further, I was numb.

I hoped something had been rearranged for him in some way, when he said, "he had been healed." He had high hopes his last year that I would meet a nice companion and he played cupid a couple of times. But all I cared about was him getting better, cupid could wait. That was something I didn't care about and hadn't for many years. He was my top priority even though I knew if this had happened it would have comforted him by knowing I wouldn't be alone. He wanted to know I had a good person in my life after he left. He wanted to know I had someone to care for me. He even fixed me up to go on a date once. I finally gave in knowing it would please him. I had a nice time but I was so anxious to be back at home to my son who I was concerned about. I couldn't feel relaxed, but acted as if I was happy about it for him.

A Bird Found in the House!

It was only a couple of weeks later, a few days before he suddenly took a final bad spell when he called me. David found a bird flying around in his house when he came home! We knew there was certainly no way a bird could get into the house! It was cold that early part of the year, still wintertime, and more than four doors would have to be open at once for anything to get in. I was really frightened, but trying to look at this as a good sign. I remembered my mother telling me years ago when I was a child of an old superstition. It was about finding a bird in the house meant a "sign of death." This terrified me so badly I shuddered, but refused to believe an old superstition in this day and age. How in wintertime could a bird get in when no one was home and the doors were all locked? This was impossible, but there it was! I was very uneasy and David agreed with me that he didn't see how a bird could get inside. The next thing was to catch and release it.

Finally, the bird landed on a broom handle and was let go. I just prayed it wasn't some kind of sign. I am not really superstitious and he never mentioned any more of what he thought, except he couldn't imagine how it got in with everything closed up. We were stumped and it bothered me greatly. I have no doubt now he knew this was a future sign for him. I was afraid it was a warning for both of us to be prepared. Did my mother have something to do with this knowing I could remember her words to me growing up? Knowing how psychic David was, I am sure he knew something was about to happen at least to one of us. There was nothing more we could do about it and what more could either one of us say?

He knew so much he did not reveal in his life. As I earlier said, he knew why he was here and knew his journey with what he was to accomplish. With both of us being psychic he would try and block my thoughts of any worry to me but it didn't keep the whole truth away from me. I always felt that knowing inside of me. One big thing he wanted to keep helping me with was our work together and helping family members through several difficult times in their lives and he certainly accomplished that. How difficult all of this must have been for him knowing that he was soon leaving with a last Heavenly healing into heaven.

I apparently was being prepared at the end of 2007 to be ready for his transition. I encountered several visions in the nights before he had his last emergency. In these emotionally painful visions he would always be missing with me frantically looking for him! I would call and call for him, searching everywhere! Stopping to ask others if anyone knew where he was, had anyone seen him? I had two last visions where I could see him up ahead of me walking away into a vast nothingness. I called as loud as I could, "David! David! Come back! Come back!" He was extremely sad looking as he slowly turned around to look at me. I could tell he didn't want to leave me. He had his head hanging down with his shoulders slumped, and he said nothing. Slowly he turned back to continue into this misty void knowing he had no choice! I woke up crying, and sobbing my heart out! When I calmed down I called him. I told him, I had the oddest experience, to see if we both shared the same one, which was common for us. I was also trying to get any kind of information I could from my son in this way. He listened intently as I told him what I had seen but he didn't comment much. He asked me a question or two but he really didn't have much to say and we let it go. I never told him my terrified feelings and I wouldn't have. I softly said, "I don't know what I would ever do without you" and he told me his same feelings too.

Both of the visions I had were nearly the same, and the pain I felt in my heart was horrible and real! I believe he knew I was being prepared with these signs from the spirit world for his departure. Most times we both have been prepared for the worse with visions of coming events, with all kind of dream states, symbols, spoken words and signs. A night later I had a third vision of what was to come. I was in New Mexico looking at the beauty of a town, and at the beautiful bright colors of skirts and tops the ladies wore. I wanted to feel happy too! I was walking along and something stopped me to look down at my clothes to see what colors I had on. I was so sad to see I wore all black! I wanted to feel happy but could not. Then it ended and I was waking up out of the vision. Those symbols told me the final prediction of David's life! We both worked with our own signs and symbols and I knew exactly what this meant and I was devastated!

This would be my final message that was different than all the rest concerning David and myself from the other side. This was shortly before David had his last critical time. In this message they said; "for me to always continue my work here on earth and to never give up." But, for the first time nothing was said about my son! I felt a chill go through me and I went weak, still refusing to think the end was near. The messages we received in all the years before, were for the both of us. In this one, the other side was preparing me in their gentle way, for what was about to happen. They were apparently preparing me this time for my son. I didn't want to acknowledge it without his name, but I had no choice. The other side hopefully wanted to help make me stronger for his day, which is the reason they said it as they did, they know the pain of suffering. Knowing all of this did not lesson it, and my broken heart from the moment he passed out of his body. They had did all they could to help me.

I have recalled so many things he wanted me to remember and what we chose. With all the sadness, and tears, and how we always made it through. Those times were full of great love for one another and our bond never ending, sprinkled with laughter, jokes, and humor. And most of all we persevered through it all.

I truly know he came from *somewhere else* that can't be explained as just the other side. He came from other places, in our universes, and for many reasons. This was for his special mission here as a human being, but not the same as most would ever think. David was something very different and more than a very advanced old soul and knowing he gladly chose to give his life for others. He also knew the suffering it would take to do this in his spiritual work. He was indeed a Spiritual Being, a Warrior, whom I know was created in the beginning as my other half soul. But, he was also a Being of Light on a mission. I know in my heart he taught what humility and humbleness is and he left me with many clues along the years to think about when he was gone. Those questions with many answers have since become clear to me. Our lives were very complex by working together with all kinds of information. It came to us from our spiritual teachers. Some of it was like a giant puzzle coming in parts for us to absorb slowly. The other side would at times tell us to use our "gifts" to figure it out, to sharpen our skills. Our whole reason for returning was very exciting and to once again be taught by the Christ like Beings of Light where only goodness and unconditional love exists.

I am sure most of you have heard the saying, "that we are already spiritual beings here for an earthly experience, not the other way around." I have complete faith in this and there are many things we can never explain that would ever make sense to all of us, just as David's and my work will not be understood by most others.

There are Angel Beings who walk among us here in human form on this earth right beside us helping in times of need. There are those who save lives and are with us in times of need, and who helps us as guardians. I am sure many of you have read stories of this. We both experienced this many times. They may appear in different forms such as a male, female, child, or animal, coming to help you in some unexpected way. We are certainly not the only Beings that were ever created. This is my truth and that I have been told from the Beings of Light. There are other places and worlds which may never be found by human beings that were created in this universe. The universe is full of other Intelligence beings that were also created.

We were taught by our universal teachers that each one of us can choose to learn and make amends anytime while we are here. Earth is a big learning school for each person to excel in. We go to school on both sides here and the Beyond to gain our experiences and rise up. David and I talked of why we came here to earth and about our missions; mostly the work we would do as a unit, mother and son. From the time he was very young small boy he knew this. He had been given the knowledge of a lifetime and knew his journey could not be altered.

I too, now completely understood my journey as well with no turning back. As time has passed I understand my daughters' directions and the part they play in how we were all connected in this life by helping one another. I believe when our work here is done it has nothing to do with age; we go home where there is no pain. There, we experience tremendous love and joy, in perfect spiritual forms. We are in perfection which is our Heaven. Here we are humans with emotions and feelings trying to find our way while here on earth. All of our feelings were given to us in order to use them and learn from them. One thing David made clear to us was he wanted to be cremated when his time came and this is what he expressed several times over the years. He didn't want the traditional funeral when his time came he wanted the easiest way for us too, with only a Celebration of life service. His wish was for people to wear bright colors and play his happy music like he had talked about to us years before. Although he and I talked this way many times of how a celebration should be, it was still a shattering part of our life for us to get through. It is never a final good-bye as many think; it is only good-bye for now, and the human physical part of us, and the outside cover we each wear through our life as a human.

Chapter 14

Evil Was Lurking in the Church
A Soldier's Spirit Appears

An Evil Minister

There were experiences David and I took on in different locations such as cleaning out bad spirits, and/or identifying who the spirit/spirits were. There was all kind of places, homes, churches, theatres, businesses, hospitals, stores, and on *holy* ground where they thrived! We always kept the, names and places confidential, of where we went unless the party did not care, but we still kept their privacy. If they wanted to express their experience this was alright with us too.

Spirits who linger only to cause fear and trouble are everywhere. They haunt all kind of locations; and some may even come with antiques or other items one may buy, which is quite common. The energy of these evil spirits can come with anything, even a location of ground where something took place hundreds of years ago. I can give an example of this in my next story.

We received an urgent call one particular day from a large church in a far away town. They were having some bad experiences going on in their church. Somehow they had gotten our names and needed any help we could give them. "Could we please come?" We agreed quickly to do what we could.

Driving up to the old church you would never have known what lurked inside of it! The exterior was mostly brick with the newer additions' added onto it over the years. All of it together made it a beautiful looking structure. The older part of the church had been built in the 1700's. This was the area where the terrible problems had originally started from, which made everything a nightmare for the congregation and others. The Minister had stated on the phone, "He didn't know what to do, and his secretaries' wanted to know what was going on in their church." It wasn't just them either; as several of the members of the congregation had been frightened away!

We met with three of the church staff members as we entered the church. We had arrived purposely on a week day. This was the best time to do our work, while no other members were there. Immediately we could see in their faces that they were having some frightful experiences. As we shook hands, the minister said, "We appreciate anything you can tell us." He mentioned that so much was happening in the church he didn't like being there alone; to work in his office day or night! He told us the other former minister was hardly there one year and left, none of them ever stayed very long. Then he told us that he was also leaving at the end of the month! The former minister, who knew we were coming, asked to be called when we were finished. He wanted to know what we found.

The current minister mentioned having large prayer sessions to try and make this dark spirit or whatever it was, LEAVE! The Minister said, "That the prayer sessions didn't work and actually seemed to backfire. Things had gotten even worse when they started! He couldn't understand how things could get worse with all of the prayers." David and I explained, they needed to know how to work with these dark entities, and it takes a lot of energy and experience. We also warned him not to *agitate* or try to do anything with this dark entity that it would continue to keep getting worse, because they aren't trained in this kind of work. The dark energy would only grow stronger due to the fear and attention it was getting that's what it wanted. The Minister agreed, since the prayer sessions only made things worse. We warned him that this also made IT more aggressive!

Prayer is the most powerful thing in the world, but one must know how to use it properly against a wicked and evil force. Some dark forces are removed from places and people, by an exorcism. This procedure can be serious and very intense even for a qualified Priest. It is not something for the amateur.

Certain priests are trained extensively for some time, and usually have a terrible fight on their hands with such an evil force! Unfortunately, Evil is around everywhere and walks among us here on earth. We both did not have the training to do this but with a much milder bad spirit, we have removed those. I can't stress the importance of never getting involved with evil beings; it is a dangerous thing which can follow one the rest of their life. One cannot move away from it because that kind of evil will go with you.

As soon as we finished our conversation we began our tour through the church and we could see that thing's began to happen, but first the two secretaries and the Minister wanted to give us some background information. The church was huge with hallways and several rooms on each floor with stairs here and there. It had been built onto over the years, it was enormous! As my son and I were walking in a downstairs hall that we were being shown, and we were drawn to a certain room. We had suddenly stopped in the hall by seeing a *ghostly* looking lady going into that room! We explained to the minister and secretaries there was a *ghost* lady with us. She had said to David and me, "she had passed over first, before her husband, and this had been their church." She said, "Her husband had built on this beautiful room; and she loved to come there often to watch him as he worked. He also did many repairs and other jobs in the church." The *ghostly* wife mentioned their names, and other information to us. She was a very sweet soul full of goodness.

The minister and secretaries knew exactly who this lady and her husband were, so they verified that this spirits information was correct. The couple was kind and loving souls and the *ghostly* lady meant no harm to anyone. She only wanted to be where they had loved spending most of their lives together. They had been an older married couple who was devoted to one another and to the church. The minister and secretaries had known them well. They were surprised with what we said, and that it was all true, and pleased they are happy, at peace and enjoyed being there.

The feelings we felt in this church were of many, such as, grief, happiness, joy, regrets, changing of hearts and souls, peace, trust, forgiveness for the better, negativity, and of the evil one! What we feel and receive runs through us at once. Think of all of those years of people's feelings, and all at once we feel them.

We had no fancy equipment, only a small regular camera and tape recorder to try and capture any sounds or images. We explained what we could both see and hear as we walked on to the end of the lower level in the church. We said "not to tell us anything." We knew by our clairvoyance where to go. David and I continued down another hall going right to the most troubled place, this is where we knew the dark entity would be! It was in the smaller children's bible class where it wanted to be! Then we both saw him! The others could not see as we could, but there he was, the Dark evil intruder!

Immediately we knew he was the very first minister of this church still here in spirit, a very bad spirit! He had begun this church in the 1700's! He moved as fast as a blur to right in front of my face hoping to terrify me! He quickly saw his attack didn't work on either one of us, and the chase began! He vanished, but we saw his dark figure fleeing down the hall, which looked like an ugly dark smoke! We took off at a run following his darkness. He was still wearing his long black robe and some kind of tall black hat ministers wore back in those days. We had now begun our job and the horrible feelings we both had told us the cruel minister was very angry that his tactics didn't work on us! We darted in and out of several rooms where we knew he had been to no avail. He stayed ahead of us, finally, we decided to check out the entire place and hope we could get him cornered.

Since the current minister had not told us where the main action was, they knew we were legitimate with all we told them, and what had happened so fast. Then they admitted there was a lot of trouble in the children's room which seemed to be the worst place in the church. Quickly then, they all decided to go back to the main office while we did our work.

The Evil one had vanished quickly to hide somewhere else, we didn't know for sure where for now. We would find him if he showed himself, or when we felt his evil presence. We went to explore the many rooms in the downstairs of the church. He still managed to stay ahead of us. We were later told some of the parish members had seen apparitions in different places in the church. And there were others who had experienced two other spirits, an older man and young child on the staircase at times. This was after we pointed out more of what had just happened to us.

We reminded the minister and secretaries not to tell us anything. We would tell them what we found. We had experienced the most evil of darkness that day, along with the good and positive spirit couple who had been past members and recently crossed over. Then there was the spirits of the older man and young boy who was bound there and afraid of the dark one. We later told the minister more information about the nice spirit couple who had passed over which he also confirmed was accurate.

We soon met up with the spirit of the small boy who wandered the church at times and was usually accompanied by the older man. The small spirit child was terrified of the dark spirit because of the connection he had with him when he went to church there long ago. The older Dark one (minister) was so cruel to the children, by beating them and doing other terrible things to them. This little boys' spirit couldn't get released because of what the evil one did to him by keeping his spirit grounded there.

We were able to tell this to the present minister and ladies. We told who these spirits were, and why they were there. There were other spirits also there who had lingered. The spirits would move to other places in the church away from the dark one if he came near to them. The good spirits do not want to be anywhere near the evil one, or have anything to do with it. They were afraid of it! Even in spirit the good doesn't want to be near evil in any way!

The minister asked, "Can you pick out the evil one if you saw him from our church pictures? We have pictures of all the ministers who have ever been here at this church." We both replied, "Yes, we can" and followed him to where the pictures hung in the church. As soon as we entered the room and at the same time we both pointed out the evil spirit in his picture, which hung on the office wall. We quickly blurted out that his name was Fredrick and he was of German decent and the oldest and first clergyman when the church was started in the 1700's. He was extremely mean and cruel and he was furious now that we had revealed his name and that we were here and we could see him! Mainly, he was furious that he could not terrify either of us. We could hear him screeching out loudly, "These are my flock! And that he wasn't going anywhere, this was his church!" We both saw him as clear as any human and it was very unpleasant. In his tormented mind he was still trying to run this church with his meanness and cruel streak, by trying to frighten everyone he could. No one could ever be comfortable there. We wanted to do more about Fredrick that day but we would need the help of a Priest.

We encountered several more experiences there that day. Even in churches, there are evil spirits that can linger for eons of time. They need to be cleaned out and sent on their way to the Christ Light, or wherever the evil go. Some, such as this one won't budge, and perhaps never will. They cause problems anywhere they are. Most people never know why they are not getting along, and there is always some kind of chaos going on.

Churches sometimes divide because of so much friction among the members. They can't figure it out because they cannot think that way, that a church could be *haunted*. The dark ones will work on a negative person there and it starts spreading throughout. They find a very negative person to latch onto who causes conflict, the rest is easy for the dark energy they unknowingly carry on the work. The evil entities want to see this happen because they are able to grow even more powerful with their bad energy. This was truly a place which needed to be cleaned out of the evilness.

The other spirits were good and bothered no one, but needed to be released. They needed to go on into the Light to join their loved ones in peace. They had been stuck there in fear, still hiding from the evil all of these years. We thought of all the poor little children the dark one had terrorized, tortured, and probably killed.

David knew there was a hidden burial place he would tell them about before we left that day.

Little Boy in Spirit

Then it was time to go to the current Minister's home next door which was now a rental house. It was haunted too! We told the people living there and the Minister who and what was in the home. The spirits who resided there were good and had passed away long ago. They had previously lived there in life and somehow all stayed on this side. They were harmless and content where they were. We spoke with them, even getting their names and they were also of German decent. Hopefully, after that day they were not afraid anymore, deciding to go to the other side, we had tried. They meant no harm reliving their lives, and as best they could they stayed clear of the dark entity from the church.

While we were in this home the radio would come on by its self with nice happy music, the lights would turn on, toys were moved around, and even a telescope that had been stored in a closet was moved to the front hall while we were in the kitchen! They did this for a special reason wanting us to give a message to the lady of the house living there now. They certainly got our attention! The message for her was good and positive to help her.

In the basement of this home there was a large teddy bear in a family room. But when we went to the basement later on the big bear had been moved to another room and sat on the floor in a corner. The bear was moved by the little boy spirit. David felt the little boy use to hide there for some reason other than playing or in fear of the old Minister from the church. The little boy loved the bear which we felt gave him comfort.

I am sure he stayed at the house most of the time since children lived there now and his positive family of spirits. This is the way he was letting us know where he used to go, and take his own toy for comfort. The spirit boy usually had the older man with him too sort of like a father figure to feel safe. This kind man had been a farmer in his life and looked after the boy. This was a great comfort to know he watched over this small child.

These positive spirits let my son and I know they were still afraid and happy we were there to help them. The spirits had positive messages for the family living there. They meant no harm to anyone. David and I offered to do more but the day was almost over with and we had a long drive home. The minister gave us his thanks and said, "The former minister would be waiting for his call to know what we found and to report back to him. He would be calling him when we left.

A Soldier's Story

There was an amazing and loving experience I want to tell you about before we left that day. This beautiful experience happened in the main part of the church, making my son and me very happy. An unexpected visit was about to take place. As we were talking to one of the secretaries' inside the sanctuary I couldn't help but notice the spirit of a young man, a soldier in uniform. I saw him standing beside the main pulpit up in front of the church on the stage. He was watching all of us, waiting for something to happen. I didn't let on then I was waiting to see what he wanted.

He said, "He was waiting for me to tell the woman standing there, that he was her son! Please tell her I am here!" His spirit had moved into *our time* and in a flash he stood alongside of her waiting. I heard him clearly say to me to tell her "he is her son!" When I told her there was a young soldier beside her, who says he is your son, and that he died in the war. she gasped! She was stunned for a few moments' then said, "Yes, her son was killed while in the army! How do you know this?" She was shocked, but her eyes had lit up! She became very excited now asking how we could know this.

I gave all of his messages to her, which she said were all true and that this was unbelievable! She wanted to know where he was. I replied "He stands right beside you! And he can hear you." She cried out with happiness and began talking to the area where I told her he stood. She expressed this was a miracle come true and she was happy. This relieved her of where he is, and to know he is happy and at peace. She said, "His dad and her had grieved over him for all of those years wondering, is he alright? Where is he? Is he at peace?" She was anxious and excited as she talked through me to him. I told her he can hear you as you speak.

I continued to relay her son's messages to her. A mother and son again reunited made my son and me happy too! She was the happiest mother you can imagine. She couldn't wait to get home to tell her husband of their sons' visit! It was such a good day knowing the soldier had been waiting for us to come, so his mother would know he was with her and his dad! This church trip was very important for them all to be reunited once again! It gave both joy and peace in reuniting so now they knew he was more alive than ever! Something the woman had never thought possible! These are the blessings we are so thankful for in our work.

The other side is absolutely fascinating in how they can orchestrate events ahead and make things happen! We not only were called there to help the conditions in the church and home, but this ladies son was waiting to get his message to his mother! To witness all of this is still amazing time after time we experience it and how these things work. This mother received information from her son we could not possibility have known of her son's death, and of the circumstances that he told her. The confirmations' the souls give to us for their loved ones' know we could not know these in any way possible. We always know the soul (all of them) wait for an opportunity to get their messages across. We also were delighted to experience how open the minister had been and were so kind to us.

Demons

On the way home we thought of how some people label this kind of work as "from the making of Demons" and that we have been called this in rare circumstances! The spirit world is a blessing, and the way God plans things for all of us. They don't have a clue they are also calling God the same name since He gave us the gifts to help others. God only wants us to be happy and give our sorrows to Him to bear for us. He knows why He made us human, complete with all of our many flaws, emotions and deep feelings. We were given all of these so we are equipped to work with them in our life here on Earth. This is how we are able to cope through our hard and happy times. The other side's expertise with arranging their visits and their unique way of reaching out to us means so much to those who understand. There are times when passed over souls use their free will to turn things around, and help us here in other ways. They are sometimes full of surprises and full of their humorous kidding in their messages.

This mother in the church had the answers she had longed for that she never expected, and now she is free of worry about where her son is. She knows her son is happy and their love is stronger than ever! She called us several times afterwards telling us that when she told her husband who was grieving deeply he was quite shocked! His son's information was so accurate he knew it was from him. His broken heart changed into a new healing heart. Both of their lives had quickly changed by knowing their son is at peace and with them. And that he has never left them and never will. He will be the one to come to take them home when their time comes!

Chapter 15

Angels, Miracles and Messages Lighting Our Way

Angels of Miracles

I shall never forget one of the many times my son was becoming critically ill. I prayed for a sign he would live and be able to get to the hospital quickly! I was hurrying through my bedroom to grab a jacket and found the sign! This was amazing; my eyes became glued to it looking down at the floor! There was no doubt that the Angels of Healing were close by my son in his ordeal! There was an *Angel drawing* in the carpet! It was absolutely perfect and phenomenal! I keep an old holy box, which belonged to my son that was used for healing a long time ago, and it sits on my dresser. The Angel figure was drawn on the floor right in front of it! I turned on the light to look closer making sure this was what I thought it was. I couldn't believe what I was seeing! I went closer to examine this phenomenon to make sure my eyes weren't deceiving me. Behold! It was an Angel with outspread wings! I knew then the Angels were already watching over him and letting me know. They were ready to protect and heal him.

The coming days in the hospital were full of doctors, nurses, and medical technicians working on my son. This was the hardest part since it never gets any better, but my faith and trust stayed strong! I knew there were these magnificent Angels assisting him and holding me up. Just the same, being his mother and seeing what he went through was hard! He never expressed pain; instead he managed to smile at me. It was all I could do to not cry, knowing how brave he was.

I rubbed his feet running energy into him which would put him to sleep for a short while. While doing this, I thanked the Creator with all my heart for letting him stay longer. We had so much to do in the future and his body was tired, but never was his strong courage and will to live weak. I told him about the sign and he also had known the Angels were with him and he was as excited as I was! After he passed the crisis, and we were back at home, I took pictures of this Angel drawing. There was something else different now about the Angel from earlier. Now the Angel had a halo over its head! We both knew this had been a wonderful sign that he would continue to prevail! I knew for sure the drawing was showing us ahead of his emergency to come.

The Angels who guided our journey would always be with him, and he would heal again! In which he did, for he shall be well, as I was always told. We both understood why we were shown the Angel ahead of this experience; he would be protected and guarded over!

The next Angel imprint drawn in the carpet was larger and looked different and also had detailed beautiful wings! David and I came home after eating out one evening and I ran upstairs for a moment. I flipped on the light to my room and what a sight to see! The ENTIRE carpeted floor was in Angel wings, which was breathtaking! They were so beautifully and perfectly drawn over the entire floor! I called for my son to come see! I tiptoed over to the bed trying not to disturb the amazing art work! I stood on top of my bed and took many pictures from different angles. We both felt teary eyed and so humbled, but we had to laugh with our tears because we were so happy to be witness to this event! The Angels were with us once again for an upcoming event. This was the second Angel sign drawn in this way in such a short time for us. The sign was showing us once more the, Angels are with you!

The third time came shortly thereafter when another Angel was drawn in the carpet in my bedroom and happened only a day or so before I was contacted about a story I had written. My story had been selected to be published in a wonderful magazine called, *Angels on Earth*, by Guidepost Magazine. This third Angel was drawn in the carpet beside my bed! This one had different types of wings and halo and was an Angel bearing happy news about David's story being selected for the magazine!

Our lives were kept busy and full of amazing and exciting events. These things helped keep us balanced and strong in our perseverance with all we were learning. Angels were all around us and bringing good news! Our spiritual earth school lessons and study combined with the Beings of Light were absolutely uplifting to us. The experiences we each were having made our strange new world ever more fascinating! I was opening my memory to what I somehow already knew from a previous time and place. A heavenly place I was remembering more and more with Alien Beings of Light.

A beautiful part of the Angel drawings was how detailed and perfect they were. The carpet is a plush and very short fibered type. Later on I tried to repeat some of the art work on the carpet myself, but I could not work it out.

I could not get one thing I drew to stay; the carpet fiber just went back together! That's how clever our Divine ones are, they can make anything happen. I treasure all of the pictures I took of the Angels drawn and they are beautiful! I have included one in this book for the reader to see.

Angel wings draw into the carpeting by the Heavenly Realm

Messages from the Spirits in the carpeting

Indiana Experience at a Church Camp
This brings to mind an experience David and I had at a large Church Camp when he lived in Indiana. He was in remission and feeling good living in

Indiana. He called us to come to visit for a few days. He wanted to take us to this special Church Camp. He was full of excitement because some of the people there had God given gifts. David had been there to visit recently.

My husband and I drove up to his home as soon as we were both free, then all three of us went to this unique place. Upon entering we drove under an arched iron gateway which opened to a community. The quaint little houses and stores along the streets were laid out in the shape of a horse shoe. Each house had a sign outside telling what gift they provided and a booklet one could sign up on if you wanted the service they provided. Some were Palm readers, card readers; and natural readers, called psychic Mediums, and so on. There was a wonderful museum and stores to brose in. They had guest housing for adults and children in the summer so they could go to classes.

The church people there reportedly had all kinds of God given gifts which I thought was a wonderful environment. In fact, I had never experienced this type of freedom in a church setting. This was because they were open to their gifts and not judged by non-believers. I couldn't get over this as I imagined how this would never go over in most places I have ever been in!

Past the small group of homes was a nice little church on the arc of the circle. This was when you were about half way up the road. After spending the day checking out the stores and places to sightsee, we checked the church schedule. We wanted to go to a service but would need to come back the next afternoon because we were too late for anymore that day.

We returned, after a lengthy drive, again the next day. After seating ourselves in church, an older lady came down the aisle to my son. The church was full by then. At this time, David had been on chemo and many medications for some time, but he felt fairly well. The woman criticized him for having his baseball cap on with a bandana under it while in the church. I could tell my son felt very hurt and embarrassed. He had had so much chemo his head was always cold so he always wore his Cardinal cap for warmth. All of his life he attended church and now, in front of everyone, this older lady clearly pointed him out. He was very polite and did remove his hat when she left. When the service ended I went to an Elder of the church and told him what had happened. The man apologized to David and said he would talk to the woman.

The church Elder understood and knew anyone who came into the church wanted to be there by choice. We did this so others who are sick wouldn't have to go through a lecture to be in church. I left the kind man by mentioning to him that this woman needs to realize how many people are very sick and taking treatments with chemo and others who are suffering with other diseases. Hopefully she wouldn't do this to someone else. It does not matter about a hat when so many people are sick; the important thing is hat or no hat, he wanted to be there. This is one of those questions, "What would Jesus do?" According to the Bible, Jesus turned no one away who came to him, especially because of a head covering. Men covered their heads in biblical times as well. People cover their heads all the time because of cancer and other illnesses to keep warm. Jesus Christ would have hugged them all!

A Reading with Thomas

All in all, we enjoyed this place very much and I met a special person there who appeared to have a strong connection to me. I had been told that day by the other side I was to meet someone there for a reason, and soon thereafter I knew who it was. Every time I passed by this one home I felt pulled to this particular place to check out the gifted person living there.

There were some Indian relics in front of the house and I just knew he was the one I was supposed to meet. I stepped up on the porch where a pad and pen lay and signed up for a reading by a man called Thomas.

I will always remember meeting this man for he recognized our psychic connection quickly. He told me this later when our visit was nearly over. Although, we had never met before, we both worked in the spiritual world along the same lines. I would find out soon that David and I were brought to this place on this day, by another man in spirit that Thomas grew up with! I had briefly met this other man I called, John the one in spirit, once at a psychic fair in another state! And now he had brought us all together for a reason! I had no idea about any of this yet and what was going to take place. This is another case of showing everything is for a reason.

Getting into the reading, Thomas told me to, "say nothing" and gave me a paper. I was told to write down whoever in spirit I would like to have come in with a message that day then fold the paper up and hold it in my hand. He left the room while I did this. I wrote my parents' names and a couple more but not John's name. I didn't think of him at all since only meeting him the one time. I had not found out yet that my reader, Thomas and John were closely connected at one time.

Thomas returned and sat down to begin my reading. He did not look at my paper at all; he only held it in his hand still folded. He began by telling me the names of my mom and dad and their dog, Iggy. He then connected with my Uncle Leo, giving me a message from him that I confirmed. He spoke to me of my main teachers and guides. He told me I was from the four directions which he said was nearly unheard of being extremely rare.

Suddenly, he got a puzzled look on his face and stopped! He fell back in his chair and I could see he was shocked and finally he said, "You know John from Kentucky?" "Yes," I said. The reader, Thomas, couldn't get over how I was led to him for a reading by John, his boyhood best friend! I told Thomas I only met John once in my life, but he had been a spiritual teacher to me since he crossed over. Thomas said, "We both knew one another from a former lifetime." I told him John is now a teacher to my son and me and that he helps guide us with our other spiritual teachers.

Then I knew why I felt so drawn and compelled to see this man, Thomas, for my reading that day. Thomas fell back again into his chair with a big grin, asking me if I knew when John crossed over? I had no information for him on this except that he had read for me once and that it couldn't have been too long ago. Now I will explain to you how John appeared to me with his messages.

I awoke one night knowing I had a visitor. There stood John on the stair landing in a type of robe like garment. He told me of a past life together when both of us were healers. He had recognized me at the Fair that day with our connection. I did not know that is why I too, felt drawn to him for the reading. He said "I will be staying close by you for the next 5 days because I have much to accomplish." He would provide me with teachings and that he would also remain close by me the rest of my earth life helping and protecting me as he had before.

No doubt we both knew instantly that John had brought the three of us together on this day and I felt sure that David and I would figure it all out later on.

Thomas told me in my reading that I was writing a book, which I was! He then described the front cover and said, "for me to "take it to the largest publisher I could find!" He also mentioned a Rainbow or an arch on the cover. Then Thomas laughed and said, "And it's not McDonalds!" My first book I mentioned earlier titled, *"Under the Rainbow Crossing"* was what Thomas meant. The front cover has a picture I took of an upside down rainbow on it! This meeting was wonderful and important for both David and me that day! It is remarkable how we each had come together again for certain reasons in our life. Everything is so orchestrated in our lives such as this meeting.

The Big Brown Teddy Bear

A few months later while still in Indiana back at his own place, David, watched a TV show about a famous reader who is an excellent psychic reader. That same evening I was watching the same show where I lived. He gave a reading for some parents who had lost a small child, a little girl. The dad did not believe in readers but was grieving so terribly for his daughter he went with his wife that night. The reader was right on the mark with his information from their child in spirit. The dad was still reluctant and said, "If you are really in touch with her what did I bury her with?" The reader replied, "Her big brown teddy bear with a red ribbon around its neck."

The father crumbled then, crying, he knew his daughter was really relaying her messages to them! That was her favorite bear he had given to her. No one other than the mother knew he had placed the bear in the casket after her funeral to be buried with her! This was such an emotional reading, but now the father had the knowledge that his daughter had spoken to him. She was ok, well, and happy with loved ones and other children there. She would be with them again one day and she loved mommy and daddy.

A very strange thing happened after the TV show. David's friend went to get something out of a closet close to the living room. He opened the door and there on the floor sat a large brown teddy bear with a red ribbon around its neck! His friend became hysterical! David immediately called me, but his friend couldn't talk he was so upset! I was astounded! We had experienced many things and knew this man was a wonderful reader but this was incredible!

I asked David to bring the bear home when he and his friend came for a visit. A few weeks later he and his friend arrived. When I met him at the door the first thing I asked was, where is it? He told me he forgot the bear because of trying to leave quickly to miss the traffic. I was so disappointed but knew he would bring it next time. I was so happy to see my son I soon forgot about it.

The next day all of us went on a short trip. Returning home, I opened the door to my bedroom and there in the middle of my bed was a large brown bear with a red ribbon around its neck! I was really in an excited state. Where had it come from? My son had forgotten to bring it, but there it was! I ran to get everyone! To say we all were in shock was an understatement!

This bear has stayed in my home all of these years and has been quite active at times. So much had been *brought* to us from the other side. I wrote to this famous psychic and sent a picture of how I found the bear.

Now, could the little spirit girl, Katie, who resides in my home whom I described earlier, have something to do with the bear? I feel sure she is the one who moves it around as she has done with other items. Could this be a case of Katie reincarnating over and over? Somehow, there is a close connection with all of us in some way. The bear has moved around the house when we've been gone and during the night. A family member opened a closet door early one day and there it sat on the shelf! I found it in my bed with the covers up around its neck several times! Then the bear sat in different chairs and so on. I have many pictures of these things from over the years. I wondered could she have been the little girl whose story was told on the television show. I do know spirits can be in more than one place at a time. This has no ending to the story as of yet.

Always Wanting to Create

One evening David called to me and said he had a surprise to show me. At the time he was legally blind. This was in late January of 2008 two months before his last emergency. He had decided to lay some antique tile around his fireplace opening. He had kept this box of antique tile stored for years always planning to use them in his home. He called me to come and see something. When I came into his living room the antique tile was all laid and he asked, "Does it look okay, mom?" It was so exquisite I could have cried! Every single piece was perfect and straight. I exclaimed to him how beautiful it was and the wonderful job he had done! The tiles were beautiful blues and creams in elaborate designs. I know he did this with his second sight.

Today, the fireplace sits in my home and I am so proud of it because it was the creative part of my son. I have so much around me in my home of things he made, created, and loved. This gives such a good feeling inside of me to have this part of him, combined with his strong energy. The work he did on the tiles while blind, the cutting and placing of them was amazing because of his sight being virtually gone. He still made every second count. He never gave up on anything and he still made beauty come alive!

Chapter 16

David's Incredible Passing into Spirit

He Lives On

It was March 13, 2008 when we took David to buy a new kitchen table, one with round corners instead of pointed corners since he had hit his sides so many times on it by not being able to see it. We took him shopping hoping to find one. My oldest daughter and I were helping him decide and he purchased the round one he wanted. This was on Saturday a week before everything began to happen. Robin was not feeling well and was sick off and on all day that Saturday. We went to a few stores and had lunch together before starting home. She first became sick at lunch and on the way home from our shopping trip she became even more sick and we needed to pull over a few times for her. The last time we pulled over was on a church parking lot. Robin said, "She had never felt like this before it was something different, it's not flu, and I can't describe it." We were relieved to get her home so she could go to bed. The next day she was better.

Exactly one week later we both would know why this happened to her. Through the next few days David and I did various things, even going out to shop in another town for cabinet doors for my kitchen. We had a nice lunch together and he wanted some chocolate ice cream for dessert but was too full after lunch. I told him, "We would stop by to get some again later that day on the way home." Then David mentioned how he shouldn't eat dessert because of Lent and that he had given up chocolate and ice cream for it! I couldn't help but smile big saying to him, "But you aren't Catholic!" We laughed then and David said he always gave up something he loved for Lent which I thought was so sweet to do. We knew you don't have to be a certain religion to give up what you want to in honor of Christ. This was our last day out together.

After that day the nightmare began for all of us and mainly for my son David. It was on Thursday, the next day, when he called me early in the morning and he sounded terrible! He had decided he was going to pick up his new table. I tried my best to get him not to go! He said he had to pick it up today. I begged him once more not to. I told him, we could call the furniture store and pick up the table next week. But he insisted, he had to get it and would be fine. I asked him once more "To please wait." I was really worried because of how he sounded. He tried to change his voice to sound all upbeat and full of energy. He said someone else was taking him to get it. I had a really bad feeling he should not go! I was worried all day long because he didn't call me. We always kept in touch by cell phone several times a day when we were apart for any length of time. I did not hear from my son all day and I called him every hour or so without an answer! Why wasn't he able to answer! By then I knew something was very wrong with a terrible sick feeling I had about him! All day I questioned myself over and over where was he? I was pacing the floor by then. He would never do anything like this! The person who took him had a cell phone and he did not answer either, no matter how much I called! What to do, should I call the police there? Where would they be able to look? I had no idea where he was by now. I would wait awhile before I called the State Police.

I knew he was in trouble or he would have called me. All I knew to do was to call him so I kept calling his cell phone. The later it got the more frightened I was. This wasn't ever like my son to do! I made his friend PROMISE to always call me if I wasn't along and he became sick. He promised, but he never did that day even when David collapsed in a store. My many calls to his home and his cell phone were never answered! Finally, after 7pm the phone was answered back at my son's house by the person who took him. He said, "David wasn't feeling very good and was back at home." I rushed to see him! He was lying on his sofa and asked me to do Reiki energy healing, saying he would be fine, but he looked terrible and was in pain! He looked worse than I had seen him in a long time. I told him he needed to go to the hospital but he said no, the Reiki would help him; he didn't want to go to the hospital.

In a short time he became much worse, so I began calling his doctor to tell her I was bringing him to the emergency room, but she was in a meeting and her assistant said she would be out soon, to call back in a short while. His doctor had said early on that when my son had an Emergency to call her and she would make arrangements for him so he would not be held up in ER. We had so many emergencies over the years because he could turn bad so quickly! We could not reach the doctor later and the nurse told us again she would be in the meeting another hour! I told her what the doctor had said about the hospital but there was never a call back.

Much time was wasted and we started for the hospital. David didn't want to go but he did it for me. I asked him to PLEASE go! I was so scared!

That's when he said very slowly trying to muster up his strength, "Oh Mom I'm so tired of doctors, needles, and hospitals." He resisted for the first time and didn't want to go. By then his color had changed and he looked even worse!

He had never said that before to me, he had always fought to live. I was so frightened, no more waiting! I ran to gas up the car and my two daughters were on their way to David's home. We loaded up the car putting him in the large back seat with pillows and blankets like he always needed to make the ride. I felt we would lose too much time waiting for an ambulance if one was even available in our small town. We had already wasted so much time waiting for the phone call. By now hours had passed! This would be faster! We all agreed and took off. Speed made little difference as far as getting a ticket, this was an emergency! I hoped all the way to be stopped so the police could lead the way for us. Why David's friend did not call me or take any of my calls, I do not know. He knew how bad my son could be in a short time yet he kept him in the city until David had collapsed! Yet the man brought him home miles to here instead of a hospital as he promised to do! They were only 10 minutes from the hospital at that time! How devastated we were!

I think David must have felt he wouldn't survive this time and was so tired of fighting and probably wanted to die at home. I don't know the answers to this one, but I am sure he wanted to be at home. If I had known, I still couldn't have let him have his wish and suffer there, but we didn't have any idea of his outcome to be. My daughters and I only knew to get him the help he needed as fast as possible! He had pulled out every time before and we thought his miracle would come again. We prayed so hard for it!

I punished myself for a long time knowing he wanted to be at home, but now I feel I made the right choice. There are times one must make a very serious choice in someone's life and we can only hope we make the right one because it's too late to take it back. I couldn't stand for my son to continue suffering and not give him a chance to get another miracle to pull him through. I would have done anything in the world to save him, as any parent would. I would never have believed this would be the end, I would not! I could not!!

Back to that excruciating night my two daughters and granddaughter, Brooke, followed one another driving as fast as possible behind me to get David to the hospital. When we arrived at the Emergency door there was no gurney available for him and he was unconscious! I ran over to get two kind strangers standing outside to help get my son out of the car and into a wheel chair. This was horrible to be without the help we desperately needed! I gratefully give thanks to those strangers who helped us. He was so tall we were trying to hold him up to keep him from falling out of the wheelchair from the car into the ER room.

Once into the hospital, it was packed full of others waiting to be seen, without a seat available. There was no time to wait! None of us could believe as critical as my son was the nurse didn't take any action at the desk except to tell us we had to wait! I couldn't believe this! Anyone could see he was passed out and needed immediate help and was still unconscious! I held his shoulders in front of him to hold him up as best I could. I knelt down on the floor facing him. My other daughter held him by his shoulders from behind the wheel chair. My oldest daughter quickly went around to the nurse again making her take notice of how serious he was. She sternly said, "My brother is dying and he needs a doctor now! If anything happens to him it will be your fault!" The nurse hurried back around the desk and listened to his heart then immediately had him rushed to a room! Much time had been wasted in the waiting room and more would be wasted in the ER room! Everything was falling apart!

There was no doctor only ONE attendant in ER to work on my son! This was a very large hospital. The male nurse immediately saw how serious David was and started working as fast as he could. He threw things out of his way, not wasting a second to get a large bag of fluid going. He was ready to put a large pack under my sons shoulder to do another procedure when he was stopped. An older man had come in across the hall having a heart attack; the male nurse quickly left David to see about him! The male nurse said, "not to touch anything not even your son, I will be back as soon as I can," and he left. We were standing there in shock and disbelief that this was happening! My son was laying there as if sleeping but was deeply unconscious. I could not believe the attendant had no one else to take over and there was no more help for him! From the very beginning I felt as though everything was working against us and my son lay as if lifeless on the cart. We sat close by my son still thinking he would pull through, he always had! He had to! We tried to reason that the male nurse wouldn't have just left him if he was critical. The nurse was gone a long time then he suddenly returned to continue on my son. After the nurse could do no more for him he said something that nearly made my heart stop, "I sure hope he makes it!" With that David was whisked away up to the trauma floor. He was still unconscious and my legs went weak with the attendant's remark! Those words made everything real! Was he past help? I still kept my faith that he would make it. We raced up to the unit on the elevator waiting until we could go in his room. I had watched my son come out of death more than a few times so I prayed this would happen again. PLEASE!

After David was sent to the trauma floor that terrible night on Friday, March 14[th,] the next day surgery was to be hoped for, but later testing results showed different. On his x-rays the damage was too great and it was too late! My daughter, Robin, saw the doctors looking at his x-rays then shaking their heads No, meaning they could not help him. We were told there was nothing more that could be done! He was on the edge of dying now; there would be no surgery or anything else for my son!

Taking my family and me into a private room we were told that there was nothing they could do for him but make him as comfortable as possible! I couldn't grasp those words that "NOTHING COULD BE DONE!" They earlier had talked of surgery to help him! "Not my son!" I cried out! But it was true and we were devastated. Everything was shutting down in him and his intestines had holes in them. The infection was spilling out into his body everywhere. He was also in Adrenal gland failure and everything in his broken body was wrong. We were told he had a small amount of time left for us to spend with him; there would be nothing else they could do! This was real, and we did not know how this could be happening so quickly. I just wanted to wake up from this nightmare and see my son laughing and kidding again. Our shock had taken over; we were as if we were in another world stumbling around. This can't be is all I could think!

The doctor later said, "David's only care was he didn't want to leave you, and he was mainly worried about you, his Mom." He had said to his doctor, "What will happen to my mom? How will my mom get by? What will she do without me?" He was so upset over our not being able to be together anymore here on earth and as a family. Just hearing these words I fell apart, I was totally helpless. He had always been so protective of me, his sisters and our family. The worst now was I could not do anything to help him! I would never be able to help him!

Still, when he could speak he kept trying to reassure us that he wasn't going anywhere yet! "Don't worry I'm not going anywhere yet, Mom." It was his time, but he and I were together for so long and our earthly work was so important to him, he wanted to stay just a little longer. He had helped all of us in his life and there would be no possible way that our bond could ever be broken. This part of us could never be taken away and would never end. We would soon be working together in another way with each of us on a different side. He was never afraid, for he knew who was waiting for him in Heaven. He would always be with us, our life work in the spirit world was also our world filled with love and there is nothing to ever fear. Our lives being the way they were sealed with our promise and plan on how we would be coming back. All that I had experienced with our spiritual knowledge couldn't help me in this time. I would later remember that shock is a helpful emotion in times such as these. Although one isn't trained to think of it in this way, shock kept us in a daze to help protect us and was helping get us through the worst time of our lives!

David and I held on to one another's hands very tightly and never let go! He opened his eyes again saying, "Mom, I'm not going anywhere yet." He was fighting to stay. He had pulled out of so many critical crises. I silently kept praying he could still do it this time again, in another Divine miracle way. I was happy in those quick moments thinking, He can do this again no matter what the doctor had said, like so many times before. But one very important part missing was that I wasn't hearing the familiar words, "for he shall be well" for the first time ever by the Heavenly voice as in all the past years! David kept trying to reassure us that he wasn't going anywhere. He would always be with us but now nothing could help my heart and soul and all of the family.

I began rubbing David's feet just like he loved me to do and I asked him if he could see me. He followed my voice looking to the end of the bed and raised his arm enough to give me a small wave like a child does with his sweet smile. I will never forget that beautiful smile full of bravery. He could tell where I was by my voice and I truly believe he could somehow see me. I have no doubt he could with his gifts. I know he was very concerned for all of us and how we were handling everything. Everyone held strong trying not to show their tears where he could see them. At least we tried to spare him this, knowing how much harder it would be for him. It didn't always work but we tried. I made sure I stayed positive and did not let him see my tears but he could see my soul dying too.

He loved us all so much he was trying to hang on longer. My daughters were on each side of his bed when I left his room for a few moments so they could say what they needed to. I stepped into the hall close by his room and called my dear friend, Alex, in Missouri to tell him David was critical and dying! When Alex picked up I began to sob so hard finally releasing my tears. Trying to tell him about David, my words were hard to come by but he finally understood what was happening. He gave me the strength I needed with his comforting words to go back in. I hurried back in to my son; we were all in that state of non-belief this was so unreal! I felt I was watching this from another time and place yet it was taking place in front of me! It is the worst nightmare and you can't come out of it! You know it is really taking place and you are helpless!

I questioned myself knowing how my son had suffered silently for all of these years and how much longer did he have to suffer for us? I knew he had stayed with us way beyond his time out of his deep love. But could I let him go now? I would have to free him now, I had no choice! He had lived fourteen years longer than was possible, the doctor told me. David said more than once, "it was through his spiritual healings and coming home to be with me is why he lived so long." He always thanked me as I thanked him for all he did for me and his family. I had memories of what he had told others, my mom made me well with God's healing or I would have been gone long ago. He always had so much faith in me and now I couldn't help him, except knowing he needed me to help him with my love. I looked at my son as who he really is, a Being of Light who would shine on forever. This is my beautiful son and brother to his sisters who is our earth Angel.

I had thoughts spinning through my mind of how he should be outside now planting his beautiful spring flowers; this was his favorite time of the year other than Christmas. Spring was here, he should be cleaning up his yard like always, not here dying! He had so much he wanted to do and give all he could! Even though I knew his soul was ready and had been for some time, he was needed in Heaven for other things. I tried to realize this but I just couldn't in the state I was in. I pictured him in his beautiful yard where he loved to be for a few seconds before reality came back once again. Nothing seemed fair at this point but this was with our agreement we made long ago, he was needed by those who sent us.

At one point all of us were told we had to leave the room for him to be checked. When we returned, the attending nurse was complaining to me that he had pulled all of his tubes out and gotten out of bed and what a mess he had made! This nurse was angry about what she had to clean up. If I had had the strength then I would have tried to make sure this nurse never worked with any patients again! We were in such shock and quickly knew all he wanted was to come home! He knew what was happening and in his mind he was going home to be with us. I knew he was fighting so hard to go home by getting up despite being as critical as he was! He had used his inner strength to get up, pull out the tubes and life support off of him! My son was fighting for his life and his independence to live! He would never take pain medicine but now he would be given this in order to relax his body. I knew he wanted to be as alert as possible for himself and us. How devastated he must have felt. How I wished I had been right there to talk to him and help calm him when he was trying to go home! This terrible thing would never have happened with the nurse had I been in the room! I was angry with myself for letting this pass by without turning her in, but I was so traumatized at the time I wasn't thinking right and she didn't matter. It was more important to be with him.

I have tried not to think back on these things knowing the past is gone, but I still mentally have punished myself by not staying right beside him when asked to leave. At a time such as this I wanted no problems in front of my son. I only wanted her out of his room and to be by his side to comfort him all I could. It was looking back later that I remembered this again and again, and thought of what my son was thinking, but I needed to let this go and not let it fester any longer. I know it is wrong to do, but then again he is and will always be my beloved son.

David heard every word said to him in those two days even if he could not always respond back. Sometimes he had a little smile or he would squeeze my hand letting me know he was sending his love to me. I must have told him I loved him hundreds of times and how proud I am of him and always have been. I was honored to be his mother and thanked him for choosing me for his mother! He held tightly to my hand too, never letting go. I managed as best I could. We were blessed to be able to say our goodbyes for now in our own words by only speaking of our love for him. There were no goodbyes that anyone said. In all reality we would be together again and again! Thank God we knew this and how God works only with great love! No one uttered a goodbye!

That night I still held tight running things through my head. I found myself again thinking that my son would make his way out of this and mend and then we could all go happily home. David always said, "He wouldn't leave me" and I banked on this with all my heart. But lurking underneath I knew. I wouldn't allow my thoughts to think that he wouldn't make it! Perhaps the mind has to sidetrack us in order to protect ourselves? I was scared, because things were moving too fast, like a blur. I couldn't and wouldn't process the truth. I rarely talked with my family because I was afraid to let go of him! We all did what we needed to be strong for him. They understood everything happening.

I don't know what I would have done without my daughters, my family and Alex, or how I would have regained the strength I needed to tell my son what he waited to hear. My one daughter, feeling so helpless asked her brother, "Oh David, what can I do for you? Just tell me." He slowly opened his eyes and said, "Eat green eggs and ham!" His comment came from his favorite childhood book of Dr. Seuss. As critical as he was, he still wanted to make her smile! My other daughter asked her brother a question for me that I couldn't. How strong they were! My granddaughters were very close to their Uncle also and stayed close by him waiting their turn.

The last hours he was here I softly spoke to my son holding onto him and him to me and in that time he managed to whisper to me, "Mom, you're going to be happy now and live a good life." I choked on my tears managing to say, "How could it ever be good without you?" I quickly had to leave the room so he couldn't see my tears as my daughters and granddaughters surrounded his bed staying close to him. I completely broke down in the hall trying to swallow my tears back so I could return to my son, but what he had said to comfort me made this all the more real!

I called Alex once more in Missouri and thanked God he was home and answered. I was crying so hard trying to tell him what David had just said to me. Alex told me to go back into his room and tell my son that I understood. That I had to let him know I understood what he said and what he needed to hear from me. David was waiting for these special words that he needed to hear from me to release him so he could go in peace. I had to understand and know that I was the one he waited for to release him and for him to know that I would be alright. Thank God, Alex again gave me the strength to do this for my son.

I went back to him and sat as close to him as I could to hold him. I softly and gently whispered to him, "Oh David, I am so sorry, I didn't understand what you meant before but I do now and I will be happy. I will live a good life and I will be happy for the both of us and you will always see through my eyes." This was the worst thing I ever had to do in my life to give those words to my son! This was what he waited to hear from me to move on to his Heaven. I would do anything in the world to help him so he could go in peace, but he had to know I would be okay and live out my life. In my reasoning I knew that once I told David what he needed to hear he would go home, that I couldn't keep him any longer! I would be letting him go! But for him I would do this and it tore my heart out. He had to know this without asking me. I don't know to this day what I would have done without my loved ones and Alex to guide me. I drew on my inner strength and all of theirs. It is very hard to relive this last tragic part of my son's story but I must do so, so that his chosen life and love for others will count and live on. What he did in life made a huge difference in ours and in many others' lives.

It was now close to the end; others left so we could be alone. My family didn't want to go and were saying their last loving words to him in his final hours. They knew their small children were waiting for them at home. I knew this was the hardest time in their lives to leave him and hopefully David knew we would all pull together and manage without him. I know this was the hardest time in his life knowing this was a final good-bye to everyone he loved with the few words he tried to muster. I feel he was very aware of those leaving even if he couldn't respond to them.

My head was coming off from the pressure of the small amount of time left for us; it was excruciating and emotionally painful! I knew my son had heard and understood me as I was saying my words to him. He squeezed my hand letting me know he loved me and knew I was with him. I tried to get closer to him to hold him in my arms but medical objects were in my way. I just wanted to hold him until his time came, we never let go of one another's hands we held on together tightly! I didn't want to lean over him to put any weight on his chest; he was laboring to breathe now. I leaned as close as I could, my eyes focused back and forth at the clock on the wall. I knew our time was so precious together and the minutes were flying by! I have never felt the way I did in those minutes about time. I wanted to stop the clock and never look at it again but couldn't help myself.

This last part was more than overwhelming with certain special last words my son waited to hear from me to help him go in peace. I knew once I told him the very last words leading him over, he would be home and I couldn't keep him any longer! I had to let him go! God help me! I was thinking "please, help me to be strong enough to say these final words!" This was the hardest thing I have ever done and it broke my heart. I could not bear to see him suffer any longer trying to keep him here any longer in his pain, how selfish would I be? I knew he would try to hold on with me as long as he could. I was realizing how hard it had been for my family to leave their brother and uncle knowing this was the end. They would never see him again in this lifetime. I had felt my family's pain of seeing and leaving him one last time.

We still held our hands clasped tightly together sending our love to one another through our touch and a squeeze of our hands. He let me know he was very aware of me, sending his love and strength to me as I was to him. I couldn't quit watching the clock on the wall because the other side had told me his time to leave would have a three in it. I thought at 3:15AM could this be it? And then that time passed. Too soon, 3:30AM came. I was panicking and holding my breath, and then it too passed. I think we were given extra time because he and I prayed for it and now he had finished everything he had come here to do.

All of a sudden David startled me as he suddenly began to shake his head very fast back and forth, No! No! He was telling the other side, No! He wasn't going, he was fighting to stay with me and I held him, our hands together like steel as if I could somehow keep my son here with me! I wanted so much to plead for him not to go yet. I am his mother who loves him with all my heart and soul, and because I am, I knew he needed to go on to peace and free his soul! I was in shock and quietly I thought "this can't be happening to him!" I knew he felt my total soul so full of love for him. Silently I thought Oh, my little boy what can I do, except what I was doing and it was excruciating, this can't be! The seconds had flown by and I dreaded the clock on the wall I wanted time to just STOP! David had squeezed my hand more times so I knew he was aware and in his way saying, "I love you, mom!" I was telling my son I loved him over and over and how proud of him I am and always have been!

I knew now without a doubt at 3:45AM on Palm Sunday and his Sister, Pam's birthday, he would be going home to the Christ Light in Heaven. The other side was trying to prepare us both as well as they could. David had squeezed my hand several more times, I love you Mom! I had begun to get very frightened as the moments ticked by; this was sheer torture for both of us! I tried to stop glancing at the clock but I couldn't!

"Oh, my beloved son, how did our lives pass by so quickly?" I thought to myself. I was continually telling my son softly over and over, "I love you! And that he was the best son I could have ever had. I could never have special ordered one like him." I have never felt so helpless and I pray I never have to feel this way ever again. I knew it was time after my son shook his head the three times, NO! I wanted to call out once more, take my life for his, but I knew it couldn't be! I was his mother, the other half of his soul, who loved him with all my heart and I know he felt my love deep in his soul as I did his! Without words, we both understood we would be together again on the other side. I wanted the monitor and equipment out of my way so I could be closer to him and to hold my son like when he was small, he was still my little boy! This was the hardest thing in my life, watching my child getting ready to cross over. I was so full of love and compassion for him and so utterly helpless! We were still holding tightly together his hand was so strong and tight holding mine; he never lost his strength, it increased! We were not letting go of one another.

I was waiting for the courage to begin what I knew I had to for him now with the last words he waited for and needed. I told him once more how much I loved him and how proud of him I have always been. And again I could feel his deep heartfelt love for me. He had never spoken again after telling me, "I would be happy now and live a good life." He must have felt he had to let me know I could manage to go on without him here.

Then mustering all the strength I could, everything became a blur as my son's spirit combined with mine, and I began softly talking my son over. We had merged together as one soul and one spirit now as in our creation. I could plainly see what my son was seeing. I was with him I could see our passed over loved ones coming to us. I first asked David if he could see grandma and grandpa. "No," he said. I waited another moment and began softly speaking again to help relax his labored breathing and he relaxed. I kept telling him, I loved him so much! I recall specifically putting the cross on his forehead saying, "Fear not for I am with thee always." Where that came from was Jesus Christ, for the words came through me by hearing them.

I slowly began crossing him over further and continued to see what he could. I was into the other side with my son! I first saw his little dog, Shorty, come running to him and jump in his arms! I said, "Oh look David, there is Shorty, she is here!" It had been a few years since she had crossed over and he had missed her so very much and grieved terribly for her, they were so devoted! She was instantly in his arms so excited to greet him! Along with Shorty were my son's twin babies, his boys, and my grandson who had passed at birth who had been named David. My son had always quietly grieved for his sons all through his life. There were his grandparents he loved so much and many other loved ones, and dear friends all waiting to greet him home! I knew then he was there and I began telling him the last words I would ever get to.

My soul was in agony and lay bare as never before! As all of this happened I could tell he was not resisting any longer. He had been moving closer into the Light, the spirit world, into our familiar heavenly home. I knew for the first time I COULDN'T go with him, and this part was killing me! Oh, how I wanted to go with him, but I could not leave my daughters and loved ones yet I needed to be with them longer. All I could think now was, "my boy, my loving son, how can our lives together be over so soon here on Earth?" As beautiful as this was where he was now I wanted to beg and beg again, my life for his, but I knew nothing was going to be changed. I knew the Heavenly Light Beings were holding me up giving me the strength to do this for him.

I could see my David continuing to float further into the spirit world that was surrounding him in a golden white Brilliance which is completely indescribable! The beautiful softness of this Illuminating White Light he was merging into was our Creator of Supreme Light! There waiting for my son in this Brilliance of light was our Creator of pure love! God the Creator was holding outstretched arms to receive my son! David was so happy and laughing as never before out of his joy, he was ecstatic as he floated right into God's arms, then God wrapped his arms around him as if tenderly embracing David to him. I was honored by being granted our crossing together and to see my son greeted in this phenomenal loving WELCOME home! Then I plainly witnessed David melting into God's arms completely. I said to him, "Now you are in GOD'S arms! GOD has his arms wrapped around you; you are in GOD'S arms!"Then he was completely absorbed completely into God and they were one!

This was the most beautiful amazing gift, a miracle that I was honored to be a part of! These moments were so amazing that I have no correct words to describe this beautiful experience in our earth language! I knew his soul had merged together with God once more as one, and he was in perfection! I knew what this represented; he was home with our Savior! He had been, David, my son here on earth, and now I was watching his magnificent ending as witness to what waited for him! He now existed in his new and perfect spirit body out of human pain and into a glorious bliss of peaceful joy! Quickly I was pulled back to Earth into my world of reality and confusion with a mixture of his love and peace to my earthly great pain and the worst sorrow I have ever known!

Now unbelievably with David's last breath he pulled my arm straight up into the air with his hand holding mine so tightly it was like steel. I was pulled partly out of my chair because he had pulled me up with such strength upwards to him, trying to take me with him! Suddenly then his arm and hand went limp and both of our arms quickly dropped, lifeless now with both landing on his chest! He had given me this last gift of his human self! I had just watched him merge within God yet I was given these last moments together holding hands. I stopped breathing for a few moments frozen in place by expecting him to move somehow. I could see his face was completely peaceful and serene; and he was glowing in light, which is indescribable! It was then I realized my beloved son was completely gone from here. I then returned to my world knowing what I had just been a very important part of. David looked as if he were just sleeping, waiting to wake up. It took me a few moments to understand what had just happened.

I cried out, "Oh David, if I could just feel your heart beat once more!" At that time my hand was still lying on his chest and I could feel the warmth of him. With my wishful comment immediately the life support machine started up on its own! It had shut down when my son had quit breathing and died. I couldn't believe what I saw! I was so in awe to see all of his vitals showing perfect once more! This was incredible, his blood pressure, heart, and the rest were perfect! I guess in those moments I thought he had returned to his body in another kind of miracle once more!

The attendant who was in the room was saying, "That can't be!" She was looking at the life support machine which was still on with his readings! I recall turning to say, "But you don't know what my son can do!" Then turning back around there he was! David was standing close to me on my left side looking at me; he was in the most beautiful form of silver glowing sparkles from head to toe! I called out, "There he is!" I was indescribably happy and overwhelmed! Even though my son had passed into spirit a second before to another time and place, there he was in spirit to comfort me! I truly believe God gave us both this extra time knowing we needed this moment together once more as I had humbly asked for, our request had been granted! Then he vanished from my sight in his new spirit body. We had been granted this glorious moment which I would keep in my soul forever, and I gave thanks.

Quickly then, I looked down at his physical face which was so peacefully beautiful still with an amazing glow I can't describe. In the wonder of these moments I realized this was his outer shell, the identity he wore as a human. The son I held tightly only a few moments ago and loved so much had entered the other world taking away his pain. And it wasn't but a few moments later all of this had happened. I was now contacting my son with my thoughts. I could hear him saying to me, "he would never leave me, always together, I will always be with you Mom our vow is eternal!" Then someone was tapping on my shoulder from the hospital and I mentally crumbled.

I had felt our special close connection once more. I wanted to keep on seeing him but he had faded away for now going back into the spirit world. You see, in spirit one can bounce back and forth faster than the blink of an eye! A spirit can move that quickly to where they want to go. They can stay close to their loved ones after their body dies. Our loved ones who are left behind in their grief are now concerned if they are okay, and where their loved one is. By my own experiences with the other world of souls for years, and now with my son, I guarantee you there is another magnificent place waiting for them. Death isn't the end; it is another beginning! There is no end! I thanked David for doing what he did to comfort me all he could that our lives would go on in this new way until we meet again for eternity.

Making it out of the hospital and to the car was a blur to me and the drive home which took over an hour. I walked into my home ready to collapse. There would be no more phone calls, today with, Hi Mom, what you doing? Always ending with I love you! It was almost 5 am.

The day my son passed over I returned home to his house around 8AM. Looking at the clock, he had only been gone barely five hours now. I knew people would be coming by to see us when they heard about him. I wanted to be where he had been and lay down on his bed. I am sure he knew he would never be in his bed again when he became violently ill the night before. This was when we rushed him to the hospital. I wanted to feel as close to him as I could, this being the last place he was. I didn't really know if people had been called and knew about him. I hoped I could be strong for my daughters and family.

My best friend, Shirley, who lives several miles away, had been called by someone who told her of David's passing and she soon, arrived. David, Shirley, and I were very close to one another. He adored her as she did him. He was always teasing her and making her laugh all the time. I was so glad to see her! She was very shocked that he had died so suddenly! She had no knowledge that he had become critical so quickly and was in the hospital. I had not been able to call her myself to give her any details. I had not told her anything about his passing or the vision I had of him. After she arrived, she asked me what time did he pass? I said at 3:45 AM this morning which was Palm Sunday, March 16th, and his sister Pam's birthday! She looked surprised with that information and said, "I need to tell you what happened to me! I had a dream or vision, whatever it was of David at that exact time! Because it was so real I opened my eyes to look at the time and it was 3:45 am!"

She told me in her vision she saw David laughing, and he was so happy, floating through a soft luminous whiteness towards a brilliant Light. Close ahead waiting was a beautiful glowing figure in a bright white robe, holding out His arms to David. She instantly knew this was God! David floated right into God's outstretched arms and was absorbed into him as the Creator's arms folded around him! She knew now he was safe in God's arms! I was so shocked! Shirley was given the exact vision just as it had actually happened, right at the very moment I saw this happening myself! Plus, with the exact words I had said to my son at the exact time! We both knew we had shared this divine blessing together. I blurted out, "I can't get over that you witnessed exactly the same way he crossed over, and with the same words I said to him!" And the last thing I saw of my son was the exact same vision of him that Shirley saw, absorbing into God's arms! And I had told David he was now in the arms of God! I was thrilled to hear this from her experience.

Shirley and I were given comfort by experiencing this amazing event at the same time. And with each of us in different places, and miles apart as it was happening, this was a gift from God! I knew the Heavenly Father our Creator and David were together in exactly the way it happened. This was a gift we each were to share and it was a great comfort and confirmation! David knew we would find this out, that Shirley would tell me to comfort me with her information! We both felt completely humbled and amazed and I was being reinforced by her experience. He had such strong love for Christ in how he lived his life and God had received him in this way welcoming him home. By going straight into God's arms my son was absorbed within Him. He had finished what he came here for and now he was *home* again with our *Creator*!

I had not been able to ask him a last time about his wish to be cremated; this was his wish through his life when he died. My daughter had to help me with the arrangements since I was still too overcome to handle it. Pam was so strong and reaffirmed with her brother that night that he did want this done.

David Comes to Hold My Hand

That same evening I had another phenomenal beautiful experience from my son. It had not been even 24 hours ago that he had crossed over. This was back at my home on the evening of his passing. I was all alone walking the floor just wanting my son. I was sobbing and crying out for him when suddenly the doorbell rang and it was my daughter, Robin. I was so glad to see her and in my sorrow she had come by to keep me company and check on me. I told her what Shirley experienced the same as I had! She was mesmerized! I had felt David around me strongly all day and I told her his spirit energy was with us in the room. I was trying to show her a ball of light that kept circling around the ceiling and was now in front of us! David's energy was this circle of glowing light moving around over to us, time and time again. "Can you see him, he is right here; his energy is the bright light! It's David!" I was saying! He is trying to let us know he is with us now and wants to help us! He knew better than anyone we needed him our heavy hearts were broken!

As we talked I watched the ball of light slowly come over me to my left hand. Both of us had been talking at the time about him coming in his light. We were so excited we had not noticed right at that moment what was happening. I felt my excitement by suddenly moving my attention to my left hand and could not believe my eyes! I called out to Robin, "Oh, look at my hand and arm!" I had no control over what was happening to me! My left hand had risen from the arm of my chair by itself! My arm and hand was moving slowly upwards! I felt nothing different at all! We sat still watching this amazing experience David was doing for us!

I asked my daughter to quickly go and grab the camera out of the car to take pictures. My arm was rising upward slowly, a little at a time and she began taking pictures! We both could plainly see my left hand was much larger than normal, much larger than the right hand and it looked like wax! We decided to have my daughter touch my hand to feel it and she exclaimed, "That it was hard as wax and wouldn't budge down as she put pressure on it! My hand couldn't be pushed down and I could not lower my arm back down!

I realized immediately that David was somehow holding my left hand up just as he did in those LAST moments before he passed over when he pulled me up and towards him not letting go of me! His spirit hand was strong like steel as before, and I could feel the pressure. He was comforting me by holding my hand now as he did less than 24 hours earlier! The color of my arm stayed normal even with the blood flow going down my arm the entire time he held it. I thanked him and our Divine Creator with all of my heart and soul for this blessed event!

I completely believe he somehow arranged this through Christ. I know he did to continue proving, "I am with you always mom!" I have the pictures showing my left hand is much larger than the right one, just as his hands were much larger than mine! This went on for at least 35 minutes with my arm and hand up in the air, it never bothered me and my arm never became tired because David was holding my arm up to him! This was how he wanted me to know he was so close to all of us and he always would be helping us all throughout my life. I recalled then when my dad was passing over and David first saw the ball of light representing my dad in his apartment that evening while he was with his friend Jim. I now was so grateful for this to happen because it helped Robin and I to know David was there to console us.

I hope you the readers can somehow understand this; it was so unbelievable even to both of us, but it happened! This was an amazing experience giving further evidence of what he was doing to show us, "I am here! I am with you both!" He knew how important this was for us and wanted to comfort us! David had managed this through the grace of God!

I was once told by a Heavenly Angel Being that when someone crosses over for the first three days they are not to touch anyone physically, why, I do not know? But later the other side confirmed once more that David did this for me through the grace of God. David had arranged this beautiful and wonderful way to reinforce, I will never leave you! This was an amazing exception that he could touch me within the 24 hours that our Creator had made possible! If I ever had any doubt that night, the pictures my daughter Robin took shows my left hand larger than the right, and it does not look real! I know what happened on that lonely sad night as my daughter does, and how we were graced with his Heavenly visit. On that night with my hand rising and changing, he also gave us strength and love though his touch. He knew we desperately needed it.

Early the next day, trying to pull myself together I could hear David talking to me before I started to the funeral home to make his arrangements. He said, "Mom, I will be standing right beside you through all of this to give you strength, remember, I am with you always!" This was how I made it through that day with my son, my sweet daughters, and loving family all standing with me. I knew he was close beside us all joining in on everything that was happening. At his celebration my daughter shared two separate letters she had written years ago about a conversation David had with her at that time. She wanted to know his wishes.

The Letter

David needed to tell her how he felt that I will share with you. It is very personal and sad as he laid bare his soul to her with what was in his heart.

June 1, 1996

My brother and I had a conversation in my parents' living room after he returned home from a hospital stay. He needed to tell me of his feelings and desires of the time when he passes over. He broke down and told me that he was dying of cancer. He said, "The most important thing was to have faith in him. He felt guilty because he knew it would hurt Mom and Dad. He worries about all of us." He cried, and I held his hand for a very long time. He knows mom is tired, and he knows she loves him so very much. He just doesn't want to watch us suffer. He wants us to be ourselves. David said, "He is happy, but has wanted to go for a very long time. And that when he was a little boy, he wouldn't live to see the year 2000, but he holds on, to be with us as long as he can." David says, "To wear all bright colors and have happy music when he leaves here. That he never felt a part of this world anyway. And that he would never leave us; he will always be with us."

On September 14, 1996

I asked David why he never complained and he told me "it's a waste of time, it doesn't change anything." This was a very hard letter for me to read. I only saw it after my son passed over when my daughter brought it to me for his celebration of life on March 19th, 2008.

The Empty House

   I went home that evening after David's celebration of life and a dear friend of ours came with me for a while that evening. I was so relieved for the company rather than going home alone. My children had families and we were all exhausted. There was a cold stillness in my big empty home walking into it after the funeral celebration was over. It had no life, no laughter, no anything, just empty and cold. I was grateful my friend, Stacy, stayed a few hours, just talking about my son whom she had known a long time and adored. She helped arrange things for us in the medical world when I first brought my son home in the beginning and that's how we met her. She came to help us with his health care. Stacy was so tender hearted and cared for him so much. Above all, she was compassionate and had a healing way of her own. She and David just loved each other and I loved her as much. Stacy was a wonderful treasure, a friend to us for those years. This meant so much to me on that sad night to have her with me. I will always remember her kindness.

   I shared with Stacy what David did the moment he crossed over. The life support machine came on by itself and he showed himself to me in a brilliant bright light of silver sparkles! She is a believer of the truth and loved hearing what he did. One of the memories that brought joy to him was when she came for her visits and especially on his birthday each year that we celebrated together. We always kidded him since he was born on Elvis Presley's birthday so when I answered the door every year, there was Stacy in a black leather pants and jacket! We laughed so much and it made his day! Every year after, she never forgot to wear her black leather like Elvis wore, on his birthday.

   My son had predicted each child ahead in Stacy's future including the gender and the names! Even when she would say "no, I'm not going to have another baby, David," he would smile big and say "Yes, you will with another baby girl ahead" and this would come to pass each time! Three new babies came into her life all beautiful and healthy with David's predictions! Stacy and her husband are very happy with their blessed family. We all shared our bond together for years.

Chapter 17

David's Many Visits in Spirit

A Sons Loving Touch

The next morning after his service I woke up by feeling a loving touch on my face which brought me out of my sleep. Opening my eyes I saw my son on his knees beside my bed! He was solid and looked so concerned for me! He was confirming he will always help and protect me. I will see this in my mind forever, his caring, humbleness, and the love shining in his face! This was in his desperation to continue letting me know he was concerned about me, and still with us to help get us through our excruciating experience.

My granddaughter, Brooke, had taken pictures of David's personal items and his photographs that were set up for his Celebration of life that evening before. When those pictures were developed we detected a bright white and blue light passing over his pictures in each shot. He was showing us all that we were not alone, just as he said he would do. Brooke had noticed this right away even though she was devastated as everyone; she was very close to her uncle David. I am sure that's why David left his energy of light on the photos she took for all to see. He was still sending out to us, "I am alive!" Many more strange things began to happen to us and to several of his close friends right away after his passing. He had begun his contact with others showing them he was very much alive in spirit. My daughters and granddaughters Casey and Brooke helped me emotionally that night and I knew David was standing with us watching over us with his love as he said he would.

After my son had passed over several people and some of our dear friends from different towns and states began calling me in the immediate days and weeks to tell me they had seen my son in one way or another. They all knew his visit was real and not a dream knowing what they had experienced. I was told of his many visits that I have kept written down and some I have included in this book for you to experience also.

Some friends said they had woken up to see David close by or at the foot of their bed with a message to some and a big smile to others. He was always happy and healthy, and looking so young to all of us. I still get calls to this day from those who have seen him in what some people call dreams, but they are without any doubt real visits. Most say he is usually solid looking in the visit, smiling and happy in a bright light; he lives on and is at peace. His visits, give those people peace, along with a belief of life after death, if they never believed it before and he is still teaching in his work from where he is.

David Making His Rounds

One day shortly after David's passing; my daughter Pam and I were at David's home packing up some of his things. I was upstairs when suddenly I heard the loud noise of a train with whistles and bells sounding as if it was running right beside me! Whirling around I realized I was only a few feet from David's little antique train and it was running by itself calling out, all aboard, everyone all aboard! The train whistles and bells were sounding out loudly!

I stood there stunned, and then I heard Pam who had been down stairs come running up, "What's going on?" I couldn't answer her, I was glued there watching the little train running around the track and going through the small tunnel! We both stepped over together to get a closer look, to what our eyes couldn't believe! We were spellbound, staring at the little train racing around the small track by itself! "It's David," we both said, laughing together! The train kept calling out, "get on board, all aboard!" We kept laughing because he broke our sadness with his presence, by making the little train run by itself around and around the track.

We both knew he was right beside us probably laughing hard with seeing us so happy with his surprise! He knew this would cheer us up with his visit and being his same funny self! The train continued to run for several minutes still calling out, all aboard, get on board and then it was over and the little train just stopped! We couldn't recall ever seeing it run before and we couldn't wait to tell everyone his latest escapade!

I believe this was a two way message. With the words that were coming from the little train, he was actually meaning for us to get back to our lives (get on board) and go forward. He did so much for us we couldn't wait for the next experience! I keep his little antique train in my home now and it has never once run again. He loved old toys and always kept the little boy inside of himself, that's why he had the train and many other objects he liked as a child that he had saved. Perhaps he kept them hoping for children to come. He still had his old keepsakes a Snoopy clock, watch, wastebasket, and other items from his childhood which had been packed away for years. Take my advice; don't ever lose the "child" inside of yourself. As we would say later, you're "Burnt Toast" if you do.

He was just getting warmed up! Everything he was doing was to let us know how close he was around us and he made our suffering more bearable. He knew we needed moments like this with the train that day to know he was there and because we were very emotional packing his things away for good or to give away. I knew he would always know when he is needed. Our spirits were lifted high that day we couldn't quit laughing with tears rolling down our faces at what he had done and we couldn't wait until the next time! David and I could never get over all the things we have seen the other side do for us and now he was showing what he could do! This was like an enormous dose of happy medicine for us!

The Palms of His Hands

One of the remarkable things David told me in the first few days after he passed over was for me to "look into the palms of his hands" and I would see him! I didn't understand what he meant and what he was trying to say, but I knew that this was a clue. I would find out what he meant and intuitively I knew the answer would be found in his house. I told my daughter, Robin, his message and we went to his home to search for what it meant. As we searched she opened a drawer in his bedroom chest and excitedly called out, "Come look…Look, Mom, here it is," she gushed out! She was holding a small plaque in her hands that we both had never seen before. The plaque says, "I will never forget you! See, I have engraved you into the palms of my hands." Isaiah 49:15 16 from the Bible verse! This was what he meant with his message about the "palms of his hands!" We were so excited I called my daughter Pam quickly! He did this to help us in a very difficult time and continued to make contact as he said he would. He made it clear that he had etched us all in his spirit forever more. This was absolute happiness and joy to know!

Back to shortly before the celebration of David's life service, Sara another very dear friend called. She had given me the beautiful figure of a pair of hands holding an Angel in its palms and now we found the plaque! This was an example of how he sent messages that helped all of us so much by knowing how close he is! How perfect this was and how clever the souls can be to reach us. He had also given Sara the "thought" of bringing the Angel to us even though she would not have known this. See how things come together and when one is open minded more comes in because of belief. My friend Sara, who had given me the Angel figure, knew nothing about David's message to me or the plaque we found. She did tell me later on that she was picking out a blouse to wear to the funeral home that evening and she pulled out a pale colored one, just as quickly she heard a voice say, "No; wear a brighter one, this is a celebration of my life not a funeral!" So needless to say, she took the brighter colored one to wear! My friend said, "This was the first time she had ever heard a spirit voice talk to her and knew it came from David, and she will never forget her experience!" She said, "At first she stood there a few minutes frozen to the spot surprised and stunned, looking around to see who was there, then she knew!" Since the plaque was found that day in his chest in his home I have heard this verse several times on TV and read it in the Bible about the palms of his hands. I know my son is arranging all of this in some unique way so we will never forget.

Friends Letting Me Know

I soon received a call from our dear friend Stacy. She called to tell me her news, that she had also seen David after he had passed over! Since Stacy and David had been being such close friends for a long time, I wasn't surprised. On this particular night Stacy said, David had woke her up in the early hours after she had been sleeping. At first, she could only sense him being there in the bedroom, but she knew it was him. She slowly got out of bed not wanting to wake her husband, knowing David wanted to connect with her. She walked out of the bedroom and down the hall. She was very aware of his presence, knowing he was following along with her; she felt his spirit growing stronger as she went down the hall and into the living room. Stacy said to him, "Now don't scare me, David" and laughed quietly.

She lay down on the sofa as not to disturb her husband and quickly closed her eyes since this was the first time she had a visit and was a little nervous, soon falling asleep. David always teased her so much she didn't know what he would do to aggravate her in fun. Suddenly, she felt a gentle slight nudging on her shoulder. With that her eyes flew open and there David was smiling down at her! He was standing directly in front of her as solid as could be, saying "Hello!"

She was so happy to see him and not at all afraid now in any way, she knew he wanted her to know he was fine and happy because she meant so much to him and he thought so highly of her. He had always been thankful for her help in his illness and this meant the world to her. I knew David had appreciated her staying with me part of the night of his celebration to comfort me. She had been in our home off and on for many years and we had many wonderful visits. Stacy said, he talked more with her that night and then he vanished.

She soon had another visit from David. She said that he would turn her TV on and off to gain her attention as if saying "Hi, I'm here!" They were both so funny and the best of friends; so he was still connecting with her. She is a special person who has helped many people through her work and this visit he made to her meant so much as she had taken David's passing very hard. He was still making his rounds to those he knew closely and loved. I get calls of his visits to this day from others. I was surprised at how many of his friends were open to have the experience of his visitation. Not one person was afraid of his visit, they were in awe and happy to know he is at peace and appears as they knew him. We still keep our own personality in the afterlife.

Another close friend, whom I mentioned earlier in this book, Bev, told me of an experience with David by calling me long distance to tell me. She was on a plane traveling to Mississippi; suddenly she noticed a reflection on her lunch tray, which had a shiny finish, of a man's face. She knew it had to be coming from the direction of the airplane window which was impossible! Since no one could possibly be outside but she quickly looked over at the window and it was David's smiling face she saw and without words he winked at her! This startled Bev at first, but then she quickly figured that something had happened to him, that he must have passed over to see him like she did. His appearance was brief but it was him and this experience made her think of all the years he had been sick and that she would miss him very much. She quickly called to tell another friend the experience of seeing his face in the reflection and to find out if her thoughts were correct about his passing and of course they were. She was sad and happy at the same time knowing he wanted to say "Hello, I'm ok" and this was the way he chose to do it!

This was one of the things he taught others while he was on earth, about how the spirit world can work to arrange many ways to show they are present. For instance, by leaving all kinds of signs to let their presence be known and to let loved ones know they are still alive. We wanted people to know what happens and not to be afraid of dying and to continue to embrace your life here on earth while you are here.

My Son's Help to Pull Me Through

My son knew I understood his help to me after he crossed over and in time I would get on my feet reminding me that we are all POWERFUL beings. He helped to build my strength, an inner strength I never knew was possible and he held me up with his strong spirit and love. I continued to see him each day and night as he came to me, helping me through my endless grief and protecting me from negative people coming around me. The negative ones were like vultures and had stolen all kinds of things from my son's home when he had only been gone a few days. Material isn't important, but the stress I was in with just experiencing the passing of him and bad people getting into his home stealing, I was fighting for my life each day to survive.

I felt my heart and soul were raw and bleeding. This was all a total nightmare! There was just so much going on, on top of my greatest loss ever. David was helping me as much as he could and he repeated several times, "for me to fight for my life, I must fight to live and get better! That I was not a victim of circumstance." I tried to do this at that lowest time in my life but with my extreme sadness and fatigue, I gave up on my fight to survive. My son was trying to hold me up with his spirit the best he could. He knew everything going on in my life and that it was too much for my broken heart and mind.

He reminded me of the work I still had to do while on earth and that we still would do it together. He was doing all he could from his side. Your loved ones can't do everything for you from where they are that we must do for ourselves. I knew I needed to draw on my own self with him helping me. I had to pull myself out of the pit I had fallen into with despair through trusting the wrong people I shouldn't have. All I wanted was to be able to carry on with my family and for the negative ones to leave us alone in peace, to begin some kind of a healing process.

Eventually, my family and I put all of this behind us with David's help and began the start of a healing process the best we could. We were all worn out by now and I was worn more than I knew. Then came the blessed experience about an Angel calendar that David had asked Beverly to bring to me about being a victim of circumstances. David soon came again early one day to see our friend, Bev. He told her, "He needed her to bring a message to me. For her to bring me a page from her Angel calendar" which sat on her dresser, so she began to remove the April page since it was April. David said, "No, take the next month of May instead, mom needs that one." Each month had a wonderful message, but Bev said, "He was very specific this was the certain page I needed. Then he gave her directions to his home telling her to take the back road through the countryside to his house. She would see three turtles on the road to his house as a confirmation that she was on the right road. Soon she saw three turtles crossing the road on her way." He also said "there would be the sign of two doves when she arrived at his home sitting on his front walk," and there they also were! She did not know where his house was, but with him guiding her, his directions were perfect.

We were originally to meet at my home and when she didn't show up I intuitively knew to drive to David's home to greet her when she didn't arrive on time. I soon arrived at David's home as she was getting out of her car, getting ready to call me when I pulled up. She told me how David directed her to his house and what he had said about the turtles. We both had a good laugh about the turtles as this was a joke they both shared once and they both loved turtles.

The first thing we did was walk around to the front walk where two beautiful doves were sitting there on the front walk just like he said they would be! Bev said, "he also wanted her to bless the inside and outside of his house while she was there." He knew the people who had caused me trouble in his home after he passed over and had her do this blessing for my safety in living there. I was now in the process of moving in to his home where he wanted me to go and begin my healing. He knew that would be where I needed to be for some time and wanted to make sure I was safe just as he wanted the Christ Light circle of protection to be put around the house and yard.

The two doves stayed on the front walk all day even when I walked around them going up and down the porch steps to get my mail without them ever moving! The next day they were still there and remained there the following day. They were gorgeous and completely unafraid of me, seeming perfectly at home. I would look out of the windows and see them many times afterwards in the following days, off and on, for the rest of the time I lived there. They were symbols of goodness, peace, and love. We both had been given the symbol of doves in our work, so I knew he was close by with sending them to me.

The Angel Calendar

This is the saying from the calendar page David asked Bev to bring me off of her Angel calendar, dated May 20th of 2008.

"You, who have the power of all of Heavens spheres within you, need never believe that you are a victim of outside circumstances."

I knew exactly why David sent this message to me at such a difficult time in my life. I had become a victim of outside circumstances. I was devastated by everything happening at once. My son was trying to get me to see where I was in my life plan to help me. Since he sent this to me I have kept this beautiful Angel page in a frame close by my bed and I treasure it with all my heart. He knew I needed to hear these important words and he chose to deliver my message through Bev, our dear and best friend. But it was already too late for me for Bev had noticed my aura was very dim.

This reminded me of how much the symbol of the doves have always meant to us coming from one of our great spiritual teachers, Edgar Cayce. The doves were our symbols as were his, he has been a spiritual teacher to both of us in our healing work. Edgar brought the both of us a long way with his teachings, healing techniques, and his insight to understanding other universal worlds, and he worked with both of us in learning the trance states he used. I cannot express enough of our love for him and his wife, Gertrude. Edgar passed over many years ago (1945) with his wife following him shortly thereafter. We always knew when he was with us and teaching us. We were his students for a long time and he is close by us to this day. If I need him I know he hears me. This is why David chose the doves that day for me to know I had his and Edgar's help coming to me, I would need them.

The Sound of Footsteps

We see our children as the Angels they are fulfilling our lives which is about the next visit David made. My daughter Pam in this next memory also connected me to my other daughter, Robin, who found the Angel plaque in the earlier experience. After this, Robin began hearing her brother in her house after he passed over. First, she would hear his footsteps on the hardwood floors and coming into her room. She told me of his visits and that his watch, which she had, kept running on its own, sounding the alarm early every morning around 3 AM!

David never really used this watch because he had gotten it right before his last emergency. He had recently been given it because of his blindness to help him when he was in training. His watches alarm had never been set to go off, especially not at 3 AM. The watch had a Rooster alarm sound that would crow and tell the time. Robin would hear the rooster sounding at 3 AM each day. Again, he was letting his sister know, "I am here and I love you!" David appreciated the watch but did not like the loud crowing because we had kidded him with our rooster calls to cheer him up. So in this way it was easy for him to quickly get her attention!

There continued to be many more visits from David to our immediate family and close friends, he wanted us to know that he was with us. One evening when Robin returned home from work and was ready to go to bed she pulled the comforter down and found a big surprise! She discovered sequins sprinkled on the sheets in her bed! She called me full of excitement to tell me her experience and that she had never seen the silver sequins before so we certainly knew who brought them! The following night there were more sequins found on the floor beside her bed. These sequins were in different colors of bronze and silvers. There was no rational explanation, except in knowing David had left his "calling card" for her.

It wasn't long when she had another visit from her brother. She had gotten up early and was walking down the hall when she saw an object on the floor. There lay a picture she had of birds (David had a love for birds) that had been on her dining room wall. It had to have been removed from there and lay some 8 feet away from the wall in the hall! Again, he let her know; I was here to see you!

On another afternoon when she returned home, she was startled to find a cereal box that had been in her kitchen cabinet hanging out of a kitchen drawer by the box top only! Surprise! All of what he did cheered her up and brought her closer into the spirit world. All I can say is to stay open minded; coincidence is not a word to go by. There is no such thing.

It is amazing how the other side can gain one's attention to let you know they are around. By David leaving his sister the sequins, I knew why. This was how I had seen my son appear immediately after he went into spirit, standing by me in the hospital room, in silver sparkles from head to toe, as I mentioned earlier. That is why he left the bright sequins in and around her bed to say, yes; it's me!

I believe if one puts the puzzle together you will find the reasoning to go with it as with our experiences. For years I have seen all kind of bright colored lights and gold/ white dazzling lights around spirits. Some are solid and some are transparent figures, some are in their light, too many ways to count. With our experiences I feel positive I know what is taking place when these strange things occur to others.

His Heavenly Angel Wings

This next beautiful experience concerns my daughter, Pam, with another visit from her brother. She was missing him so very much and wanting to see him again. I told her to ask him if he could come to her in a vision, or dream state and soon he did. It was late evening when he came to her by suddenly appearing when she least expected it! She knew this was real and he gave her the big hugs that she had waited for so long. Even though he was not physically solid as in this world, never the less she felt him and his visit washed away her sadness. He had heard her words and knew she needed him. Pam told me that he flashed his big smile lovingly at her and although he never spoke in words as we know them, he used telepathy with his thoughts, mind to mind, which is the usual way we hear them.

After they had greeted one another she suddenly noticed behind him he had beautiful tall wings attached to his shoulders! They were from way above his head on down to the ground behind his heels! She was spellbound taking in these beautiful wings! Then what seemed like moments to her, he began to slowly move upwards up off of the ground to above her, where he stayed floating gently as he hovered in a stationary position. His huge wings sparkled in dazzling blended shades of whites, creams, gold's, and bronzy browns. She said "he was just floating in place and looking down at her, as she watched him, then he looked straight up, stiffened his arms at his sides, and zoom, he was gone!" She felt wonderful he had left her in such peace and her wish was fulfilled; she had gotten to see her brother and share his hugs! Pam will never forget this amazing experience of her brother and the love he passed to her heart. Pam has said many times, that David knows when I need to see him and afterwards I feel so good for days. He gives me a calmness and happiness filled with his love. Between our friends, family and me, he has come to us with his visits many times.

In our homes and other places I can still see these beautiful sparkles of light and in my son's home there are hundreds of them in silvers and blues.

At night the room looks as if there are a million stars that fill it up and I say thank you! I can look at my own beautiful Universe! All through the years David and I could identify other spirits in this way, which we call spirit lights. To us, the outside world generally looks like snow or rain in movement, even on sunny days we can see what we called the eons and molecule patterns and they are quite beautiful. We both see the world in an amazing and different way than what most others are able to. Maybe it is for reasons that involve our work. The first time I saw these patterns I called Bev as fast as I could. I wasn't sure why and what they were. She explained how rare this was and had heard of some people who could see in this way. This helped me to understand. My son and I had the same vision such as this in the same way being one soul.

Another experience came to Bev as she was having coffee with her husband early one morning as they both were reading the newspaper. She put her paper in the middle of the table folded over when she was finished with that section for her husband to read. As soon as she did this the paper suddenly flew off the table and landed on the floor! This certainly got their attention and her husband yelled out, "What was that?" He was quite startled of course. Bev went to pick up the paper and put it back on the table. She had just sat back down and the paper took off again in mid-air landing further away in front of the refrigerator. Now, they both were really surprised!

She knew a spirit was among them, first thinking of her brother who had recently passed away right before David. She went over to get the paper again and looking down she couldn't help noticing a nice size ad staring up at her in large letters, *David, Sunflowers by David*! This is a company advertisement for selling sunflower seeds. Bev knew immediately that her close friend, David, was making his visit! She knew sunflowers were his favorite flowers and the clue for her was with his name. Both she and David had planted flowers together in the early spring many times at her home. He certainly got their attention with his visit to say his, hello! We laughed about this quite a while when she told me about it. I have always been so grateful to hear from others with their stories of my son's visits. Bev loved him very much and was very connected with both of us with her gifts of clairvoyance. We were certainly like a three party system with our gifts and laughed often about the strange worlds we lived in. We had each other and understood our work together. We had one another to lean on in good and hard times. That alone raised our spirits on many occasions.

David's Past School Friend

A young woman whose name is Janice called me one evening to talk. She had gone to grade and high school with David and best friend Roger. She slowly began telling me she had something strange happen to her recently and it was about my son. I had not had contact with Janice in a long time except at David's celebration of life services and she had not been in contact with my son for many years. They had drifted apart while he was in the service and living in different states. Janice had taken his passing very sadly. She continued telling me that something astounding had happened to her and wanted to know if it would bother me to talk about him. "No, I would like to hear what you have to tell me!" I was excited to know!

She began, "When she had woken up one morning he was standing in her room with a big smile on his face! David said, "He had come to check on her to see how she was doing." She was quite startled at first, but quickly settled down and realized he came to visit with her for a reason and it felt just like old times again! He looked the same as he did in high school and especially with his big smile. Then he was gone! She felt so good after his visit, she explained. He had befriended her all through grade and high school; he was a protector to her and apparently still is!

She had been going through a difficult time in her life when this happened and he knew she needed him. Since that time, she has had a couple more visits where he greets her, lets her know he is fine, and to know he is always there for her. I urged her to call me anytime when he shows up again to visit her. This made me as happy as she was feeling. She told me "she hoped he would soon come again; this was a wonderful experience for her to have happen!" I know he is her guardian and will always watch over her. I was eager to hear of his visits from anyone who wanted to share them with me.

With those in the spirit world, distance is not a barrier to go to anyone, anywhere. Our loved ones in spirit can extend their vision and hearing to us here knowing when we need them, coming in all kinds of amazing ways to help and guide us in our lives. They know what's going on in our lives and want to help us all they can, but are limited to an extent. We all need to learn from our own lessons and hurdles. Life wasn't meant to be easy; it was the learning ground that we chose. They can only do so much.

The Best of Friends

David's dearest friend Jim lives in Dallas. He would call me from time to time to tell me of David's visits with him. They both had worked at the same place and shared an apartment together for a few years after David's service life. Jim loves antiques like my son did so they had much in common. A couple of years after my son had crossed over Jim went antique hunting one weekend to a nice shop where they both had enjoyed going to. After looking awhile he decided it was time to go home. Jim was walking to the door, getting ready to leave, when a thought came to him for no apparent reason to go back inside. He explained "He felt as if he was pulled to go down a certain aisle and to the very end of it. He waited, looked around quickly for a moment, and then turned around to leave once more. Suddenly, he stopped in his tracks by seeing an old street sign for sale. Then he knew why this happened, the old sign had David's former street name on it!"

My son was there with Jim as if saying, "Hey, this is like old times again looking for antiques." Jim left feeling very happy because he missed my son very much. Every so often I hear from him relaying another experience of seeing David and at times my mother, who he had a good relationship with too! Jim certainly knew what David had done to connect with him on that lonely day.

The other side is very clever and can make things happen for us. Talk to them they can hear you. Use your thoughts or speak out loud, either way you connect, they know even if you can hear nothing back. Don't be discouraged if everything seems the same after you talk with them, just know and believe your contact has been made.

David knows when I need to hear from him and sometimes while driving alone I know he hears my thoughts. All of a sudden a big truck has rolled up beside me as I'm driving with a familiar ad, *David, Sunflowers by David*! Inside my car quietly I call out to him, "Hello, my sweet son, thank-you for being here!" I feel so good knowing we are in touch with so many ways.

Now you may think that is the old coincidence, a word that explains nothing, but things such as this are arranged by your loved one. We both used to laugh at how clever the other side can be, so unbelievable! Since then, I have seen this happen several times and I know my son is sending his message of love in this way! Our loved ones are very clever and many have such humor bringing a peace and love with them. The other side is very clever in their way to reach you with a message that is why David and I say to be observant.

You may see or hear a message that would not mean anything to anyone else, but to you it will. This may be in a book, movie, news report, a sentence someone says even from a total stranger, a license plate, a phone call, a sermon in church, or just a few words from a friend, that would mean nothing to someone else, but to you it has a special meaning.

It was about two weeks before David had his last crisis and I was driving to the store. All of a sudden the most beautiful song came on the radio by George Harrison called *My Sweet Lord*. I was mesmerized by it going straight to my heart. I later asked my son if he had ever heard of this song and if he liked it. He told me he knew it and liked it very much. This is the song I choose at his celebration of life with the others he liked. I knew then why I was so compelled to use this song and why the day I first heard it I loved it so much. Many times after he crossed over I turned the radio on it would play! I know he had somehow arranged this to be on at that time. Yes, they can do anything and our loved ones do these things to let us know they are with us and hear our words to them.

There is a certain visit that David makes to me quite often. The doorbell rings, I open the door and no one is there that you can see! This happens again and again, usually a third time with no one there! My friend changed the doorbell just in case and the new one rings just as often! I had to say, "I told you so." Each time there is no one (that you can see) anywhere in the yard or street! It is David's calling card he likes to use. He knows I am aware of him even if anyone else is or not.

One day a few weeks later Bev called to tell me that David was standing in her doorway when she woke up. He was plain to see and he began to walk (glide) over to her and sat down on her bed smiling and happy. He talked with her like always, laughing and telling her something funny and then he was gone like a flash! He was off to another place. Have you ever wondered what your loved one is doing? What it is like where they are? It is amazing what they are doing. Remember, my dear friend, Bev, was very clairvoyant too. She loved David very much, so of course he would see her often. Being clairvoyant has been such a blessed gift to my son and me. We are able to be in their world and with those in spirit after they pass. Everything we experience now, we have before! The souls come in different ways even different ages; usually looking great, healthy and younger. They love to come at a younger age and I don't blame them! Some will appear the way you would recognize them the best, it's all different for each one by their choice.

The Big Collapse

I didn't know how to live without David being with us. Life had completely stopped for me. For days and long periods of time I lay in bed not leaving the house, not combing my hair or eating. I wasn't feeling like talking to anyone, but family and a few friends. I didn't know how to live any more. I was in a collapsed world of my own, yet connecting spiritually with my son. It was too painful to wake up and have to face a minute, let alone a day! It had happened and I had to get myself together as I promised David, my daughters, and family.

I would try to pretend I was better as time passed when they called and came over to check on me. And although I could *see* my son and hear his words to me, I naturally wanted to hug him as he was before. I missed him so much, and the house had lost his energy of laughter and joking. Amazingly his complete essence was still with me, thank God. If I held something of his I felt his strong energy go through me, and I knew he was with me. I felt so small in my agony, in an unknown vast and empty place I had never before been! I would ask myself questions, "How will I feel in a month, six months, a year, five, ten years, how will things be?" I was searching my mind for when relief would come, and wondered if it ever would. We had spent many years together 24/7 in hospitals, with his doctors, and the medical world. This was our life in his illness. Then life changed so fast and came to a halt.

It was soon after Bev's visit with the calendar page that I collapsed. I couldn't get better because I worked around the clock moving from my home to my son's home, afraid to stop, trying to block out the thoughts of my son not being here. I would be so exhausted by late evening I hoped to sleep. It was probably too late for me when Bev came with her visit and the calendar Angel page. I didn't know it yet, but apparently my son did try his best to slow me down knowing what was getting ready to take place and hoping I would understand what he meant by the Angel calendar he sent to me.

Bev knew my body was still in shock and tired beyond belief and she also wanted to see me slow down. I knew my aura was very dim by now and so did Bev. I thought if I could keep working every day at David's home, I could forget for a while, which never worked. No matter how many hours I worked moving my things, the thoughts of missing my son continued.

The thing was, I was not remembering to eat and drink fluids; so my illness crept up on me without my even noticing. I was thinking it was only exhaustion with him leaving. It wasn't long that my daughters found me one evening and I quickly ended up in the ER at a hospital some miles from home. I barely had a blood pressure; had double pneumonia; was severely dehydrated; and was very low on potassium; not to mention my badly broken heart. Even though I had been perked up by Bev's visit, I apparently had already broken down too far in my physical body with grief.

My loving daughters had been very concerned about me all along. I kept things from them as if I was doing fine and as not to worry them. But they were worried! They told me later they didn't know what to do with me to help me. I had lost at least 29 pounds since David passed, which was about five weeks earlier. My daughters found me at my home in bed with a very high fever and out of touch with reality. It was then I had no choice, this was going to be a new fight for me and a GREAT gift in my life. There is always good in some way that comes from what one may consider a bad time. I recall I could see the fear in my daughters' eyes that evening in the ER and I felt so badly they had to be afraid for me now when their brother had only been gone a few weeks.

This was what he was trying to tell me by the page he sent to me through Bev's Angel calendar. He knew my health was going down; he was trying to help me pull myself up to get better; to not let myself become a *victim* of outside circumstances due to all that had happened by others wrong doings. My daughters was with me from the start of my illness in ER and David in all of the following days and nights telling me I had to get well. He said, "that I had too much to do yet; I had to fight, fight, Mom, fight! Mom, do this for me if you won't for yourself." Each time I was conscious I could see him with me telling me this. I was too weak to let my daughters know their brother was beside me. My daughters were there with me too. David never left my side.

On one day when I awoke, he showed me himself as he was in another lifetime as a Cardinal in the Catholic Church. This explained without a doubt, why he was so drawn to that life by the many objects and pictures of Mary and Jesus that he collected from the time he was a small boy. Bev said, "He loved who he had been then being able to help others. He also was drawn to the whole orchestration of how the communion was done and the beauty of it all." He had many lifetimes of service to others. As I watched him that day standing before me in the red garments he wore, I thought of how young he was when he was a Cardinal in that life. His blond hair and facial features when he was that age and in that time were the same as he looked in this one. For him to show himself in this way to me was to be a very significant and special meaning coming in my life.

I didn't plan to leave my daughters and beautiful families putting them through what we had just experienced with their brother. David stayed with me even though only I could see him and he encouraged me strongly to keep fighting over and over! He smiled with words of love telling me it was not my time yet. He kept coming to me and saying this. He stood before me in beautiful golden light with the Angels all around the room radiating this light and love to me sending healing energy to me as he did. He never left me and when my eyes opened he would always be there watching over me.

He showed me past lives of himself which made me understand his life here even more and why we would never be able to reveal many of the spiritual messages we had been given that were for our eyes only. I felt I fully understood our contract and work together much more clearly now. I had crossed over into a new level. I loved those days in the hospital not thinking of what all had transpired with the heart break and agony. I had some relief now that I was helpless and too weak to do anything but rest with my daughters and son helping me. I began to realize my keeping busy around the clock and trying to forget for long hours at a time each day is why this happened to me. I had become deathly sick and needed rest. I had been stopped by the grace of God and would have to face my life now. I had no choice if I was to continue living for my loved ones. I made up my mind

I wouldn't leave my beloved family. I would do my best now. I truly know in my heart, sleep is a great healing tool for a broken mind and body, I had surrendered at last! I slept most all of the time day and night, knowing my son would still be there when I opened my eyes. With my daughters' care I was blessed. I felt and knew deeply we were all working together.

As soon as I was able to, I made notes of all the things David told me in the hospital, writing down the experiences as best I could of the Angels and everything he said. By his presence each day and night he was still with me as in life, so solid and concerned for me. I wasn't able to tell my daughters in the hospital what he was saying, I was too tired and sick, but later I would explain this to them.

Time passed, it was good to be back at home in my son's house. This was where I would live for the next two years, although at the time I expected to be there the rest of my life. I continued to sleep as much as I could. I was content to sleep away the days and nights so I could communicate with my son more often. Waking in the nights he was there and I listened to his words. I began to realize he wanted me to do more, to live again, and to find my desire to do this. I had a beautiful world outside I needed to find once more. This is what he was waiting on me to do.

A Long Way Home in the Blizzard

I have had many visions of David since his passing and one that I will remember more than others turned into a visit by him. In this visit, I was with my daughter Robin and we were in a terrible snowstorm up very high on a mountain. With me being afraid of heights, I kept falling back behind her as we climbed this snow covered mountain trying to get to the top. The fear of falling kept coming over me. I felt that if I let go of this large rock I had my arms tightly around I would certainly fall! I was even afraid to look down behind me. I somehow knew that when we reached the top I would be able to look over the ridge and see below the beautiful green grass close to my home. I knew then I would be back at home again to safety and everything would be okay again. But right now I was terrified!

My daughter had gone on ahead of me thinking I was right behind her. She turned around to check on me and could see I was holding onto the big rock too afraid to let go. My daughter kept calling to me, "Come on mom!" She was waiting for me to catch up. I recall looking up at her in the blizzard and she had her hand reaching out for me as if she was going to come back down for me. She was trying to coach me upward to her and I just couldn't let go of the rock. As long as I didn't let go, I felt grounded and safe.

All of a sudden I heard my son, David, call out to his sister Robin, "I'll have to help her. I'll pull her up!" With that I felt him take hold of my hand and he began to pull me up! I felt so safe with his hand holding mine and I knew I would be okay now; he would take me to the top near Robin and then to home. I recall then, in a blink I was at the top of this mountain and the blizzard was gone! I felt such a peace as I looked down from the top of it to see the beautiful green grass below. I wasn't afraid anymore.

David and Robin were in this amazing experience to help me know that everything would be alright. Not to keep looking back and being afraid to go on. I could go on in my life and be strong enough without my son in his physical body; he would always be with me in spirit. I was back at home once more and everything would be fine I would go on. David would always help me up back on my feet with my daughters.

I realized later when coming out of this vision that this experience had more than one meaning for me. It was reinforcing to me that David would always be there helping me in the times I needed him. He had always been my rock! I was afraid to let myself (let go of the rock) go on without him! I didn't think I ever could and that's why I held onto the rock so tightly. He was helping me, through my daughter because she was at a point of not knowing how to help me anymore. I then realized this message and in my state of mind from the left over depression, he was reinforcing his healing message, "I will always be there for you!" He was showing me I would conquer my mountain in life, get to the top again and let my life take off as I had promised.

The night before the mountain vision came about, Robin later told me she was praying and asking her brother to help her get me going again to doing more. She was at her wits end not knowing how else to do this and was feeling helpless! Needless to say he heard her words to him. I know she felt helpless not knowing what to do in order to pull me back into life quicker; the vision carried a double meaning. This told me she was also working in my life to pull me up as well. This was an important turn around through my daughter and son's help.

All of this transpired between the three of us at the same time sharing the same experience. By this I mean the amazing part of the vision was that Robin remembered everything when I first began to tell her early the next day! I couldn't wait to call her and as I started to speak the first few words she said, "Wait, I know what happened too! I was there and I remember it all!" We had shared this important transition together on the same night, and at the same time, all together, how extraordinary! Robin explained she had clearly saw David when he said, "I'll have to help her, I will pull her up!" Then he took my hand in his and began pulling me up to the top of the mountain! He and Robin rescued me together as he always had in life and now my daughter was learning from him. I would make it over my mountain now and onto a new life with much to come. I had come along way but I still had stumbling blocks yet to conquer.

The Holy Temple

One night in David's visit to me, he took me to a Holy Temple where we had lived near in one of our past lifetimes. I was walking up a dirt path and passed my daughter Pam. She was wearing a simple light brown colored robe with a cord tied at her waist as women wore during the Biblical days. We hugged and greeted one another happily then she continued on the path which led down to a small village. I then stood at the doorway of the Temple looking inside it was so dark in the Temple that I could not see anything. I walked slowly foreword as I heard a strong loving voice ringing out to me "let there be Light!"

Golden rays of light came down from above lighting up the room as I looked down at the stone floor. I could see names carved into the stones and mine was in the stone at my feet! I was overwhelmed and in awe as the bright light shined across it! Soon then the vision ended but my emotions were high with humbleness and love. I will never forget this and these blessed moments with the memory of this lifetime. I thanked my son and the Creator for this extraordinary experience for bringing our lifetime back into my memory. How extraordinary this has been to me! The Bible tells us of many miracles and wonderful events but it seems in today's period of time some people think these things cannot happen, that it was only in those days. Nothing is ever impossible!

As a parent dealing with loss, it is almost impossible to move on each day and do the smallest things for a long time. Our normal routines are not important anymore; only our loved ones that are in our world. There will be times of being so afraid that something may happen to another child or loved one, which is frightening. All kinds of thoughts pop into your head that never had before, that is what fear can do. We feel guilt with the thoughts of thinking we could have done something ahead as a loved one, friend, or relation to have prevented the outcome. This is a normal reaction to ponder over and over as we progress more in healing our wounded hearts. So in saying this, so much depends on how deep one's feelings stay buried. But know that you can and you will continue on and this makes the soul of your loved one on the other side very happy. They can then let go of their deep concern over us to work on their own spiritual life now. They have been waiting to do this and they are not mourning as we do here. They have no time to go by and they know we will all be together in what is a blink of an eye to them. In the meantime we are saddled with this earth thing called time, and to us it seems like forever before we will meet our loved ones again.

The White Moth on the glass panel storm door.

The White Moth

The first year after my son crossed over, I was living in his home and I had an exciting experience. One early morning I found a solid white moth on his storm door glass! I had never heard of a white moth, so I checked on my computer to see what kind it was. The information was that white moths are only in Asia! There are no white ones in the United States. It was a beautiful all white and very furry moth with coal black eyes. The moth didn't look like the usual gray/brown ones at all. I took pictures from both sides of the glass door and it never moved.

All day long it never moved. Later on the next day I became afraid something would harm it, so I gently took it off the glass and placed it where I thought it would be safe outside. The next day I went to check on it but it was gone! I knew this was a beautiful greeting to me from my son. I knew this when I first saw the moth that it was from him. While the moth had still been on the storm door before I moved it, my daughters came by to see this amazing mystery and one of them took pictures of the white moth too. One thing certain we knew, it didn't fly here from Asia! You can see the white moth in the picture on the previous page.

Rain and the Teardrop

One morning I had woken up to loud thunder and a gloomy rain filled day. I lay there listening to the sound of heavy rain pounding down on the roof and hitting the windows. I relaxed back into my pillows and quickly, as if by magic, I began to have a vision. Suddenly, I felt my son's presence with me. He began talking to me and clearly told me to remember "that in every drop of rain that fell, it would be filled with his love." How beautiful I thought and his words made me smile because I could feel his strong love. Soon, he was gone once more and I would never forget what he had said to me. From that time on with his message stored in my heart I have loved the rain and looked forward to it knowing his love is showering down on us. I immediately told my daughters and family so now they can feel the same way. He is just the same as he was on earth full of loving comfort and concern about us.

It wasn't long after this had happened that one of my daughters Robin had a vision one evening after she fell asleep. She looked up into the sky to see a bright shimmering white and golden light coming closer and closer to her. She could see the light was forming into the shape of a large shining tear drop. The tear drop slowly floated closer finding its way to a tree limb. There it stopped, softly settling on the limb. The tear glistened with such radiance and light, like a shimmering crystal would look. My daughter looked closer and longingly at this beautiful, glistening drop slowly examining its beauty, and suddenly she felt her brother's deep love washing over her heart and soul. She began to hear his words to her about sending his love in every raindrop that fell. With this amazing and wonderful confirmation from him she knew he was there in those special and precious moments. This was a continuing message from what he said to me about his love being in every drop of rain to us, as a confirmation to all of us! We love the clever way he orchestrates his messages and visits in the way he does. Since that day when it begins to sprinkle and those first drops of rain touch my face I feel his gentle kiss on my cheek saying, "I love you, Mom!" And my daughters feel the same way.

A Visit to Little Max

There have been so many wonderful experiences with visits from David that I must tell you of one special visit. It is very unusual and involves my granddaughter, Brooke, and little grandson, Max. Keep in mind that Max was about three or so then and never knew his Uncle David; he was a baby when David left us.

One fall day Brooke was talking to a friend outside and Max was in the back seat of their car. Brooke said, "That Max just kept talking and laughing like a game was being played with another person outside the window of the car. She finally asked him, "Who are you talking to, Max?" Very clearly Max said, "Uncle David!" He had never seen David! Brooke was startled, ready to ask him more questions, but her attention was caught by a large leaf slowly floating to the car window where Max was talking. It settled on the window glass where it stopped, not moving or sliding off! It was fall, so the dry leaf had nothing to hold it onto the window. It should have floated off, but it didn't and the breeze couldn't budge it.

Brooke continued to observe this as she was slowly putting things together by then. How could this happen she thought? Little Max giggled again loudly continuing to talk and play with the invisible person he called David. She couldn't explain what was going on but knew it had to be her uncle David, only Max did not know who he was. He couldn't have remembered David when he passed. Brooke knew Max was seeing him and they were playing a game! This was amazing to her.

Later she thought of an idea to test Max. She took out pictures of several people one with my son included and asked Max if he saw anyone he knew. Little Max pointed out my son and called him by name, David! Brooke, her husband, and two small daughters were living in his home by then and both girls would not have remembered David either. But the youngest one talked of Uncle David being in the house. Brooke showed both girls pictures of him one day with the question, "Do you know who this is?" They both answered, Uncle David because they said they see him!

Ever since they moved into his home Brooke could hear footsteps going up the stairs to where my son slept. The last step at the top of the stairs always squeaked when David put his weight on it. She has told me many times in the night when it is quiet and everyone is in bed she can hear his footsteps coming upstairs and at the top on the last step, squeak!

A few times she has caught a glimpse of David. Even her children had experiences when they would lock the dog in his big cage at night and later find the door open, even when they were gone for a while. The cage sat right where David kept his dog's cage when he was gone for a while. Once, Brooke was cleaning and actually saw the cage door open on its own! It has to be opened by an adult because it has two latches top and bottom, which are difficult to move out of place. Brooke said, "She knows it was her favorite Uncle David letting her know that he was there." There were other signs of him, even in the basement, which makes them feel protected.

None of us are afraid of these events. We all know he comes to say hello, and to check on us. He loved his home and I recall how many times he saw my parents (his grandparents) while living there himself. One day a dear friend was in the yard talking to David asking him who the older man was in the kitchen window. David said, "He turned around and was looking right at his grandfather in the window!" The family feels they are protected by David and that he is their Guardian.

Inspiration

One Sunday morning as I was sitting up awhile I realized my world was beginning to change even though I did not fully see it yet. Then something happened to me in a wonderful way. Little did I know I would be turned slowly around to the big part of my rescue? I soon came to know this was meant to be in my recovery. I had flipped through several TV channels as usual that day not wanting to watch any of them and then by chance, I happen to notice a program that caught my complete interest. There in front of me was a man whose name was Joel Osteen. I had heard of him before and for some reason he said something I knew came from my son.

I took strength from his words and wonderful spirit! There were certain messages I would catch in his words which I knew came through from my son speaking to me. One time on this show suddenly I was shocked to see the house numbers of my home at the top of the TV screen! Just the numbers, but I knew to listen closely that Sunday morning. I could always find my son in his messages to me. I had found the words from Joel that my son was sending to me, he was working through Joel Osteen to reach me.

I began to listen intently each Sunday now for my message. I am sure many people have found their messages in life through a person, newspaper article, a sentence, and so on. David and I knew this is how things can work if one pays attention. We received messages in all kinds of ways in our work, so I knew what was happening. I couldn't wait to hear what would come next on these Sunday mornings!

I began to feel empowered little by little with knowledge that I was growing stronger once more. I was being lifted by David through Joel and his lessons. I had heard of this man before but I had not watched him until now. He empowers people and lifts the spirit letting them know how precious they are. He doesn't tear anyone down in any way. This is the real love for others David also taught.

There is a world of difference for those who are uplifted in their spirit instead of being afraid they are not good enough by being taught fear. As a child, I thought I had done something bad by such strict church teachings. I almost felt as if I looked the wrong way, I had to be careful. We were taught not to wear shorts, show our legs and so on. None of this is important when we get on the other side. Manmade religion is harmful when out of hand.

I could understand why there was some unrest over Joel by some ministers who spoke ill of him (they judged) because his theological schooling was missing. But, his father had been a minister and he grew up in the church helping his father. He knew the right way to help people grow to do their best and like Joel, sometimes people are called to do their life work differently. The papers, certificates, licenses, do not always make the teacher or person; it is the amazing knowledge inside of one, and good common sense. It is always about what one came here to do and not to be afraid of doing it. Joel Osteen was different with his teachings in a good and gentle way laced at times with his good humor. What a refreshing experience to hear his words. I was so stirred I felt great HOPE now!

He didn't need to bang his fists and yell out his messages. People seemed to hang onto his every word. He was gentle and conveyed beautiful and powerful words to all. He empowered people instead of putting them down with fear and guilt. He also carries a wonderful sense of humor that people love. As we all know laughter is good for the soul, especially in our world today.

In him, I could see his gifts INSPIRING others with his words. In his way of talking he doesn't just go over the scripture, he has a unique way of teaching on how to reach others in a loving way with it. I was totally surprised with his gentle being and love for all. When I say work, his work, our work, it is only a word to describe our job on earth. A beloved job we can cherish, a rewarding and loving God given one. I give Joel my thanks for being a bridge for my son in order for him to reach me in that way when I needed the extra help to begin my awaking.

Joel has no idea how important a roll he has played in my life with his words, caring for others and his wisdom and strength. I know everything is in the timing and this was my new beginning to the way back. In my own opinion, many ministers could benefit and learn from Joel, a person who does not carry jealousy or greed. He is a true minister of spiritual healing. I have never heard him judge or put down another person in any of his messages. He helped me to rebuild my life again. I would get stronger and continue on, which still took time but I knew in my heart I would!

I felt such a strong love in my son's home, his energy is everywhere and beautiful! I could hear David moving around, walking on the floors and going up and down the stairs. At times, I would be standing in the house in the kitchen or bedroom and he would say to me, "mom, step into my energy and I will give you more." He is always close by watching over me, my Guardian Angel. I thank him for leading me to Joel Osteen that day.

My Awaking to Life

In our work that David and I were doing, we had agreed to remain silent about these activities. We had our spiritual protection beside us, which we have always been grateful for. We have been guarded since birth here. God gave us this protection for our journey into earth and a safe return back home. One day perhaps I will be able to reveal more of where home is.

When my son David crossed over we were completely numb for some time. Everything stopped, even my heart it seemed. I am sure millions of others have felt the same way. We thought over and over what will we do without him? David would know if he were here to erase the troubles away in our lives. How do we do this without him? He helped run things so smoothly, no matter how life was. I felt like a baby who had no direction in my life now, the shock was too strong to think about anything. I didn't care anymore. In those times I felt like a robot for a long period of time. He orchestrated so much in all our lives because he was so efficient at handling problems when we came to a hard spot in our lives. Our cement foundation was not here among us as a son and brother anymore and never would be!

His voice, so full of laughter would never be heard again in human form; this was unbearable to all of us. Those of you who have experienced a great loss, all understand the emptiness.

When I was alone, I realized I had lost my way and that I had given up. I felt I was emotionally dying as only a parent would know with the passing of a child. It doesn't matter how old your child ever gets, they are still our children. This pain is the deepest one can imagine with the loss of a loved one. You feel like your life has also ended. I was totally out of reality for quite a long time. So if you are suffering from a loss, however you fight it, it is the way that is right for you. Everyone is different in how we handle a broken heart and when we start to try and mend it as best we can.

Our lives together had been 24-7 and most years were in and out of hospitals together. I was now without my son and so very thankful for my blessed daughters. I thank God for my daughters who stood beside me helping me along, watching over me while also in their own pain. I would think if one of my daughters had anything happen to them it would be completely unbearable. I love them so much.

I was at a loss as how to go on. We all suffered the same hurt and pain as many of you have. I feel sadness for all parents who have lost children. The heart breaks; our heart cords are completely torn away and ripped apart; and the hurt and despair can't be put into words. I don't know if the mind ever stops going over the last days and moments of a loved one's life or not. I have always heard of how a child should never go first, but I know when God calls us we go home. Age doesn't seem to be a part of what we think it is to be. Some lives are cut short but we need to know that the soul is in the best place a soul could ever be and they are safe now. Our loved ones are safe. Even with knowing this, we are still deeply wounded as never before.

I try to see the good in all people first and sometimes get crushed in the process as David did knowing the negative ones were lost and badly off track. Sometimes you feel as if you are drowning with them, some try to pull you down. Their aura looks like tentacles reaching out to you. That's another one of my lessons, to always pay attention to my intuition and quit trying to trust a person who is negative. They must learn themselves; hopefully they will down the line. Whatever they do is usually just for themselves in a selfish way. They want things in their control and not anyone else's. It is best to always mind your own business and it can be a very hurtful experience to watch those people struggle. We sometimes need to stand back, be there for them, as best we could but stand back. Our human nature is to help others all we can, but do we simply want things our way with what we think is best in order to orchestrate others' lives without always realizing it?

By going through my entire negative trauma I had to get back on track and sharpen my old positive outlook, but I would need time on my side. I knew I had protection from God and the Universal Beings of Light and my dear loved ones. I also knew I had it in me to survive. I just needed to rest awhile and store up my energy and I would. I had made a promise and I would keep it, I would be ok in the long run. I am writing all of this in hope that others who have suffered a loss know that it is okay with whatever way one feels. There are loved ones who are told to just get over it; some people say they have had this way expressed to them! How devastating this comment can be! However slow or fast one takes to heal is right for them and no matter how one does this.

Reflecting Back

After so many years of doctors, hospitals, and watching David suffer most of his life, I had made myself be strong so he wouldn't worry over me. I suppose the years of holding my feelings in and not crying in front of him did a lot of damage, more than I ever knew trying to be strong. I had felt helpless at times but I had never given up! I held my son's secret inside of me most of the years he was terminal. I had made him a promise and I kept it. He knew he could always depend on me as I could him. We would get through the illness as long as possible together.

It's that I never dreamt the end would come so soon or unexpectedly, because I wouldn't let myself. I tried to stay completely blind to that part, as long as he pretended, so did I. I never really faced the reality of the situation. We kept one another up in spirit and so did his sisters along with us. We had our trust in everything we got, and believed 100 percent in what came from the Heavenly Spiritual Beings. We had come a long way on this journey with the love of the Creator.

Maybe it was because he had so many miracle healings' over many years and that's what we expected to happen again. What I didn't want to think about was how his human body could only stand so much after so many years. I don't know how he stayed so long in his broken body, but I know with his great inner strength he did because he loved us so much.

When his work was finished he didn't want to leave us. He breathed life into all of us around him; he gave us so much of himself. I believe he still felt strongly that he needed to be here to help us with many things coming into our future lives. He knew how to make people feel like a million dollars with just a few words, a touch, or smile, that's how he was. During the times he was better, we all felt like a million dollars! Money, material things, meant nothing to us. It was about David feeling better and having him longer with even another day.

He was unique as all our children are. I had never heard him ever talk back to me or use a curse word in his life. He only wanted to please with his special love and joy, sharing it wherever he went. He could go into a room full of people and like a magnet someone who sat alone and upset was where he was headed. The next thing I knew he would be walking over to them and warm them up in a short time. Soon, both of them were laughing and talking. He had an ability to empower others no matter their circumstance or self-worth. When he left them with his presence they held their head up high.

He knew who to help all his life and the UNDERDOG in him was where his work was. He knew every human being was a special child of God and he could bring that part out of most he met. I believe those people could see the compassion and light in his eyes, and yet not know why they opened up to him. They just knew he cared about them, truly cared no matter how they were feeling. He did so much of this in the hospital waiting rooms where we waited endless hours. Even when his blood was taken the nurse could only shake her head laughing at his words. His doctors looked forward to his appointments and enjoyed him coming in! One doctor came to me outside of her office one day where I waited she wanted to tell me once more what a joy he was! How he never once complained to her. She said, "We don't meet many patients like him, his words are always happy and I feel fine!

He had a natural ability to heal people in whatever way they needed with his love and personality. He knew how to help the spiritual, physical, mental, and emotional side in others. He was a spiritual healer to those suffering with incurable illnesses. He was a healer in his lifetime.

There were several times over the years that I became sick and snapped a bone out of place. And once shingles popped out on a Thursday, that evening he gave me healing and said, "Mom they will be gone in three days," and they were! Whatever he got I knew was true from the Divine healers who worked with both of us. He could help me in my sickness and I could help my son with his, that's the way we worked together and with others. With all of this David lived many years longer than said possible for him. His soul was full of spiritually.

How thankful I am to God, knowing we are all a part of Him. With my son's free will, he appeared to me off and on in the days and nights that followed and still appears to me now. He continues to be with me since he has left. I could see and hear him speaking to me and it was such a comfort. He told me "he would be there for me as he promised me." He was still my coat of armor and strength, and continues to be. He promised and I promised, always together and that will never change.

A loved one's passing takes the very essence out of your humanness. Time helps, but cannot heal in the way we may pray for. One never really heals in the heart and soul as we hope to do. The other side told me to live the life God gave me. Our loved ones are in a place of splendor with the knowledge and knowing we will be together sooner than we think. They are at peace, but are still concerned over us here, in their new life now. They are taking in so much in their new transition coming *home to heaven* and celebrating their return with all who waits for them. This transition is full of many events for the new soul. They are looking ahead not behind right now, although they can be in more than one place at a time now.

I would go over the visions I had had and remembered that David had used his beautiful gifts as a reader and healer for all he could. I am sure he had to have hoped I didn't pick up that he may be leaving here soon. Just the same, I was being prepared ahead. I have recalled so much about his last week and other important moments in his life. One such statement that I always found very profound was when he said, "I am NOTHING, Mom, neither male nor female; I am something not from here. You know what I mean don't you?" Not hesitating I was replying, "YES, YES I DO!" We both knew who we were and from where we came. This was the secret part of our lives I knew what he meant. He figured I would remember all of our journey together now in other times and places. He wanted to make sure I would remember our bond on earth, and that his life here would be ending. I know that he came here by his own free will and choice with his chosen mission as a human being, but not the same as most. He was here as a different entity all together in the role as a human being, and yes, I knew exactly who he and I was without saying more.

How did he know his whole life ahead at the time? And as a child that he would die so young? That he would go through his life to suffer, in order to help and teach others? There aren't really other ways to explain him other than as who he was not of earth.

He left me with so many clues to know more about our lives before he was gone. There were also the messages from the other side about our work on earth. The answers now have long become clear for me. As the saying goes, "We are all spiritual beings who come here to lead an earthly life as a human," instead of the other way around. I have complete faith in this.

Those who are trying to pick up and go on to get their lives back together seem futile after a loss. How empty and quiet the house feels when your loved one is not there anymore. There is a whole different depressing energy in it. I didn't want to move anything on a table or any of my son's personal items such as his towels, soap, his clothes, pictures, and so on. I wanted everything left just as he left it. There is no way to explain this behavior in human words, except to another parent, sweetheart, wife, husband, or other loved ones. It all takes time to start any kind of a healing process.

My son came to remind me again, "Not to make a *shrine* out of his house. We must live our lives and go on and treasure each day." Thank goodness for my daughters and all my family who were also trying to start again, we all stuck together. I write these experiences to hopefully let others know we all heal differently and in a certain time. And whatever one does it is the way they need to. The process can't be hurried. But our life needs to go on the best we can.

Our life is unending that follows our death. It is a progression for those who seek our Supreme Intelligence, Christ, Creator, God or the name your higher being is known by you. On the other side there are many levels of higher existence as; in my Father's house there are many mansions. I knew in my learning from the Creator and Heavenly teachers we can choose what we want to do and learn there. In time, we may even decide to be born again to come back to Earth or to another learning place someplace else.

Death does not separate loved ones from one another, we only think it does. This is a question I long ago would keep asking myself. This privilege was revealed to me from the Beings of Light, that I may tell the world something of what we are being taught so others may learn not to fear. That God is indeed LOVE and the key to all things is LOVE! David and I have been shown that which others cannot see and we are well guarded by our

Creator and have nothing to FEAR. Our story isn't in a text book but we were living our truth with the Creators help guiding us both.

Few will be able to understand our life completely with how we both were created and with our own desires to come back again. Our sight was multi-dimensional, seeing into the future with what awaited those on Earth. This was not an easy emotion to carry but in the big picture we understood. There was so much ongoing information which sometimes confused me about what was the meaning of the unknown worlds which I asked my many questions about. One common one was did I really see that? Was this double exposure real in our world? Did we see what we thought we did? This is because we experienced so much of these many worlds simultaneously together.

Many multiple worlds overlap with other dimensions that we were connected with. We sometimes questioned, "Were these things to come in the future or had this occurred in the past or transpiring at the same time?" Times such as these, our minds were full and our world intermixed, it was hard to keep focused until we received more direction. So the best thing to do was to stay patient and wait. David knew the answers but I had to remember, so he patiently went along with my questions. I was to understand these things in time. This had been the way for unknown reasons we had set up our plan this time.

David gave me all the comfort he could, but I still felt my body and spirit was torn apart, and torn away from him. He knew the mental pain I would be in. Blessedly, he said "we are still together, but in a different way now." I knew we would always continue working together with him on one side, and me the other. David clearly expressed that he could help me more from where he was going than on this side when he was here.

Chapter 18

How David Would Care For Everything

The Torch That Lit His Way Home
My heart still stings with the memory of my son and his protection of me. After he had been crossed over for some time, I found a big branch with a flashlight taped to the bottom hidden in the bushes by my back door. I had to figure out why this would be there and suddenly I knew. I sat down on the porch and visualized him on the road. He would walk in the early AM hours from his home to mine. This was his TORCH of light that he carried.

He was going blind in the last years and could see very little. I found out after he was gone that every night, rain or shine, he would walk to my house. He was checking to make sure I was okay. This usually happened around 3 AM. He carried this long branch with this flash light taped to the bottom of it to see the best he could. I realized he put it there the last time he used it. Realizing this, I knew again how much my son loved me as his mother. I was ready to burst into tears and my heart just sank.

I believe he recognized where the light fell on the roadside, hoping not to fall in the night. Plus, cars passing by would hopefully see him on the side of the road. He was always concerned about my safety once he moved into his own home. He was very good at telling me, not to open the door to anyone! I still get overwhelmed and sad knowing what he risked doing for others and me. I also found out that on his way back home he stopped and checked on an elderly lady who lived alone.

I know he was divinely led and guided on those dark nights. The road he walked had no side-walks, only a rocked road. I know that God kept him safe with his blindness. If I had known then I would have tried to keep him from taking such a big chance, but I doubt he would have quit. He may have been blind in our world, but intuitively he was not. I could picture him clearly on those nights in my mind with his *staff* to make sure I was safe.

After moving into my son's home after he crossed over. It took quite a while with deciding to leave most of my things in my home. I didn't know what to do or how to think clearly. I still had my home to take care of. Each day I was back and forth for about two years. I had yards to keep at both places along with other upkeep to do.

One day not long after he left, I had gone to clean my house. I always put my house keys in his boot while I was there which was a safe place when outside. After I finished for the day, I went to leave and my keys were gone and his boot was empty! No one was there that day but me! Luckily I had another set at the other house. My daughter drove up about that time and I told her about the keys being gone. I thought either David or one of the friendly spirits had taken them as a joke. We both looked again and she checked his empty boot once more. I asked, "Please return the keys. I needed them." No luck, she would give me a ride home. For some unknown reason Pam decided to check out the boot one last time, and there they were! My daughter couldn't believe how fast this happened! We were standing right there by his boot, we laughed with relief and I drove my own car back to his house. I gave many a thank you all the way home.

Remembering David's Gift of Giving

I would like to recount a time in David's life that should provide you with an understanding of how generous David's caring was toward others. When David had one of his earlier near death experiences and had pulled through but became bed-ridden for some time, he did something very wonderful. It was such an expression of his love. He was in his room, but being so quiet I thought he was sleeping. He had made something for me a little at a time in secret.

I collected Victorian dolls and I had the body of one tucked away with the head, but no arms or legs just the parts. One day he handed me a gift wrapped in newspaper. I couldn't believe my eyes when I opened it! He had put the dolls arms and legs on it, found scraps of material someplace in a box and hand sewn a dress with a lace collar as best he could! My heart just melted to see how hard this must have been for him at that time!

I have kept this doll all of these years and each time I look at it I think of what he did. My sewing box was in his room in a closet so apparently while he was bedridden he somehow got up making it to the closet. He made this as best as he could to surprise me! He must have wanted to give me something so badly, and I will never forget this gift was made with pure love. Every time I move the doll in its buggy to dust, the legs or arms fall off and I gently replace them. I treasure this doll more than anything and a fortune couldn't buy it from me. I know how much this meant to him wanting to give me a gift. He was always a gift by being my son as my daughters are gifts to me.

He made all of us around him happy with his thoughtfulness. He gave the best birthday celebrations for us, his family and friends, which he did by himself as he wanted to do, this made him feel good and he knew the "secret to living." As long as he could give and do for others he was happy within.

One day not long after David had passed over, I met a lady we both knew. She began to tell me about the help he gave to her family. She and her husband were both in bad health and did not have much. It was on Thanksgiving Day when she heard a knock at the door and there stood David with a large roasted turkey, all the trimmings and desserts for them. She said, "The family wouldn't have had a Thanksgiving without this meal he had prepared for them and she would never forget this," with tears in her eyes. I knew on that same day he had also prepared a meal for a mother and her son also, this way they had a good Thanksgiving too. You know he never said anything about doing what he did for others he was very humble. He never felt he had to tell what he did, he wanted to do it and I honor this in him, he never bragged of anything he did. Since then I have been told several similar stories which he did for others even up to now. He didn't need a pat on the back it was all about helping others.

He loved Christmas with a passion, not about getting gifts, but with his GIVING of gifts to others. His life was his love for our Creator /Jesus Christ, and Mother Mary, all of the Christ Light Beings and family. He loved to give gifts and listen to Christmas music, the peace and love, with all of us together, this was his life. Going to his home was a treat for all of us and our friends. Beautiful Christmas music would be playing and there would be the aroma of delicious foods prepared along with glowing candles everywhere. The tables were set with beautiful table cloths, china and silverware, Christmas decorations, linen napkins, crystal goblets, all kinds of lush desserts and home-made candy. How blessed we all have been to have such a loving bond.

David would have his Christmas village out with all the details and lights on in the displays. A miniature train would be running around the village full of people, cars, beautiful landscapes and snow. This exhibit filled the entire top of his grand parlor piano along with miniature ice skaters and figures. His 12 foot Christmas tree was gorgeous and full of exotic figures and treasures. It stood from floor to ceiling next to the decorated parlor mirror. The room looked like a storybook!

Since his cross over, it has never been set up again, but I hope one day we do this. It took him weeks to set everything up for the family and the little children to enjoy. I don't know how he did this by himself. I know he started on his Christmas festivities right after Thanksgiving. When he stayed focused on something he worked to accomplish it every moment. He never wanted any help even the last Christmas.

He knew what was important in life and it wasn't about wanting material things. He never owned a new car or fancy clothes; in fact he never was close to having a new car in his life, just a couple of old cars. While he could still see, he drove my car and my 20 year old pickup and you would have thought it was a new one to him! He always said, "New cars and trucks are not important to me, life is." It's not to say he wouldn't have been happy to have a newer car when he could drive I am sure he would have enjoyed it very much. Living in the cities so much before his illness he didn't need one anyway he said. He knew what was coming in his life and never wanted much, just life.

David gave all of us special beautiful celebrations for the family to be together; it didn't have to be a special occasion he knew every day was special. He surprised others with gifts and special treats he made for any day. His whole life was giving. We all recall his famous Halloween parties and giving out treats to all the kids around. We all wore costumes, played Halloween music, had chili, pie, and cake with punch, not to mention all the candy! He had the most decorations I have ever seen! He was so much fun any time we were together! Our memories are endless to us and he lives on through all of us. That's the important part of knowing our loved ones live on! They leave us with their legacy no matter how young or old our loved one is.

The holidays have never been the same without him but we try to do our best so he is proud of us. We have fun and good food as always, but we do feel the void. He is a big part of each and every get together where we enjoy reminiscing memories of him. I know he is present at everything we do. Our loved ones are happy when we keep their memories alive which helped us.

David's Spring Flowers

Again, recounting one of David's precious moments involved his love for flowers, especially sunflowers. This was just a couple of months before he became ill for the last time. He was getting anxious for the weather to get better so he could begin his spring gardening. One day we were shopping and almost like a little child who had found a special toy that they wanted, David came up to so bubbly and happy and called out, "Mom, look what I got!" He had found packages of flower seeds. He was holding up packages of sunflower seeds that he purchased to plant. He was grinning and shaking the packages to show me. He was counting the days until he could plant them. You would have thought he had won the jack pot by the look on his face! He was planning his garden and happy over such little things in life... I will never forget that day! I can still picture him doing this as clear as can be and the happiness shining from his face like a little kid! He loved to grow everything and at that time I thought he would never get to plant them. I had not yet had the visions of him crossing.

As 2008 moved into March, David started to plant some of his spring flowers much earlier than usual than in previous years. This was not long before he passed away. Each day he was in the yard before 3 AM as usual, finding something to do. His love was for the sunflowers and the color of flowers my mother loved, pink roses. He would care for his pink roses in her honor. He adored his grandparents, and taking care of this home was special to David. The home had first been my parents' home and where I grew up, and now it was David's. I would tell him often how my parents came to me saying they loved everything he did with all of his hard work! My mother loved the pink roses and how beautiful he had made the yard. The roses hung over the white picket fence. The flowering trees he planted were in the front yard along with mom's orange tiger lilies and purple flags beside the walks. The beautiful tulips he planted lined up the front walk to the steps. In the backyard was a huge tree, hundreds of years old where he planted flowers at the base of it around the trunk in soft yellows with lavender and purple moss.

After David left us, I tried keeping all of the yard and house the way he did, but it never looked the same after he crossed over and it finally all died! I was really crushed, nothing I did worked like his magic touch. He had a little pear/peach tree still stood in the corner of the back yard where Shorty was buried, it was his Magical Tree, but it wasn't doing well either. The little tree was barren. When his flowers did not do well, that hurt me. And now his tree wasn't doing well. This was such a part of him which he had tended to and grown, I tried everything, but it was as if all of these things had no energy to grow anymore. I know this may sound silly but I was really down and upset with this part of him also leaving now in the way of the beauty he had created was now gone. It was as if it all died with him. Everything or most anything can bother a person in time of a loss. We want to keep holding on to the past and the things they loved, which is only human nature.

By now my parents had been crossed over many years. David had loved this home because of all the special memories in it; his grandparents' energy was still strong and loving throughout the house. My mother and dad came often to tell me how much they loved their home and all David had done there, making it beautiful! They were happy he had the house and grew the beautiful flowers in honor of them. They made themselves known to get attention all of the time he lived there. He was happy they stayed nearby to him and he laughed at the funny things mom and dad did. He was proud to have the little Victorian house for his own, and had worked hard inside and out for all of the years he was there. The yard was neat and beautifully trimmed with the gorgeous colors of plants and flowers; it looked like a picture.

After he was gone and I would be working outside, several people passing by would stop even those who never knew him except by sight to tell me how much they enjoyed his yard. They would mention how they always saw him working in his yard, even in the dark. They had no idea he was blind and had been sick. He never wanted others to feel he was any different by being sick. People coming by missed their visits with him. They had really enjoyed having conversations together. He had designed the little garage in back of the house with a small tower on top of it with Victorian trim and shutters. You would not believe how many people stopped, thinking it was church! David being so spiritual always said he loved that and I feel he will always be remembered in that way.

The police were so used to seeing him outside in his yard at all hours for many years; they would beep at him while passing by and wave. Since his sight was all but gone he amazed me of how well he did things. Most people did not know he had an eyesight problem at all. He followed their voice when they talked to him and walked with perfect posture like he could see as well as anyone.

He was the Block Captain and loved being one to keep things safe in the neighborhood, which he took very seriously. He would laugh all the time about being the Block Captain because no one knew about his sight, and this job meant so much to him. He was so proud to do his best to keep crime out of the neighborhood. He could sense things perfectly; and he made a great one with his intuition. He would know when anyone was lurking around.

One night we were watching TV and David sensed someone in his yard. He grabbed his huge flashlight which looked like a spotlight! The person who was prowling ran away. I laughed so much with him he sure could do his job. I think he had the brightest spot light anyone could buy. David use to say, "The most important things he missed, was seeing all of the beauty outside, the stars, being able to read his books, and seeing our faces and other people clearly." These things most of us take for granted.

The Magical Tree

There is another experience that David had which was amazing about his *magical* tree! This is what I called it because of what happened. David had planted a little fruit tree many years ago which proved to be quite a phenomenal. This small tree kept producing fruit of a different kind! It produced two different types; pears and peaches!

Early one day he excitedly called me, it was about his peach tree. He had endured a bad night of being sick and went out into his yard very early in the morning to get some fresh air. He bent under his fruit tree in the dark to pick up a shiny object he thought he could see; when he rose up he said something had grazed his shoulder. Looking back at the tree he made out objects on a limb. Touching it he was shocked to feel fruit! He went in to get a flashlight and to his amazement he could see what seemed to be pears on his peach tree! This was the first time that had happened.

He explained how the tree had nothing on it days before, and it was not pear season anyway! He brought 14 pears to me. The 14th was also my mother's birth date, so we each ate one. It was delicious! I have pictures of the pears and of many strange things that happened with this tree over the years! Why would the little tree produce two different fruits on different years and out of season? Later on in a different year it produced peaches again, and it was not a hybrid tree. No one can tell me the other side can't do unbelievable things! David said, "His grandmother did this for all of us to see and the fruit was truly an amazing gift from her." Those were from my mother and the number 14 was the way she let us know they were from her.

On a separate occasion when I came home one day I found 14 pears arranged in one of my large bowls sitting on the kitchen table! The bowl had been in my kitchen cabinet but was now on the counter filled with pears.

Without wasting a second I called David so he could witness my surprise! I took pictures and added this amazing event of photos to all the others. This again was from my mother as if she said, "Hello, how do you like the pears I brought?" There is no way to explain these things that continued to happen.

Chapter 19

Spirits Messages

What a Wonder

Every time, I think of how our loved ones can arrange events and it fills my heart full of love and happiness! With help from others in the spirit world where our loved ones go to after leaving here they soon learn the ropes. Sometimes it is difficult at first for those who have crossed over, and for some it remains difficult for a long period of time. It may be to get adjusted or for other reasons of trying to get through a loved one's grief. However, they are in spirit and have an adjustment period with plenty of help waiting to assist them.

A child trying to get through to a parent or a loved one's grieving is very hard, if not impossible to do sometimes, because of the parent's emotions of being grief stricken. I see this like a heavy fog in my way and if the parent or loved one is open to this or not can make a big difference. Sometimes, one may suddenly see their child for a quick moment out of the corner of their eye in a room, inside or outside, where they played. It could be anywhere.

A friend of mine experienced her son in spirit when she was sitting outside one evening after his passing. She was devastated in her grief and asking for him to please give her a sign! She explained that suddenly she thought she could see something in his truck nearby. A form of fog had appeared in his truck in the driveway! She couldn't believe her eyes, thinking, am I really seeing this? A second later she saw this whitish fog move from the truck into the trees close by her and then his face formed in this mist! Since then, she has had several experiences of her son, Michael. She has grown to another level and is absolutely certain he comes to visit the family. This has helped her and given her so much peace in her heart. She and her daughter have both had several experiences now.

Mysteries work in so many ways in the spirit world and in the earthly world. Our loved ones are closer than you can imagine and able to move freely to other places, in less than a thought. When your loved one is close to you doing what they can for you to notice them, they cannot always make themselves known by a solid visual sign of themselves. Although, they are with you more than you can ever imagine. They want you to know so much that they are here; if you don't, they will try again when you are hopefully more susceptible to it. You may see a shadow, a mist, a figure, or even in solid form; they can use their energy in different manners to get your attention.

David and I worked in the spirit world throughout our lives using our extra senses, our gifts, to see and hear them. This has been a huge part of our work here. We have been connected to other dimensions which make it easier for us to pick up on all kind of phenomenon happenings. I have seen many new spirits do amazing things to reach loved ones right away. This can depend on many circumstances. They too, learn how to make their "visits" and come to their loved ones. I can describe this as riding a bicycle, some are fast learners and some need extra time and help.

Meeting Great Grandfather

I will never forget how I met my great-grandfather. In a vision one night I found myself entering a long building. Looking far to the end of it I could see an old fashioned bed with an elderly man and woman in it. They were sitting up leaning against the head board which seemed odd to me. When I moved in spirit I was beside their bed in a blink! I first noticed the older white haired man had amazing beautiful blue eyes and I definitely knew he was Indian, and soon to find out he was my Great-Grandfather! The elderly woman beside him was my Great-Grandmother. My Uncle who had passed over a few years earlier sat on the end of the bed never saying a word.

Great-Grandfather first took my hand and looked into my eyes with a steady gaze and said, "I am your Great Grandpa Powell." I was mesmerized and said, "How can you have blue eyes and be Indian?" He lovingly answered, "Yes, and they are BLUE the SAME as your son's." I felt a strong connection between David, great-grandfather and me with his love radiating out to me.

We seemed to have talked quite a while when suddenly I knew I had to go back! As I walked to the front of the building I looked down studying my clothing. I wore buckskin, Indian clothing with beads and trimmings of fringe! Then I knew what had happened and why we were to meet. I could see my own self in that time period and David as great grandfather! I was then close to the doorway, which I knew would take me back into my world. Suddenly I fell backwards! Right before my head hit the hard ground, someone grabbed my hand and pulled me up! It was Great-Grandfather! He said, "To always remember, I will be there for you to help pull you up!" Then I returned to my world.

I never knew him in my life or anything about him. The next day I called my older Aunt and asked her "what is our Great-Grandfather's name and what color were his eyes?" She confirmed they were blue, his last name was Powell and that he was Indian! I had now met my Great-Grandparents finding out he was a Guide and Protector to me. Later my Aunt brought me his picture. It was time for me to know him and why he wanted this meeting to introduce himself. What a wonderful way to meet him in that way back then.

David and I taught for years about the other side and passed messages back and forth from both worlds for others. We knew what we came here for, working as a connection to the other side, called by most people a spiritual medium. To us it was just part of our beloved job on earth.

I had firsthand experience that the spirit world is able to do anything and now you know more of why I say nothing is impossible! David and I discussed this subject of nothing being impossible so much over the years by being involved as witness to spirits on the other side and the things they can do. Plus, those who had a wonderful humor about them on earth are still extremely humorous!

This kind of phenomenon can either give comfort or fear to those who have never experienced it or believed in this. Some people have changed their lives with their new view on death, realizing they will go on, only in a different way. I have heard some people express things such as this would scare me to death! That is their fear talking. Then I explain what has happened as my son would to others. I need to remind myself that this is my life and I see spirits all the time, they are everywhere, so it is normal for me and was to David, but isn't to most people.

It is a shock when a person experiences their loved one in spirit although some say, I was not afraid at all I only felt happiness knowing my loved one is fine. There are many who are never afraid again and feel great comfort in this process of seeing a loved one once more. Your child, mother, father, husband, or loved one does not want to hurt you, they love you! But I must try to remember and realize many people are taught from a child on to be afraid. What one doesn't understand or is taught about to fear is what they will usually experience, at least for a few moments. Others can't wait until another time comes to meet their loved one again with their visit. Everyone is different on how this affects them.

Passed Over Souls at Their Funerals

There were many times at funerals my son and I both wished we could help those in mourning, but we could not tell them of their deceased loved ones presence. When some people pass over into spirit, we could see many of them at their own funerals! They, in spirit, are very aware of what is going on with everything. I have heard some spirits comment; I never knew that person even liked me! or vise-versa. Some express they had no idea how many people cared so much for them while watching the people coming and going. The one there in spirit usually stay close by to their loved ones or may move around here and there. They enjoy seeing everyone and their celebration.

The first big experience I had was a long time ago when I was attending my cousin's funeral. She had passed away of cancer. I was sitting alone in the back row when suddenly I felt a cool breeze brush by my left side. It was strong enough to get my attention. I immediately turned to see what caused this and there she stood! She looked beautiful, and glowing then she smiled at me and said, "don't worry about me I am just fine," and poof, she was gone! I had been sad before this happened because in her sickness she was terribly thin and worn from her cancer, looking badly when she died. I was surprised that she was in an open casket. Now her body was completely restored, young, beautiful and vibrant! Back then I wished I could tell her family but I knew they were already dealing with the shock of loss.

Messages of Help and Peace

The messages continued coming in from our friends which made us feel wonderful knowing how close in spirit David was by making his rounds and visiting those close to him. In the future there would be times my son would intervene to help us when he knew we needed him. On many occasions, David helped us in certain other situations, always looking out for us. He could give me words I needed to use for others and he gave me warnings when driving to a certain place for my safety or a coming event. He helped with many things in my daily life, helping to protect me and my family. He is with me in my work as a reader (medium), and in my spiritual healing work with the sick, and so on.

In very sad or difficult times he would help me through by coming to talk with me of what was coming up in the future so that I could be better prepared as much as I possibly could be. He gave me extra energy to face what I had to deal with that day or what would be a negative person crossing my path. He began to let me know certain positive words to use if I needed them in a negative situation. He helped me to start standing my ground instead of being a door mat. This can be done in a positive way.

I learned long ago that we have control, more than we think over our lives due to our free will. This is the control we use daily; we really do design our days and hope we make the best choices we can. But our mistakes are the most IMPORTANT way to learn by. That is how we learn since these are our stepping stones to grow by. We choose them without knowing this, which can elevate one to a higher learning level on the other side, to advance closer to the Creator.

There Will Be No More Tears in Heaven

One of the things I strongly recall and appreciated so much was when the other side said to my son and me, "There is no room here in Heaven for sad songs, and this is a place of joy! Only joy, peace, forgiveness and happiness await those who believe with an open and good heart!" These are our choices here on earth and I feel the choice of music a person wants at the end of life is their preference, but once in the other side there will be only happy, serene and peaceful music, for there are "no more tears in Heaven" just as the song says. Remember, this is a place of joy, not tears and this is the only way in our human words I have to describe this.

Something else you may be surprised at that I have mentioned is the humor on the other side; but this is not as I was taught in organized religion growing up, where everything in church was so serious! Absolutely, there is joy and laughter on the other side and I am so happy to be able to experience this. Through my own passing over and my lessons, moving back and forth, I know how joy is through the Christ Light Beings and Spiritual Teachers. This is NOT how some organized religions teach it. It seems to me that some churches preach more on sin, torment and hell, rather than love and forgiveness in their sermons. Some people are kept afraid and in fear of a great punishment lying ahead for them for the least little thing, how sad this is. I know this is not true from being there in my spiritual experiences and from my spiritual teachers and the mighty Council.

The other side has worked with my son and I all of our lives and I know this is why the Creator told me to write The Story of David after he crossed over. This was in the plan before we arrived here. I was told to tell the world of his life to hopefully help others who live in fear with the old ways of death and passing, to learn what a wonderful place awaits us. That is why this book is being written as a tool for others. It has taken me some time to get to where I could begin to even work on it, because I relive David's last days over and over in order to write his story. I am humbly doing this as I was asked to do by my Divine Creator in Heaven and I am honored to write the real truth we both have been taught. Death is the celebration by leaving the hard earth lessons behind, they are over. Of all people, I know how happy David is and how blessed we were to have him. I will always be his earth Mom and we all will miss him terribly as a human being and he understands all of this.

Chapter 20

What Happens When We Leave Earth, Questions Answered

What Happens When We Cross Over

David and I were taught long ago through our own experiences in the spirit world, when physical death of the body happens we each return to spirit. Once the body is shed we are in a new unseen spirit body of energy, unseen to our loved ones and others in this earthly world. But, we still remain the same person we have always been. After the transition, there are spiritual teachers who will be helping on the other side; everyone doesn't just change into a better person because they cross over. We keep our same mind, intelligence, joy, humor and our same emotions. Those who are grouchy, hateful, mean, or whatever, may stay the same as they were in physical life, at least for awhile, but change is always very possible.

Our soul is still who we are, but most loved ones left behind cannot see or hear their loved ones words to them. Passing does not transform one to become different, but with their free will there is much to choose from on the other side. We may want to learn more to advance, or want to make amends in some way truly from the heart and soul. There are souls who want to go to higher learning levels. There are those who want to make up for something on earth, or help a loved one in their grieving.

Some in spirit try to find a way to help themselves communicate, make contact, or perhaps are seen in a vision. Many souls can't reach the one they want to because a loved one's grief may be too hard to get through. If this is the case, the soul may be able to make contact through another person in the family or a friend, whoever they can. This is in hopes that the person will relay their messages to them and tell others. The soul can find help in their newness of crossing on how to make this happen.

There is always help waiting for the souls because our learning is continuous. My son and I had been taught this concept long ago and once more with our own NDE's and/or deaths by going into the spirit world to unite with the Creator. I would never have any doubt of our spiritual information with all of the experience and proof we have received. It is all in truth from the Holy Creator. Having been there is an amazing and beautiful experience! There are no words to really tell how it is, its unexplainable! Most people cannot find the right words to explain this phenomenal change to them!

When we get to the other side we still have our free will and go on learning. This is a promise to all of us who were created. We are all given free will for eternity. On the other side, one can look back at their life to review it and learn from how we lived it. In this review of our experiences our lives roll by like watching a movie. This goes by exceedingly fast, but souls understand it all including the positive and negative ones, and the lessons we learned on earth; and how we lived and treated others. We watch the goodness and the anger expressed. We have learned what a human being is and the emotions which drive us. Then when we are ready to begin a new journey or type of work the soul wants to continue on.

Once in the spirit world and still with our human feelings, some souls have a kind of regret. They may want contact to let others know they are ok and at peace. Information is there on the different processes that can be use, even on how to use their new spirit body to travel to other places in our huge Universe. I call it, learning the ropes, since everything is different for now.

We can each learn in our Heaven how to find what we want to fulfill and have been searching for. This can cover a broad area such as forgiveness from loved ones left behind and of things said and done in our life on earth. But regardless, you have a new life on the other side and anything is possible there. I was told by the spirit world, that some loved ones who had passed from a traumatic illness or a sudden accidental passing, may go into a resting period on the other side as if wrapped in a cocoon of love and peace, until they feel ready to begin their spirit life. That is as close as I can explain this.

Confused Spirits

David and I have had experiences working with spirits who did not know they had passed over. After seeing their own bodies, they begin to understand why no one can see or hear them. Some have trouble not being able to realize they are dead for some time. Those may not know it for some time, thinking they are still living. They repeat their daily lives in our dimension over and over; this is when they cannot move forward. These souls may be afraid to go on because of fear of what will happen to them.

Some who have passed are totally confused and do not realize they are in spirit and not still living. They can easily create a haunting to gain your attention, or be seen as a ghost by the living. They may have left here without being able to express what they wanted, or feel what they needed to accomplish. Perhaps, they simply want to bring a message of love to let those still on earth know that love never dies.

There have been cases where the one in spirit may give important information to where an important paper, will, jewelry, money, or something else can be located and found. This information to gain one's attention may come in the way of dreams, or a visit, hearing their voice, the scent of tobacco smoke, fragrance, food smells, or maybe with an object laid out where it can easily be found. They are very inventive and creative! It is a different process for each soul to choose from. We can choose our new life of what one wants to accomplish in order to advance on the other side.

In the work David and I have done, we gently tell those confused souls that they have died and are now in spirit. We show them they can join their loved ones by going on into the Light where loved ones are waiting for them. At times, we lovingly guide those who need help. Once, they get the idea and are not afraid of punishment or fear they hold on to, they will let go. They free themselves to pass into the universal Light through the doorway.

If not, then they are still here repeating their lives until they want to move forward if they ever want to. This is where one's belief of ghosts may only be loved ones trying, in the only way they know how, to communicate and get your attention. Many spirits can be attached to a certain place by the people, ground, home, and furniture, antiques, where they once worked, or where they loved to be. Some ghosts are malevolent and there are those who are benevolent.

The people still here can scare themselves badly, with an experience such as this which is normal. They are afraid, full of man-made fear, and some are without knowledge of the unseen spirit world. This attaches more fear to what is the unknown world to them. The spirit world is only a breath away mingling with the earth world in overlapping dimensions. And there is no doubt of very bad negative spirits who may try to weave their way into some people's lives at times. Each person probably knows the sign a loved one would use for them, knowing where it comes from. If you don't, and it is doing bad things you do not identify with, get some help from a person in this field. They can track the negative energy and get rid of it! This is something to take very seriously. The evil dark entities count on a person scaring themselves to death, or destroying their life. It is nothing to play around with.

All of this may sound absurd to some people who have not had experiences into the other side or received a message from a loved one there. Others have said, "By the grace of God what a wonderful thing to experience with a loved one's passing." Many people may later receive a message or hear the voice of their loved one. Some may smell roses, lavender, or perhaps experience the strong feeling of a presence or see a vision of their loved one! Some spirits move objects, turn on lights or make sounds which may give the bereaved comfort or a shock! Even though they know it is a loved one, this may be accompanied by fright. This is because of the way many of us have been raised and taught to believe this is just nonsense because one is grieving.

Just to know our children and loved ones go on gives one a much better understanding of where they are and that they are fine. There is so much more to look forward to when we return to our Heavenly home knowing loved ones are waiting for us and we will be together again.

Phantom Cars

One thing that absolutely stunned me years ago when I was first learning about the other world was seeing souls who had passed over still doing their daily chores as they did here on Earth! They are everywhere doing things they use to! David and I have witnessed souls driving their phantom cars, which really threw me! After my son-in-law Charley passed over he was seen in his Trans Am! He still went through the motions of driving it. On one of those days my son had his back to the road working in his yard. Suddenly, he heard a car stopping and gunning the motor then honking the horn. He looked up to see Charley, my son-in-law, with the biggest smile on his face and with a wave of his hand he drove off! Charley had passed over a year or so before! The direction he went in was where he and my daughter had lived in his life.

I recall my friend, Shirley, who was driving along the highway coming home from a trip one day when a car passed her just as she mentioned a family name and on the license plate it had that same one word, Cole. The name she mentioned a moment before was not coincidence. You may think of this as silly, but this happening was something special and a sign for her.

Some time passed and we both decided to meet for lunch. As we sat eating I felt her husband in spirit with us. I began to tell her what he wanted to say to her. Then I asked her if he played the harmonica because he just said he did!" She became excited and nodded yes and laughing. Then he quit talking to me for a minute and suddenly from an empty booth by us the song, *Old Suzanna* was playing on a harmonica! The place was empty there was no one anywhere around us. Shirley got up and looked around the booth behind us to be sure no one was there! You have to know her late husband was always a big kidder and was always joking around with her. We laughed all afternoon about what he had done for her on their anniversary that day and it sure cheered her up! This was a first for me too, unbelievable! I had not heard a harmonica played before by a spirit! I have experience many things but this was great!

An older man I knew surprised me a few days after he passed over when I saw him driving past me. I was sitting in a restaurant looking out of the window when he drove by! I then drove to his house where his wife still lived. I had to see if his car was there as usual, it was! He showed me himself in his "phantom" car so I knew for sure it was him. A vision is as real as anything here on earth that you see, at least ours are. I was so happy he wanted me to know he was happy and fine going on with his new life.

Your Soul is Immortal

My son and I have seen so many spirits over the years and passed on their messages to loved ones, there is no doubt whatsoever that life goes on. Your soul is the part of you that is immortal, it never dies, and we are eternal. Your child and others are watched over and are with other loved ones and other children, they are wise beyond our understanding. They generally will be very close to you, moving back and forth. They just want you to be okay, and for you to know they are at peace and they love you the same as always. They will be there waiting for you when your time comes. Nothing can break love apart, love is forever.

There is only one Supreme Intelligence who is our Creator, and there are countless high orders of Spiritual Beings of the Christ Light, High Councils, Heavenly Teachers and Guides. There are also Archangels and Angel Beings of every kind who can help in the new process there. Other spiritual beings of love and devotion exist in the Universes and there are other worlds that can also help. God did not create only us. We definitely reunite with loved ones who greet us there. There are loved ones in spirit who come to welcome us, and those who may help a loved one depart Earth by guiding that soul home. This transition we all make at death is a big celebration. When we return home we are filled full of happiness, ecstatic with the greatest love, joy, and peace. A soul is free of the heavy human body and hard life on earth! Earth is known by the souls as being the hardest place in the universe we come to in order to learn, and/or teach whatever one has chosen to do.

Children Who Cross Over

All of our children are precious. Each one has a special gift and are on a special journey while they are here, even when they pass before or at birth. No matter how long or short that journey, it is very important. Our children more than touch our lives forever leaving us with their beautiful memories and with a broken spirit when they leave. They are not meaning to, it is a part of life. The main thing is to live and enjoy life, that is what our passed over children want for us so badly. It is just so very hard for us as parents and other loved ones to realize this that we can do this in time to at least survive and be okay even though we never forget. This is so important for those souls to know so they can move on They have so much waiting for them to go forward with where they are now. Their soul may return at a different time to the same family. They have free will and only they each know how they will use it.

Consoling Others

With others who were going through this with loved ones who have passed over; David, no matter how busy he was, would make time to sit down, listen, and console the person with whom he spoke. He knew how important it was for people to pour their hearts out and be understood with sympathy. Like I mentioned earlier, he did not care what race, culture, color, rich or poor, religion, bad or good; what illness they had; if they were gay or straight; he wanted to help them and he reached out to them. How proud I was that he did not judge others as different and speak of a torturous hell to put fear into those who made mistakes. Cast the first stone if you have not made mistakes. We knew this was wrong to do; our God is a Supreme Intelligence, forgiving those who need forgiveness with their very heart and soul. We both knew we have a forgiving and loving Creator, not a Creator who is waiting around to point out who is the next one to destroy and condemn. I have trouble with even thinking of having a cruel Creator just waiting to punish each one of us according to some man-made teachings. The negative man-made teachings bring fear into people. It's not about fear, it is about love which is forever and all there is. Always know you are loved more than you can know. Remember, if you are taught to live in your fears, praying to be saved from a devil you are giving your energy to that. Give your energy and prayers to the love of God, a Heavenly Universal force of the greatest divine love. With David's compassion, positive messages and love he helped those who were grieving get through so much.

Chapter 21

Escorts for Souls

Helping to Guide Appointed One's to
The Other Side

David and I both felt enlightened in our journey by being escorts for some of the souls into the other side when they crossed over from death. Through the years we attended to many souls we never knew on earth and were quickly connected with a soul passing over to the other side. We both felt honored in this work by calming and steering the deceased one in spirit, taking them home and into the Christ Light they went. One I was surprised at was a famous person. I was taken to a football stadium in this vision. I was standing in the middle of it on the field looking around at the empty stadium wondering why I was here. Almost up to the top I could see a blond headed woman with her head in her hands and she was sobbing.

Suddenly, I was standing beside of her wanting to comfort her. Looking up at me I could tell she was extremely sad and upset, and had not made her transition to the other side. She told me about her famous husband who had played there and that she was worried about her children and her husband with what had happened to her! My heart just broke for her. I then escorted her home to the other side. Later in the news the next day I saw her face and recognized knew who she was by her picture.

Time Traveling Into Other Times

Much of our universal traveling was going back in time! David was showing me examples of our work throughout different periods and times. I recalled moving through these different periods in time travel seeing, Joan of Arc, Aristotle, Albert Einstein, Egyptian Kings, Rome, and many others from past history including the Bible days. I was getting to experience how we on earth overlap with other dimensions. It was amazing to experience the past in these experiences! Yes, David, was giving me even more information to tell of one day and hopefully to get across for others to learn, or perhaps plant a seed for now. Now, I am continuing our experiences to carry on, his and ours together for those who can understand this. Things aren't even close as to how we are taught on earth like they really are. The speed of light was the way they chose to move us through the many dimensions when we were learning about space travel and worm holes, with other Beings and places never known to us. As I write this, I can only speculate how many others will think how unheard of our our lives have been, but it is all true! This kind of travel had to do with the breaking up of molecules into Light!

Quite often some spirits would come to us to relay something about what had happened to them, how they died and so on. How did they find us? I was once told by a Being of Light that we omitted a certain light to the spirit world so those there who wanted to could send their messages through us to loved ones here. With the light we omitted, the spirits knew we would help them in this way. We were a link, a bridge, and both of us have been grateful to serve and help as long as they needed our help. Some spirits had been involved with negative others and some were ordinary positive loving people when on earth. Some had led a life of fame and politics all kind of souls came for help. We were in awe at times, but no matter whom they had been, rich or poor, all were important.

Ruthie a Special Soul

I will always remember one special lovely little lady my son helped who he knew when he was working in Tulsa, Oklahoma years ago. He just loved this little older lady named Ruthie, who was like a grandmother to him. Ruthie was also getting up in years but still had to work to have some income. Ruthie and David both worked at the same place together for the same business and that's how they met this time around.

David told me about giving Ruthie that first ride home one day after work. When they got there, he noticed her grass was very tall and filled with weeds. He knew she did not have the means to have the work done to keep it cut and taken care of. David also told me that many other things were also needed both inside and out. He started to go to her home on his weekends, mowing her yard, painting her house, planting flowers, and doing errands and other things she needed and could not do herself. He was happy to help her and never took a cent, this came from his heart to help Ruthie. He had an attachment to her as his friend and a grandmother and his help gave Ruthie less worry over the needed repairs. I know he thought the world of her. He mentioned her to me often.

One very early morning David called me before he left for work to tell me he had seen Ruthie in the night, she had died and he helped to escort her over to the other side. He said, "Ruthie was so happy and dressed in a beautiful blue dress. Her spirit was free now and they celebrated by dancing together into the beauty of the Universe and the most beautiful music flowed throughout the Heavens for her and they shared her passing together." He was happy for her and that Ruthie had him lead her home for her celebration with loved ones who were waiting for her! David told me that he would miss her as his friend on earth, but was overjoyed at her happiness! He was honored to help her to where she resided now in great peace and joy, she had no cares any longer. He loved Ruthie like a grandmother and she knew he did.

This part of both their lives was in their life plan to meet again on earth in their promise. I felt very happy hearing of Ruthie's beautiful crossing over with my son escorting her home to the other side! I wish I could have met her. See, how we meet those we have planned to, if it is a good or bad person there is always a reason and you will know the answers when it is time. Sometimes, it is to help one another hoping we make a right choice we had made a commitment to doing. This is where our contract or promise is fulfilled. You likely have no idea of what you have promised to do here but hopefully your inner self will lead you the right way. Everyone knows when they should or should not do something that really matters, because most of us use our conscious decisions in life. As an Native American Indian friend of mine has explained it to me, although some may not want to use their conscious decision making abilities in their life which may lead to their life going up in a puff of smoke one day, leaving nothing behind to show in their lives.

In most of these times we both were working together crossing people over on the same missions which are when our spirit bodies were out of our physical while the physical body is sleeping. There were a few instances when I woke up the next day feeling drained and very tired from what had expired during the night. This would happen especially when we passed through the terrible underworld which made me feel this way. But, I felt happy for what I had experienced on the other side as David did. There are so many places in our vast Universal systems that have never yet been discovered and in a way I hope they never are, because of how destructive man is today, I would fear future destruction.

One particular time when we were in the other world in our spirit bodies, the next day David told me I really scared him! Why, I asked? He said, "I went too far and he thought I wasn't coming back! He called and called to me and I finally I returned." I had no idea I went too far, I was in a blissful state. I began to wonder if perhaps this may be why at times, a person may be found passed away and was otherwise in good health; like Denise my dear friend, who was a young school teacher and collapsed at school one day. She died immediately with no known cause. She had been in good health at the time. The autopsy did not show the cause or any cause of why she died.

Spiritual teachings on this kind of an unknown early passing was now coming to me and I was a little overwhelmed. The lessons on how things are planned ahead and how one leaves here make up a big part of each one's life commitment. I realized then that our work explored further out than I ever realized into other realms and universes in all kinds of ways. Life was more than fantastic in our work by learning so much of how our lives really were meant to be. But, we also carried the human part of our emotions by feeling people would never understand our strange lives, when and if we were to expose them some day. This would have to be when the other side told us it was time. Soon, I was at ease with this because it was our lives and no one else's, our challenges, lessons and the work we both were dedicated to do, from the other side. That's what mattered; we didn't have to please anyone with how we lived our life in service to our Creator with our promise.

The more David taught me of past memories, the more anxious I became in our work, I couldn't learn fast enough! Every day became a new joy of discovery and the mundane work became pretty non-exciting to me most days. I was forgetting to live more of my life on this side I was so caught up in all I was learning. But, not by ever neglecting my family, just meaning my everyday living in general in the years to come. There were so many treasures and secrets to be told about still and I never really thought I would be allowed to tell the world! I was devoted to doing my beloved work the most.

Those Crossing Over

As time passed through the years, we both felt familiar with the process of helping loved ones crossing over to the other side. There were many of those souls we did not know, but it did not matter. The souls who returned were meant to come back. Some were those who had experienced being DOA (dead on arrival) and those who had had NDE (near death experiences).

Everything I experienced was in my awaking to the wonders and memories of other times, and to other places through my son. I knew we had done these things before in other times. It felt wonderful to be able to resume our work taking away the new souls fear of passing and bringing them into their Heaven and other Universal places.

I was also strongly drawn to study one subject after another more than ever. The fascinating Ancient world, the Mayans, Emperors, Huns, the Amazon, Egyptians, American Indians and so much more. I studied the different cultures and teachings of their healing techniques in our world; there was so much to relearn. I was like a sponge, for all I could find and learn through my son and our universal teachers and guides. I loved being in the Heavenly realms in my astral travel and visions and filled with their spiritual information. Each discovery made it clearer for me to remember about some of the events my son had explained to me earlier in my astral travel. I couldn't learn fast enough!

We lived in amazing worlds, if only we could share all of this somehow with everyone! The Heavenly Beings said, "No, It was not yet time for many to understand, so be patient. The old ways on earth were strong and had been taught to this world for ages. History was not going to change what has been written in books." The more I thought about this, the more it made perfect sense. History would not be changed! To say a large amount of it was wrong would be unheard of to the world!

I was hard pressed to find another person who was interested in my discoveries other than family that I could trust. My attempts to converse with very few others on these subjects were futile. Once in awhile, I would meet another person who I felt was familiar to me who was another seeker such as my son and myself.

One day, I was told by one of my Spiritual guides to slow down and not rush my earth life by so fast. I was here to enjoy it as much as in the spiritual realm and to live my earthly life to learn what I chose to this time around. I have learned to look at problems in a new and better way knowing I am in a big learning process. It is easy to do this by simply taking notice of what is important and what is not. My loved ones are the most important thing to me ever; they are my heart and soul, my completeness on earth.

My son, knowing our plan also tried to tell me to slow down and smell the roses. He and I enjoyed everything created in nature and the cherished gifts of beauty given to every person to see for free. I often tell others, just look out your window at all the beauty money can't buy. It is unbelievable the people who think money is everything, some worship it! And that's a whole another story, greed. We are earthly beings of great wealth with this beautiful planet all around us and this has nothing to do with money. Life isn't easy, it is hard, but through knowing, we each can conquer our hurdles turning those into our lessons, painting a wonderful and positive picture. The big picture is only what matters in the end. Life is about how we handle the problems we came here for and the love we pass on to others.

It is the separation of our loved ones and our children who leave us which is our worst nightmare and greatest hurdle to bear; making our struggle seem impossible to get through. The magic they have left us with will always be our own treasures to keep; no one can ever take those away. This is the hardest hurdle we try to heal from.

My son and I always knew our lives were very complex to say the least. We lived a duel life every single day. We were fine with it most of the time, learning to accept an important fact, not to ask the why or have the answers. Knowing if and when we were meant to understand more we would be told. I was sometimes impatient for answers but learned to understand how to relax and not rush this part. I must confess all of this took time as I still slip getting ahead of myself. I know why I feel this way, I love my work. David would laugh and remind me again to be patient.

We accepted our learning with grace, excitement and knowing this was a big part of our work to keep trust and believe. I do not ask anyone to understand all of this; I can only tell you of the way we chose to live. Through the Angels and Christ like Beings which, covers a lot of territory and we knew something greater than we could fathom was being woven into our very soul, why else were we this way? There were instances when certain Archangels: Michael, Gabriel, Raphael and sometimes others stepped in to help us depending on the mission that came to us. We were always in awe and completely humbled of how this worked. I cannot explain more of this to you the readers, there is so much I cannot explain now, or am permitted too. Even when I was on my way to the hospital or other places, I visualized the Angels around us to keep us safe knowing they were near. We felt blessed and honored for their protection and were also guided by our spiritual teachers and guides.

If you ever experience an Angel or Divine Being of Light you will feel so very small and insignificant, yet filled with the most powerful love you can't explain and you will never forget the amazing experience. Angels come in many different ways, it would surprise you. They do not always appear as we think they should look, with wings and so on. But they are ready to protect and help someone in less than a thought. They can come to us in disguise depending on the circumstances, even as a human being when needed, walking among us. They can adapt to all kind of situations. Even as a homeless person, a drug addict, an intoxicated person, someone you may have treated badly. This is your test sometimes. How did you treat this person? Hopefully, without a negative comment to them or look of disgust. To pass by without being mean is the test of success. We don't know, but can learn to have compassion for others. Be careful who you judge. You may be judging yourself.

Denise Was a Treasure

I did not know heartbreak was in front of me on the trip back home with a very close and dear friend, Denise, who was the sister I always wanted and never had. We met when I taught Reiki at a local college near where she lived. Instantly, we each knew we had been family before. We went together to see the Dali Lama a few years ago which was her dream to do and was on both of our bucket lists. We had such a fascinating trip at this event to see him and to hear his words. My son was too sick to attend and could not sit that long and I didn't want to go without him but he insisted I do and I wished he had been there with us.

Some of the older Tibetan children whose entire families had been destroyed in front of them by the communists were along with him. The older children who were in the higher grades of the University spoke of their horrific lives; some broke down in tears and could not continue. We here, could not imagine living as they had and our hearts went out to them. This was a once in a lifetime experience for us.

The Dali Lama spoke with his gentle and powerful words of love and humility. He appears as love himself and for the human race. They are an extremely gentle people and I learned from those there. Once you experience how their lives were destroyed and yet they went on with their strength by picking themselves back up, it is amazing! These Tibetans have suffered greatly and the young were left alone without parents. This place is not a warring country; they are gentle people who never thought of being taken over, killed, or tortured. These people did not know what a war was! We left after the day was over with learning about them and their small country, and the feeling of great compassion for them. We realized those who escaped were very fortunate.

On our trip home something happened after seeing the Dali Lama. Denise told me about her dealing with cancer years back. She told me of certain spiritual signs she received when she was in the hospital which let her know she would be healed. She spoke of the miracle of her healing and she had been free of cancer for several years now. The more she talked of this wonderful time in her life for reasons unknown right then, I felt something was wrong with her. I didn't want to let this information coming to me to continue on, I was afraid for her! She looked so happy and bright eyed on this trip so I blocked out my thoughts! I didn't want to know what the other side said. She pointed out churches we passed by along the way. She explained her signs, when sick those years, were always around churches, letting her know she would be healed. I have had those types of signs before when my son was so sick, which I thought was odd we both had. I didn't let on that I felt the way I did and told her to continue with her get well story that was beautiful! Why did I feel something was wrong, but what? I was like Denise, on a high from this wonderful event we had just experienced with the Dali Lama! We had the best time together. This was a once in a life time experience for anyone!

Denise always felt we had been sisters in another time, which reminded me of a vision I had one night. In the vision I saw us playing together in a tiny village in Tibet. We were both little girls, very poor but happy and loved one another. I recall so clearly we were playing in the dirt drawing pictures and giggling together. This confirmed what we both felt.

Almost two weeks later I had just gotten home from getting out of the hospital and David answered a phone call. He hesitated, and then hung up before telling me Denise had just been taken to the hospital; he knew she was already gone, he later told me. I also felt this as soon as he told me she had collapsed at school and they had taken her to the hospital. I then asked David and my daughter to pick me up a few things so I could be alone while thinking of her. While I waited for more information to hear back on Denise, for some reason I decided to take a shower hoping I would feel better. That was not a good idea.

At first I had trouble with the water getting warm which was a mystery since all the plumbing was new and I was having no trouble before with it. Later, I found out why. Getting into the shower I became very weak and felt myself starting to get dizzy. Suddenly, I knew Denise was with me! I called out for her to help me, "Denise, please help me!" I recall seeing her face clearly above me just as I started to faint. The next memory I had was sitting on a small chair in the bath room, just sitting straight up! I reached the towel bar pulling a large towel around myself, then made it a few steps trying to walk into another room to lie down and passed out again! When I came to, I was sitting with my back against the wall which I barely recall doing. Denise was helping me again, I know she did. I sat there wrapped up in my towel until my daughter and son returned and helped me to bed. I couldn't get her out of my mind.

A second call about Denise soon came with the details. She had collapsed at school at 8:15 that day and died immediately in the hallway. Her husband, child, and family were crushed! She wasted no time in appearing to me with messages for her family. She wanted me to go to her family with her messages so they would know she lives on and is at peace. This is a story of how once again the souls passed on can help us here in many ways. I am positive Denise saved my life; in the shower since I had seen her before I passed out. That night she came to me constantly and in the following days and nights, and each time I opened my eyes she was there. I wrote down messages from her for her family. She had a small son who she was very sad to leave, a good husband and family.

Her messages to my son and me were very important for her; she was relying on us to tell her loved ones she was okay. She was very anxious to connect as soon as possible with them to give them relief. I knew I couldn't go to them until I could travel but I did call them immediately to tell them. Thank God, they knew Denise was a very spiritual person and open to life after life since they heard her speak of this subject often.

After an autopsy, there was never a reason given for her death! The autopsy showed no reason what so ever. She was 42 years old and the school teacher every child would love to have, she was the kindest and sweetest person one could meet. She had been trying to call me the day before she collapsed and I had not gotten back to her. I have felt so guilty since then, but I know she understands. I feel strongly she had something on her mind she wanted to say to me, perhaps of how she felt, like a coming doom. She was intuitive as well. I treasure a picture of her meditating in her beautiful card that her mother gave to me later on.

At the time of her funeral I was too sick to attend. I was honored to know her family had placed the first book I had written, *Under the Rainbow Crossing*, beside her picture at the funeral this had been a gift to Denise from me. I had recently given her a beautiful Tibetan jacket as a gift that she was cremated in. I felt honored once more and respectful to the family for doing this. Denise and I were very close like sisters as I mentioned, even though we had not known one another very long. As I thought of our friendship, I remembered a week before Denise had said, "She had been getting so tired every day. She stayed in bed on the weekends to rest up enough to teach through the week." As much as she loved life and her loved ones, I knew her soul was tired.

Denise was so strong around me the day in the shower because she was trying to keep me out of it so I wouldn't get hurt. Somehow she controlled not letting the water get warm, hoping I would change my mind to get in. Denise intervened and saved my life, my head could have hit the hard tub and who knows what would have happened? I figured later on that this was the way she would come to me quickly after she had crossed over to help save my life! It was in the first couple of hours after she passed that she appeared to me in the shower. She also knew my heart was broken over her passing. I was welcoming her messages each and every one of them.

As soon as I became well enough to travel and drive I gave Denise's family her many messages over the weeks while she came to me. Up to that point, I was still getting messages from her. I continually kept writing them down as she talked to me. She certainly loved her family with all of her heart and was very concerned about her son, who was only 12 then. The readings with Denise's messages were profound and everything she said to me was right on target for her family. They were more at peace knowing only they and Denise could know the information she gave to me for them.

She had described many items to me to let her family know that this was coming from her. Things like a bracelet she had given to her mother as a gift on Mother's day and the colors of tiny stones in it. She also described a high school play she was in, The King and I, and the part she played in it. She described a certain picture of her class room that she had given to her brother, and the art work her students made that was in it. She also told me there was a ball of light in her palm in the school picture; this was some kind of a phenomenal picture which couldn't be explained! Sure enough, he showed me this picture and the light was clearly in her palm!

She gave me pages of information about her life that I could never have known. Every message she had me write down to tell her loved ones was exactly right and a confirmation to them. Her mother even pulled the bracelet out of her purse I described that Denise told me about. She had brought it in her purse hoping Denise would mention it. I knew nothing about the information she gave me in her messages, but her family knew all of it! I had several pages written of what Denise needed to tell her family so they would know she was at peace. This gave some closure to them proving she was okay.

But even the messages don't take away the pain of a loss. They help, but the hurt still lies deep within and always will. They, on the other side try to get us to realize we need to continue on with our lives here and they will be waiting for each one of us when our time comes. Denise had a mission as we all do.

David said, "When Denise was with us both; she was giving him messages too which he relayed also for her family. To tell them she was happy where she was now, but her main concern was still about her small son and she would become his guardian from now on." The only clue I had about her passing so soon was on our trip and when she confided in me that she was so tired. Her energy was depleted. I have known since she crossed over that her physical body was worn out and her job here on earth was over. Apparently that was the way it was meant to be. I will be reunited with my loved ones and Sister, Denise, some day.

BEV and More Wonderful Visits

There were soon more experiences going on, constantly between here and there, and my son came again to visit Bev. He was so excited one day when he appeared to her. David told her he was so happy because he was going to see the King! That he wouldn't be around for a while and as quick as a blink he was gone!" I was so excited for him my heart leaped in my chest when she told me this experience! This was the ultimate, and so wonderful; I couldn't imagine how excited he was, especially to have the honor of going to see the King! I felt humbled as I knew he was! This would be his greatest wish since he merged with the Creator and now it was time to see the King! I quickly thought of the words in his celebration song, "My Sweet Lord, I just want to know you; I just want to be with you, I just want to see you, My Sweet Lord, but it takes so long…" This made me feel absolutely complete as a human and thankful for my son's happiness and honor! He was with his Sweet Lord from the very beginning and to the end of his life here and then merged with him for eternity.

It wasn't long until Bev had another short visit one evening when David simply said to her, "I have to go check on my mom!" And zoom, he was gone! Bev and David kidded around so much that she had to laugh when she told me what he said so quickly and poof, he was gone! How sweet to know he was always checking on me, even though I saw him day and night. He knew she would tell me what he said. Actually, he had just made a quick check on Bev too!

On David's first year in the Hereafter, my girls and I decided to release balloons into the sky to celebrate his one-year on the other side, on March 16th. Each one was in a different color and one was even a cartoon style balloon. We held onto our balloons getting ready to release them, we were anxious to start and made the countdown, then let go, and all of the balloons floated off at once. I took pictures as they floated up into the sky and far away as we stood outside of his house. We watched until they were gone out of sight. We knew he would like this very much and I felt sure he was right there laughing with us.

Pam, Me, and Robin releasing the balloons

When I went to pick up the pictures I had taken, I saw what I had hoped for that day. I had silently asked David if he could do something to show he was with us when we released our balloons. There was my answer right in front of me as plain as day; there were the three balloons we sent off, but one extra balloon was also in the picture! The extra balloon now made four balloons and it was cobalt blue in color floating above the roofline of his home! He made us very happy showing he was with us watching and joining in on the celebration just as I hoped he would! We sent our devoted love to him on his special day and I can just see him laughing. I have no idea where this cobalt blue balloon ever went, or how he did this, we didn't see it anywhere that day because it wasn't for our eyes to see!

There is still more to this story. Something else wonderful happened one year later when my daughter Pam found her balloon that she had sent up to her brother lying flat in her front yard! She lives in the country a few miles from David's home where we released the original balloons and it appeared to be the same balloon with the same cartoon and colors on it that we had purchased. One year later he was letting her know I GOT IT, and now I am letting you know by sending it back to you!

I thought of all the months through winter, wind, rain, and snow and how he brought the balloon back after 12 months! But really, considering all that the other side can do, would I think differently? I cannot tell you how much this lifted our spirits, but David sure knew. Where was this balloon for over one year? Disappeared into the universe I suppose I am sure it was nothing for him to arrange this surprise for her. This may give one something to think about, how do they do these things? They seem to be masters at moving things, as well as making themselves appear. I loved his amazing balloon experience for her!

It was also right at a year later, when I saw my son's hands move over my face as I woke up. There were orbs of pink light floating around the room, which represents love to me. Then my son said four important words to me, "Green Eggs and Ham!" I broke into laughter with his words and softly fell back into a contented sleep knowing he was happy and making me feel happy. He lifted my very soul; he had used these very words often through his lifetime joking with me and his sisters many times. He came to cheer me up on this his crossing over anniversary. He had said these very words to Robin as he was dying that sad night one year ago. We had always broke into laughter every time he kidded us with those words coming from his old Dr. Seuss children's book he had when he was small and growing up!

Another message occurred nine days later when I clearly heard the Heavenly voice say to me one day, "Ruth, take a little time for yourself", and the Being was gone. When my mail arrived on the same day a Midwest Living magazine also came. I did not subscribe to the magazine at that time! The sticker on it said, "It was from David to me as a gift book!" I was stunned, even though I know the other side can do anything, it made me emotional to experience his marvelous surprises to cheer me up. How wonderful to be a large part of these different worlds, I cannot express this enough to you!

Before Christmas I had another amazing vision. I had fallen asleep one evening and quickly found myself in a traveling experience. I was sitting in a big chair of some sort and I could see a big beautiful Lion. The feeling of love I had for it indicated this was a very special pet to me, one that I loved so very much. I felt very close and bonded to my pet and I knew it was guarding and protecting me and the Lion sat right beside me at my feet. All of a sudden an object flew into its eye and quickly a sharp piece of wood flew into its face! I was extremely upset and quickly I picked my lion up to rush him to the Vet for help and to get the pieces removed! I was so very sad and upset it was injured.

The next thing I saw looking into the Lion's face was my son's face in place of the Lion's face! Then I was given the clear understanding that David and I were going home to his Heaven together. He wanted me to see something and was taking me back with him to the spirit world. In what seemed like a moment, I was in another place which was very familiar to me, now we were in a Biblical time I somehow knew. I could see many people on each side of a dirt road lined all the way up ahead on both sides. Then I saw what seemed to be a large Temple at the end of this road. My son and I walked up the middle of the road toward the temple. There were crowds of people and all of them had been waiting for us to come! They were expecting us in honor of something grand; they were waving and cheering at us. I said excitedly to David, "Oh Look, they are all here!"

I seemed to understand all of this at that moment and I could see many of our loved ones and friends who had passed over! I had such an unexplainable feeling of exciting joy. I was home and I was so happy! I was given the meaning of this special event then and I knew what it meant. David, in life, had a Lion's heart and courage. He walked without fear through his life even when he was so sick and now he was taking me to see where he lived and the many loved ones he is with. That in his life he had to be strong for all of us while he was on earth, no matter what happened. He was our Lion with a Lion's heart and strength. He conquered life and he represented King David!

I came out of this vision an excited and a very happy mother to have this honor by knowing where his new home is now. He had given me my wish that I had asked for! I thanked my son for this amazing and loving trip together and I will remember this experience all the rest of my life with complete love and humbleness. My son, to me King David! I would repeat this to myself to come. He had always protected us.

I know that those in spirit can move in any direction to anyplace they want in blink of an eye and we had done this *together* so many times. This is what he wanted me to know and experience. I had asked him once before if he could show me where he is now when the timing was right for him and me. This is what the vision is all about. He had taken me to see that he is with many of our loved ones and friends. We have always stayed together in life after life, and in different time periods. This is where I will go back to one day.

In a double visit, my CD player began playing at 2 am the same morning by itself! This was the music sent to me from my dear Indian friend, Alex who crossed over in May of 2014. It soon soothed me into a deep sleep and I remembered no more, except that I received great peace, away from my sadness. I have felt this was from my son and Alex together with their spirits both combined.

Phone Calls from the Dead

Another way of contact that David and I have both experienced is with phone calls from the dead. It is surprising how well we could understand them; their voice is usually quite clear. David and I have each had these phone calls from the dead where Heavenly voices and crossed over souls speak just as anyone would. Their voices are hard to describe and you feel mesmerized, yet know something is going on that you can't explain at the same time. There is something holding you onto their words that you are hearing and you don't seem to be able to control even your own thoughts. Words are hard to come by as if your mind knows to be still and listen. I will tell you some of our experiences of when we have received telephone calls from souls that happened close together. The two I will tell you about were from a Being of Light I call the amazing Celestial calls, and two more were from David's friend, John, who committed suicide. There have been many others too.

John was a very depressed young man who my son was urging to seek help. He tried his best to get him to go for help and offered to take him but he refused. David talked with him every day and went to see him as often as possible knowing that John was not making progress and he was very worried about his friend. John kindly listened to him but explained he could not see a way out of his troubles. David told me he was very concerned that John would kill himself. Within a few days his friend was found dead by his own hand in his yard.

The next evening after John crossed over, David found a message from him on his answering machine! John said, "Trying to reach David and something about thanking him for his help!" Then I had an experience with his friend myself. I had only briefly met John maybe three days before he killed himself. He came by to look at something at David's house and I was there. We were introduced and other than a nice warm hello and so glad to meet you, that was all that was said between us. I felt strongly he was a very nice man who had a beautiful smile and a big and gentle heart. I knew he was going through many hard times in his life.

On my birthday a short time after John passed over, I found a message on my e-mail which said, "Happy birthday, Ruth Ann, been trying to reach David!" It was John and he was again trying to reach my son! He desperately wanted David to hear from him. I was actually shocked because I didn't get to know him, but I was very happy he could manage his message to both of us so soon. How did John know my e-mail address let alone when my birthday was? Like I said, they know everything!

We both knew John somehow quickly learned how to get his messages to us both. I was mostly surprised that he knew how to connect to us immediately in this way so fast! He needed to get his messages to us and he did. The main thing was his strong desire to send them. Many adjusted older souls seem to have a way to show new ones how to use their own voice on telephone calls and in all kinds of ways to make contact quickly. It seems unlimited as to what can be done once we leave here. I will remember John all my life and know how much relief he is in now than when he was on earth suffering.

I would certainly think this kind of proof does confirm how alive our loved ones are on the other side and how they can make contact in these different ways. John, for his own reason gave me this message because it was so important for him to get through to David. He wanted to thank David for standing by him being his friend, and in John's compassion, to wish me a happy birthday! I felt wonderful and happy getting his sweet message, a blessed soul who was now at peace. This is the kind of contact that proves how alive our loved ones are and a suicide contact is no different. We both were surprised by the phone calls and my e-mail message which helped take away some of our sadness knowing John was happy where he is now. I made sure to say a big thank you to him for my birthday message and we would miss him until we all meet again.

Celestial Calls from Heaven

One of the times this happened to me was early one evening when I made a call to my daughter's home. The phone rang and a strange voice answered who I did not recognize and began talking to me and it was not my daughter! I felt totally surprised since it was not her, but the voice made me want to hear it! I was frozen, yet stayed on the line intrigued. I couldn't think to say anything. I gave all of my attention to what I seemed to know was a Heavenly voice. I was thrown off for seconds, feeling compelled to listen. I could not seem to comprehend what was taking place and what exactly was going on with the voice. This voice was full of Angels' sweetness; soft and different.

This beautiful sounding voice was telling me how much I was loved, more than I could ever imagine and how much God loves me! All of the words I was hearing were so beautiful! This was a voice I had never heard like this before. I couldn't comprehend what was taking place so I finally stuttered, "I am sorry, I must have the wrong number," and hung up. I asked myself, "Why did I do that?" I decided quickly to call my daughter's number back again wondering what had just taken place. The same voice answered once more and talked to me about how much God loves me again and also told me other beautiful words. I was stunned! I can't believe what I did out of confusion, I actually said, "I must have the wrong number again!" The loving voice said, "No, do you want it to be?"

I finally hung up more confused and called back again a third time planning to ask questions. The phone rang until an automated message said the telephone was disconnected! Then I knew for sure what had just taken place! This was definitely a Heavenly Being talking to me with such love and who was reinforcing me in my work. This happened at a time I needed to have this amazing experience. I felt such happiness surge throughout my entire body with God's love. I felt so sorry with a deep regret that I had not realized this before. This experience and message would always be locked in my heart!

I later remembered that I had forgotten my daughter, Robin, had changed her number. I quickly called my daughter's new number and told her about what had just happened when I called her old number. She had no idea how her old number could possibly work. She, in turn, called her old number to see what would happen, which was nothing! She called the phone company only to find out that NO one had her old phone number yet! The phone company said they wait one year before giving a number out again to a new person! This really made me feel better knowing I was right, and I needed this uplifting message. I was in a slump at that time and I feel strongly that is why the Heavenly call came, to bring my spirit up.

We hoped one day to get more of these calls and we did. David and I noticed calls from the Beyond always seem to come in a time of our need and gave us extra support. We have experienced more than I could ever dream of, filling us each time with their compassion and love. The other side can always surprise us! I am amazed to this day the many messages and experiences my son and I both have received through the Christ Beings of Light. They always come in some way when we need to be lifted up and put at peace; afterwards we are powered up again to persevere on the journey.

Even though Angels have no gender, they come in the way that is best for us at the time and they don't always come the way one may think. Many Angels that we have seen who have come to help us look completely human in regular clothing such as the Phantom nurse and guide at the bus stop who helped us home.

Chapter 22

Experiencing Beings of Light
Spirits Caught on Camera

Keeping Records

You can probably understand now why we were not sharing our strange lives with others more than ever. We did not believe others could possibly believe what had been happening to us and that it is still happening. All of the messages ever given to each one of us have been full of love, spiritual knowledge, and wisdom from our Creator. I have recorded messages we have received, except those given directly in voice and in visions, when a recorder wasn't turned on. I put those messages that are taped on video as soon as possible. I also made records in my notebooks that I keep very secure. The video, notebooks, photos and those on cassettes are all backed up in case something ever happens to any of the pictures and notebooks. I knew one day they would tell us what to do with them.

This makes me remember an important vision where I was having a conversation with the Creator, and I was in the brightest light! I recall hearing roaring laughter when I was told I would be his secretary! I was so dumbfounded I couldn't comprehend this at the time. Suddenly I came out of the vision wondering what this clue could possibly mean! After all of these years that have gone by, now I know the answer to the statement made to me. It hit me one day thinking of how for these many years I have documented everything we have experienced. I have faithfully used my notebooks, cassettes, camera, and video making records through our lives! Now I know the answer. Yes, I knew the meaning at last! With the records I had made and kept over the many years I was very much like a secretary!

It wasn't long and our messages increased more from the other side. They were coming to us in every kind of way; some came three to four times per day and evening. This was eventually common for us and it would continue through the following years. Not only were the messages daily, but some of the voices I continued to record on cassette players, and on video recordings. I recorded everything that I was allowed to. I kept my note book beside my bed day and night, writing down any messages I received.

So much of our work was given to us in visions which were very powerful from the Christ. I sometimes scribbled down their message as the spirits or The Christ Light Being appeared close to my bed. At other times, I had to tell them to slow down with their words as I wrote. David told me he could remember his visits, but for our record I would write his down too as we went over our information each day. If he was at his home we called one another first thing, going over what we each received in the night. When we analyzed our day of new information, sometimes we would joke about how we felt, which seemed as if we lived in a snow globe that only we could see out of.

In our promise I knew we would never forsake our work unless we were told differently. I knew we had been given all we received for a huge purpose and that's all we needed to understand. Looking back, David knew when my information would be told to me and why I was keeping track of it in my notebooks without me knowing the whole picture yet. Those times I had to try and remember my past by slowly filling in the pieces on my own. He would remind me to be patient; it would all come...learn to be patient. I was like a sponge soaking up all I was taught from the other side and here, and I always tried to keep a balance with my busy life the best I could.

A Message Appears Mysteriously

There will never come a time for me to forget finding the first messages that came to us in my notebooks! When I found the first one in the very beginning, my notebook was found lying on my bed open with a message! I called out for my son to come quickly from his room! David and I were nearly jumping up and down! Try to imagine the excitement we felt! How can this be happening I thought! It took a while to calm down, almost two days! This was unheard of to us and probably to most people. How could this kind of connection to the other side ever be made public in order to share with others how the other side worked with us? With that thought, again I heard the word, patient! I felt I heard familiar soft laughter too!

Our lives were completely woven in accordance, existing partly in other places without time and space, and yet here, trying to understand the overwhelming changes so fast in our human lives. We were being given a massive storehouse of knowledge, going beyond the lifting of the veil to more than one world that would impede understanding of the psychic sciences. We had moved from our mundane daily world to some kind of spiritual evolution, but while waiting, we kept our spiritual work going. In time we would understand more of the reasons we were chosen for what we were doing. If we knew anything, we both realized we were sincere seekers learning to empower our spirit and others, with knowledge and wisdom being taught to us. This was in order to rise up and use every chance we got with the real truth of unconditional love and peace. It had taken the early years to learn my many symbols, designs, and some languages with the soul's words in their way, and getting to use to hearing their whispers to me in the early years. David helped me figure out many of my signs which would be critical to know. It was about being in school once more and it would always continue. I was allowed to see souls in most ways in all kind of settings as they wanted to orchestrate for me to best understand them in our work.

Beings of Light

Our notebook messages kept coming from the Christ Light Beings and our loved ones with a new journey beginning. These journeys were to be with new Beings and unidentified places. But now, with the new lessons we were starting, it wouldn't be so easy to learn new symbols and designs plus, a new spiritual language all combined.

The first new information we could partially read was clear enough for us to see. But not knowing what the new symbols and designs meant, they were mostly guesses on our part. The messages were always signed in some kind of script we called *Alien* since that's what it seemed to look like to us by the symbols and because we didn't have a clue as to what was exactly happening.

In those times we felt as if we needed to learn to be code breakers to understand it. In time, we finally began to understand some of what the Beings meant. Eventually the new signs and symbols we understood that they had been trying to slowly teach us their language from another dimension and world! I wish I could say that I knew what they were clearly saying but, no! It was going to be on a long learning journey with this one! They let us work at it and know school classes were back in! We were filled with their patience and love. Now we would be getting their information in this different way of communication.

I kept busy recording everything I could. Once in a while the new information would be made clear "that this was for our eyes only" and later it would be gone, disappeared off of the note book paper and computer!

Clearly we knew that these things were never to be seen by anyone else. The messages were mainly holy, beautiful, important world information, our teachings and sometimes answered Bible questions that we asked.

Also, at times we were allowed to tape and video those who came in their light form, and others who were transparent and who came in a different type of solid matter. I vividly recall one experience of my dad when he came to see me. He was in golden lines of bright light with a cobalt blue circle of light where the third eye is located. I was stunned; he was so beautiful in his light, his spiritual light! Then he told me he loved me.

Our schooling now also came to us from a new source of Christ Light Spiritual Beings that exist in other Universes and Worlds. This was very encouraging with extraordinary material for us, the students. We didn't have any idea yet as to what it all meant. We just knew this was phenomenal! In the beginning, right before all of this started with the new Beings, I found my scarf and my moon necklace hanging on my ceiling fanlight! The moon necklace was a gift from my son. It had been placed facing the direction of the North! The scarf was placed in a beautiful perfectly placed design! This indicated to us the Christ Light Beings would come from our north directions. The label inside the scarf said made by Dimensions! This would become very important, with new information.

This scarf was placed here by one of the Spiritual teachers.

Past Life in Egypt

Close to this time we experienced a phenomenal event very clearly. This was about another past life in Egypt. I wore Egyptian clothing moving as fast as possible deep down inside of a pyramid holding something in my hands which was of great importance. I was running from Egyptian soldiers and somehow knew just where to go. I was running even faster now down the stone steps into a lower level. The objects I carried were something so precious they had to be hidden quickly before the soldiers found me! The chance of survival was non-existent, but it didn't matter, the sacred objects had to be hidden in this special place where they could never be found by anyone for now.

I heard the soldier's step's coming closer now; they were almost right behind me! There were only moments left to find the secret opening where the objects were to go. Suddenly there it was, I shoved the precious objects into the space and the stone to cover them fell perfectly in place. They were safe!

The soldiers captured me without a fight; they would never know where the scared treasure was. I was so happy to do what was needed. This was something very important to the world to be found some day in the future. I knew that there were only moments left to live, but it did not matter. This was a very important treasure that would never get into the wrong hands now. Whatever it was had something to do with world events in the future. I did not feel my immediate death, but I gladly gave my life knowing I had achieved my purpose for man-kinds future. For some reason, I was to see and remember this; it is still crystal clear in my mind today as to when it happened. The fear I held inside of myself was that they would catch me before the items could be hidden for all time.

Later, in another memory that came to me of David and myself, we were together in Egypt once again. I had beautiful clothing on such as worn in a palace and I was in a large Temple where the Priests and Healers gathered with others. I remember looking up high and there was a beautiful golden bridge and David my son was walking across the bridge in a long golden robe with a high Egyptian head dress on that was all in gold. He was carrying a golden rod in his one hand and I knew he was a High Priest of Healing. Being my son, I was feeling very proud of him. Everything was very quiet and remained this way in respect of this event. I knew he had always been a Healer in each life time, and I was his mother once more in this lifetime. This was told to me at that moment and I shall always remember this time in Egypt. We had experiences living several life times in Egypt and both of us have always been intrigued with Egyptian culture and events. I knew why I had been shown this clearly, as my son did. In these past lives the things we are strongly drawn to and the people we meet we have usually been connected with in some way, the good and the bad.

Continuing to Learn

Still to this day I am reliving the story of David with our information I am now allowed to write in this book, I sometimes marvel at it! So much was going on in so many different directions to teach us. Growing up, I never thought about any of this. I had never heard of these things. Of course, I know now I was here to learn all of my life working with David together for our various reasons.

More recently, people everywhere are becoming more curious about what's out there in our universe. More now than we ever thought possible. So much is going on in our world and people want some kind of direction and answers to the best they can find. Others in this world are also changing how they think. They are searching out all kinds of advancements from shuttles in space, carbon dating, and new discoveries over the world. Technology has become amazing and the brilliant minds who bring it to life. Common sense years ago told me we aren't the only Beings who were ever created in this vast Universe.

Never did I dream for the first years my son and I would be doing this kind of work and traveling in spirit. We are experiencing amazing places that sound like fantasy, and moving faster than the speed of light, passing through time warps where time bends and shapes! All of these things we have at one time known about before coming here, but I had forgotten. Experiencing all of this I felt as though I was in a secret science fiction movie, and who would believe it! An ordinary house wife was my earth cover, but underneath I was someone else as my son was. I was to learn over and over, things are not always as they seem. This was told to both of us many times for our own peace of our human mind.

I did not know the opinion some man-made organizations would have on this information and it really didn't matter. I later became curious as to how shocking this information would affect most church doctrine and belief, which has been passed down for centuries. I am sure our work would be shocking to most. I do know everyone is on a different path and we are all learning in different ways but no matter what path we each choose, the key is love. We have always embraced our teachings from our Creator knowing that He had lined out an unusual plan for the two of us to accomplish on earth. I only know the most important thing is to keep the key of love open and in your heart so you can pass it on to others. I know we both are happy to be led in the Creator's way.

As I stated before, our messages are always of great love, spiritual knowledge, and truth. Any warnings given to us are to protect ourselves. Also, for in the future, we both were told to never forget we are always protected in our work. This continued message helped us to grow stronger without fear of any ridicule. The Heavenly Beings reinforced once more that we were their honorable students. We were grateful the Beings of the Christ Light were lighting our path. This spiritual message let us know we were on track in our lives.

At times, all of us get off track, the main thing is to get back on and keep on persevering. Getting off track didn't last long, but once in a while this happened when we were overwhelmed, it would happen, but we got back up and went on. This is the part for anyone which is so important, keep going! It too shall pass! We were fulfilled to be doing our work on earth! In our unusual life I had so many questions and David was so good with his patience telling me what he was allowed to. A few times he also waited for answers. If it was not time for me to know something yet, he simply told me, it will come.

We were certainly happy making contact with so many of our loved ones on the other side. Our spiritual teachers are full of love with such indescribable humor at times. I certainly don't want to forget the humor the other side has. There were occasions I could hear thunderous laughter rolling through the heavens and this was usually to my never ending questions for them. I was raised to think everything was so serious and solemn in my old way of growing up. In our excitement we felt so much joy coming from the Higher Beings of Light!

When David first tried to describe this to me many years ago I soon found out who to talk to, and who not to talk to about our work. Life is too judgmental and some minds are too closed to new thinking. An open mind is a seeker who wants to learn and never stops seeking. We are all so different and on separate paths. Each person is where they should be with their own free will. This does not make one person better than another. That is what free will is all about, I choose, you choose. The last thing in the world I would ever want is for any person to think that we are patting ourselves on the back. We are only different by making our choice to get this information out that we promised. Experiences were recorded to pass on as we were told to do by the beings on the other side. We both have been very grateful, and know we risk a great deal but it does not matter.

Every human has important work to do if they realize it or not. Even the worst humans have shown us NOT to do the things they have and have no idea they are teaching others this. Everyone will use their life as a lesson to others in some way. It was not easy to leave old ways and many manmade beliefs behind at first. We know without a doubt to follow Christ's words to us. Because we have experienced all we have, why would we ever doubt? I do not expect others to change anything they believe. Most of us live by what we are told, taught, written, changed, experienced, and passed down through beliefs of people from centuries ago. This is because that is what was taught and written into books. The certain thing we both knew is where our work came from.

When a person expresses an amazing experience they had on the other side, you can see it in their eyes and life changes for them. Do you deny their truth because you have not been open to it or because of how you have been taught? On the other hand, some people have an open mind and know in their heart there is so much to learn in our world of other things. Even most church doctrines will not believe this story due to their schooling. It would be foreign to them without having this experience themselves.

Now, thank God, many others have shared their unusual true stories of their experiences to pass on everywhere. There are many innocent children who are telling where they went when they died and what they experienced. There would need to be thousands in our world everywhere who are lying if this had no truth. Famous and ordinary people put themselves on the line having much to lose by telling their story. They know they must in order to let others know that there is more going on than ever imagined. Yes, God is good, and not ready to throw us to the wolves as many may think because of their fear and misconceptions they hear and read.

Years ago, people were afraid to come forward worrying too much about what others would think, which is not even important. What is important in life is to do what you know you were brought here for! I was learning that timing is where it is supposed to be for each person. People are becoming more open and wanting more and searching for the truth.

Now you can understand more of the why we were not sharing our unusual lives with others for many years. We did not think most people could possibly understand. All of the messages we received are full of love, caring, and directing us with spiritual knowledge and wisdom. This all comes from our Heavenly Creator and Beings of Light. This was a daily learning experience that we encountered as hard as this may seem to you. It is not as if the spiritual teachers were standing in front of us in a solid form, however; they would briefly appear nearly in solid form to us during some of our learning experiences. We can see and hear what many others cannot. We were busy day and night, no matter where we were since time and distance makes no difference in our work.

Dimensions

In thinking of distance, when my son was healthy and lived in other places, I would go to see him. I was always taking pictures of his home which would be full of dimensions. I have several of those pictures which has part of his rooms mixed with my rooms from my house in one photo! My chairs may be upside down beside his TV and some of his furniture all combined together! I can't take doubles on my newer camera or what use to be called double negatives.

In my own home pictures I have taken some of my furniture from two different rooms is mingling together in all directions. Clocks may be sideways, light fixtures showing through pictures (dimensional), furniture upside down in a bathroom, and all kinds of ways. Some things are transparent or see through, and some are sideways and upside down! Several pictures have my son's furniture in mine, sideways and see through, but in my house!

What I do know is that the other side was big on teaching us dimensions for at least three years. I guess the pictures were another way to explain the idea to us. I have some spirit pictures showing the form of one of my main spiritual teachers coming out of the television in his light! And on my web site at Universal Conversations.com there are several spirit pictures to see including the one I just mentioned.

Try to remember God makes no mistakes, no matter how life seems at times, and the main thing is to never give up! What's important in life is to do what you know you were brought here to do. If you don't know what it is, just be a loving and good person because you are here doing what you are suppose to. No matter what we are each made of, in the big picture it works out. When we live the best we can that's what counts.

Capturing Spirits on Video and in Photographs

We connected with all kinds of spirits inside and outside, and in other places into the *Beyond*, capturing the pictures when we could. We have many pictures of spirit activity and movement from in my home and in other locations that both David and I took. I was allowed to take these pictures or I wouldn't have them. I knew who several of these spirits were. There were only a few that I didn't know and those became our teachers and friends too.

On one of the videos that I treasure, there is a long parade of people walking by in a line on the screen of the TV. They seem to be as solid as we are. I was videoing this right in the living room. They are all dressed as they do in India and some are wearing turbans on their head and many have animals walking beside them. Some are moving slowly together, others are walking by quickly. All at once, one of the people stopped, turned, and looked straight at me then he smiled and waved! I couldn't believe it! We were all in shock! Then it happened again! I have to say we watched this over and over. We began laughing so hard because it was so unbelievable and yet genuine! Most of the people were simply dressed in white tunic tops, white pants and some were without the white turbans. There were goats and dogs mainly beside of them. Some are walking fast and some slowly.

Uncle Leo

The one person that really took us by surprise who walked along in this parade of people is a favorite Uncle in our family! He had passed over recently and had lived nearby. He spoke many languages and had traveled around the world teaching. He had written a number of books and befriended important individuals in a number of countries. He had been a teacher and taught several languages. While he was living, I was used to seeing him in a white dress shirt and dress pants. This is what he had on when I saw him with the India people as I videoed. Uncle Leo had his sleeves rolled up to beneath his elbows without his usual tie, but there he was big as life!

I have thought of why he would show us himself in this way and then it hit me; he taught parapsychology among many other subjects in his life! I felt as if he was simply showing me his afterlife and that he has continued on in this way. Uncle Leo had many friends in many locations around the world.

We have an oil painting portrait of Uncle Leo that was painted by a Philippine artist who did not have hands and used only her feet to paint! She captured the very image of him in the painting. It is beautiful as if he is standing there in person. Although Uncle Leo's son had died as a young boy, he expressed to me many times afterwards how he wished David was also his son. He wrote David many heartwarming letters over many years.

David and Uncle Leo had many traits and likes in common. They would talk on the phone as much as possible and once David moved back to his hometown they spent much time together. With Uncle Leo having taught Paranormal studies, he and David were able to have great conversations on the subject

When I videoed I used a regular video camera with the television off and cable line unplugged, using the TV as a monitor only. In that way the TV could not work to bring in any programs. I loved doing this because we were able to learn about unknown dimensions, other worlds, other beings, and Universal Beings in their beautiful light working together with us! They gave us these lessons on the television screen like a movie! I have on video universal travel that we would be shown while taping it! This amazing travel was shown to us moving at a tremendous speed as if we were traveling in space. These were lessons for us about the speed of light and worm holes. It is amazing to see!

When I would take pictures, usually with an inexpensive store bought disposal camera, a loved one, guide or friend in spirit would normally be in the picture. Each time after getting the pictures back after the film was developed it was a real treat! Sometimes there are Universal objects I don't understand yet. When my main teacher comes, he is from another dimension and is in a form of Light. He once changed into a more solid human form as I videoed! I have a great picture of this. We couldn't wait each day to see what was going to happen next! Our friend, Bev, came by one day to see some of these phenomenal videos and pictures and even she became perplexed and excited over them. She could not believe what David and I were being taught daily.

This was an amazing and exciting learning school beyond earth that we were absolutely enthralled about! We had the best school a person could ever imagine from the Spiritual Teachers from the Other Side.

David had so much enjoyment out of my excitement because he already knew what I would be seeing and what would happen in our visits with the Beings of Light. He knew what I would be experiencing in my lessons as we worked side by side, but he didn't let me on, for he was my Earth Teacher. These happenings were the many secrets we were living with by being different. And we were thankful we had one another to share our way of life with by being connected to the other side, and using the same gifts. To have had all of this happen with no one who could understand and not be able to share with would have been very hard! I really can't imagine what life would have been like.

Fear and Darkness

There is one word which carries power over people everywhere and can terrorize those over our world. Do you know what that one word it is? This word, fear, can control lives even until a person takes their last breath. There are many descriptions of this emotion, and the worst is a fear of burning in a Hell along with the darkest entity called the Devil. According to some, many things can be caused by the Devil. This entity is an evil and dark negative entity, which instills a superior fear in many people. The name alone gives this dark energy a powerful focus to help build it stronger, so it keeps growing and growing. That's why it is so popular.

Where I am going with this is? There is no doubt in my mind that any dark energy that gets so much attention and energy from people, is the very power it needs. Now, we know what one focuses on, goes out into the universe and the universe will send, or give you what you keep your attention on. That is the way energy works. God our Creator is of love which is the most powerful of all! And those two emotions can never be combined because they are completely opposite energies. The Dark energy and God's Love and Light cannot co-exist together in the same space and time.

I believe you have to personally in some way invite darkness into your life before it can come into your life. Is it tricky? Oh yes, evil and darkness do exist and I have seen it more than once and it can fool those who cannot detect an evil presence. David and I are true believers and followers that Christ is sending our love and energy to the Supreme intelligence of Creation over everything. We knew that we had no room to bring any kind of darkness in with a constant focus on it. So be careful where you put your energy and focus.

Do I believe in a burning hell? David and I both have never seen or heard anything as a burning pit with pitch forks, the devil and so on from the Christ Light Beings. Never, have we been told this by the spirit world. I know it speaks of this in the Bible. We do have information there are many levels on the other side of darkness and the worst are the very lowest in a solid agony of darkness. There are many souls who go there reliving what they did in their life over and over in agony. This is what they expect. With the way we have been talked to about this is that we create our own hell on earth.

When we pass over, things are taken care of on many levels. We don't have all the answers, no one human on earth has. But this is one worth standing my ground on knowing where it came from. We think many things can be misinterpreted in many ways. Information can be left out and changed and all kinds of confusion can occur. We have gotten information from the other side on how forgiveness, combined with an immeasurable love is absolutely vital for change. Who knows what awaits us each in our transition other than wonder and love. I know everything is taken care of on the other side in a certain way. There are many Evil souls who walk among us here every day on earth in many places, that's for sure. I understand how our "hell" is on earth that we create ourselves. After passing over our energy can go to so many places in our vast universes and worlds.

We were in spiritual classes daily and learning through astral travel at night in our sleep. This is what most people only think of as dreams. They may be dreams to most, but the travel and visions for us were full of information. If a person is open minded and ready to receive, your world can change to a much better one. On occasion, we both were told "we were their *honorable students*" and we were in awe of this! We were so grateful for what we were learning. Any warnings of negativity we were ever given was to prepare us both and was always correct. There was nothing but positive told to either of us by the Benevolent Beings. We tried to stay around positive people, and all of this combined helped us grow more spiritually and stronger each time.

There were many times we needed to work with extremely negative people, which was a challenge. In this world one good true friend may be all one can count on, and that is a blessing and a treasure to have. One must be aware of the intentions of a negative person. They can sometimes act so charming at first to gain your trust. Bless them and go on away from them.

Spiritual Guides and Teachers

I had noticed for some time there would be new Spiritual teachers and Guides step in for a certain kind of a detailed work to help us. It depends on what we are working on when we would get new teachers. You wouldn't believe who some of them have been, and who some of the Guides were while living on earth. There are spiritual teachers on the other side who simply work with new souls arriving and there are others who guide and help us on Earth. A guide is someone who led an earthly life. An Angel or Arch Angel has not led a life on Earth, but can appear as a human to help someone. Our children who pass over to us become our Angels in heaven. Some become our guides, guardians, and protectors if they so choose. We always have our main teachers and guides working together with us, but others may step in for other things we are doing or to help. Each soul has one main Guide who comes in with them at birth. They stay with you until death and some even after. In time you may know who your guides are.

I had begun noticing this more when I was about to begin teaching college classes. I was trying to go to sleep the night before and was a little nervous; my first class would start the next day. My prayers were answered that night. I received the help I needed to direct me by a wonderful spirit teacher who was an important scientist in his earth life!

He came to me by appearing that night before my first class telling me, "not to worry, that he would be with me in every class I taught. My class would be well received by many." I was mesmerized! I couldn't believe this man who had gone down in history, had appeared to me! He was being my guide now. With his information I knew everything would go well and it did. We always thank the spirits and all the rest who work with us. I certainly thanked this brilliant man many times over!

Chapter 23

Death Experiences

My son and I wished others could know how wonderful the other side is in so many ways. We had hoped that perhaps one day some religions could be taught to listen more closely to others who have been DOA or had NDE and returned. Those souls hopefully return with not only the experience but with a new understanding that not all our beliefs are always as we think and are taught. That is part of why we are sent back here to tell others more of what REALLY happens on the other side. There is so much more going on than we as humans are taught on earth and that is another reason I am to tell David's story to the world. Everything is not in a book that a human believes as the right way; there can be misunderstandings in how words are misinterpreted and taught to others. Experience is the best way to learn, if it is available or from an informed person and teacher. What my son and I have been taught comes from the Christ Light Beings and has been from their information in order to teach us.

Above all we are not trying to change anyone's view in any way or your belief in what you choose. We all are where we should be in our lives in this moment. We learn from one another what is right and what is wrong in how we live and treat others. I learn every day and hope to always keep learning on this earth and from the other side.

My world changed completely after my death as a young woman where I went to heaven and came back because my mission here on earth wasn't completed. There my spirit was free and happy I was home! And more importantly, by knowing we have the most loving and forgiving Universal Supreme Intelligence, God, looking out for us, that you cannot imagine! It was when I set my spirit free of the labels and old ways here on earth that I found my way with Jesus Christ. Under His teachings and direction came my spiritual work. After I died in the wreck, my life changed big time, a little at a time, as I grew older and along my path.

With my son's teachings I was told I would grow stronger into the future. My trip to heaven was filled with many messages of things to come, more than I could ever embrace all at once in my memory. My soul overflowed with Christ's compassionate love and direction. Nothing would ever be the same; I knew I was feeling the ultimate by happily being committed to my promise and our covenant in this life. I know that I am a part of everything there is; I am a Universal Light Being. The universes are my real home as they are David's too.

It is a blessing and a gift for some people who have death experiences (DOA) and are sent back to tell of their experience to the other side. I know that is why many of us return, we are to tell what happened while we had those moments, minutes, hours, or days in the spirit world. Some people are away from their body in comas for months and years and one day they Wake up!

The experiences sometimes make some people afraid to speak of them. This especially goes back to years ago with being more conditioned by fear. David and I believe without a doubt, anyone's frame of mind greatly depends on what we each have been conditioned to living with, what has been put into our minds growing up with man-made control. Any person can be sinned to pieces in some places of worship and in the very home they reside. Take for instance; if one is afraid of a devil force as their worst fear, they are giving their energy to a complete focus of fear. It is what we create in our minds because of this fear. It is the difference of focusing between the positive and the negative.

If one thinks in the positive, powerful, love of God, with belief, trust, and forgiveness that is what we will experience. The love we both have experienced all of these years from God our Creator let us know we are surrounded in this as the spiritual beings we each are here for. We have always known a loving presence, not one passing out threats of hell and fire for every little thing. This doesn't exist in our Heaven in that way and we each can only speak with experience by being on the other side, in a beautiful indescribable divine place, taught by Christ and the Great Council.

What happens on earth will be put into balance, the good, bad, and evil. If we, as humans did not make our mistakes we would never learn and grow. We all need to stumble, fall, get up, and persevere, in order to strive to be a better person. The other side said to us, "In that way each one will hopefully learn to do better and live in a more positive way." The other side knows better than we do how as a human, we need to have hurdles to grow by. The other side also realizes we are stumbling around like little children in *earth school*. Some misbehave and some want to mind and excel to do better.

I can understand how the mind can be conditioned with all kinds of ideas carried down through the ages, with manmade belief systems. This emotion can eat one up and it helps negative forces grow stronger, it can even destroy the human mind. I am talking of this kind of fear, not the fear one feels and needs to protect them. Fear is good as a warning to help one in a bad situation, which is the good fear in order to keep one safe. David and I together have seen terrible fear situations and knew how to protect ourselves as we learned to do.

Beat Down

I remember a kind man who had been a good church member living his life with a compassionate heart doing well to others. In time, he developed a terminal illness. After church one day he stopped at our home and confided to us that he was afraid. He felt he hadn't lived a good enough life. He had tears in his eyes and I could see he was clearly upset. I told him no one is perfect but God, we all do things and make mistakes, we are humans and that part of us is understood on the other side. This seemed to help him; I hope it did so he could pass over in peace.

He couldn't see himself as the good person that he was. When a person tries to live by very strict rules to please others, they sometimes believe they can never be good enough. One can get beat down with words very quickly and made to feel like a failure all of their life. Being human isn't easy as most of us know, but once a death experience, dead on arrival, or near death experience happens to a person most say, they never fear death again.

In another instance, through the years I had been friends with a nice elderly man who worried deeply about what would happen to him when he died and he was so afraid! He felt guilty because of his role as a Sergeant in the Army during WWII. He gave the orders to his men and he killed many enemy soldiers in the war. He told me stories of war, the freezing cold, no medicine, food or water for long periods, and some of his men froze to death! But the worst was the killing he said.

I explained to him to realize he was a very young man who was drafted and made to fight, he had no choice. He was a soldier who obeyed his orders and this was his mission at that time in his life. As a young man, he did the best he could. We talked of this a few times then suddenly one day, he passed away. Through our talks he found relief in his heart and felt much less fear. I was thankful for our meeting and brief time as friends to help him move on. I remember how disappointed he was because his other men friends were giving him a hard time about his grief. They did not believe his stories and this alone, had defeated his soul. He saw I believed him, understanding what he was going through. I thank God we met and know we did at just the right time. I like to think he was given his peace, for he helped me so much by sharing these things with his compassion and who he was as a human. I am proud we met one another once more.

Those of us who have experienced a DOA do not want to return here, but are told we must to finish out our life. This can give those people a new positive and fearless way to finish out life with a new attitude, less worry, and a new appreciation for the gift of life. Many find out there is nothing to fear and what really is important in life. The other side taught David and I there are two main "sins" if you want to use that word, which are fear and guilt…Think about that, with fear and guilt one cannot learn what positive living is. We were taught to not condemn those who do not attend any church. It is the love they have in their heart and soul and share with others which counts.

Some who experience NDE's or DOA's ask to return to be with their loved ones again and are not yet finished here. If they were meant to cross over to end their earth life they would not be back. I believe without a doubt there are different times we each can go home. The DOA's (dead on arrival) of some people who have very rigid beliefs and who are afraid of a devil force waiting for them, is like this, what you expect, you will experience. Your mind is the builder. The power of the mind is so great we only use a tiny portion of it! Our mind can do us in if we can't find a dividing line.

Another myth we could not understand is why some people and places condemn cremation with the belief that it is a sin. It's not! Are the people who perish by fire creating a sin, of course not! The body decays and goes to dust; a cremation does the same thing. It is a choice one can freely make; it is one's own body and when this shell that we each wear while here on earth dies, the soul leaves it. The body no longer matters if it is cremated or buried. Do you know that fire purifies the body by a quick way of burial; the soul is long gone out of it and into new energy. Nothing can destroy the soul spirit, it is forever. But this choice is anyone's right to make and what they want to do. I have been taught this from the other side, the Christ Light Beings, that cremation is NOT a sin. When I asked the other side, "What is the deceased body good for after one passes away?" The answer is the body is only a covering for the soul to wear while as a human being on earth. Nothing more…

Chapter 24

Coming Back

Determination

This record of our journey hopefully will be an inspirational, profound and phenomenal way to help the bereaved and others in their pain of loss. Even as I write our story, I have no fear of telling it. There will be those who will understand and then there will be the non-believers, it doesn't matter. Non-believers are ordinary people learning just as we all do. It is hard for those to be open to new thinking and directions. There is nothing wrong in that because we all are learning here. We all go through different levels, but I do know when the pupil is ready, the teacher will come, with a life changing enlightened new path.

My son and I chose our spiritual work in this time period knowing how hard it would be for many others to believe our worlds, but this was to be. It would not matter to us for this is our promised work to the Creator, our Divine Intelligence and only a fool would make fun of God's work. In the future my promise here will be fulfilled and then I will be joining my son. In time there will be even greater changes worldwide with more information.

People will begin to realize most of us have lived our lives mostly by man-made rules. There are many people who are seekers and on similar journeys as we are, so never be concerned with what others think because your ways are different! Know that anything is possible and a few people can make huge changes in time. Experience is so much more important and credible than old man-made rules. One main thing I have been learning is if you are tied down feeling depressed, worthless, or just not living good enough to please everyone, don't try to please everyone, live your own life!

Use your inner strength to move forward, let your soul go free and live a good life. Pleasing others should be used wisely. To try and please just because it is your church, friends, a relationship, job, race, or whatever may not be good. If it is highly negative, sometimes it is best to stay away, but be kind to others and to yourself and live the best you can in life. By keeping a good love filled heart with faith, compassion and forgiveness for others you have most of what you need. Love is the key to all good things. In this world we live in now wars and destruction is all around us. Peoples' hearts have been hardened in various places over the planet. We want peace, not to destroy our world on earth. I wonder how much more our earth and the people on it can take. But, change can always come when you least expect it. Persevere above all and never give up!

There is no one in this world that can ever tell me our loved ones aren't so close to us that we can just walk right through them and sometimes we do. Their spirit walks among us in hospitals, our homes, outside events, graduations, school programs, churches, universities, at birthdays, births, death, and on and on. If you could only see what my son and I can, your life would immediately change to a better view without the fear of death.

I have given much thought to these things mentioned above as I put myself back into this world again. This world and my other worlds have been my life and I don't know any other way to exist than this. I have been taught to live with caring, gentleness, and love to others. I have all of the emotions anyone has and I certainly don't think I am any better.

We all have so much we can do on this earth to pass on love. If you hold an old person's hand sharing your love or helping those who need help that is a beautiful thing! If you smile at someone, that is also a beautiful thing. Small things count as much as large. We all say and do things we are sorry for, but we can all learn and forgive.

I get upset with myself many times wishing I had handled something differently with my expressions or blundering of words. We can punish ourselves to pieces, but realize that everyone can find the strength to pick up, learn and go on. God loves you! So go easy on your flaws we are supposed to have them and with them we have the opportunity to make changes. Thank God for good friends who are our treasures who understand and stand by us in the worst of times!

They Continued to Watch Over Me

My family; beloved friend, Shirley; and my Indian friend, Alex, continued to watch over me closely by phone checking on me after David left. Alex would call me first thing early in the morning and several more times day and night. He would kid me getting me to laugh and feel life again. Alex and I had serious talks about the other side and David. I would cry a lot and he understood. He kept my attention and I was very close to him. He is very wise and always wanted to meet my son. He sent me music to begin healing me without telling me what it would do. On the most part, Indian music is beautiful. It is very soft and relaxing; however there is some that can be very sad.

I remember each time I played it before going to sleep; I would cry my heart out. I didn't need to know what the words meant; I could feel them in my heart. I let out the pain for my son over and over in this way. Alex is still my beloved friend now on the other side, and still a strong hold for me along with Shirley and others. We remembered our lifetimes together and had made our pact as friends in this earthly time. I am blessed to have had them all in my life.

Before David crossed over, Alex told me to send him something of his and mine, anything, and for each of us to say a prayer over our objects before I put them in the mail to him. He took these objects with our prayers far off to a sacred place and hung them in a sacred tree and they still hang there today. That means so much to me knowing our prayers continue on to the Heavenly Creator and are still in this scared place. I know Alex traveled a distance to do this for us, which is a wonderful sacred Indian custom.

David used to tell me he knew when Alex was with him in spirit at his home before he crossed over. He liked Alex's gentle spirit so much and knew what a good man Alex is. He also wanted to be able to meet him and we had plans to do that in the summer, but David couldn't last. Alex told me he always wanted to shake David's hand and meet him.

Alex lifted me up tremendously in these times of my healing and in my life. He had me read books he sent to me full of beautiful true stories of Indian culture. This brought back my interest in doing something besides sleeping so much. I still loved sleeping because I had so many visions of my son and of my Indian life in another time, during those long months. My Indian background is very important to me and we discussed it often.

My past lives visions came day and night and I felt great peace with them. Alex spoke to me about long ago when I lived in another time, I had been a Brave who protected my family and Alex told me I had also been a great hunter and that it was time for me to be brave once more and become who I am and be who I have always been. David was working alongside of Alex in spirit and both Alex and I knew this.

All of the books Alex sent to me were full of healing words. One of his books was quite different than the others; it was *Illusions* by Richard Bash. Alex wanted me to find what I needed to help me through my sorrowful times in this book. It had important information for me and is now one of my most favorite books. There are lessons to learn for anyone. This unusual story is full of truth only expressed in a different, yet humorous way. Bash is also the author of *Jonathan Livingston Seagull*. I absolutely treasure this book. Alex sent me more wonderful enlightening books to read, which I enjoyed very much and helped me to relax and sleep. I had noticed I was interested in all of these things now so I had made big steps in the right direction in my life once more. Alex helped me in amazing ways which was putting me back on track. I was feeling stronger and growing once more in my inner strength.

Awakening

All of this help was certainly repairing my body and mind. I had the time to organize myself more again. It had taken all of this healing assistance and words of encouragement to help mend my soul. After the second Christmas of David's passing, I began to feel some of the beauty inside my soul flicker. I was waking up! I felt hope once more! I was like a candle being lit for the first time again.

I began to notice the warm sunshine pouring through the window panes each day and melting into my body like a sponge, restoring my energy. I felt the Light in my soul beaming outside of my body again, and my Aura was becoming brighter, as if a light switch had been turned on! I was listening to the sounds of the rain washing Mother earth clean, and the gentle wind of spring with the lovely sounds of nature. I listened to the birds singing sweetly each day and the old owl in the big tree made his voice heard at night. How long it had been since I had noticed this beautiful world around me? I was healing my heart and soul, and I was getting ready to continue my contract as I had promised.

My world was slowly changing and it had been there all along, but I had been tucked away someplace else in my own different world. I knew now I would go on doing my spiritual healing work and readings. I had a mission to fulfill and books to write. I was in a new phase of life and a good one, getting better, because this is what David told me I would do and I promised him. My change also made my daughters feel better, with them knowing that I was doing better. It allowed me to see a change in all of us. We were all finding life in us continuing to go forward once more just as most people do in time.

I found pleasure in my awakening with the enjoyment of this new world outside my door. I slept upstairs where I could open the door getting a breeze at night, then awaking to the sounds of those beautiful little birds in early morning. I felt like I had been coming out of a nightmare and into the light of life! This was the world I wanted to stay in and I had found the flickering flame in my soul! I wanted to make my family happy knowing I was on my way to catching up with them. I knew my son was with us in a new way.

I had found out it was okay to not be working every minute, as I tried to do before my down fall of trying to find a way to forget. I had decided I only wanted to keep remembering the happy times together and keep David's memories with us forever. My family and I included him in everything to keep his memory alive with us. He was talked about and laughed about, with his funny sense of humor and the wonderful things he did. He was alive with us in this way and in his own spiritual way. We would have him forever in our hearts and souls knowing we would all be together someday in the Hereafter. I knew David was very aware of every occasion we had, and would be with us in our lonely times. All of this let him feel he could soon let go of us a little more to move forward in his chosen work on the other side. We, in our sadness, hold our loved ones back somewhat until we can let go then, then they feel that bit of freedom to do what they need to. They will never leave you but have a new world they are adjusting in.

I would have days that I slip back to that sad night when everything crushed our lives, which is normal. Over and over in those times, I reviewed that last night thinking and dissecting each moment to find out if there was anything I didn't say to my son. I knew everything was right in his world but I wasn't quite able to quit going over these things with myself sometimes. Everything goes the way it was set up to be and I knew that, but the shock of a tragedy means we become such wounded human beings until we can start the separation process. After we dig down deep long enough we find the new strength to heal and go forth with our lives. It will never be the same, but we need to do this for our loved one and ourselves.

Chapter 25

Suicide

No Soul is Ever Lost

During the time of our learning with the Blessed Beings of Light, my son and I were taught about suicide. We met many souls who had departed in this way. The aftermath of a suicide is one subject that many parents and loved ones can NEVER move on from. For those living with the loss of a child or adult who chooses suicide, to die by their own hand it is NOT a sin! Those who die by suicide and go this route are in deep despair and feel as if there is no way out. It is no one's fault so do not blame them or yourself, please! A person who leaves in this manner also leaves their loved ones in shock not knowing why they did this! How could this happen? There will never be a peace and most of those who are left here are filled with questions that will haunt them for the rest of their lives.

Depression can do many things to a person and when one is not in their right mind a choice can sometimes be made too quickly, or it may have been planned for a long time. All kinds of reasons happen with each person who chooses this path to end their life. There may be medical factors involved that have been present since birth which even treatment could not help because their brain is not wired right. A person may have been abused, or have a terminal or painful illness; you never know what is going on in another person's mind. It has to do with them, no one else.

With the shock of a suicide, loved ones are stunned and confused! There will be repeated conversations within the family and circle of friends as to, WHY? All are trying to figure out the reason why it happened. You may hear comments such as, but I just talked to her an hour before she killed herself! I was supposed to go to his house in 30 minutes, I just talked to him! All kinds of situations may happen right before a person leaves in this way where it makes no sense to anyone, but it does to the one who died.

First, in the big picture, we couldn't have changed a thing in that person's life and we can't understand taking this way out either when we don't understand how it feels to be in their state of mind. We only have control over ourselves and it is hard to understand our own actions at times, but that doesn't make things any easier dealing with this kind of loss. Regardless, on the other side there is NO punishment for a suicide and there are no shortcuts either. This was something the person felt they had to do to get relief for themselves from living a daily torturous life. It doesn't matter if their life looked perfect and happy; they were trying to get through each day and night as best they could, eventually not fighting it anymore. The suicides are people who at this moment believe that the best alternative is to end their life and they have generally planned to commit this act for a long time. Perhaps all their life they have felt this way since they were small and have kept it hidden. Try to understand how tormented they were to get through each day.

Our soldiers with PTSD coming home from war with what they had to do to survive may feel no other alternative. Several of them have taken this way out when they return home, more than we want to consider. Thankfully, the military is beginning to understand this and are doing something about it compared to previous wars or conflicts. Suicides will need to finish out their journey in some other way, in their next life or on the other side, where these things are UNDERSTOOD there. They will be taken care of with great love and understanding. They will have much to catch up on on the other side and help will be there for them in the way of Spiritual teachers and higher up Beings of the Light. They are safe now, and DO feel the pain they left behind for loved ones. They only hope for those left will be to not feel responsible for what they did. Most have so much remorse even though they felt there was no choice which could help them.

In one year David and I gave readings for five different young teens and adults who died by taking their life. One young boy who used suicide as his way out came through in a reading to his parents saying, "He was so afraid for them and that is why he took his own life." He was 14 and had recently joined a gang of young kids his age and older adults. Some of these older individuals were well known and pillars of their community and supposedly nice people, but he said they were the ones conducting a hidden cult. He had wanted friends, but got in with the wrong group. They told him that there was no way out once you join!

The young man knew they meant business when they killed his dog and did other things around his home. They told him, they would kill his parents and sister's if he tried to get out! What a nightmare for him! He was so terrified and scared that he told no one! He said, "He decided to kill himself so his family would be safe!" This was a sad choice and by feeling completely helpless this is how his suicide happened. He wanted his family to know he was sorry and fine and safe on the other side. People can get into something so quickly, not realizing what it really is, especially when they are so young.

When we gave this reading, David told the parents their son said, "They would find something from their son, a sign, when they returned home." When they reached home we got a quick call back. The mother looked inside her purse and found a paper bird (Origami) just like the type their son had loved to make! This had not come up in the reading and you will understand why. He had done this as a hobby in his life and was saying I love you! He knew his parents would know it had come from him! It was his surprise to them.

There are so many reasons a person is suffering and can see no way out. There are those who are mentally troubled and may tell someone before they do commit suicide and then get helped in time, at least temporary. The thing is, their relief may only be temporary and they will try again. But those who have left in this way are not punished by a HELL, just the opposite; they are being helped on the other side by highly evolved spiritual Teachers, Guides, and Christ Light Beings working with them. They will learn the lessons they came to earth for, eventually picking up where they left off.

That's what I mean by there are no short cuts in earth school. Most souls who have relayed messages back to us have a deep sadness and unrest from watching loved ones they left behind in their sadness. They blame themselves for what happened. They can even feel their loved ones sadness so they suffer as well, if not more. We feel those spirits did their best to survive on earth the best they could, it's no one's fault. They are loved just the same as anyone else by our Creator. They are totally loved beyond measure. They will heal and learn where they are now in a perfect place where they are completely loved and safe.

Chapter 26

Getting Through Time

Holidays

The first year of holidays without a loved one is the worst and most difficult to get through. All together we managed rather well with the children making those days full of laughter. This is why, it is very important to keep family and friends close by, they will be a calming inspiration during this period of time. They tend to keep the mind occupied with other activities and conversation, but when talk involves a passed over soul, the togetherness of everyone helps relieve the pain.

It is the rest of the year that takes a toll. Everyone comes together for the holidays, but what about all of the remaining days of the year. Family members need to help the most hurt throughout the year and not just on the holidays. In our case, everyone pulled together really well; this was so helpful to me. Holidays will get better as time passes on. It is important to understand that your passed over loved one's will come and be with you in spirit during the holidays since they know that they are so missed and want to be with you. They will come and oversee what is going on and in some cases leave a special message to be enjoyed.

Thanksgiving

David was the organizer and host for our family. He would have the big holidays at his house, inviting everyone over for dinner and celebration. He loved making the big, big dinners with all the fixing's and he would decorate his home for that holiday season. So this was going to be different for us with my daughters picking up with some of the hosting of the dinners and activities.

The first Thanksgiving that David was not here was going to be very hard. I missed him every moment. During that night before the Thanksgiving holiday I lay awake with thoughts of the past year running through my mind of all of us together. I did this over and over with every detail I could remember. I then sent my thoughts to him asking if he could make me a special Thanksgiving visit, I missed him so badly!

It was around three a.m. Thanksgiving morning when I suddenly woke up wide awake! I knew someone was close by my bed. I gazed over to my left to see my son standing there with the biggest smile! He wore his suit, complete with a white shirt and his favorite tie! This was an outfit he wore when he absolutely had to for special times and I was one of them! I could hear his loving thoughts to me "Happy Thanksgiving, Mom! I love you!" I could see his happiness by knowing how aware of him I was and that he was here sharing our special day too! Then in a moment he faded away with me calling out, don't go David! As long as he knew I was aware of him that was his goal. I knew he had to leave and he had let me know he was with me. I was feeling so happy my soul felt like it was bursting with love as I thanked my beautiful son for coming. We had an easier time that day by talking about their brother's visit and what had happened with him coming to share our day! We all knew he was with us in spirit celebrating as well!

Christmas

That first Christmas without David, my daughter, Robin, gave me a very special, beautiful round silver ornament. When I pushed down on the top of the ornament, David's voice is heard saying "I love you!" This message came from Robin's telephone recorded messages that she had kept. I remembered this call he had made to her. He was trying to help her find a car for her son Shae, and these were the last few words of his message. We knew without a doubt that he was saying I love you, on this Christmas day to all of us. As long as this small silver ornament worked, we could hear his voice.

We passed the ornament around to each family member. He found this way to tell us each and I felt him with all of us. I treasure this gift and hope it never wears out. I listen once in a while to hear I love you, but I do not want to chance breaking it and I have a feeling that it will play forever. I treasure to hear those special words said to all of us and this made our Christmas special for everyone. We were remembering David with that special sparkle in his eyes on Christmas that lasted all his life. He loved being with us more than anything in the world.

I had been working on a new book long before David passed over but I was told to put it away for the time being by the other side and to write The Story of David. Even though I had been in a long healing period by now I was not ready to write. I still couldn't find the extra energy at that sad time, and they understood, but now I write in honor of my son and our work together for our Creator. The other side said, "to tell others his story and of the teachings he lived by, they were to be shared." I know there is a reason for all of this and hopefully people will be able to be helped by me writing his story. I am proud to do this so some people can be led onto their road of recovery and healing. There are many of us in this world who are sharing our stories and feelings wanting to help others and in this way we also help ourselves in this way.

What it's Like

Just know in your heart we will all be united one day and that the other side calls our day of passing, a very big celebration! We are home again in our real home and all the human sadness and pain is gone.

My son has said, "It is beyond human words where he is. The other side to where we each go is pure love and bliss which is indescribable!" No one seems to be able to find any kind of right words to describe how the other side is, except with what we have available in our human language. From my experience, the other side is impossible to describe, it is so magnificent! A person has their same intelligence, humor, and the way they were on earth. We just lose our heavy physical body. We are still in a learning school on the other side where we each choose what we want to learn and what we plan to do. At some point some make a new contract for when or if they decide to return here or someplace else in the universe for further growth. We continue on and on, we are eternal. There are important things waiting for each one of us and with answers to our questions to start our new life wherever it will be. We have the choice of where to go, plan the details of when we will be born; choose our parents, and what lessons we want to learn on earth. Sometimes a soul backs out at the last moment as a still born baby, called a still birth and returns when circumstances are more right for that soul's life pattern. This is all by our free will.

Many of us make some very hard choices for our future new life if we come back again. We do this in order to advance to a higher level when we return back to the other side moving closer to God, our Supreme Universal Intelligence. We each have lessons to learn and until we learn them, we keep evolving back to earth or a place we choose over and over by choice. My son and I used to laugh and kid about what all we took on before returning here. I can remember saying, why did I want to do all of this, was I out of my mind? It was just a joke of course, and we both would double over with laughter. I have always thought by both of us being the same soul and sharing everything together in our work was wonderful because we understood it and we had one another to share it with. One mind and soul working together.

My son and I have been given all kind of various information most of our lives on the mysteries of many unknown worlds and our work with different types of Angels, and Universal Beings. This is why we are in a learning school, by going through our lives on earth between our joy and hard hurdles in order to keep learning, teaching and healing. It is all there for those of us who want to move higher on the other side continuing to learn. There comes a time when one is as high as you can go joining the Creator! It is clear that it is not just cut and dry on the other side with spirits waiting around doing nothing. Long ago the other side said, "What a waste that would be." They are busy on the other side always learning as we are here. The other side also told my son and me, "They also learn and grow as they watch us grow. As we grow, they grow," and this statement amazed me. I am still sometimes surprised when they speak to us on how we can still choose what we want to do on the other side because it's all about free will.

Doing What!

After my mother and father had long crossed over, they came to me saying, "Sorry, we have not been around for a while, but we have been helping the soldiers in Iraq!" I was dumbfounded on this one! "WHAT!" David and I both were absolutely shocked; never in a million years would we have thought we would get a message like this! We were blown away; at least we were not expecting this.

My mother and father were helping the souls in Iraq, How? Then we knew what they were doing. They were helping the souls of those who were passing over to the other side and at death's door. Here was something I had to absorb for days and I felt proud to know some of what they had taken on. We thought of how great their work is over there on the other side! This was very important and something we were completely thrown by at first. My parents didn't get out much in life to go anywhere in life, and now this. I am so proud of them to choose this kind of work. Like I said they all have a selected agenda on the other side they are choosing to do, that you cannot imagine! In life my dad was a railroader and mom a housewife, and now we were given this amazing information. They had no idea in their life time of a war in Iraq, or the technical world to come. We never got over this message and are so proud of them.

In spirit they escorted the soldiers' souls' home to peace and to loved ones waiting for them to be reunited in Heaven. This was one of the things they had chosen to do. They also stayed close by in spirit with those injured in battle to keep the soldiers' spirits going with hope and strength until help came. The soldier may not see them, but the thoughts were given to him/her to hang on, keep up hope and strength while waiting for help, it is coming! It does not matter if a person remembers this or not, it is the outcome of what the spirit is to be able do to help. This may be very hard for you to understand but this is one of the miracles one can do from the other side. This is a part of the way we live in a magical and mysterious world.

What we had completed so far was in our contract and agreement accordingly. We are here yet have been existing with the Angels, Christ like Beings of Light, Heavenly Teachers, Guides, Aliens, The Council, and our loved ones on the other side, and the enormous Universal Spirit world. There are many important things waiting for all of us on the other side and there will be the reasons for one to understand why we chose certain things on Earth. Actually, we will begin to remember everything clearly when we get home. If we knew all there is to know now, how would we learn more to grow, make amends and gain experience through our spiritual lessons that we came here for? We wouldn't!

Our souls yearn for our Heavenly home throughout our earthly life and there are some of us who are aware of this restless feeling stirring within our hearts, and we have a knowing that we are of something much more we can't explain! You may feel restless much of the time not knowing why you feel this way and are without a clue. If you don't know or believe we evolve at times, our past life experiences can surface with what you think is a dream. One way to find out may be with hypnosis to discover who you have been, or why you have certain hang ups. Even certain health problems can surface life after life, along with certain fears.

We each can carry over past experiences that may be positive and aid us or negative and create problems in our present life. In a past life with unique gifts you may have had which may be present again in this present life that give one joy or a talent creating the impression that you had it naturally in your present life. We may have had these talents all along in life after life and now to enjoy once more. Have you ever questioned where an unknown, amazing talent comes from? How does a small child graduate years early from college or become the youngest doctor in history? Young prodigies, what creates them? Do not worry about these past lives unless you need council because what matters now is THIS life and what you do with it. Live this one now and learn as you go.

Your loved ones, your friends, and others you meet in life, have more than likely been with you in other times before in some way. We are drawn to one another and tend to stay in the same groups each time we come back. Some may need to make amends with one another for the growth of their soul and spiritual development, and this will hopefully and maybe finally provide an understanding of what we need to do to overcome our flaws, and how to advance to higher and higher levels of perfection. We will know who our soul really is, what we are inside, and what we need to do to become closer and higher to our God. Remember, In My House there are Many Mansions! There are other levels of existence far higher than any of us can know. Because David and I both had death experiences into the other side we knew these were a blessing in disguise, we were being prepared for other experiences in life and there is nothing to ever be afraid of.

Kindred Souls

One day I met a wonderful lady sales manager while buying furniture. We recognized one another instantly, although we had never met before! We seem to know one another as if we had been best friends for years. She knew instantly we were kindred souls, meeting again in this lifetime. The woman knew this as I was trying to figure out how I remembered her. This meeting happened in a faraway city while I was shopping and little did I know then that the meeting had been planned long ago in another time and place.

A kindred soul is a person one has been very close to before in another life. This can be a family member, friend, loved one or someone you helped in another lifetime and are bonded to. I am sure you have met a person at some time feeling as if you had known them all your life. I believe most of us have. This is how your feelings come into play thinking, this is the first time I have ever had ever saw this person but yet, I know them! It happens to most people in some way. I only saw my kindred friend once more, and never again. She helped me with something which meant a lot to me, and to see her once more was wonderful! Sometimes these meetings are only a one-time thing, it depends how it was agreed upon. Other times it can be a life time. It all boils down to the agreement we make and it is for important reasons.

I was always searching for others who were working in the capacity of the other side such as we were. I could spot people easily who had a loving compassionate heart and who reached out to others. We seem to know one another by who we meet on our journey in this way. This connects us to one another in the way of what I am writing about. I was always hoping for that certain person who mentioned something familiar, knowing we had a connection to one another. There is a world full of other dedicated people who are bound to their spiritual work which I call a network. When we meet in our different paths on earth we know instantly, we are kindred souls. When we part to go our ways, there is a feeling inside I cannot describe of great happiness.

Choices We Make

One such choice in David's contract was being a spiritual teacher, a humble humanitarian, and minister of healing filled with God's love, and grace, and to persevere in all he chose to do no matter the pain or consequences he would go through. He chose to come back as an invalid and would go the length for many years as he fought to live the time out with his terminal illness. In his complete faith he knew one day that he would be set free. Through his death experiences and by his passing over the many times he did and was sent back, he never gave up showing his faith, love and trust in our Creator. He never complained one time in his life not even with a headache, let alone his pain riddled body for so many years. He is to me, the strongest human I have ever witnessed.

That he never gave up or doubted his true belief and trust in God to sacrificing himself. This was all in his promise to teach others a better way of life in the best way he could and to finish his time here as he had offered too.

People had seemed to look at him with how he lived more than I realized. He lived through Christ and he gave his life to be an example of his work. I thank God that he came back each and every time from his DOA's and NDEs.

I looked at David as how I really knew him, a Being of Light teaching me through himself and our Creator. I know he came back to earth each time in his past lives to work beside me in our covenant, continuing to teach of love and forgiveness. His work always came from the other side to help crush the fear of old man-made rules and as an example of unconditional love.

All lives are important and if everyone could only know the real truth, how much freedom they would feel and know. Through his bad times of terminal suffering and sickness on earth and in his past lives before this one, he gained more knowledge, wisdom, and strength. He had returned each time with a giant courage, faith, and perseverance, to help others with their difficulties. He came back knowing what others needed most, as he had suffered with his illness, which developed into a higher spirituality each time, bringing out the best in each life. He talked to others of how each person is unique and precious; he lifted them and he loved them. He understood how the sick and hopeless feel and gave them comfort with a high degree of great understanding and love.

The years of my teaching at the college served many purposes. There were things others could never understand if they had known the answers. For instance, several of my students and other people we knew said "they had on occasion, experienced David and me at their bedside during the night hours working on them in a healing way." They were very serious about this. They explained what we did and where we sent the energy of God's healing to them. I asked David, "Do we actually ever sleep?" According to those people neither one of us did, with reports coming back to us of how much we were seen in other locations. We traveled in spirit, while in astral travel when the body sleeps, and did not always remember where or what happened. We were given all the strength we needed to do our beloved healing. This would always be our dedicated life. These things can't be explained in a simple way our lives being how they are. There are others who work in astral travel over the world. There may be all kind of reasons one may be doing things in astral travel.

There are people who use different techniques such as remote viewing it is a remarkable tool and used over the world to mainly help the military. A person who does this can be anywhere at the present time, but is out of range of the physical eyes. They can relate what is happening at that time and location, without ever leaving home or where ever they may be. Remote viewing can be done from any distance. There are so many things some people have not heard about that are phenomenal and this ability is in the Psychic area, it is pretty amazing! A friend of mine sometimes found missing children with remote viewing. She crossed over a few years back and this is the ability she used to find them. In remote viewing the spirit travels to the destination and looks around to report back.

I mentioned back in my story about the Praying mantis on David's door that was dying and he was very upset. This is how he made himself be known when I was in Tombstone Arizona last year, it began raining there and my partner went to get the car to pick me up at the edge of town. I waited in a store for a few minutes talking to the owner. Then I could see him coming up the street in the car so I stepped outside. There were a group of Bikers there and one quickly brushed my hair back with his hand! "Sorry" he said, "but you had a praying MANTIS in your hair!" I know it wasn't there before as I talked to the lady in the store! Also, where would it come from? I was in the dessert without trees or anything else around me! I had a chill then and I felt my son's presence with me! He had such love for Praying Mantis and other small beings I knew he had arranged this to happen so I would know he was with me! He knew I would recall the one on his door...

Chapter 27

Spiritual Growth

We all pray for our loved ones who are ill hoping that death will never happen but it does and nothing can stop their time to return back home to the other side. This is because their soul is READY to go home. The soul is tired and knows when it is time to leave and nothing can stop it from going. When a loved one's soul is tired and exhausted; they deserve to rest and become whole once more in our real home without pain. Someone with missing limbs will be whole once again. Those who cross may look as young as they want to appear. Those who are mentally challenged will have superior intelligence; everything is taken care of by being made whole again in a new spiritual body surrounded by love and joy!

David had said as a small child, "He never wanted to come here in the first place and that he would die young." But yet, he needed and wanted to accomplish this journey in order to be with us and he held his promise as long as he could. There were others he knew he would meet again that he would minister to and help. There was so much he chose to do, so much that his body gave out even though he felt he was still not finished. He was constantly moving so fast all of his life as if he had to do everything tomorrow.

A soul who is going home so young seems to have this drive in life, to get all they can finished as fast as possible and they seem to always have a new list to accomplish every day. Work or play it doesn't matter, they make it all work out for them. Their energy is high and when they lose it they find it extremely hard to come to a stop because their way of living has slowed down so much. Their vibrations are much higher than others and they give so much of themselves to make others' lives a little easier. They are given amazing courage to do what they are driven to; even a bedridden person is doing what they came here for. This may be by showing strength through the illness that they have, or to encourage others with their own compassion to not give up! There are many reasons, everything has a purpose.

The Ministers Who Believed

Over the years we discussed the process and transition of death in our world. How it is viewed here and how we were being taught by the Spiritual

Beings on the other side. I was searching in that period of my life hoping to find someone who was open minded to share our unusual lives with and who could understand ours. My son lived away at this time and was still healthy and doing well in his job. I was led to find the right person to talk with one day when a thought came to me, that I should search out and talk to a few ministers about our lives.

I found stumbling blocks that day because except for one of them I could not find a minister who was able to comprehend this kind of life. This one knowledgeable minister was able to understand me because of his own experiences, I was so thankful for this! I knew I had been led to him in my search. This minister was a true believer in others having gifts as the Bible says. He was not afraid and had a fair understanding of these things. The others I spoke with had no comprehension of a different life or worlds. They had little patience and no connection to my life or work except with a negative view. Of course, everything around seemed to be caused by evil or the Devil. Everything also seemed to revolve about how much one attends church. They had closed their eyes and ears to my truth and beliefs because they had not experienced it, or perhaps been taught of life after life in this way in school. What one has not experienced one cannot always imagine.

All I searched for was a kind and understanding person to share my story with, to listen and not judge me first. I do believe that currently more ministers are beginning to understand and accept non-traditional beliefs, realizing they have not learned everything in school. The Bible says nothing is impossible and it was written by telling all kinds of mysteries no one really can understand. These mysteries still happen to people all over the world that cannot be explained, they occur now, NOT just in Bible days. The regular answers I had gotten revolved around, if you came to church more and so on. They did not understand our connection with God our Creator. I think they were without answers, but I felt they could have been open to one's experiences without judging. I hoped for that even without their belief in my stories since I was to share them.

I am still concerned over churches that have no bereavement groups. They have other agendas and this one is one most people will need or do need now. I went to many churches offering to tell of the experiences my son and I have both had of being a DOA and what happens on the other side to give peace. The ministers didn't really want to even consider a group talk, even once! The last lady minister I met with greeted me at the door and immediately she said no! I offered to be of any assistance to their group and she did not reply. I asked her perspective on what I spoke of and she replied that it did not go with their church's doctrine!" I thought how can dying not go with her church's beliefs! Wow! But I knew I would be given a no! I told her I was to share my story but it made no difference to her. The other side made it clear to us that a person is not judged for where they worship, what label they wear, or what religion they practice, or even if they do. Everyone is on a different level of learning.

I was quite surprised when at last I found one enlightened Minister who listened. He told me he and his wife had some amazing spiritual experiences, but if he stood upon his pulpit and told any of this to them he would be looking for another job! How Sad! This brought tears to my eyes thinking of how we grow up with so many strict man-made rules and those who have closed their ears because they could not open their eyes long enough. I am not judging, just explaining this part of my story.

I think now-a-days, more religions and churches are beginning to learn they do not have all the pieces of the puzzle. They find that miracles and mysteries do occur to different people all over the world. In our Heaven, these other worlds, dimensions, universal places, and planets, have souls that are not judged for what label they wear or what religion they practiced, but how they live their life. Everyone is on a different level of learning on earth and people need to make a good change quickly in order to keep this beautiful planet. Do you ever notice how easy it is for some people to condemn others, to tear them down because of their views, or because they are different? Living in this time in our world today many people the world over have opened their heart to a DOA or NDE experience, Aliens, Universes, and so on, which shows more spiritual growth.

I was raised in a strict religion and never felt I was in the right place even when I was small. I was not at peace, but I found my place and peace after my DOA (dead on arrival) experience. The blessing of being into the other side put me on course to my chosen field of work with my son and the promise we made long ago. It set me free! I know the value of enlightened people and places over this earth. I am a Spiritualist, meaning I have no specific label in regards to religious type. My label will mean nothing when I leave here. I try to be open to churches who teach of love without so much judgment. I want to learn and grow in my spiritual life and I am happy for those who have their beliefs the same as I do. Our world needs to get close to our Creator in these times of such atrocities. The Bible tells us Jesus ministered to his followers in the dessert, villages, by the water, anyplace he chose. Know you are fine wherever you pray and I hope you who are searching find a good Bible based church. GOD is LOVE! I know our answers are in the stars and the heavens, our creations of life.

I believe what my son and I have been shown and taught from the Christ like Beings of Light. I will never go by any other teacher on this side. The best teacher I found has complete experience and all knowledge which is my Creator and Beings of Light. This is where my peace and spiritual love comes from to continue my work here. Our spiritual teachers are from the Creator. I would be a complete fool to ignore the blessings I have received. I cannot express how thankful and richly blessed I have become because of these Spiritual Beings. I thank my son for his blessings to me as a teacher of the Christ Light from the time he was born. There will be soon to come in my future a new and exciting way I would understand more about the Beings of Light! Something most of you will be astounded at!

Be sure to know that the beautiful positive words I hear do not come from any devil type of darkness who I do not let exist in my world of Council. That is the worst pure fear that some people carry all through their upbringing. I sometimes cannot believe the fear that has been pushed into our brain and into one's life. As long as my messages are of such love and full of only a positive nature, why would I question my Savior? Especially when combined with our travel to the Heavens and all of our experiences of these many years to learn by. Not to mention our help from the Angel Beings and higher up Beings of Light who saved my son and I.

If a person thrives on a Devil's dark force, they create their own fear, they help to empower any dark negative force and make "it" stronger. Yes, there are very dark negative forces in this world and in the Universes, who walk among us daily. I have seen them! Every single thing is made of energy and can be used for a positive or negative purpose. We were taught early on from our Heavenly teacher how to stay away from negative energy and what to do when one comes into our reality. We had no use for it or to come near to it. I hope people give their positive energy to the highest God force in your life with your prayers and empower only the good and Divine. I advise anyone not to feed the dark forces with your energy by keeping your attention fixed on them; this is what the darkness wants from you!

The more one constantly uses their focus on anything; they can eventually invite it into their life in that way! I hope with the information in this book it helps to move some souls to begin a new level of thinking and progress in their own learning by moving away from this type of fear created by man. We are all learning and hopefully trying to do the best we can in life, try to learn all you can, stay open minded, and then decide what positive route to take that you only feel empowered by. A pure heart and goodness will overcome evil when you hold your ground with the Creator. Because of our spiritual work and the negative thoughts of some people about the subject of prophets speaking against those in their fear I want to express how the bible speaks of this saying that the church should respect the prophets in 1 Corinthians 14:1. Also it speaks of those with gifts they have been given they are to use.

In another way to express the love for the Creator that was provided to me from my dear Native American friends is a piece written for the church people from Charles Alexander Eastman (Ohiyesa) Santee Sioux.

When in the course of the daily hunt, the hunter comes upon a scene that is striking beautiful, or sublime. A black thunder cloud with the rainbows glowing arch above the mountain, a white waterfall in the heart of a green gorge. A vast prairie tinged with the blood red of the sunset, he pauses for an instant in the attitude of worship. He sees no setting apart one day in seven as a holy day, because to him all days are holy and is in the presents of God.

Through these many years I was learning my true identity, things were falling more into place and into my life. My learning started out through the spirits in my home, to other dimensions and Universes. My worlds are many.

David and I traveled to our real home on the other side often over the years and I know among the reasons was partly preparing me more for the future. He wanted to strengthen my soul to carry on without him by going home first. He protected me and tried to take away any hurt to his sisters and myself during his life with us, just as we did him. He knew inside of himself that when he left here he would not want us to suffer over him, but knew we would. That again, concerned him deeply; he never could stand to see us hurt. My precious daughters, David, and I have a bond that is incredible between us. Everyone has loved ones watching over them if we know this or not! Life may seem like a long hard time to some, but life is a marvelous miracle teaching each one of us. We all have chosen to be here, so live your life with as much happiness you can muster.

Life for me has been like an ongoing dream year after year. We both have always been thankful for everything and to live in our worlds which are very complex. We became use to this kind of life and on the other sides, always looking forward to our studies from the Heavenly Beings of Light and Teachers. We both took on a great responsibility with our service on earth and doing so with a full heart. To see the joy in a smile, a child tasting their first ice cream, an elderly person telling of their garden and the flowers they grew, a new puppy or kitten licking your face, the trees, nature and its beauty inside and out, no matter what it is that's sweet and beautiful, you have fulfilled your heart and soul. We are here for such a short time try to make it count. This can be the smallest thing, live good and treat others with kindness. There will be some people who you will side step knowing not to go there, but bless them anyway, send a prayer for them to find their way. Some unknowingly push others away by being crude and mean in their lives. Words can hurt like a knife if you let them. You are your own person, know who you are inside. Even with this ammunition life can still be very hard just don't give up on it!

Chapter 28

A New World

My son and I both knew what spirit energy can do by experiencing our own past death experiences plus being schooled for many years by the spirit world. We understood a small part of the mystery of life since we were given a good look at what happens when our soul leaves the body and goes into soul spirit. Life goes on and hopefully we will keep learning what we need to until we get it right and rise above our lessons on earth. The other side told us "that in the future people will learn to live together in a loving way and there will not be all of the different religions. There would only be one United Spiritual togetherness all over the world. No more wars and fighting, with everyone learning to live in peace." This may not be any time soon but it gives us hope and great promise for our future and that of our children to come. This may or may not occur until after an earth cleansing in the future, which will bring a complete new world in order for man to start over in a new and clean Spiritual world of love for one another.

Mother Earth has been terribly mistreated with man's destruction over time. Something has to change! We have wars, kill others, kill and eat our animals, destroy and pollute the water, land, and air, all in the name of better living. There are parents fighting their own children. People living in fear of food and water shortages, while preparing for massive societal unrest. It has continued rapidly. Now children are killing other children in schools. Something will have to happen to stop this insane world we live in. Eventually there will be a new world with love for one another.

Speaking of their new world to come, my son and I were sent back from death to tell of our experiences to those who are afraid. Again, our spirits don't die only the physical body does; we go on in our energy soul to a spiritual life with knowledge of the past. The other side is a special place that would be hard to describe in human words, some call it the *Beyond*, the *Other Side*, or *Heaven*. But, there are many places we call home in the other Universes and on other Planets and Worlds.

Many people who have had an experience from a NDE's (near death experience) have come forward to describe them to others. This alone tells me things are changing with others' attitude for learning about the unknown in our world. The thing is there are no shortcuts to one's learning. But a soul can do this in the way they may choose to and with love. It's up to you, to each human being and the Being of Light working with you. We have been instructed to express this process as we were told and there is much more than this which is both good and positive.

I can only hope this story gives a comfort and confidence that with change, man can make our world be a better place. I can only hope the Story of David will help those with the experiences we both have shared. He is guiding me on my way and creating events to show my family and others he is here with his visits. His life story is to pass comfort and healing to others that are grieving. He always thought of others first. I would be extremely saddened if I thought we each just end when we die! There is no death in the Big Picture…life goes on and on.

I feel his spirit in the rain, sun, wind, flowers, evening breeze, and beautiful sunsets. He is everywhere around me and my family. I hear his words to me daily and through the night. I know when a flower appears in the dead of winter, he has signaled that he is lifting my spirit up. Our loved ones are closer than you think. They know when we need them especially in the tough times in our lives. They will never let us down. There are signs if you stay in tune and open your mind to notice. I feel the glory of the spirit I am just by life itself, knowing how precious time here is. Try walking barefoot like when you were a child with the warm earth beneath your toes and feet. Be like a child again, laugh and love more, forgive, dance the gift of life. Find out that you really are an important part of this Universe and infinite!

After our loved ones arrive on the other side for a while of learning or whatever they choose to do, they may not come back as often. Sooner or later, those of us who are left behind may feel the absent presence of their loved one. But, all that has happened is that we each let go of them just a little every day without realizing and you have done them a great favor. We here go back to work, school, and the many things we do in life. Even though our hearts are still breaking for them, life goes on. This doesn't mean we aren't still missing them with all our hearts. This means we are finding a way to go on and live without them here even in our agony.

Our loved ones on the other side need their freedom from us in order to move forward into their life there. They know how we are and when to come to us, which is when we need them. They have an agenda where they are now, some are teaching, learning; orchestrating events for loved ones here and other places, which can guide and help us. They at times give us our thoughts we think are our own ideas and sometimes make things happen by guiding us to the right path at the right time. They keep busy with all sorts of jobs on the other side, plus what they need to do for their own self in order to grow. They need for us to progress in life here as well. This gives them relief! They want you to be happy, they want your happiness to be here on earth until you meet again, and you will!

Coincidence

A very long time ago I learned there is no such thing as coincidence and it makes perfect sense. It is a word that cannot explain the happening of an unusual event (no known cause and effect) so one just thinks of it as a coincidence. A coincidence has no real explanation because there isn't any. We humans use this common word much of the time when we can't explain an unusual occurrence. This brings me to the stories of my son and I being seen by others in two different places, at the same time! How can it happen with each one of us being a great distance apart making no difference at all, when others have seen us? One of us could be in Europe and one in South America, it does not matter. But by using the word coincidence it makes it an easy way to justify anything unexplainable. This will explain itself in the story below.

This part of my story is hard to explain and perhaps for you to come to a final conclusion on I will continue as best I can. David and I were told by other people over the years that they had seen us both in locations where they were at, but we were far away from them on that day! One particular time a nurse who came to the house for his treatments asked one day, "How did you two know where I lived?" David and I answered, "We don't!" The nurse first looked at us unbelieving then burst into laughter as if we were joking with her and then she knew we weren't kidding. She continued on but, I passed you and we all waved at one another, I could have reached out and touched your car! This certainly got our attention and hers! She knew we had no idea of what she said.

The nurse told us she had recently moved to a place in the country and we had no idea of this or knew where her home was. She went on to say she was on an old and narrow country road which leads to her home and that we passed one another, each going a different direction. She said, "Our cars were passing one another and were only inches apart and that David and I had smiled and waved at her as she did, looking right at one another!" We explained to her that we were in the hospital on that day with David's appointments miles away from her location. She was speechless for a moment and said, "But I saw you both! I know your car and I saw your faces clearly!" She looked stunned and was staring as if trying to figure this out, but there was no answer for this! We had no information on how we sometimes were seen in other places and were someplace else at the same time. How could we explain this? We knew this had to do with Time Travel which most talk of being in the night time hours, but we knew that was not the case, at least for us.

By then we had heard so much about our strange visits from others, we chalked it up to Time Travel, being in two different places at the same time. This has been reported by other people over the years and there are several books on the subject. I know my son and I Astral traveled for as long as I can remember and we knew the mechanics of how this happened. This was amazing to those who had seen us in our visits. When I was teaching, some students at different times had told me this same thing about seeing my son and me working on healing them and from other people while they had been sleeping. Nothing is impossible that's for sure. We were traveling in our healing work when the spirit is capable of moving and being where it needs to go. There are books with the subject of others moving about in this way.

One well known story is about a man named Arthur Ford who was a brilliant author and psychic. He was sometimes reported being seen in two places at the same time. He was seen in Europe with several friends on one occasion and at the same time in New York! Most people have no idea when they sleep and dream that they may be out in spirit traveling. But in our phenomenal experience we were seen in a solid body as Mr. Ford was! This happened several times from what we were told by those who saw us.

This takes me back to our lessons for years by experiencing and being shown many messages printed into the carpet from our loved ones and our teachers in spirit. I have included that photo on page 179 for you to see that was from my loved ones in spirit and how the messages looked. This one is for my aunt (living) from my dad and their mother and father (my grandparents.) One day after picking up my photos I found an amazing one which I did not take! It has my heavy crystal ball flowing through the AIR by itself! You can see the ceiling in the room and if anything had held it up you would see it! It had to be as high as 5 to 6 feet up! It does not look real inside glowing and full of sparkling light.

Crystal ball floating as described above.

Our Own Perspective

My experiences continue with visits from David and this helps the healing in my heart. I am very grateful for the information and knowledge from him and the spirit world, knowing what to expect when I leave here. I am absolutely positive all of the information we have been taught and what we have received from the *Beyond* with our experiences is how it will be. In all of the years of what the spirit world has taught each of us we have never experienced, seen, or been told of a burning hell. My own thoughts along with information from the other side are that we DO create our own hell on earth, and this is what I believe to be absolute truth. I know many beliefs can be interpreted with all kinds of ideas and each person's perspective. I can only tell you mine. I am not trying to change the way anyone believes. I feel there is a strong possibility that huge amounts of missing information was left out of books because it was not recorded, taught, or happened as we think it was in the ancient recordings over the years. Who Knows?

Like I mentioned earlier, things are taken care of in the spirit world in many different ways. It is as my friend, Bev, would say, "What a person does with their life on earth is no one's business but their own; no one else can live it for them." Sometimes, by being human there are those who want to run other's lives instead of taking care of their own. We have most likely all experienced this in some way. This can cause emotions to flare and this is not appreciated.

In more of our lessons from the Beyond I know that God's love CANNOT co-exist with terror and torture. God, our Creator is pure love! Who knows how much of our old information is man-made, handed down to keep people in fear and to keep control of them? Where there is forgiveness, there is hope, and a way out of what is created on Earth, but only with the deepest regret and change to a pure heart, and this may involve a long learning process. This may mean that after one crawl's out of the deepest of darkness's levels wanting forgiveness, only then the Creator will know if they deserve to be forgiven. This is my own perspective through my spiritual lessons. I don't begin to have any information but what I receive. I wonder if in the BIG picture, if there is anything to be worried about at all when we move on? From what I've been shown and taught, there is NOT!

I have a very deep involvement in my work with the spirit world, which is with God our Supreme Intelligence; plus with any being ever working alongside of me with a great purpose in my life from the Light. Nothing I do is without direction from this highly intelligent source. I also truly believe that when a person asks for forgiveness, our Creator listens and knows if you really mean it from your heart and soul. I sure don't have all the answers by a long shot, but this is the one time you can't fool or talk your way out of your own untruths when one is dealing with our Creator.

I understand a negative person may sometimes work their way back out of the lowest dense plane to a higher plane with true deep regret of their actions and the help of Divine Spiritual Teachers working with them on the other side. These spiritual lessons and learning may take eons of time before they can move forward even a small amount out of the terrible darkness and agony they are in. I only know what I have been shown and I continue to believe our hell is right here on earth, the one that we make for ourselves. These are my personal thoughts and what I have learned with the information David and I have received so far. This is my reality. We seem to repeat over and over until our lessons are learned in order to move forward to newer horizons. This opinion is my own and what I understand from spirit information and where they are now. Everything gets balanced out in one way or another, nothing is left undone. The Universe is balanced, nothing more or less.

There are spirits who learn nothing on the other side and never ask for forgiveness, who stay on the darkest lower level suffering in their own misery. But they can move forward if they use their free will and work with the Beings of Light. Many will never leave this darkest of all levels and always feel the deep pain they have caused over and over, non-stop. God cannot co-exist with a burning hell, fire, torture, pitchforks, and blood. God is Love and Light! We will all have the choice of where to move to after we cross into the cosmos. Souls can move on to other dimensions' and places.

Akashi Records

My son and I experienced many different levels in our learning from the other side. One main lesson was very real to us and as if we were sitting watching a movie where everything shown to us flew by at a tremendous speed! I was told the speed didn't matter; the information had all been inserted into our brain stems to use when needed! We experienced this more than once.

Now the Akashi records are of each person and happenings of our earth arranged to earth's history. These impressions are wholly in the domain of Supreme Intelligence; one can enter into a conscious recognition of these Akashi impressions if one is in close contact with the Holy Spirit, when every thought vibration is instantly felt in every fiber of their being. Then these impressions can be translated into any language the reader is familiar with. And can sometimes be perceived by psychics. In other words, our information sometimes comes through to us like a movie being shown in the mind. This history of information was stored there in the Akashi records. I do recall this happening very clearly and using it.

When asking for help from our spiritual beings, their answers can sometimes come in a sentence, a book, a sign, a spiritual voice, and other ways. On occasion we both were in the Holy presence of Jesus Christ through our death experiences; in the process of working healing on others; and as I worked on my son through his life. Mother Mary has appeared on separate occasions to help us and still has at times to help me here. I take none of this lightly, it is the most amazing and beautiful experience one could ever imagine!

These are the grandest true experiences and times that occurred in our work. There can be no way to describe this. We saw the real world in those moments of truth without any fear, only indescribable love! To realize this was really the truth of all things taking my breath away with tears of happiness. I was astounded to have received this knowledge. I was now also recalling Beings past the times of Jesus Christ, from the Universes, Planets, and Star systems; things I cannot yet describe to tell plainly of that my son and I became familiar with from another time.

I firmly believe that when we pass over from this illusionary world of existence we live in, we are provided opportunities to evolve further and to learn more and become one with everything. We are tempted to think of life as just a time of suffering perhaps sprinkled with happiness to be followed by our Heaven where all our tears will be washed away. My eyes have been opened to a small part of a vast universe of information, on this side and the other. We all have our jobs to do and whatever they are, we are in the right place at the right time. As the Angel Messenger said to me, "Blessed be those who open their hearts and eyes to the beauty of it all, for we are a part of this great mystery of life and hearts are for sharing the love they hold inside." I firmly believe that perhaps we can teach here on Earth that there is nothing to fear, but fear itself.

David and I were told long ago "to not give messages to people who are not ready," but at times we tried thinking we could begin to help them. The non-believers are not ready to accept and learn and no one can make them open their eyes to a new path of enlightenment. The time must be right for each of us to learn and make our own transition on our own paths. It is true that my son and I became so excited in our learning we wanted to spread the word with joy, and teach spiritual information to others. But we both understood to listen to our teachers on the other side and not go to those who are non-believers as we were told about, for they do not want to change from a life of fear.

Perhaps one day they will be ready and on a different path with their free will. It is not right to try and push anyone to do something they aren't ready for. It has to be with each one's own free will and own time in life. We are all different and on different learning levels and the time must be ready in life for change, or not to want change, this is everyone's right to choose. A non-believer is not a bad person just because they have a different view; it is their choice, such as my son and I made ours.

During our times of wanting others to have these same spiritual teachings that we wanted to share with them so much, we sometimes jumped too far ahead. After a few times of this we learned not to push the teachings and we knew more on how to use our energy on the positive ones to help those grow. You probably know how it feels to want to share good things, but I certainly learned on this one without a doubt. Because this is my learning ground, my world, my spiritual world, and teachings, it is not everyone who would want this and who is ready. I truly think each person is on their own path, in their own time, and many may never be ready.

A person who is truly searching in their life will learn to be alert and open to new directions and new opportunities and to stay around positive people, read positive books and materials, and do positive things. No matter what your own ideas and beliefs, it is wise to hear what others have to say that may interest you or not, even if their beliefs and ideas seem outside of the box to you. You may just learn something new by letting your guard down for a few minutes. What does it hurt to listen? We are all different and we each can learn from one another. We are all teachers to one another in some way.

When a negative person can't rationalize what they can't understand anymore, perhaps then they may choose to open their eyes and let the Heavenly light find the opening into their soul and become more opened minded. One may even become a seeker of other amazing experiences wanting to learn all they can, to soak up their new world like a sponge. Some people say I'm not into all that stuff, that's fine and okay, but someday they may change their mind.

This sometimes happens after an illness, huge loss, some disappointment in life, or something else like a vision and one begins to reach out for answers and comfort. Something may shake them to their very soul in a good and positive way in order to rethink their old way of thinking. It does happen and if not, there is choice with their free will to accept or not. Each person is on the right level for them to choose.

How sad for those who do not have faith, but by learning through our hardships, one can create faith. And if not, it is everyone's free will to accept whatever they want to. Everyone doesn't have to feel my way, or anyone else's, but it is a blessing to know that without a doubt we continue on to another life when we leave here. We are not just buried under the dirt. What gets buried is the body we once knew someone by. Their total real self, the soul, has gone on to another place. To my way of thinking, how wonderful it is to know that there is so much more, we have only just begun!

The Angels and the spirit world told me several times, "Don't ever let anyone take your truth and dreams away, believe in yourself and keep your faith. There are those who will try to pull you down to their level, don't let them! Your truth is yours, no one else's. Your experiences are yours, no one else's." The Angel Beings also told me, "Disbelievers will believe when they have to face the truth, those humans are on a different level to hopefully learn from."

I knew part of why I was getting this lesson. I was afraid to write of my own experiences at that time, but the Angels helped me, knowing I needed assurance; they certainly gave me the strength to do what I had agreed to with love eternal. I felt much stronger from then on with the Angels' wonderful, amazing, empowering, words by delivering their messages to me. I became much more confident of myself inside as a human being. David was happy for me with these important messages that he had waited for me to hear. He always knew this was one of the weaker points in my life that I needed reminding of, to tell it all!

He was always watching my growth in our work and in the spiritual worlds, but I did not know this at the time. We were a team with him like the parent, and me the learning child. Many times I would remember those very important words from the Angels when I was around hurtful and negative people. I knew they could not harm me in my work or any way. They could laugh and make fun, but it didn't matter to either one of us. We knew what was important and forgave them. David and the Christ Beings reminded me to remember the key I hold. One day I would understand their repeated words, "You hold the key!" I do know now why I hold the key!

Honored by the Heavenly Council

One day when David and I returned home, I opened the front door and got a big surprise! Six soft pillows had been taken off of my sofa and put in a circle on the floor! With that, we began to receive information from the other side on a script of paper left beside the pillows! The Heavenly Beings of the Christ Light and High Council said "too be ready at a certain time that night as this would be a joyous celebration of us throughout the Universe! This celebration was for the son to name the mother and the mother shall name thy son, then we would be known throughout the universe by our Universal names forever! We were to sit facing the east and would not have the memory of this afterward until they chose to let us. We would only remember this experience happened, until later on." WOW!" We exclaimed when we could think clearly.

We were so excited it was absolutely UNBELIEVABLE to us both! We wasted no time and went to each ones private place in the house to select our names without telling the other one what we had chosen! That night as we were told to, we went to our rooms as usual to go to sleep. Everything went as the Beings and Council told us it would without our remembering anything. After this grand celebration was over we would both know our Universal given names and we were ecstatic, honored, and humbled over this greatest honor! Then we could tell one another what name we had chosen.

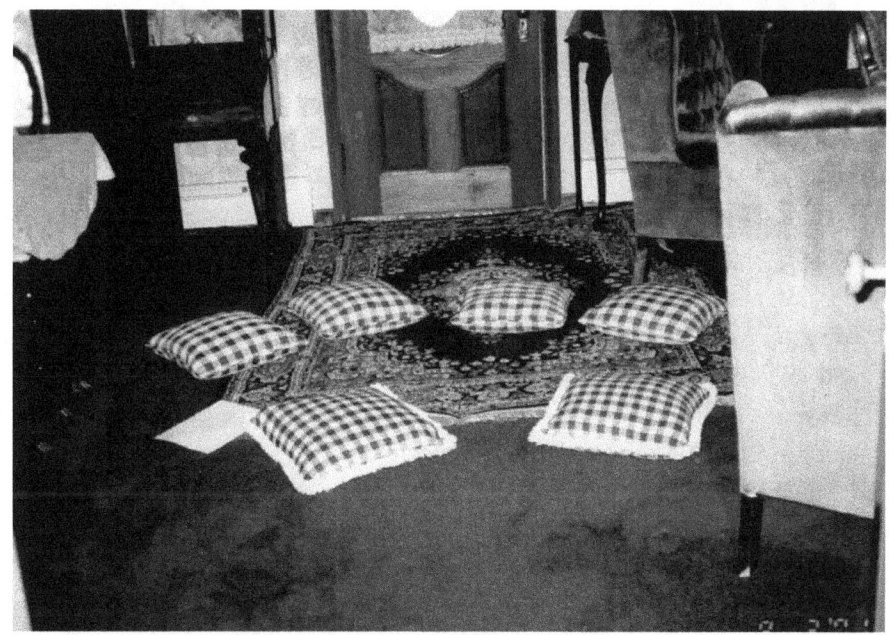

Our grand Universal celebration with the Heavenly Council

Since this night we both are known by our Universal names throughout the Universe! For whatever all of this celebration meant we are completely in awe! This was extraordinary to us and we were completely in sort of shock! What did this all mean to come, with new our work through the Universal Creator?" I took pictures of the setting they had chosen for us in the circle the next day. Nothing seemed different or moved the pillows were still in place so I put the pillows back on the sofa. There was the page of script still there we had found the day before still lying in the same place. By the count of six pillows we knew four beings of Light had come from the high

Council for our chosen celebration. I will never forget this! I felt we were highly honored, but why? I didn't have a clue. Later I would know. David already knew but did not say.

I am not afraid because David and I are different in this way. We both have been lovingly guided to do our spiritual work. David was and still is my spiritual teacher. He and I work hand in hand and never cared who poked fun at us. For as the Angel said, "Only a fool makes fun of God's work." This alone keeps me knowing all that matters here is to love our work. Don't feel down or afraid if you are different in mind and body. You are a precious human being created by your higher power. Each person is unique and precious in their own way. We are all powerful human beings, and if you only knew how powerful you are!

In the history of this world David and I are certainly not the only ones who have been labeled in a certain way. Unfortunately, labels are everywhere for everybody some are good and some can devastate another person. We feel blessed that we chose this work. I can't imagine not doing what we have so lovingly taken on in our lives. It has been as important as breathing to both of us. Our Supreme Intelligence God, the Creator has provided us with this mission and we both have stayed humbled and grateful. At one point in my life after my son crossed over he came to me and told me to read Psalm 34 and 37 and that this was very important for me so I quickly did. There were messages in these scripture verses for me to absorb. The Psalms have always had great meaning for both of us in our lives.

To tell of your experiences in your life can be scary, you put your character, stability, everything on the line. You know in your very heart this is a large part of the life you have dedicated yourself to do. It is a promise made to ourselves and the Heavenly Creator through the other side long ago. A sincere heart goes forth and completes a job regardless of what lies ahead. In this line of work, never be concerned with what others think, it is your life, what you desire doing that will fulfill your heart and soul. If you capture what you yearn to do, you will be content and happy, if you don't, you will spend your time wishing on what you missed out on, because you didn't grab the happiness you deserve. There are millions who have a similar decision to make and overcome all over the world. One can't sit around and let others change your mind or you will be regretting what you were to do. They are the ones who can hold you back.

Readings

Doing readings can take a toll on one after a length of time in this work. A Reader hopefully will protect themselves with the Christ Light of protection and not hold the information they get as if it belongs to them. You feel many emotions of others in passing messages, but need to move on; leaving the emotions with the person behind. We could not change anything for anyone; we all have our lives to go through. Although, it is hard to leave the sad feelings we pick up from the person we are reading for, we must, to protect ourself. I have been warned a few times to slow down, live my life here as well as the other side.

When I give a reading, which is when I pass a message from the other side to a person here, I visually see, hear, and feel the emotions of the spirit/spirits that are sending it. They are sometimes asking for forgiveness from a loved one who is still on earth for a certain thing they did or for the way they lived their life on Earth. What may bother the spirit is that they want to make things right, seeking forgiveness to move on.

They have many reasons to want to connect to a loved one still here. It could be mainly to send their love; let them know they are happy and at peace; give a message of concern; or perhaps to just say hello, I am fine here! The souls keep their same personality and many mention they are watching over loved ones as a Guardian, and want their loved ones to know this.

Some are still as stubborn and angry as they were in life and are not advancing on the other side and who knows how long before they do, it's up to them. It could be millions of years in our time or a simple decision to want the spiritual teachers to help them. Then at some point; they may be able to move on to a higher level into peace. The spirits who stay bitter sometimes never change and some have tremendous remorse of themselves of how they lived on earth. Once home we will all look back at how we lived our lives here and what direction to take now. There are many other places to learn in. Whatever we need to do, help is there for us with love and concern.

Let me give you a small example of what we hear every day. Wherever we were sitting, could be a public place, beside or behind someone in line, in a gathering, it doesn't matter where, thoughts bounce back and forth from people. I have now learned how to tune out some of the buzzing around me.

We who are clairvoyant can hear them and most times see them. Then a connection is made between them and us. This is some of how we work with the other side and live in this one. Once in awhile we got a big headache!

The soul's messages are sometimes like pulling teeth and other souls talk, non- stop! Accept what you get it may not make sense to you in a reading but it will to the one you are reading for if they realize this now or years later. Any reading one does it is none of our business, it is for that person only unless they don't mind sharing them. We only pass the information. You never know what you will get in a reading for someone. There are souls who still use the same rough language as they did in their life. I tell what they say in their way I change nothing. I will not back down on any reading I get. I learnt early on to hold my ground and that's what I do because I know where the reading comes from.

Driving my car I get free riders (spirits) who I at times find beside me or in the back seat! They usually have something to tell me which is important in some way. David and my life have been full of this day and night and we are conditioned easily since this is all we have ever known. It doesn't bother me unless I need my rest and most spirits are usually kind about my needing sleep. There is only one thing I ask, supply me with some extra energy for the next day. I have had visitors drop in who are terrible, dark, and evil ones who I try to get rid of fast! I can't always control who passes through but I can protect myself with our heavenly help.

When I was growing up I was really scared at night to go to sleep! I was picking up on passed over souls then. I would cover my head to go to sleep even after my babies were born! Thinking back, I can see why I was afraid being intuitive. I remember doing some odd things before going to bed you may laugh about. I actually scattered a small amount of cereal in the hall in front of my bedroom door a few times! My husband knew something was going on I couldn't explain. I hoped to hear any noises coming close to me! That's not the way spirits come to see me anyway, by invisible feet crunching on cereal! So after several of these clean ups in the morning I quit my non-sense. I have laughed at this many times since, but I was just beginning on my journey of learning. I still can't believe I did that! That's what the fear factor can do! I didn't think I would ever share that one either.

It was hard to believe in myself at first. David worked with me to understand what I knew all along and had forgotten. I questioned myself then when getting information from the spirit world "Did I hear this or that right?" In the beginning one questions themselves which is natural to do. People who receive readings leave with a peace in their hearts or with a more positive feeling, which helps their grief. They are very happy for the connection that was made. After contact with a loved one they let the tears they have held go free in relief. Many have the confirmations they have needed. I never know what will come through for them or who. It may not be the one they want to come through but they can still get confirmations or good information. It is like when you open the door on a crowd the spirits all want in at once. The strongest speaker gets there first! Some souls say very little and I never know until a reading starts. The souls who had a fantastic humor still have it! Some things they have said are really funny. Before meeting with most people I know in advance from the other side I will be seeing them for a reading. It is so amazing on how the spirits sit things up! They orchestrate so much in our lives here it's unbelievable!

In one case where David and I gave a reading to a couple that had a tragic event with the death of their little daughter. A friend of theirs that had heard about us called to ask if she could bring this couple to see us and we agreed. They traveled from several miles away. We knew nothing, not even the names or why they were coming for this reading.

The first thing we saw was a small child around 4 years old beside the mother, clutching onto her leg as small children do. David and I knew this was a spirit child belonging to her. We could hear the child call her mommy. We began the reading and explained there was a small child beside her who called her mommy. The mother began to cry but was in awe and excited. We continued on explaining that the child doesn't seem to know she is any different now than she was before. The little girl told us about her room decorated with butterflies and dragon flies on the walls and the different colors. She told us when mommy and daddy are outside they sometimes go for walks and she wants them to be happy again so she sends them the dragon flies and butterflies. The mother told us this was true, that they are surrounded by them when they take a walk. She still doesn't understand she is not still present with them.

The reading was extra long and full of relief for the mother who was crying from the messages. At the end of the reading the child told David and I to tell mommy and daddy a surprise was coming to them! The little girl had only passed over about 6 weeks before. When we told them of the surprise, it shocked them that her mommy and daddy were getting a new baby! They asked what would the new baby be and at the same time we both said, a girl. We explained in this way that their little girl was coming back and she could be with them again, she loved being held and loved by mommy and daddy. The mother could not believe she was pregnant but knew it must be true.

The husband was close to suicide because he blamed himself for the death of his little girl. He had his small daughter on the riding mower with him that day and as he went up the small ramp to load it into back of the truck she fell off backwards. He tried reaching for her but the mower rolled backwards and he couldn't stop it! The little girl rolled to the bottom onto the ground up against a concrete lawn roller and was crushed between the lawn mower and concrete roller. They were so devastated they couldn't even function at her funeral. This was their only child. By the way the mother went to her doctor right away after the reading to find out if she was pregnant, what a happy day! She called to verify this and asked if it would be ok to name the new baby after David's nieces and my two granddaughters Nevaeh and Grace. We were very happy about this and they also called us when the baby was born, she was back!

Our worlds are dealt with in the way we have been taught, not to let all of this interfere if possible, with our regular life. We have been shown how to protect ourselves and work in other worlds with other Beings without carrying it all together. This seemed normal to me before I knew it with my son's help. We didn't know any other way to live and neither one of us wanted to be any other way. We have our agreements to the other side and we both felt blessed to go through whatever it took in order to keep our promise to our Creator. What could be better than this? We knew we were really different beings but that is why we do what we do.

One very important part we have been grateful for was that we could always share and discuss our unusual lives and the information we received with each other. How hard it would be to not be able to share this with someone! We both were careful with our deep caring of others and their many different emotions. If we let this affect our life completely with others' feelings, it would be too hard to handle the work.

The information given to us always has a reason; we don't have to know what it is for. That is the trusting bond we have with the other side, knowing in time answers for us will be given. Everyone we work with in a reading and the messages we receive are none of our business. We only pass their messages. This explains where the word bridge comes in.

We gave readings over the telephone with a first name only, and no information. We call this a cold reading. It is best this way to confirm we know nothing about them. Many times it is normal for me to make the appointment for the reading and write out the reading before they call back. When they call it is ready for them on paper so I can first tell them what I have gotten from the other side. Most of these people we had never met. They call knowing us only by word of mouth. Those people usually live in different cities, towns, and states.

One can't turn this ability off and on and it takes time to learn how to cope with everything going on around us. We learn the best we can because some souls in the spirit world do not give up on contacting us. We both were so happy if we could help them. They are counting on us to give a message to someone here. Then we proceed and do the best we can to deliver it.

Chapter 29

Conclusion and Final Thoughts

My Final Thoughts

Since my son has gone home I have asked myself many times who he really was all a part of I knew there was more to him. What did he still want to teach me before he left or was it finished? I believe his job was more than completely done, and I firmly believe he has taught me even more now from his side. He had those lessons he sends to me now but couldn't hold out any longer. After he crossed over, he has continued to be at my side. In all reality, I knew clearly who he and I were. He wanted to be assured I clearly remembered why we both chose our path together this time around and had again and again. He needed to hear me say that "I did" once more before he left this earth and he needed to know I fully remembered the covenant we made for all eternity. I had remembered everything clearly for a long time by then.

We were like fish out of water for our new experiences here, but our perseverance kept us going and our loved ones who were close by us gave us strength. I know that I will carry our truth in my heart and soul forever and I knew why my son needed to know I would never forget our journey here. I feel positive he wanted and needed to hear me say one more time that, "I had not forgotten any part of who we were, what we came to do and where we came from." That is what I let him know before he left I knew in my heart and through my soul.

I knew his complete plan then from a small child, why he came to this earth, what he was to do with his life and all the people he met. But, I was meant to forget parts of our plan for a while through my years of raising my family until it was time to recall it. This was because the other side knew I was being busy as a mother with my mind focused on the family. Our different lives also explain why he and I were so easily hurt in this world of human cruelty. We had to adjust to human life once more; this was very difficult for the both of us. We had come from peace, love and the freedom of our soul. There were many hardened hearts to try and reach to soften. There were specific people on our list to hopefully guide in their own way to where they belonged in life.

I still marvel at what he accomplished in his short time with complete humbleness, love, and forgiveness to others. He did so much in so little time, until the very end of his life. I know his life experiences were hard and full of hurdles with the experiences he had chosen to accomplish. He almost bit off more than he could chew, but by the grace of God he worked it out. He checked them off of his mental list as the hurdles came, looking forward to the next one with understanding why. His soul was strong but yet fragile and easily hurt by watching how mankind keeps changing, going into a downward spiral with many hurtful, greedy, and harmful people who walk this earth.

He gladly offered to take on a devastating illness to teach others around him love, compassion, faith, forgiveness, trust, hope, humbleness, and perseverance. And he never gave up on the negative people; he wouldn't have, he took each one into his heart. His life was cut short with his time to go back, but in my heart I know he is doing certain work in his own way from the other side. With our visits together back and forth to our real home makes me happy! Our complete life here was about sharing and helping others and with my daughters and family. I have it all in my mind clearly. I have been given the time to raise my children and help my family as I chose.

THE WARRIORS

There are many children who are great teachers to us, who come here only for a short time, suffering for others to learn by. I am sure many never need to come back, but agree for reasons we wouldn't understand. Some want a turnaround, meaning to hurry back to be born again, to be with their loved ones once more. Those souls want to be held and loved again. These choices are by free will and understanding. Looking into a child's eyes is a beautiful thing, look closely and you will see the beauty of the soul.

I often think of all the other parents who have had a child cross over, young or old. There must be millions of stories and we as parents can only try to help one another by sharing our thoughts. We have this in common and have been in these same shoes in one way or another. And there are many parents who lose more than one child, or whole families, which can't be imaged! They are still our beloved children, our treasures, and we will never be the same without them.

Life is full of pain and suffering, and wonderful love, and we need to keep hope alive by keeping our hearts open and not being bitter with the loss of our loved ones. It does no good to ever become bitter and loved ones on the other side are actually waiting for us to go on with our life here. God never TAKES anyone until our time is over. We each plan our own time to leave this earth plane with our free will. It is very important to the one in spirit that we here continue on with our lives. They understand our pain and once we begin to heal this also releases' those who are on the other side. They want us to enjoy life, they know we will be together again in time. They told me that what seems like years to us is only a blink to them there. There is no such thing as time there. In the other world, they in spirit are on different levels of learning and working on their own spiritual agenda. They know when we need them the most.

People who come to earth with a life mission to teach others through their health problems such as abuse, disabilities, soldiers of war, and other tragedies are true Warriors. They are Warriors who are here teaching many things to each of us if we just listen, watch, and open our eyes and hearts. These special earthly souls choose their missions while on the other side with their life plan on earth. Usually they will not remember what teachers and warriors they will be once they enter earth life since the memory is erased in a short time after birth. Many of these people are only here a second, days, weeks and so on. This is where David and my memory were different; he was to remember it all after he came here as he planned and as he had chosen. I remembered with him as time went by with the Christ Light Beings of Light leading us on Earth. I was given extra time being a mother with glimpses of those memories when I was very young.

Hard Lives

You may think why would anyone choose a hard life to suffer through? The Warriors who come here are with their free and will come for many different reasons for their spiritual growth. Some may come to advance higher and faster on the other side to go through teaching here. Some come as teachers for those who have never known love to one another, or loved before, or who even knows the true meaning of love. There will be those who may be teachers of compassion, to teach the value of life and for those who need to learn respect for unfortunate others. Only they know one day why they chose what they each one did.

I believe we take on certain responsibilities teaching and guiding others and ourselves to learn from one another and make necessary connections to certain people. There are so many reasons why one chooses whatever we have come here to do for certain lessons to either us or to help someone else. However we choose is for whatever we need to do. The hard lessons we take on for ourselves are to learn from so we can elevate to a higher level when we return to the other side. This may be something you have never heard about, but this is what we have been taught from the Christ Beings of Light.

Have you ever noticed how brave little children are, such little soldiers who love unconditionally, and stay happy even when going through a terminally or devastating illness? They can accept what happens to them with wisdom knowing beyond what an adult can understand. They are truly our Angels on Earth from birth on for they can teach us so much. They love and trust with all their hearts. We are all teachers of some kind and hopefully we learn through the experiences we and others go through. We have to do our best by going through these hardships to grow stronger and closer to our Heaven.

Life isn't about all the hard times, there are the good times to enjoy the same, but the hardest is our testing grounds that can knock us down. That's when we need to persevere and get back up. All of our hurdles will come and go through our life. I have taught my daughters "this too shall pass". I believe this with all my heart. Life may not be a "bowl of cherries" as the old term used at one time implies, but it is a wonderful opportunity to advance in our life. Each day I get up the first thing I do is look outside. All of natures' beauty is there before me. I appreciate everything created in our world there is so much to be thankful for.

The joyful bliss David received by being with those who care and love others made his work very happy. He loved their kindness, love, positive attitudes, their faith and caring. His laughter was contagious to all he met. He enjoyed making lives happier helping those who others shun that he treated kindly, for he never gave up on anyone. The ultimate place he wanted to be was when he touched the heart of a person so hard hearted and who did things with bad intent. That is where his work was the most rewarding and important to him. He did not suffer without making his life count to the many he ministered on his path.

He loved working with the sick and supporting the poor with his kindness and caring, especially the children and outcasts. He stood strong beside those he knew needed his help and did this with conviction. He was always happy to help and assist others in need. I don't think he knew the word no in his life. He would always comment, "How can I help?" Or simply surprise others with his help before they could ask. He was the most unselfish person I have ever met. Even when he lay dying he would ask when he could, "How are you doing, are you ok?" His main concern was us, his loved ones. He never made complaints about himself, his sickness or his life. It wasn't only humans he helped in his life; his love for animals was amazing! He was a protector of the helpless.

When our own family of loved ones get ready to go home I know David will be the first to escort each one of us there with his loving big hug. We will all be together once again and this will be a giant of a celebration! Going home is a beautiful transition and not something to be afraid of facing. Once a person passes the barrier of fear and releases the soul it becomes free, moving gracefully and happily into spirit. The deep sadness will stay in those left behind, but we here can grow closer to our loved ones if we open our hearts and minds and not be afraid that we will never see them again.

Hoping to Have Helped

I hope what I have written will help to free your mind of death and of making the transition one day. This is to give you a new view to know everyone's mission is important and that each one of us is an important part of the whole. We are part of one another regardless of anything and we were all created at the same time. There is an abundant amount of information to read about that can confuse a person, and each one of us makes a choice which creates our views on our separate beliefs. Try to remember, if you are not happy with one choice try another until you feel your peace, then you are on the right path for yourself. We each do the best we can in our own way.

What we have certainly learned from our Creator is that the key to life is one simple word, LOVE! Love is all there is. Love is the key! On your journey you will find there are many people who are unlovable to us by what they do with their lives and how they treat others. But remember, the best you can to forgive them and as Jesus said, "For they know not what they do." This can be a very hard thing to accomplish but this frees your own soul. The negative ones will be taken care of in the spirit world in a different way on a different level. It seems justice is so lax and wrong at times on Earth, but there is a Universal way that will handle everything.

This doesn't always ease the pain at the time, but be assured nothing is left undone. We all move on to other places and start again on a new journey.

Our Children

When it is our children who leave here first paving our way, this is the hardest thing to try and understand. Our hearts are bursting with the deepest sadness we will ever know and feel. But remember, our children will always be our children and they will always be with us in spirit and we will be reunited again! You will see your children again, their love is even stronger for us and they will never forget you! You are etched in their soul forevermore. Each and every child who leaves us is very precious and has left us the story of their life, no matter the imprint of how short or long it was. This is their legacy to us here and they each are so important and special in our lives. They are the treasures and gifts to us, but no parent owns them, only God does. No one child is any more special than another, our children are all special and how they each live their life counts more than you can know.

Your loved ones on the other side are definitely concerned over your grief for them and how you are handling this. They want to comfort and give you peace, to see you happy again and go on with your life. This way they can also be at peace to move on to where they need to in their glory, to higher levels waiting for them. We may not understand now but everything counts and is important in this imperfect world. Please, don't punish yourself if you think you could have changed your child's or another loved one's time here. We all have a certain time to leave when our work is finished and we aren't to have all the answers now, but trust that you will have them one day to your many questions.

We have all agreed to our lifetime of lessons and learning before we come to earth for all kinds of reasons for ourselves and others we will be with. You will to be able to rise above your Earthly life and begin to plan your new agenda. Everything in life is already planned, a soul chooses what they need to do when they return and why. It is hard enough to come to Earth ONCE to learn, but without our mistakes we wouldn't learn anything in order to gain knowledge and knowledge brings wisdom. Our lives as a human mean so much more than I can say.

Many years ago before I remembered, I often wondered why David and I were given the gifts we were and the answer that came to me was simple, we asked! Because we wanted this life by choice, we were sent back to earth with our agenda and work. What a glorious gift to work in service here again. This was our mission from the Creator, Christ, and working alongside of The Beings of Light, Angels on Earth, and our loved ones on the other side, to tell the world this message. "When our lives end here we still lead a life that goes on and on, hopefully wanting to progress higher and higher. No one ever dies." It is as a spirit said in a reading once, "Think of me as living far away in another place but one day we will see one another again." I hope this helps you and I know this is true, we all live on and I have been there. It is a different life now for most here with the souls living in another space you cannot see, but at times you may know and feel their presence. Their world is simultaneous with ours and they are closer than you can ever imagine.

I hope David's life and his experiences can help those who question, "What happens when we pass from life into our spiritual body and living in a different realm we know as our Heaven?" Keep in mind that your loved ones still love you and always will. Our loved ones keep their memories of us; all the love they were given in life; and all the love they gave back to us. They feel our pain and sorrow and are with us in difficult times and in times of joy, with the choice of going back and forth at will. They are limited in what they can do for us because we have to work through our own problems.

We go on learning in the Hereafter and our Free Will is a forever gift. Let's hope we always use it to the best of our ability and if not the mistakes are valuable in order to learn from. We will always have this gift to use in the way we want. Hopefully, we will continue to make mistakes, learn and choose the right direction we want to go. We have the choice to rise to other higher levels and places as we progress on the other side until we are so close to the Creator we can stay right there.

I know in my heart and soul that I will continue my search and pursuit of my work for we become what we learn in life. It is never too late to be forgiven, just ask your Creator, from your heart and soul. And importantly, we need to forgive others and ourselves. Forgiveness is a beautiful gift and it is our responsibility in our behalf and within us to do.

After I wrote my first small book of true stories a few years ago, David urged me the next time to use my name instead of a pen name to be proud that I was completing my spiritual work. I promised him I would. This helped me to go public later on to begin telling our story that we have lived.

They also reinforced their words with this following advice, "Non-believers who laugh and make fun can never be told anything, for non-believers never learn. But those who are open and believe are blessed." And from this time on I will always use my own name on all my work. All of this isn't happening to us without a reason so I want to always continue on as a worker of the Heavenly LIGHT.

I am eager for whatever awaits me and thankful to have accepted my responsibility to do what I promised to do. I have fulfilled this part of my quest as I was told to do by the other side and in writing this story. I know clearly why my son chose to go through his choice of pain and suffering that he did. He was here to serve others with his love and goodness, helping to guide them and for the hearts he touched, to teach that we are all important souls. We come here to live an earthly life to explore and learn in order to grow closer to our Universal Heaven and our Creator.

I thank my son for all he taught me, his sisters, his family, his many friends, and the total strangers he helped. I realize and know that he sincerely gave his life for all he met with his choice and as they grew, he grew. I thank God for trusting me by loaning me my children and loved ones once more. I know they are only loaned to us as parents hoping to do our best and that we will always be united in some way and be together.

Those of you who read David's story I can only hope it gives you a more peaceful view of your children (wife, husband, sweetheart, your parents, siblings, relatives and dear friends) where they are and that they are safe in the arms of God. Every child is a precious soul and our connection to that child is through our heart by being parents. Every one of them is a gift to us and we have been truly blessed if we only have them for a moment, a day, or many years to come, it is never long enough. And no matter how old they become they are still our children.

My words have traveled across this paper as given to me in my memories and notebooks over time. How can anything really be explained any clearer as to why David chose his life to take place again in this world? He chose to reincarnate, he chose. There is no need to spend time on how many people may think how bizarre our chosen lives have been with the experiences we shared as mother and son. We could never have imagined our lives any different. We were in love with the experiences of our worlds and determined to do the best we could in each one. This was normal to us even though we had to hide our truth for so long.

Know it does take a strong heart and courage to write the truth. How blessed and grateful we both have been to be led by the Heavenly Beings, all holding our hands along the way. Christ said, "Follow Me for I shall show you the way." We did and we never looked back!

David and I have found our service on Earth to be a glorious experience. Even with all the suffering and pain, there is always the joy, happiness, excitement, and the love we experience. It is how one looks at life and to know that this place we live in is only temporary, with many lessons to learn from. We have a beautiful world full of precious life in every form created by an Amazing Intelligence no one can describe exactly, which I call God, my Creator. My son and I both have been graced to encounter our blessed Christ many times and this is the ultimate experience everyone searches for in life. I can say in all truth, Christ is always with you and stays in your heart forever, all you need do is ask. There are many names for God, our Creator, and Jesus Christ according to where one lives in this world. As Christ said, "It does not matter what title one uses in life, it is all about love for one another and everything!" That is the key.

Epilogue

The Sunflower That Wouldn't Die

Towards the end of writing David's story this past summer, David appeared to me one day. He told me that he was bringing me something special and laughing softly, he said, I would really like the surprise.

Soon after, around the first of August I noticed a plant or weed of some type growing quickly beside the fence in the front yard. I dared to think, was this sunflower or something else? Though it was growing in a flower garden, there had been no sunflowers planted in the front of the house and there had never been any planted there.

The plant grew to be rather tall and though it looked like a sunflower stalk it had not produced any blooms, plus, it was being covered by all the other flowers that were in that part of the garden. So one day early, I decided that it must have been some type of weed and I cut it down close to the ground with only a little bit of a thin outer piece of the stalk barely holding on. It was about four feet high by then and it was not too unusual to get some pretty big growing weeds.

The moment I cut it, I sensed with my intuition that this was a sunflower and that I had just killed it! You may wonder why I felt so emotional and I became heart-broken since I knew this was David's most favorite flower. The stalk was now bent over lying on its side, part-way into the grass yard, only being attached by shreds of stalk and the juices had begun to run out of it. I watched the life force run out of it and I was devastated! What had I done! I knew then that this was the special gift from David he had sent to me and since we had never planted any sunflowers near this area.

I was deeply saddened all day and through the night. I kept telling David how sorry I was, that I thought it was some type of weed. I was so overwrought with sadness. It was near early morning when David came to me in a vision. He told me not to worry, that the sunflower he sent would grow and be beautiful and not to be sad, that it would be fine. He knew I was heartbroken. Then he was gone.

With this I was happy again and each day I checked the sunflower since I knew it was special to me. Immediately, it seemed as if a miracle was developing with this sunflower. The plant kept growing ever larger with stems jotting out in all different directions, even though it was still lying on its side. The stems were shooting up to get sunlight and flower buds were forming on the different stems coming from the one stalk. At the break in the stalk, it was beginning to rot, but the remaining stems were all growing nicely. It was almost beginning to look like a bush the way it was growing all over. There are over 25 or so flowers on it from this one stalk. They just keep blooming, with more blooming again!

This sunflower is still blooming even though it is the very beginning of November and we have had some fairly chilly days for the central Midwest. Strangely, all of the sunflowers in the backyard have died well over 4 weeks ago and all of these (there were several varieties that were planted) were only a single bloom per stalk sunflower. The sunflower in the front yard is truly amazing still blooming through two complete frosts now which have killed all the flowers. I have taken pictures all along of this magic sunflower bush.

Many friends and passer-bys have asked about this sunflower since it is so unusual with so many flowers on it. I do not know how much longer I will get to keep my special gift from my son, and it has been so beautiful and so heartwarming with its amazing life and story. I am including some pictures since it has given me such joy that I want to share this with you the reader. I will keep the seeds from it to plant next year. Thank you David for such a wonderful blessing with the gift of your love, I love you.

Mom

About the Pictures

The following pages have a few pictures of the sunflowers with a brief explanation of when the picture was taken and the condition of the sunflower plant. The first picture is after I had cut the stalk which then began rotting. We thought it would die right away. This was in August.

Picture 2 is from early September after the plant began to thrive, growing big leaves and sun flowers on its new stems straight up off the ground towards the sun!

Picture 3 is in October and the sunflowers were blooming all the time with well over 36 flowers looking like a bush of them.

Picture 4 is in November and after three frosts. The sunflower was still looking beautiful, but all the rest of flowers everywhere had long died. By the middle of November we had another very hard frost and the sunflower died.

APPENDIX

Among the many messages David and I received from the other side over the years is this one below. I am passing it on to share with you.

THE ESSENCE

Receiving the essence of life is so very simple, keeping the mind, body and spirit open to the love of God then we are totally filled with his great LOVE, TO LOVE OURSELVES AND MANKIND.

Life is so very wonderful in our experiences when one has been opened to this level through faith, love and wisdom. Knowing that fear is only the illusion, we ourselves create in this mystical material world. There is nothing to really fear but fear itself, what man has taught us through the ages. We will never forsake you both; we are the Light everlasting sent from the Father. We are your strength and power to help you. See us all about thy selves thy will be done.

This humbling and extraordinary message was given to my son and me from the Light Beings from the other side and is beyond anything we could ever imagine! This helped the both of us so much on our journey and will for the rest of my natural life to remain stronger than ever. David continues to this very day to guide and help me. He is our special Angel watching over us. I thank God for my life, my children, and all of my beloved family. Today and everyday if possible give your children a BIG hug and praise them well; one never knows how long they will be in your care.

My son was so good to all of us, telling his sisters and me that he appreciated everything we did. I was given several beautiful messages from him that he had written to me over the years, even when he could hardly see any longer that I want to share with you. I want him to be remembered with love.

Mom,

Although I do not express it as often as I would like, I want you to know that I love you! God has certainly graced me with the gift of being your son. You are the Light that only shines bright throughout heaven, for all to find their way home. I am so proud of you and all the love you show to everyone, with honor and dignity. Just know that you have taught me what love, strength, honor, and grace are all about…

I bow before you,
And with all my love I thank you!!!
David

My book was coming along and I had nearly finished half of The Story of David. Christmas was near and I had such a feeling of emptiness with me missing him so much. This familiar feeling was moving strongly into my heart. Suddenly, I knew inside of me my son and I was going to meet very soon. I knew the two of us would be merging into one soul once more as in our beginning and we did! This happened in the night in my vision of our visit. This was also my Christmas with him and I fell deeply into a vision…

Later in the night hours my spirit began soaring into the Heavens to my son, our two spirits meeting as one soul once more. In an instant, there David stood in a black tuxedo so young and beautiful in spirit. He began by taking my hand in his and beautiful soft music began to play. As the notes floated into the soft colors surrounding us we began dancing to the gift of life throughout billions of brilliant stars, which lit our way across the Universe. My heart burst with joy and happiness in this celebration where I was lost in eternity. Then knowing all too soon I had to go back but forever knowing that love and life never dies, we are all eternal and our loved ones live on more alive than ever. Thank you my son for this magnificent gift that I will always cherish and will never forget at the Christmas season. Merry Christmas David we love you so very much and know you are with us.

Your honored mother.

My son was very sick when he wrote this beautiful message to me below and is another treasure he left for me. I am baring my heart to all of you who have had the experience of loss. I feel we can strengthen one another by knowing we share this part of our life together in understanding how devastating loss is. We have one another to lean on by sharing our feelings.

YOU ARE
Mom,

The Universe awaited your birth, there never has been nor will ever again be
Someone exactly like you.
You are unique.
No one can bring into being the thoughts, the beliefs, the love, and the sharing that you can.
Know who you are and follow the path that allows for the expression of life that can only come within you.
You can change the world.
You have at your command a vast array of talents perhaps as yet undiscovered, ready to create, that which you wish.
Look for what makes your heart quiver, look to make it better.
You feel that empathy because within you there is knowledge that reaches out from the depths of your soul, answers struggling to be brought forth.
Listen.
Joy will invade you as you give free rein to that which is you and that which is highest and most Nobel.
Look to bring that joy to where joy is not.
Some people live within the darkness of their thoughts, not knowing other realities are possible.
Love is everywhere, everything.

You need not search for it, simply recognize it.

The perfection of a drift of clouds, the softness of a Child's hand holding yours, a thirst-quenching drink of water, the beauty of an old woman's face, the majesty of an oak tree.

That are all saying, "I LOVE YOU" in their own way.

Let Love overwhelm you. Express love in all you do, from the humblest task to your highest aspiration. Imagine a world where everyone did the same. You always make this happen, thanks for being you!!! Love David

I cannot express to you how uplifted my son's messages makes me feel and I hope to inspire each person who reads his story as he has empowered me and his sisters. I have related to you what I have learned and experienced. I can only describe these things to you with the knowledge of what we experienced. How is it to live on the other side? For us it is filled with tremdeous love and the tranquility we all search for.

About the Author

Ruth Ann Friend

Still lives in a small community in the Midwest continuing her work in the Reiki energy healing field for well over 24 years. Ruth Ann also works as a Medium and Spiritual Adviser to others by passing messages from souls on the other side to their loved ones here on Earth. She hopes to reach people who are enduring the loss and heartbreak of a child or an adult with answers to help them in their grieving. Her experience comes from her work in the other worlds, the souls of loved ones, and spirits seeking to give comfort. She was born into this work by choice with her connection to other realms and worlds, and the true experiences she and her son have experienced over time. She has written her books in order to help those grieving and to take away the fear of living in our world.

She is the first one who brought Reiki energy healing classes to a college not far from her home. She also teaches parapsychology and psychic development in her own workshops, along with Hypnosis.

Ruth Ann's first book was, *Under the Rainbow Crossing,* in which she used the pen name of Ann Hart. In 2013, a second revised edition was released under her real name, Ruth Ann Friend. Her first written article was in Guideposts, Angels on Earth, called, *End of The Line.* Her second book, *The Story of David,* explains many of the mind blowing reasons of why mother and son both came back into our world again. It is based on true accounts and true events which are amazing and extremely rare. These are combinations of experiences with her son and herself through their extraordinary gifts. Their accounts have opened a door into what one could never imagine with both of them working as one mind and one soul on Earth. This story is absolutely phenomenal with not only the amazing experiences, but with both working together in more than duel worlds. This has been a huge breakthrough for the human mind and as a tool of comfort to the bereaved with proof of life after life, and finding out the Other Side can arrange anything, even our thoughts.

Her third book, coming out in the future, reaches out much further into other Universes and unknown places with a phenomenal twist.

David and his mother Ruth Ann

www.ingramcontent.com/pod-product-compliance
Lightning Source LLC
Chambersburg PA
CBHW071235160426
43196CB00009B/1075